PSYCHOLOGICAL DIFFERENTIATION

PSYCHOLOGICAL

DIFFERENTIATION

Studies of Development

H. A. WITKIN

R. B. DYK

H. F. FATERSON

D. R. GOODENOUGH

S. A. KARP

Department of Psychiatry of the State University
of New York College of Medicine at New York City

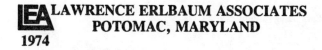LAWRENCE ERLBAUM ASSOCIATES
POTOMAC, MARYLAND
1974

THE HALSTED PRESS DIVISION OF

JOHN WILEY & SONS
New York   Toronto   London   Sydney

Lawrence Erlbaum Associates, Publishers
12736 Lincolnshire Drive
Potomac, Maryland 20854

Distributed solely by Halsted Press Division
John Wiley & Sons, Inc., New York.

Library of Congress Cataloging in Publication Data

Witkin, Herman A
    Psychological differentiation.

    Bibliography: p.
    1. Developmental psychology. 2. Cognition.
I. Title. [DNLM: 1. Child development. 2. Psy-
chology. BF701 W825p 1974]
BF713.W57 1974   155.2'2   73-22329
ISBN 0-470-95755-7
ISBN 0-470-95756-5 (pbk.)

FOREWORD

The psychological approach to the problem of human growth, from its inception in the last century as a topic of empirical inquiry up to the present, has undergone remarkable shifts which mirror the changing interests of the students of behavior. Emerging within the evolutionary framework of nineteenth century thought, the notion of human development was enthusiastically promoted by philosophically minded investigators such as Mark Baldwin, G. Stanley Hall, and others who looked upon ontogenetic inquiry as holding a key to the understanding of man. Soon, however, experimental work concerned with child growth fell prey to certain trends which, though not without merit in themselves, were rather adverse to the integral understanding of human development: we refer, in particular, to the trend toward an atheoretical collecting and ordering of detailed empirical data, and the trend toward practical ends such as entailed in mental testing.

Only relatively recently are we witnessing a "spiral" turn in the approach to child behavior and the formation of personality: that is, a return to the earlier view of the necessity of a theoretical network within which ontogenetic facts must be placed and evaluated—coupled, however, with the utilization of modern tools provided by general experimental psychology and quantitative methods of analysis. The pioneering work of Witkin, Dyk, Faterson, Goodenough, and Karp, presented in this book, truly reflects that new spirit.

As their basic conceptual framework Witkin and his co-investigators

adopt the tenet of developmental theory that human ontogenesis progresses in terms of an increasing polarity between the self and the
nonself; implied in this view is the notion of a reciprocal relation of
self-differentiation and nonself(social, objective)-differentiation. In
synthesizing the empirical data by developmental conceptualization,
the authors avail themselves of a powerful intellectual device for the
understanding of cognitive behavior and the individual differences in
cognitive mode.

As I see it, the application of a developmental notion such as differentiation to the study is of fourfold significance: Firstly, the concept
of differentiation refers to *formal* rather than to *material* properties of
organization; it thus makes it possible to interrelate the various functional areas and their unfolding in an individual in terms of formal as
against content characteristics. Secondly, it is a concept dynamic
rather than static in its essence; it thus makes possible the study of
ways of experiencing and behavioral patterning in terms of processes
rather than achievement. Thirdly, it implies a temporal element: it
ties together present behavioral and experiential characteristics—of individuals or groups—with those of the past; in other words, it binds
the state of being to that of becoming. Fourthly, it is a concept capable
of defining ways of behavior in terms of their universality and generality as well as in terms of their specificity and individuality; that is,
it makes it possible to characterize behavior by a developmental principle which, defined as a basic law, refers to the uniform nature of
genetic change—but, at the same time, allows for multiformity of experience and articulation.

Now, the developmental conceptualization to which the authors
subscribe is for them not a mere means of post-hoc theoretical interpretation of gathered facts; with the instinct of the explorer bent toward
the acquisition of empirical knowledge they transform the genetic-
theoretical axiom of self-nonself-differentiation into a hypothesis—
the "differentiation hypothesis"—which in their skillful hands becomes
capable of channeling the inquiry toward significant particular questions, as well as recruiting powerful and relevant experimental
methods; moreover, in spite of its generality, the hypothesis is sufficiently incisive to be validated and tested against the findings without
undue ambiguity.

For this undertaking the authors did not have to build on virgin
ground; they brought to their task an already impressive array of
evidence discovered in many years of previous experimentation by
Witkin and co-workers, and summarized in the book *Personality
through Perception*.

For one who—as the writer of this foreword—has always been fascinated by the genesis and the formation of fertile ideas in the history of scientific thought, it is interesting to follow the development of the notions underlying the work of Witkin and his collaborators and the interaction of these notions with concrete experimentation briefly referred to in the introductory chapter of this book.

The beginnings of these investigations can be traced back to the work of Gestalt psychologists who were in constant search for perceptual situations that would demonstrate the dependency of perceptual properties of parts of the field on the (visual) field structure as a whole. In exploring such situations involving the perceptual property of the "upright" and using (in collaboration with Dr. Asch) the famous mirror set-up of Wertheimer, Witkin soon discovered that neither the interpretation in terms of universal visual Gestalt principles, such as that of part-whole relation, nor the interpretation in terms of postural factors (Gibson) suffices to account fully for the behavioral effects in the subjects. Moving away from an orthodox Gestalt-view as one "encapsulated within the organism" (Brunswik), Witkin showed that a rather satisfactory explanation could only be attained through an analysis in terms of individual differences. Thus the findings reported in the earlier book clearly pointed to the existence of two individual modes of perception, labeled "field-dependent" and "field-independent." Now, in order to arrive at the position reflected in the more recent work, two more steps had to be taken. One consisted in the extension of the early work, far beyond the rather restricted inquiry into different modes of perceptual orientation; these later studies aimed at a differential analysis of a comprehensive variety of cognitive functions as they pertain to the articulation of the inner self and the outer world, as well as the interaction between both. The other important step entailed the placing of the inquiry explicitly within a developmental framework: this made it possible to bring the dichotomy in mode of orientation under a uniform principle. That principle of differentiation has guided Witkin, Dyk, Faterson, Goodenough, and Karp in their quest toward such important problems as self-consistency in functional patterning, the contribution of early life experience to the establishment of individual patterns, the stability and constancy of such patterns during growth.

This is a book of prime importance. It gives reassurance to those of us who believe that the understanding of man cannot advance through the mere gathering and ordering of data, but only through the search for facts under the guidance of theoretical notions. These explorations into the little-known represent an achievement of no mean proportions: solid in method, exciting in outlook, profound in meaning.

HEINZ WERNER

PREFACE

The last decade and a half has witnessed a strong revival of interest in problems of cognition. Research has centered particularly on functional aspects of cognitive processes. The renewed concern with cognition has had many sources. These have been as diverse as, for example, the growing attention of psychoanalytic theory to problems of ego psychology; the accumulating evidence, from laboratory studies, of stable individual differences in perception; and the increasingly successful use of cognitive techniques in many kinds of personal assessment. The channels through which interest in cognition has found expression have been as diverse. One line of interest, in which considerable research effort has been invested, has been in styles of cognitive functioning as related to individual patterns of adaptation. The research of our laboratory, described particularly in an earlier book, *Personality through Perception,* has been in this tradition.

The present research has substantially confirmed the work reported in that book and has extended it in several directions. The main new departure has been the pursuit of problems of cognition in the context of development, maintaining, however, the concern with individuality that characterized the earlier work. The path followed has led far beyond cognition, both in research and conceptualization. In time particular clusters of complexly interrelated characteristics (including cognitive characteristics) in children became the main concern. The nature and basis of these clusters and their origin during development are the central issues of the present book.

We deal in this book with a wide range of areas of psychological functioning, a fact apparent in the list of chapter headings. Furthermore, a large body of evidence is presented, derived from our own studies, and also from numerous studies by others, concerned with the field-dependence-independence dimension of perception with which our work began. In addition, a theoretical framework is offered, dealing with relations among diverse aspects of individual functioning. Though the scope of the areas, evidence, and concepts dealt with is thus extensive, we have sought to make the book as a whole readable, regardless of the background of the reader. As an aid to this objective we have put in small type material of a more technical nature for readers with special interests in particular areas.

Our work has been greatly aided by many individuals and groups. It is a pleasure to acknowledge their help.

We wish, first of all, to express our gratitude to members of the staff of the Psychology Laboratory who, at different times, contributed, in a variety of ways, to the conduct of these studies. Hanna Marlens, Jane Schick, and Meta Steiner aided us in the development and application of a number of rating scales and served as independent judges in several analyses. Their specific contributions, as well as that of Elaine Karp, who also acted as an independent judge, are identified at appropriate places in the text. To Meta Steiner also goes our very warm appreciation for bringing her rich clinical knowledge and sensitivity to bear, in numerous discussions with us, upon the theoretical problems we were seeking to clarify. A special debt is acknowledged to Hanna Marlens, who, over a period of five years, helped very creatively in devising scales for evaluating several kinds of complex qualitative data. The large tasks of test administration and statistical analyses were greatly aided by our research assistants, Lillian Conn, Carol Johnson Eagle, Marvin Frankel, Beverly Goodman, Sheila Hafter, Richard Loeff, Shifra Nathan, Frank Plumeau, and Peggy Plumeau. The special quality of their relationships to the children we studied was of incalculable value in maintaining the cooperation of the children during the extended periods of testing required of them. Peggy Plumeau, over an eight-year period, helped particularly in preserving contacts with the children in the longitudinal studies and in dealing with the innumerable details which such studies inevitably entail. Carol Johnson Eagle was responsible for organizing and carrying out the testing program, in Topeka, Kansas, of the children who were the original subjects in the Topeka Infancy Study. Arno Gruen and Zelda Klapper, staff members from 1952 to 1954 and 1952 to 1955, respectively, participated in the initial preparation for some of the studies and in the testing of children in several of the early investigations. We are indebted to our secretaries, especially Wilhelmina Fleming, Sally Schneeweis, and Lillian Woronoff, who patiently and skillfully worked with the manuscript through its many revisions. Shifra Nathan aided greatly by her perceptive work on the index.

To Dr. Howard W. Potter, Chairman of the Department of Psychiatry and Dean of the Medical School during the time these studies were carried out, we are indebted for the warm support he gave our work.

A number of colleagues have helped us greatly by their critical reading of all or parts of the manuscript-in-progress. We are especially indebted to Abraham Edel, Rosalind Gould, Norman Harway, Bernard Kaplan, Sheldon Korchin, Weston La Barre, Helen Lewis, Gardner Murphy, Walter Riss, Leonard Saltzman, T. C. Schneirla, Meta Steiner, Edmund Weil, and Edith Weisskopf-Joelson; however, the authors alone take responsibility for the final work.

The studies we have done would not have been possible without the cooperation of the Board of Education of the City of New York. We are particularly indebted to Dr. Eleanor Harrington, principal, and Miss Fannie Cohen, former principal, of P.S. 152, Dr. Irwin Sulo Hecht, former principal of Andries Hudde Junior High School, and Dr. Jacob Ross, former principal of Midwood High School, who helped us make the initial contacts with the children and their parents, and who in many ways assisted us in maintaining our relations with the families.

This work has been supported by a grant (M-628) from the United States Public Health Service, National Institutes of Health. That support is gratefully acknowledged. The apparatus for the tilting-room–tilting-chair test was originally constructed under a grant from the Office of Naval Research, and its use in the present studies made possible by an equipment-loan contract.

Finally there are the indispensable collaborators in a study of this kind, the children who were our subjects and their parents. The boys and girls gave freely of their time and afforded us much pleasure as we worked with them. Their parents were most generous in sharing with us the unique experiences they had with their growing children.

H. A. W.
R. B. D.
H. F. F.
D. R. G.
S. A. K.

Psychology Laboratory
State University of New York
College of Medicine at New York City
January 1962

CONTENTS

1

INTRODUCTION

This book is concerned with the nature and sources of divergent directions of psychological development. Our interest in the problem can be traced back to an observation made almost two decades ago, at the start of this general program of research. We found then that people differ in the way they orient themselves in space. This observation appears, on the surface, quite remote from the issues of personal growth with which we shall here be concerned. Yet, our present interest in these issues has developed from the earlier finding about individual differences in space orientation.

Many new results, emerging as the investigations progressed, contributed to this transition. One such result—to us the most dramatic of all our findings—was particularly responsible for directing our work toward the problem of divergent psychological growth trends. It became clear, at a certain point in the investigations, that the way in which each person orients himself in space is an expression of a more general preferred mode of perceiving which, in turn, is linked to a broad and varied array of personal characteristics involving a great many areas of psychological functioning.

The scope of individual consistency in this respect is suggested by a brief consideration of some of the attributes of people who show, in their orientation, what we call a "field-dependent" way of perceiving. This kind of orientation, observable in any of a series of tests devised for our early studies, may be illustrated by performance in the rod-and-frame test. The subject in this test sits in complete darkness, facing a luminous rod surrounded by a luminous frame. Rod and frame can be independently tilted, to one side or the other; the subject sees them first in tilted positions. Then, while the frame remains tilted, he moves the rod (through his directions to the experimenter) until it appears to him that it is vertical. Some subjects tip the rod far to-

1

wards the angle of tilt of the frame in order to perceive it as upright, thus determining its position mainly in relation to the visual field that immediately surrounds it. Here and in other perceptual situations these subjects find it difficult to overcome the influence of the surrounding field or to separate an item from its context. It is because of this characteristic that their perception has been designated field dependent. Other subjects, in contrast, are able to bring the rod close to the true upright, perceiving it independently of the surrounding field and determining its location with reference to body position. In perceptual situations generally, such people are able to distinguish an item from its context. Their perception is field independent. In the general population performances reflecting the extent of people's field dependence or independence are ranged in a continuum rather than falling into two distinct categories.

On the basis of our own studies as well as those from other laboratories using the rod-and-frame test or closely related perceptual techniques, it is now possible to offer a fairly comprehensive characterization of people who show a typically field-dependent orientation in the rod-and-frame test. The attributes given are selected from a larger constellation to be presented in the course of this book.

Field-dependent people take a rather long time to locate a familiar figure hidden in a complex design. Because they are less likely to attempt to structure ambiguous stimuli, as Rorschach inkblots, they usually experience such stimuli as vague and indefinite. They often find difficulty with the block-design, picture-completion, and object-assembly parts of standard intelligence tests. Yet, they are no different from more field-independent people on other portions of intelligence tests which require concentrated attention; and they may even do better on portions concerned with vocabulary, information, and comprehension. They are also not different from field-independent people in the ability to learn new material. In Duncker's well-known insight problems they may not readily see alternative uses for items serving a familiar function.

Sitting in a tilted chair within a markedly tilted experimental room, with room and chair aligned, they are likely to experience themselves as upright. Their judgments under these circumstances are thus apt to be very inaccurate. However, the very tendency reflected by this way of performing, to be guided by the axes of the surrounding visual field rather than by sensations from within the body, causes these people to be highly accurate in determining body position in a centrifuge type of situation, where the experimental room in which they are seated is upright, and the body is pulled to one side by a strong centrifugal force. They are apt to experience themselves as appreciably shorter than they really are. When asked to draw a person, the figures they produce are likely to show few characteristics of masculinity or femininity.

These people are likely to change their stated views on a particular social issue in the direction of the attitudes of an authority. They are also particularly attentive to the faces of those around them and, as a result, tend to be better than relatively field-independent persons at recognizing people they have seen only briefly before. Their impressions of people are usually based on the physical characteristics these people show and the actions they engage in. On the whole, they favor occupations that involve contact with people and that are popular within their group.

When shown a TAT picture that portrays an aggressive act, field-dependent people are likely to give immediate expression to the ideas and feelings of aggression stimulated by the picture. Under conditions of stress, they will probably show labile psychogalvanic skin responses. The central characters they create for TAT stories are not likely to have a driving interest in achievement. In their over-all adjustment they are clearly no more prone to disturbances or pathology than field-independent perceivers, although the disturbances they show are likely to take a very different form.

People whose performances in the rod-and-frame test indicate a predominantly field-independent way of perceiving present a direct contrast in many of these attributes. Not always, however, are the characteristics common to field-independent perceivers polar opposites of those found among field-dependent perceivers, and they may or may not contribute to optimal adjustment. Thus, although field-independent people are often able to function with a fair degree of autonomy from others, some of them are strikingly isolated individuals, overcontrolled, cold and distant, and unaware of their social stimulus value. We have in fact frequently encountered field-independent performances among hospitalized psychiatric patients who were actively delusional and apparently destined to remain in an institution for the remainder of their lives.

The characteristics cited, each referring to a quite specific segment of behavior, fall into several definite clusters. These reflect the quality of the person's experience of his surroundings, his way of perceiving and using his body, the nature of his relation to other people, and aspects of his controls and defenses. It may be apparent, even by a superficial view of the items of which they are composed, that these clusters are not a random agglomeration but fall into intrinsically coherent patterns. These patterns suggest consistency in psychological functioning which pervades the individual's perceptual, intellectual, emotional, motivational, defensive, and social operations. In addition to this cross-sectional consistency, we have been able to demonstrate through longitudinal studies of development a marked continuity in some of these aspects of personal functioning over long periods of time.

With findings such as these, an investigation that had dealt with individual differences in a seemingly narrow perceptual activity developed into a study of broad differences among people in what seemed to add up to a "style of life." Once it became clear that we were in fact dealing with variations among people in patterns of characteristics the problem became more than one of "individual differences," in the usual sense of variation in a particular attribute. The identification of self-consistent patterns of functioning made the essential problem one of psychological *individuality*. As the issue of individuality came to the fore, we necessarily became concerned with such questions as the scope of the contrasting patterns that had been identified, the origin of these patterns in the course of individual development, and their stability over time. Thus, the ever-mounting body of evidence on individual self-consistency gave our work a particular push toward problems of the nature and source of divergent directions of psychological development.

It is reasonable to suppose that the clusters of characteristics composing each of the contrasting patterns have some salient features in common. We now conceive of greater differentiation or more limited differentiation as the common denominator of the characteristics in each pattern. This conception, outlined in the next chapter, emerged gradually with the accumulation of new evidence and, as it grew and became refined, it provided in turn a guide for further studies. The continuous interchange between developing theory and new evidence from ongoing research stimulated an ever-expanding series of investigations radiating from the early studies of perception. Though they eventually moved far from their starting point, these investigations remained anchored throughout to the observations we had made initially of how people perceive.

We may illustrate this sequence by considering very briefly a few of the pathways along which our investigations proceeded in this kind of radiating fashion.

One example comes from a series of studies which had their start in observations made in the body-adjustment test, used to evaluate an individual's perception of the position of his body in space. In this test, the person is seated in a tilted room and required to adjust his chair to a position he experiences as upright. Some people, in carrying out this task, tend to align the body with the tilted room; others bring their bodies close to the true upright, regardless of the position of the surrounding room; most people adjust their bodies to an intermediate position. The inability to hold the body apart from the field, the apparent "fusion" of both in experience, reflected in the first (field-dependent) kind of performance, early suggested the possibility of a relatively poorly developed body concept. The ready ability to separate body from field reflected in the second (field-independent) way of performing suggested, on the face of it, a relatively well-developed conception of the body. Subsequent studies, stimulated in part by this kind of analysis of actual ways of performing the body-adjustment task, in fact revealed important differences in nature of the body concept among children and adults with different modes of perceiving.

Other evidence suggested that ability to experience the body as a discrete entity was a special manifestation of a more general capacity to "keep things apart" in experience. Thus, people who were able to bring the body close to the upright, regardless of the position of the surrounding room, were also able to determine rod position independently of the tilted frame in the rod-and-frame test already described. They could also quickly detect a previously seen simple geometric figure within a complexly organized design. Some communality was thus demonstrated between how the person experiences his body and how he experiences neutral objects outside himself. If, in experience, he readily "loses" his body in the field, he is also apt to "lose" any neutral external object. This relatively global, unarticulated way of experiencing manifests itself not only in performance in special laboratory situations, but also in the quality of the person's awareness of the social world around him.

The dynamic linkage that exists between sense of body and sense of self suggested that the ready fusion of body and field in experience may in turn signify a self which is limited both as to segregation and inner structure. Evidence from subsequent studies in fact showed, as we see later, that people with a relatively field-dependent way of perceiving have a less developed sense of their identity and of their separateness from others than do more field-independent perceivers. A self which is only limitedly segregated from the field—or which, in experience, easily "loses" itself in the field—is characteristic of people who tend to experience the body or any object as "fused" with its surroundings. If we think of the self as corresponding to a segment of experience, we may consider that greater or more limited articulation represents a common quality running through much of a person's experience.

Still farther from our starting point in perception were the studies which sought to determine the sources of the contrasting psychological patterns. These studies, reported toward the end of the book, investigated particularly the effects of children's relations with their mothers while growing up. The evidence from these studies demonstrated that the nature of these relations is important for a child's progress toward greater differentiation, and it threw some light on the processes involved.

This brief preview of the work reported illustrates the way in which a study of individual variations in a specific perceptual process eventually became a study of differences among people in broad psychological patterns and of the underlying bases and origins of these patterns during development. There is perhaps a suggestion too, in this account, of how a theoretical framework geared to the concept of differentiation led the studies in the particular direction they took and how, at the same time, the results obtained contributed to the strengthening and enlargement of the conceptual framework. This becomes more evident in the chapter that follows, which is concerned with the concept of differentiation.

2

THE CONCEPT OF
DIFFERENTIATION

The broad contrasting patterns of interrelated characteristics touched upon in the first chapter appear to us now to reflect differences in extent of psychological differentiation. It is a quality of greater or more limited differentiation that the characteristics in each pattern appear to have in common.

We review in this chapter some of the considerations which gradually led the concept of differentiation to move into the central position it has come to occupy in our studies. We also present a brief account of the sense in which we use the concept and compare the characteristics of a more differentiated and less differentiated psychological state.

A. BACKGROUND EVIDENCE

In long-range programmatic research the starting conceptual framework inevitably undergoes continuous revision and enlargement as new facts emerge and new relationships are identified. The emerging framework in turn continually modifies research effort and focuses it in new directions. The conceptual framework which is presented has had this kind of history in our work, as noted.

A major finding of our earlier studies (Witkin, Lewis, Hertzman, Machover, Meissner, and Wapner, 1954) was that young children tend to perceive in a relatively field-dependent fashion, and, as they grow older, their perception assumes a generally more field-independent form. This finding is consistent with the results of a number of other investigations which have shown that for younger children the over-all structure of a given configuration strongly dominates the manner in which constituent parts are perceived.

The fact that field-dependent perception is associated with earlier stages of development implied that it may be more rudimentary. Conversely, field-independent perception appeared to represent a developmentally more advanced level of functioning. Placing mode of perception in a developmental context suggested that children who persist in an ontogenetically earlier way of perceiving may have made less progress in some general aspect of their psychological development. At the same time, other evidence suggested that the aspect involved might be extent of differentiation.

First, early studies of adults and children with different ways of perceiving showed clearly that *content* features of personality were usually not discriminating with regard to perceptual style. On the other hand, *formal* features—that is, characteristic ways of functioning based on given structural arrangements in personality—were critical.[1] Thus, people who were grouped together on the basis of a common perceptual style resembled one another in particular aspects of *how* they satisfied their needs, resolved their conflicts, handled their aggressions, formed their attitudes. But they differed in *what* they wanted, were in conflict about, became angry over, believed in, as well as the life themes that ran through their histories.

The demonstrated importance of formal aspects of personality directed attention to differentiation and integration, the main characteristics to be considered in viewing a system from the standpoint of its formal properties. In many ways it gradually became clear that the constellations with which we were dealing might best be conceived in terms of differentiation.

One indication was the nature of the personality attributes found to distinguish people with a more field-dependent way of perceiving from those with a more field-independent way of perceiving. Such discriminating attributes as extent of definition of self-concept, articulateness of body image, and method of impulse regulation formed an interrelated cluster which is apt to be considered in evaluating people as more differentiated or less differentiated. At the same time we en-

---

[1] To the extent that a particular way of functioning may be predisposing toward a particular kind of content, the formal and content aspects of personality are of course related. Thus, a person who shows a strong tendency to rely on others for support and guidance is apt to hold attitudes which, in their content, are conventional and favored by society. In turn, nature of content may influence manner of functioning. A severe unresolved Oedipal problem may affect the kinds of defenses that are developed.

countered varied kinds of integration among relatively field-dependent and relatively field-independent people. Moreover, the patterns of integration found in both kinds of people might be effective or impaired. Our studies of hospitalized psychiatric patients showed that pathology, of a kind which spoke most of all on severe impairment of integration, was not the prerogative of individuals with a particular mode of perception. People with a more field-independent way of perceiving seem no less prone to pathology than relatively field-dependent people, although they differ in kinds of pathology.

In these and other ways it came to appear that the patterns of cognitive and personality characteristics identified in our previous studies could be conceived as reflecting particularly differences in extent of differentiation.

B. THE NATURE OF DIFFERENTIATION

The concept of differentiation has been widely used both in biology and psychology. Its most extensive treatment in psychology is to be found in the theories of Werner (1948) and Lewin (1935). We do not attempt any systematic review of past usages of the concept but limit ourselves to an account of the meaning in which it is employed in this book.

Degree of differentiation is an important characteristic of the structure of any system, whether psychological, biological, or social. In broadest terms differentiation refers to the complexity of a system's structure. A less differentiated system is in a relatively homogeneous structural state; a more differentiated system in a relatively heterogeneous state. The emphasis on "relative" is important for even the most rudimentary system is to some degree differentiated. This is implicit in the very definition of "system."

The description of a system as more differentiated or less differentiated carries definite implications about how it functions. In fact it is mainly through particular functional manifestations that extent of differentiation of a system may be judged. Before the differentiation concept can be applied to the description of individual behavior or the study of psychological problems its implications for function must be delineated.

Among the major characteristics of the functioning of a highly differentiated system is specialization. The subsystems which are present within the general system are capable of mediating specific functions which, in a relatively undifferentiated state, are not possible or are performed in a more rudimentary way by the system as a whole.

When used to describe an individual's psychological system specialization means a degree of separation of psychological areas, as feeling from perceiving, thinking from acting. It means as well specificity in manner of functioning within an area. Specific reactions are apt to occur in response to specific stimuli as opposed to diffuse reaction to any of a variety of stimuli. Parts of a perceptual field are experienced as discrete, rather than fused with their background. Impulses are channelized, contrasting with the easy "spilling over" characteristic of the relatively undifferentiated state. More or less discrete feelings and needs are likely to be present.

Psychological systems, like biological ones, are open, in the sense that they are in continuous commerce with the environment (see von Bertalanffy, 1950; Allport, 1960). With respect to relation with the surrounding field, a high level of differentiation implies clear separation of what is identified as belonging to the self and what is identified as external to the self. The self is experienced as having definite limits or boundaries. Segregation of the self helps make possible greater determination of functioning from within, as opposed to a more or less enforced reliance on external nurturance and support for maintenance, typical of the relatively undifferentiated state.[2]

Degree of differentiation also has implications for the way in which a system is integrated. Integration is an essential property of any system, again by definition. It refers particularly to the form of the functional relationships among system components and so speaks first of all on the patterning of the total system. When we are dealing with open systems, as in psychology, integration also refers to the form of the relationships between the system and its surroundings.

Complexity of integration and effectiveness of integration are two important characteristics of a system that need to be carefully distinguished.

To say that integration is *effective* means that there is a more or less harmonious working together of system components with each other and of the total system with its environment, thereby contributing to the adaptation of the organism. In psychological systems effectiveness of integration is reflected in adequacy of adjustment. To say that integration is *complex* means that the relationships among system components and between the system and its environment are elaborate. Integrations that may be considered effective—or ineffective—may take a variety of forms; and similarly with integrations that may be considered complex.

[2] Segregation does not of course mean lessened contact with or reduced importance of the environment.

Complexity of integration of a system is determined in part by its level of differentiation. It seems reasonable to suppose that more complex relationships among system components, and between the system and its environment, are possible in a system with many varied components than in a system whose components are few and relatively unspecialized. Psychological development toward greater differentiation must be accompanied by successively more complex reintegrations of the system. For example, the integration of ideas and feelings, a function performed by mechanisms of control and defense, necessarily becomes more complex as ideas and feelings become more discrete, that is as differentiation develops. To the extent that more complex integration is a function of greater differentiation, the presence of relatively complex modes of integration may in effect be taken as evidence of developed differentiation, along with specialization and segregation.

While complexity of integration appears to be a function of level of differentiation, effectiveness of integration is not as directly related. At any level of differentiation a variety of modes of integration is possible, and at each level both effective and ineffective integrations may be found. A particular mode of integration at a relatively rudimentary level of differentiation may be entirely adequate for that level, though not complex. On the other hand, a highly differentiated system may have a particular mode of integration which, though complex, is inadequate. A high level of differentiation clearly does not imply effective integration.

C. COMPARISON OF MORE DIFFERENTIATED AND LESS DIFFERENTIATED PSYCHOLOGICAL STATES

Both in biology and psychology the differentiation concept has most often been applied in a developmental context.

Although any psychological system is differentiated to some extent, it is clearly in its most undifferentiated state early in development, and becomes more differentiated as development progresses. The difference between the psychological pictures found in infancy and at later stages of development provides the maximal contrast between a low and high level of differentiation; the difference is obviously greater than that which exists between adults most widely separated with regard to extent of differentiation. As a further step toward putting the differentiation concept into a form useful for the description and study of behavior, it may be helpful to compare the individual in infancy and at later stages of development, with particular reference to differentiation. The highly schematized account given is intended only as a description of some of the highlights of more differentiated and less differentiated functioning in several salient psychological areas; the causes of development toward greater differentiation are left for later consideration. Major themes running through this account are the development of specialization and segregation, and, with these, of complexity of integration, which, we suggested, are manifestations of developed differentiation. The discussion is not specifically organized around these themes, however, but centers rather on the development of articulation of experience of the world, of self-differentiation, and of controls and defenses.

It is reasonable to presume that very early in development a child experiences himself and his environment mainly as a more or less amorphous, continuous "mass." Although direct evidence on this point is unobtainable, it seems likely that, even if the young infant at the very outset experiences feelings from within and from the surface of his body as already somehow "special," the segregation of self from field is at best very limited. One of the very early developments in the crystallization of experience is the growing awareness of a difference between inner and outer within the original body-field matrix. Boundaries between the body—the early representation of self [3]—and the outer world are formed and continue to become stronger during the course of development. Along with the formation of boundaries, the child develops an awareness of the various parts of the body and their interrelatedness. The developing sense of self is rooted in but obviously not limited to sensations generated by body functions and activities (as hunger, satisfaction of thirst, change in position, pain). Various other kinds of experiences (as emotions, ideas, memories) come to be perceived as emanating particularly from within and are distinguished from experiences which have their source "out there." The registrations of activities and attributes which the child experiences as belonging to him do not remain discrete bits—the pull of an eye muscle, a flash of anger, a feeling of contentment, an ache in a joint—but early form a complex, invested with special feelings and experienced as a bounded "inner core."

An important feature of the development of differentiation is the movement away from the initial inevitable state of unity with the mother toward some degree of separation. In the course of this evolv-

---

[3] The term, "self," has been used in a variety of ways in the literature, and often interchangeably with "ego." (See Chein, 1944, for example.) We use the term "self" to refer to the systematized awareness the person has of activities and qualities he identifies as his own.

ing relation with the mother and other people the child identifies and internalizes particular values and standards ("internal frames of reference") which help determine his view of himself. The child develops a growing sense of what he is like (whether objectively correct or not) and how he is different from and similar to others; we may refer to the outcome of this double trend in the development of the self as the achievement of a "sense of separate identity."

Thus, formation of the self involves the more or less simultaneous development of an "inner core" of experience and the segregation of this core from the field. There is a progression from an initial relatively unstructured state, with segregation of self from environment at best very limited, to a more structured [4] state, with greater segregation of self. The self becomes more differentiated as it develops.

The achievement of a relatively differentiated self implies that in the area of experience where the person's own activities and attributes are the source, experience is relatively articulated—that is, it is analyzed and structured, rather than global.[5] Experience which has the field outside the person as its source may also be conceived as showing development toward greater articulation. Early in development perception of parts of the field is likely to be dominated by the organization of the immediate context in which the parts are contained. During the course of development the influence of the immediate context is reduced.

In visual perception, for example, early in development the geometrical relationship among the parts of a stimulus field is a dominant determinant of perceptual organization. Stimulus fields in which the parts have little systematic geometrical relationship to each other

---

[4] "Structure" was used previously in juxtaposition to "function." In keeping with common usage in psychology, "structured" is employed here and later on to describe the functioning of a system or subsystem with regard to both extent of differentiation and complexity of integration. Variations along this dimension are designated as more complexly or less complexly structured. Finally, in discussing experience, again following common usage, we employ the term "structuring" to refer to the imposition of organization on a field, internal or external, and the term "structured" to refer to the outcome of this process.

To illustrate the application of these terms, when we consider the self as a subsystem of personality we use "structured" in the sense of differentiated and complexly integrated. When we discuss the self with reference to experience of one's own activities and attributes, the term "structured" implies organization of experience.

The context in which these terms occur will make their particular meanings obvious.

[5] We employ the term "global" in describing experience in contrast to each of the following: analytical, structured, articulated.

are perceived as relatively unorganized. During development stimulus objects gain function and meaning as a consequence of continuous, varied dealings with them. This acquired functional significance may contribute to the developing discreteness of objects and may serve as the basis for the formation of nongeometrical integrations of the field. We may refer to the increasing discreteness of objects and to the use of more complex principles of field integration as an increase in the articulateness of experience. The person who experiences in articulated fashion has the ability to perceive items as discrete from their backgrounds, or to reorganize a field, when the field is organized; and to impose structure on a field, and so perceive it as organized, when the field has relatively little inherent structure. In this view the ability to analyze experience and the ability to structure experience are both aspects of increasing articulation.

Just as the concept of increasing articulation has been applied to experience of an immediately present stimulus configuration (perception), so may it be applied to experience of symbolic material (thinking).

In summary, experience of the body-field matrix is early essentially global, and during development becomes progressively more articulated so that body, self, and objects in general are experienced as segregated. Segregation, or analysis, and with it structuring of experience —of what is outside and of what is inside—are manifestations of developed psychological differentiation. The growth of a segregated, structured self—or self-differentiation [6]—is in this view part of the process of articulation of experience.

Development toward greater psychological differentiation is also manifested in the formation of controls and defenses for the channeling of impulse and the expenditure of energy. Early in life impulse, as it accumulates, "floods" the organism and finds expression in diffuse, systemwide reactions. Raised stimulus barriers or heightened neural thresholds may provide the infant with a rudimentary form of defense against the adverse effects of prolonged intense stimulation. During growth specialized, structured systems of control and defense are developed. These make possible specific channeling of impulse, delayed expression, and protection against some of its disturbing effects. They also aid in the directed expenditure of energy in the pursuit of specific goals.

The establishment of internalized values and standards contributes

[6] The account given has been limited to one aspect of the development of the self, its differentiation. A comprehensive account of the self would need to consider other aspects as well.

to the process of control. Early in the child's development the primary "seat of moral authority," the source of rewarding and punishing forces, is lodged outside himself. The values and standards set by parents and society at large, and the consequences that follow upon their violation, provide an important basis for the regulation of impulse expression and behavior in general. With internalization of values and standards this regulative function shifts increasingly to the inside.

Among systems of defense, some may be conceived as reflecting less developed differentiation than others. Thus, massive repression and primitive denial [7] involve an indiscriminate, general turning away from or "banging the door shut" against perception of stimuli and memory for past experiences. Compared to such mechanisms as intellectualization and sublimation, they reflect relatively nonspecific ways of functioning and less complex integration.

D. THE DIFFERENTIATION HYPOTHESIS

We have examined several areas of psychological functioning at early and later stages of development as a means of determining the form which developed differentiation is likely to take in each area. Identification of the characteristics of a more differentiated or less differentiated psychological state—or "indicators" of differentiation, as we shall call them—has been important for our research strategy. Our conception of the nature of these indicators helped both in the formulation of hypotheses that guided our main investigations and in the systematic interpretation of the large body of evidence provided by our own studies and many studies by others.

Our analysis of the growth of experience of the self and the world led us to postulate that progress toward differentiation would be expressed in increasing articulation (that is, analysis and structuring) of experience. Included in this is a more articulated way of experiencing the world; also included are a more clearly defined body concept, and a growing sense of separate identity, which together reflect particularly the development of self-differentiation. Our brief discussion of the development of impulse regulation identified the achievement of specialized, structured defenses and controls as another major manifestation of development toward greater differentiation.

[7] Massive, indiscriminate repression is to be distinguished from repression used, for instance, by the overintellectual person in his attempts to maintain distance from his own impulses. In the same way, primitive denial would be contrasted to active, directed avoidance of particular stimuli through an attitude of wariness or evasiveness.

It follows from the preceding account of development that children of the same age differ in the extent to which they are differentiated, reflecting individual differences in pace of development in this important dimension. Also inherent in that account is the idea that greater or lesser progress toward developed differentiation in a given child is likely to be apparent in each of the indicators considered. We do not suppose that these indicators are products of development in "separate channels." We regard them rather as different expressions of an underlying process of development toward greater psychological complexity. On this basis we would expect measures of these indicators for any group of children to be significantly interrelated. This expectation is the *differentiation hypothesis* which guided most of the studies we have carried out. "Differentiation" thus serves as a construct for conceptualizing communality in behavior in several areas of psychological functioning.

Specifically, the differentiation hypothesis proposes an association among the characteristics of greater or more limited differentiation, identified in the comparison of early and later functioning in each of several psychological areas: degree of articulation of experience of the world; degree of articulation of experience of the self, reflected particularly in nature of the body concept and extent of development of a sense of separate identity; and extent of development of specialized, structured controls and defenses. Implicit in this hypothesis is the view that greater inner differentiation is associated with greater articulation of experience of the world.

We consider the differentiation hypothesis to be tenable though some limitations are readily apparent. First, the widely recognized principle of uneven development would lead us to anticipate that in individual children progress toward developed differentiation may be greater in some areas than others. In particular children, the discrepancy from area to area may be very marked. Second, a loss of differentiation (dedifferentiation), resulting, for example, from brain damage or not yet fully understood psychological causes, may affect functioning irregularly from one area to another, again making for a picture of unevenness. This kind of problem is more likely to exist, however, in studies of adults than in studies of children, where dedifferentiation is not apt to be common. Third, because any segment of behavior is the product of many determinants, inevitably, the segment we may consider in seeking concrete evidence of differentiation reflects the influence of other determinants as well. "Pure" manifestations of differentiation are inconceivable. Seeking evidence of level of differentiation involves focusing, within a complex behavior matrix, upon those aspects of functioning which seem particularly relevant to differentiation. Finally, it is possible for a person to operate at different levels of differentiation at different times, or even at the same time. We would consider, however, that a more differentiated person is *capable* of functioning at a relatively high level if required and motivated to do so in a particular situation.[8] As suggested, even with these limitations, we consider the differentiation hypothesis a supportable one, although we would not expect the relations predicted by the hypothesis to be of a very high order.

The proposal that greater or more limited differentiation is apt to be characteristic of many areas of individual psychological functioning is a way of *describing* a particular kind of psychological consistency. Questions of *causal* relations remain to be answered. How does this consistency arise and how is it maintained during development? What are the determinants of individual differences in pace of development of differentiation? The second question is considered in the next section. The answer to the first requires specification of the ways in which functioning in the areas considered are dynamically linked, both during development and at any particular time. In these specifications account must also be taken of linkages which, judged according to expectations from the differentiation hypothesis, make for inconsistency from one area to another. The nature of the linkages involved is inordinately complex. We discuss some of them in subsequent chapters.

For the moment, brief speculation about these linkages as they are apt to occur in the course of development offers reasonable grounds for expecting the relations proposed by the differentiation hypothesis. For example, it is difficult to imagine rapid progress in development of an articulated way of experiencing the world without àccompanying development of self-differentiation. The achievement of a segregated, structured self provides internal frames of reference for viewing, interpreting, and dealing with the world from the position of an autonomous agency, enjoying an existence apart from the field, rather than fused with it. This in turn is likely to aid in the development of an articulated way of experiencing the world. At the same time, a tendency for experience of the field to be articulated as it registers from moment to moment is likely to contribute to articulation of experience of the self. Again, as we have already suggested, the establishment of internal standards provides an important basis for

[8] As shown in Chapter 4, our perceptual tests provide examples of situations which force the subject to function in a more differentiated (specifically, analytical) way, if he is capable of such functioning.

regulation of impulse and direction of activity. Conversely, development of means for channeling impulse is apt to aid in the development of articulation of experience. One way in which developed controls may help bring about such a result is through their contribution to the regulation of attention. The relations resulting from the linkages mentioned seem consistent with the differentiation hypothesis.

E. DETERMINANTS AND STABILITY OF PACE OF DEVELOPMENT OF DIFFERENTIATION

The existence of individual differences in rate of progress toward psychological differentiation raises the question of possible sources of such differences. An interaction approach offers the most reasonable route for seeking an answer to such a question.

This approach, which is considered in some detail in Chapter 16, may be sketched in most general terms as follows: Variations in constitutional characteristics are without doubt crucial in determining individual differences, although at present the nature of these characteristics can only be a matter of speculation. The particular circumstances under which the child grows up are also critical. Differences in pace of progress toward greater differentiation thus derive from differences in patterns of contributions made to development by constitutional characteristics and by particular life experiences. We may for example conceive of an infant whose endowment greatly aids the development of differentiation. In such a case, it may suffice that the environment not seriously interfere for a high level of differentiation to be achieved; and it may require a strongly hampering environment to inhibit the forces toward development of differentiation which the initial endowment carries with it. On the other hand, an infant poorly endowed in this regard may achieve only limited differentiation, even under life circumstances which strongly foster its development. Such a child cannot "do" with a laissez-faire environment, and conditions which strongly hamper the development of differentiation will be vastly more damaging in his case than for a child who is well endowed. The eventual contribution of different kinds of life circumstances— whether they are in the nature of hampering, just allowing, positively helping, or even forcibly pushing the child's growth toward differentiation—is affected by his initial make-up.

This brief sketch of some pathways of interaction between starting characteristics and life experiences is suggestive of the possible sources of individual differences in rate of development of differentiation.

These pathways are identified more specifically later, when the studies we have done on this problem are described.

Consideration of sources of differences in extent of differentiation leads to the question of stability in pace of development of differentiation during growth. We may suppose that formal aspects of a psychological system, of the kind represented by differentiation, are particularly apt to be stable, in contrast to content aspects. It is therefore reasonable to expect that the child who shows greater differentiation than his peers at one stage of development will show it at later stages as well.

F. DIFFERENTIATION IN RELATION TO INTEGRATION, ADJUSTMENT, PATHOLOGY, AND MATURITY

We need to comment further, with particular reference to psychological functioning, on the distinction drawn earlier between differentiation and various aspects of integration.

At each level of differentiation, we noted, varied modes of integration are possible, although more complex integrations are likely to be associated with developed differentiation. Adjustment is mainly a function of effectiveness of integration.[9] Not one but many modes of effective integration, and therefore adequate adjustment, are possible at any given level of differentiation. Moreover, adequate adjustment is to be found at different levels of differentiation, resulting from integration which is effective for the particular level, although the nature of adjustment that may be considered adequate necessarily varies from one level to another. Pathology resulting from poorly developed or impaired integration may be expected to take different forms in highly differentiated persons and persons with limited differentiation. Thus, we may conceive that among differentiated persons, impairment is often apt to involve too great a separation or faulty connection of subsystems and/or isolation from the environment. Among relatively undifferentiated persons, in whom boundaries between subsystems, as well as between inside and outside, are weak, impairment is perhaps prone to take the form of dissolution of boundaries.

[9] Poorly developed differentiation may of course sometimes be a primary source of psychopathology. This may be true, for example, when the nervous system has been inadequately formed. Such impairment hampers the development of the kinds of integration needed for adjustment to many life situations. Limitedly developed differentiation may thus contribute to pathology through hindering effective integration.

The complex relation between differentiation and adjustment is particularly apparent when considered in connection with some of the specific indicators of differentiation. Though the development of differentiation in each indicator area may be of value to adjustment, these developments may be used in ways which hamper adjustment.

Thus, a person may have an articulated body concept, but because of the way in which his personality is integrated, he may overinvest in body boundaries, with considerable insulation a result. Again, a sense of separate identity may be found in individuals who show narcissistic self-involvement and extreme isolation from others or, on the other hand, in individuals who are capable of warm human relations. Awareness may be articulated and so make for clear perception of oneself and others. Though articulated, it may be markedly circumscribed through diminished contact with inner experiences and reduced ties to the environment. Articulation does not necessarily imply accuracy of awareness. Knowledge that the self is more differentiated or less differentiated is not a sufficient basis for evaluating it in adaptive terms.

Again, the achievement of differentiation in the area of controls and defenses carries no guarantee of effective adjustment. As one example, extreme reliance on intellectualization as a characteristic defense may thwart the development of an individual's emotional life. In other cases, intellectualization may aid in the maintenance of appropriate balance between the ideational and affective spheres. As another example, a developed conscience may operate in a way which makes it a harsh, unyielding master. If many feelings, actions, and needs are stamped as unacceptable, the result may be severe constriction both of activity and awareness of inner life. On the other hand, a developed conscience may contribute to socialization in ways that aid the person to live in harmony with his fellow men.

Another concept to be carefully separated from differentiation is that of maturity. Maturity, as commonly conceived, connotes both developed differentiation and effective integration. It is therefore among those who are highly differentiated that we are likely to find mature persons. But because highly differentiated people may vary in effectiveness of integration, not all those who are differentiated are necessarily mature.

G. THE PROBLEM OF VALUE JUDGMENTS

Consideration of development inevitably leads to questions of the value of different achievements of development. It is therefore important to identify clearly the value judgments implicit in the concept of differentiation, and the bases on which these judgments are made. It is equally important to specify the value dimensions toward which the differentiation concept is neutral.

Individual variations along the differentiation dimension are ordered from rudimentary to complex structure. Within limits, the achievement of complex structure is to be valued over fixation at a more rudimentary level. A developing system is endowed with a given potential. The diverse end-points of the growth of an individual developing system are broadly predictable. On the quite specific basis that it represents "fulfillment of its fate," development which brings the system close to the achievement of these potential end-points is apt to be assigned positive value. Differentiated structure is one of these end-points and therefore likely to be valued. This seems justified since, other things being equal, the differentiated person has richer, more diversified resources for coping than the less differentiated person.

It must be emphasized that in assigning a positive value judgment to achievement of a differentiated state it is only the rudimentary-complex dimension that is being considered. Effectiveness of integration, adjustment, maturity, all carry value judgments as well, but these are derived on other bases.[10] The designation of a given person as differentiated implies no direct value judgment with regard to these other areas.[11]

It is inordinately difficult to delimit the application of value judgments. Inevitably, they are subject to a "spreading effect"; a person considered "good" in one regard is apt to be considered "good" in general. This difficulty may be the source of misguided research effort, as we have found in our own work. The halo inevitably created by implied value judgments makes for difficulty both in doing research and interpreting results.

Another related difficulty is that some of the descriptive psychological terms we employ have an everyday usage, and as a result they carry value significance not intended in our use of them. "Conformity" is an example. The use of this term to describe a particular way of behaving, though not so intended, may be taken by some as generally

[10] Judgments in these areas, particularly adjustment and maturity, involve estimates of "fittingness to the environment" to a greater extent, and so are based to an important degree on the values and standards of society.

[11] To the extent that developed differentiation contributes to some of these other dimensions, there is an indirect connection.

derogatory of the person who shows it. We have chosen to employ commonly used terms, rather than create new ones; in doing so, we have attempted to make their meaning quite explicit.

H. SUMMARY

The theoretical framework that has been presented, based on the concept of differentiation, emerged gradually in the course of our studies; it both guided investigations and became more explicit through the results the investigations yielded.

Differentiation refers to the formal, as contrasted to the content aspects of a system and represents one of the two major characteristics of a system, viewed from the standpoint of its formal properties. The other is integration. Development toward greater differentiation involves progress from an initial relatively unstructured state, which has only limited segregation from the environment, to a more structured state, which has relatively definite boundaries, and which is capable of greater specificity of function. Though the development of differentiation and the development of integration proceed together in closely interwoven ways, the achievement of a high level of differentiation carries no necessary implication as to effectiveness of integration, adequacy of adjustment, or degree of maturity, although it is likely to be associated with more complex integrations. Developed differentiation may be found in effectively functioning people or people with marked pathology.

In a brief account of psychological growth, oriented particularly toward the development of differentiation, some of the salient ways in which the achievement of a differentiated state may be manifested in various areas of functioning were identified. These postulated "indicators" of differentiation, dynamically interrelated and ordinarily difficult to separate, include an articulated way of experiencing the world; a differentiated self as reflected particularly in a clearly defined body concept and a developed sense of separate identity; and specialized, structured controls and defenses.

As children grow older they tend to become more differentiated. We may expect, however, that at any age level, children would differ in extent of differentiation and that greater or more limited differentiation would be manifested in a given child in each of the indicator areas, although in varying degree. This expectation has been called the differentiation hypothesis. Some of the pathways of interaction between constitutional characteristics and various kinds of life experiences were

·sketched in order to identify the directions to be taken in a search for the sources of individual differences in pace of development of differentiation.

In the next chapter we outline the plan of the studies carried out in the setting of the conceptual framework presented.

3

METHOD OF STUDY

The investigations to be considered fall into three major areas: self-consistency in individual functioning as an expression of extent of differentiation; the contribution of life experiences and characteristics present in early infancy to pace of development of differentiation; and stability of individual patterns of functioning during development. The studies we report are mainly our own, although a number of relevant studies by others are also reviewed. The present chapter outlines the design of the studies we have ourselves performed.

We already noted that our theoretical framework emerged gradually, and as it developed our hypotheses and research design became ever more sharply focused. This change toward greater specificity becomes apparent as the account of the studies is unfolded.

We now believe that a field-dependent or field-independent way of perceiving is one of a large constellation of interrelated characteristics, which together reflect an individual's level of differentiation. In retrospect, it is conceivable that we might eventually have identified the same constellation and arrived at differentiation as a central concept had we started with studies of individual differences in any of the other characteristics which compose the constellation. In this sense it is perhaps an historical accident that our research design involves the field-dependence dimension in the central way it does. Yet, from a practical point of view, the fact that our work began in perception has been inordinately helpful to subsequent investigations. Not only is style of experiencing a central characteristic of psychological differentiation, but it is also a characteristic that can be evaluated in the laboratory under controlled conditions. From the studies of perception came the tests we have used to define the field-dependence dimension, which in turn has come to serve as a "tracer element" in identifying level of psychological differentiation more generally. The effectiveness of these tests is due in part to the fact that their development was preceded by intensive investigation, over a period of years, of the situational determinants of field dependence.[1]

Under the guidance of the problem-centered approach we followed, we were led to use many of the techniques which psychology has developed in its different branches—projective techniques, intelligence tests, interviews, behavioral observations, learning and memory techniques, and others. Had we curtailed our efforts either at the point where the issues were no longer those of "pure" perception or at the point where proven laboratory methods were no longer available, our most interesting and important findings would not have come to light.

The decision to use children as subjects in these studies was based on several considerations. First, our theoretical framework, with differentiation as a central concept, quite naturally made the developmental period the most fruitful one to investigate. Second, because of the greater lability of psychological structure in children, diverse areas of psychological activity are less likely to be insulated from each other, so that relationships among them stand out more sharply. For example, whereas in an adult intellectual functions may remain relatively immune from characterological difficulties or passing emotional storms, in a child the effects of such stresses are likely to "spill over" into the cognitive sphere. Finally, we were interested in going beyond the sheer determination of "what is associated with what," to an understanding of how the relations among diverse psychological areas arise. This objective could best be met by studying the development of these relations "in process" during the period of growing up.

A. GENERAL DESIGN OF THE STUDIES

1. Self-Consistency as a Function of Extent of Differentiation

In the preceding chapter some of the ways in which extent of differentiation may be expressed in various areas of psychological functioning were identified. It was suggested that a child's achievement of a fairly high level of differentiation would be manifested principally in an articulated way of experiencing the world and himself, including a relatively developed body concept and a sense of separate identity, which reflect particularly the development of self-differentiation. It is also likely to be manifested in structured controls and defenses. These characteristics we have labeled "indicators of differentiation," and we

---

[1] These tests, briefly mentioned in the first chapter, are described in detail in Chapter 4.

postulated that measures of them would be significantly interrelated. This expectation of self-consistency has been called the *differentiation hypothesis.*

The sequence of studies we have done bearing on this hypothesis reflects our early interest in individual differences in extent of field dependence. This sequence does not necessarily correspond to the order in which various salient concepts were introduced in the discussion of differentiation in Chapter 2. As noted, the field-dependence-independence dimension had been very intensively studied in our earlier work, and an effective laboratory methodology for its evaluation had been developed. In our research design we accordingly used performance in the tests of perceptual field dependence as a "reference standard." We considered measures from these tests to represent the analytical aspect of articulated experience. In testing the differentiation hypothesis, we first investigated the relation of measures of field dependence to other measures of articulation of experience and to measures of structure of defenses and controls. Then we explored the relation of all these measures to one another, with the expectation that they would be significantly interrelated.

Our main studies of self-consistency as a function of extent of differentiation were conducted with three groups of 10-year-old boys: [2] Group I, consisting of 14 boys drawn from a larger sample used in the longitudinal studies to be described in Section 3; Group II, consisting of 24 boys; and Group III, consisting of 30 boys. (For some special studies groups of 12-year-olds were used as well.) To obtain evidence on self-consistency the Rorschach, figure-drawing test, and Thematic Apperception Test (TAT) [3] were given to all three groups of children, and the children in Groups II and III were interviewed as well. All the children also received our battery of perceptual tests. Those in Groups II and III were given standard intelligence tests and children in the latter group were tested in special situations devised to evaluate particular hypotheses. The miniature-toys-play test was also used with

[2] Because of the consistent finding of sex differences in the cognitive functions with which we are particularly concerned (Chapter 13) results for boys and girls cannot be properly combined. The study of adequately sized samples of boys and girls in each problem area would mean considerable work, both in testing and analysis of data. Under these circumstances, we have chosen to conduct our main studies with boys. For some problems girls have been studied as well.

[3] All children were given cards 1, 3BM, 4, 5, 10, 12M, 18GF, 8BM, and 17BM of the TAT. The boys in Groups II and III were also given cards 2, 7BM, 11, and 14; card 16 was used with Group III only. These cards were selected since they appeared likely to elicit material of particular relevance to the issues we were studying.

Groups I and II (Karp and Marlens, 1958). Finally, each contact with the child—whether it took place in the course of a formal test session, the car trip to and from the laboratory, during lunch, or via telephone conversation—was used as an opportunity to observe him and to obtain further information about him.

Our first studies of self-consistency were in the area of articulateness of experience. Within this area we expected to find individuals consistent in their tendency to experience in a more articulated or less articulated fashion. Our investigations began with a study of the relation between perceptual and intellectual functioning. As background for these studies we had the clear demonstration, both from our own earlier investigations and more recent work of others, that at the core of the field-dependence dimension is the capacity for analysis of experience. Accordingly, we undertook these studies in the anticipation that people would be consistent in their performance of cognitive tasks—perceptual and intellectual—which require analytical functioning.

As a first approach to the study of consistency in perceptual and intellectual activities, the Revised Stanford-Binet (Form L) was administered to the Group-II 10-year-old boys who had also received the perceptual tests. When a significant relationship was found between Binet IQs and extent of field independence, a more extensive series of studies was undertaken in order to determine more precisely the basis of the relation. For this purpose, the Wechsler Intelligence Scale for Children (WISC) was administered, along with the perceptual test battery, to the Group-III 10-year-old boys and to a group of 12-year-old boys and girls. Because of its organization into subtests, the WISC lends itself more readily than the Binet to an evaluation of specific aspects of intellectual functioning.

As another approach to the study of consistency in perceptual and intellectual functioning, we tested a number of specific hypotheses, suggested by our earlier work, using special problem-solving situations we had developed.

In a further extension of the studies of self-consistency we investigated the relation between capacity for analysis of experience (in the sense that parts of a field are apprehended as discrete from their backgrounds) and capacity for structuring of experience (in the sense that organization is imposed upon a field that lacks it). These studies demonstrated, as expected, that analysis and structuring, which together represent articulation of experience, tend to be associated. Next we undertook studies of the relation between extent of articulation of experience of the external field and extent of articulation of experience of the self. Investigations in the latter area focused on the nature of the body concept and extent of development of sense of separate identity. Finally, the study of self-consistency was extended to an investigation of structure of defenses and controls. Evidence on body concept, sense of separate identity, and nature of controls and defenses came mainly from the projective tests, interviews, and observations of behavior, although these techniques were used to obtain information on other aspects of functioning as well.

With Group III, all the Rorschachs were conducted and evaluated by one staff member, all the TATs by a second staff member, and all the interviews by a third. This procedure was not always followed with Groups I and II, however. The figure-drawing test was administered by several staff members, but in no instance by those responsible for the Rorschach, TAT, or interview.

Some general aspects of the procedures followed in gathering and treating the data from the various personality-assessment techniques need to be described.

Each of the techniques was administered for our particular research purpose, and its results evaluated with specific hypotheses in view. As a first step in analysis of data, special methods were developed for evaluating the characteristics in which we were interested. The test material itself determined, to some extent, the particular procedure to be used. In some instances the frequency of occurrence of a highly specific feature of the test production served as the basis of a scale, in other instances a global rating seemed most appropriate. Some of the scales were based on data from a single test (in the case of the TAT, even a single card), others on all the personality test material available for a child. At times, separate scales, based on different tests, were used to evaluate a particular characteristic.

The general plan in developing scales for the Rorschach, TAT, figure-drawing test, and interview was to devise and apply them on the test productions of the children of Groups I and II. The scaling procedures were then reviewed with knowledge of the children's perceptual performances. Such a review often led us to revise the definition of the variables and the rationale for their scaling. Finally, in most instances these revised scales were cross-validated with the children of Group III.

Studies of objectivity or verifiability were conducted for most of the scales.[4] A second judge applied the scales and reliability measures

---

[4] In several instances, our findings had been replicated in other laboratories, using the same or similar scales, making it unnecessary for us to conduct such studies.

(coefficients of objectivity) were computed. In some cases, the second judge was not only totally unfamiliar with the child, but he was deliberately kept ignorant of the nature and purpose of the study.

A research design which calls for independent evaluation of test data without access to other information about individual subjects, or about the success of analyses already completed, demands careful precautions against possible data contamination. We attempted to meet this problem in several ways. First, perceptual and intellectual tests were given by research assistants. These assistants were not involved in any of the blind analyses of projective test and interview data. A strictly observed rule of the laboratory was an enforced lack of communication between them and the senior staff members concerning what these children were like, as seen either in informal contact, or during test performance. Second, senior staff members who were responsible for analysis of projective test data did not discuss the children or the data with one another, until the analyses were completed. This prohibition was rigidly carried out, in spite of the cost in staff morale. A more serious cost was the loss of the deeper understanding we might have obtained of each child had we been free to pool and integrate all the data about him while he and his test material were still "fresh."

A third major procedure for maintaining "anonymity" of the data was to secure for data analyses the services of four psychologists who had not otherwise participated in the study. They were kept entirely in the dark about specific hypotheses, results of analyses already completed, information concerning individual children, and even reasons why they were asked to undertake certain analyses.

These four psychologists carried out a number of specific analyses of projective tests and interviews and applied rating scales developed by our staff. The data given them were coded, with different codes used for various test productions of the same children. When one of these psychologists worked on separate sets of data for the same group on different occasions, she did not know that the same group was involved. Nor were the psychologists told how many different groups were being studied. In no case, of course, did they know other test results of the subjects or the outcome of analyses of any other test data.

When two judges rated a set of test records according to a given scale, the following procedures were adopted in relating these ratings to other test measures. In the case of the TAT we used pooled ratings with differences reconciled in conference. This method was possible with the TAT since both judges were members of our staff so that the joint meetings required to reconcile discrepancies were practicable.

With the other personality-assessment techniques, the second judge, when available, was not a staff member and joint meetings were difficult to arrange. In these instances, we used the ratings of the second judge, rather than of the original judge who had developed the scale.

Case conferences were held on most of the children in an attempt to integrate all the information available for each child. The material considered at these conferences included all the projective test records, the results of the perceptual and intellectual tests, and, when available, the protocols of interviews conducted with the children and their mothers. The ratings made of each child on the scales that had been devised were also available. Case conferences were of course held *after* the development and application of the various scales.

2. Role of Early Life Experiences and of Constitutional Factors in Pace of Development of Differentiation

The results that emerged from the studies outlined above directed us to the question of the origins of individual differences in extent of differentiation.

In one series of studies we investigated the role of children's early home environment in contributing to such differences. The general hypothesis which guided the study of the home environment was that the quality of mother-child interaction patterns was important in hampering or fostering the child's development of differentiation. Evidence for the evaluation of mother-child interaction came from both mother and child. That from the mother, which was our main source, was obtained through an interview with her. The child's view of his parents was appraised through his TAT productions, and through an interview with him.

Interviews were conducted with the mothers of the 10-year-old boys of Groups II and III. When conducting interviews and analyzing interview data, the interviewer had no knowledge of any of the child's test results. The method of evaluating the home-interview data was developed on the interview records of the mothers of Group-II children and cross-validated on the records of mothers of Group-III children. The mothers of the Group-I 10-year-olds were interviewed when their children were 14 years of age. The records of these interviews were also submitted to "blind" analyses, thus providing another opportunity for cross-validation of the home-interview scale.

As a further step in the study of parent-child interaction patterns, 26 of the 30 mothers of the Group-III boys were revisited 2 to 3 years after the first contact with them and were given a short form of the embedded-figures test and the figure-drawing test. This study was guided by the hypothesis, growing out of the home-interview findings, that the more highly differentiated children would tend to have mothers who themselves were more differentiated.

A second major study of parent-child interaction patterns was conducted with a group of children and their mothers in Topeka, Kansas. This study is described in the next section.

3. Stability of Growth Patterns

We suggested that the formal aspects of an individual's psychological make-up are apt to be relatively stable in comparison to content aspects. During young adulthood, we would expect a given level of differentiation to remain a more or less constant characteristic of an individual over time, despite wide fluctuations in life circumstances and in content aspects of his make-up. During the growth years, there is, of course, a general trend toward greater differentiation, but it is possible that as a child grows older he may maintain his position on the differentiation dimension relative to his age group.

Our investigations in this area have involved the longitudinal study of three groups of children. One group of 30 boys and 30 girls was first tested at 10 years of age and again at 14 and 17 years. (Fourteen of the boys constituted the Group-I 10-year-old sample, described in Section 1.) A second group of 26 boys and 27 girls was first tested at 8 and retested at 13 years.[5] The third group consisted of children in Topeka, Kansas, studied by other investigators in infancy and again by us in the 6- to 9-year period. The analyses of the data from these studies are only partially completed.

All subjects in the 10-14-17-year and 8-13-year longitudinal studies were given the standard battery of perceptual tests.[6] Intensive personality studies were made of all these children and family backgrounds were explored in most instances. To date, however, analyses have been completed only of stability of mode of perceiving and of characteristics of the body concept.

The Topeka study was made possible through the cooperation of Dr. Sibylle Escalona and of Dr. Lois Murphy and the staff of the "Coping Project" (1960a, 1960b) at the Menninger Foundation. They made available to us extensive data gathered for a different purpose (Escalona, Leitch, et al., 1952) on infant behavior in the 4- to 32-week period, and facilitated our contact with these subjects several years

[5] We have available cross-sectional data for seven groups of boys and girls of 8, 10, 11, 12, 13, 15, and 17 years. These data permit us to check the effects of practice, due to repeated testing, in the longitudinal study.

[6] The embedded-figures test was too difficult to use with the 8-year-olds.

later. Seventy-two of these children were studied in Topeka, when they were between 6 and 9 years of age, with a battery of tests of field dependence and projective tests. Home interviews with the mothers of the children were also conducted. These data, when analyzed, will permit an investigation of stability of growth patterns and of parent-child interactions from infancy to later childhood.

B. SUBJECTS

All the subjects with the exception of the Topeka group were drawn from public schools located in the Flatbush section of Brooklyn, New York. They constituted a fairly homogeneous group. Thus, the 10-year-old children lived in approximately the same neighborhood, within walking distance of the school. The area provides some opportunities for free play and recreation on the street and in playgrounds, temples, and churches. For the most part, time outside of school was heavily scheduled with religious classes, Scouts, after school clubs, or music lessons.

The cultural backgrounds of the children were quite similar. Of the 68 10-year-old boys, 59 were Jewish. Almost all the parents were American born, but of foreign parentage. With a few exceptions, they have lived in New York City all their lives.

At the time they were studied in the laboratory 59 of the 68 boys were living with both parents. Four whose parents were separated or divorced and one whose father had died were living with their mothers. One, whose mother had deserted the family, was living with his father. Two were living with their mothers and stepfathers and one was living with his father and a stepmother. Subsequent to the testing of the children, but before interviews and testing of mothers was completed, two mothers died.

All fathers were employed at the time of the study, and all families were self-sustaining, although income levels varied considerably. Approximately one-third of the fathers were in professions or were owners of factories or businesses. About two-thirds of the families belonged to a middle-income group, with fathers employed as salesmen, transport workers, accountants, skilled factory workers, or in clerical positions. Only a few were unskilled laborers in low-income brackets. About one-third were home owners, mostly of quite large and elaborate homes. Families who did not own their homes lived in small apartments. With the exception of families who had moved into homes of their own, many lived in the same apartment where the children were born. Most of the families had two children at the time of the study.

Some indication of the value placed on home life by these parents was given by the well-kept, clean, adequately to extremely well-furnished homes. All of the children were receiving some form of religious instruction at the time of the study, though, for a few parents, such instruction had cultural rather than religious value. Nearly all parents placed great emphasis on education and hoped for upward social mobility for their children.

Our method of recruiting subjects from elementary and high schools was to send a letter and consent form to the parents of all children in classes appropriate for the age range we were interested in studying. This material was distributed to the children at the school. The letter described our study in very general terms. An effort was made to get as many volunteers as possible from each class that had been approached. As an aid to this purpose a signed message from the principal, urging parents to permit their children to take part in the study, was appended to our own letter.

After arrangements had been made for a child's participation in the study a staff member called for him at school or home, by car, and returned him to his home after the test session. This procedure was followed in each of the half dozen or so sessions required of the child. A small gift was given the child at the end of each visit to the laboratory. Over a period of time these procedures led to an atmosphere of willing cooperation on the part of the children and parents of the community, with the result that many more volunteers were obtained than we needed.

In selecting subjects from the groups of volunteers, age was used as the only criterion. Each age group we sought to fill was composed, with few exceptions, of children ranging from 6 months under to 6 months over the specified age. Thus the 10-year-old groups included children between 9 years, 7 months and 10 years, 6 months. Preference was given to children in the desired age range whose birthdays were close to the testing date.

C. GENERAL STATISTICAL PROCEDURES

The correlations to be reported are Pearson product-moment, point-biserial, or phi coefficients, unless otherwise noted. One-tailed tests of significance were used when the study had a strict cross-validation design. In all other cases two-tailed tests were used, even though the direction of the outcome was predicted on a priori theoretical grounds. In describing work reported by others, the decision of the authors on this point was generally accepted.

D. SUMMARY

The studies in this book are concerned with three major problems. The first problem is that of individual self-consistency. The studies here were guided by the differentiation hypothesis, which led us to expect that measures of the indicators we had postulated of more de-

veloped or less developed differentiation in various areas of functioning would tend to be significantly interrelated. Three groups of 10-
year-old boys served as subjects in the main studies, although other
age-sex groups were used as well. Data needed for testing the differentiation hypothesis were obtained from a battery of tests of perceptual field dependence, a series of problem-solving and intelligence
tests, projective tests (TAT, Rorschach, and figure-drawing test), and
an interview.

The second problem is the contribution of life experiences and characteristics present in infancy to individual differences in pace of development of differentiation. The study primarily concerned with the
role of early characteristics has already been carried out but its results not yet analyzed. In this study a group of children observed in
infancy by Escalona and others were studied again by us when they
were 6 to 8 years old. In a second series of studies mother-child interactions were investigated among the 10-year-old boys evaluated from
the standpoint of extent of differentiation. It was our expectation that
differences in extent of differentiation in the children would be related
to opportunities for the development of differentiation provided by
interactions with their mothers. On the premise that more differentiated children are likely to have mothers who are themselves relatively
differentiated we have begun studies of mothers, using some of the
procedures employed in evaluating extent of differentiation in their
children.

The third problem is stability of individual patterns of functioning
during development and in adulthood. For this problem longitudinal
studies were carried out. In addition to the groups studied in infancy
and again at 6 to 8 years, already mentioned, we also had a group
studied at the ages of 10, 14, and 17, and another group studied at 8
and again at 13. The latter two groups received on each test occasion
a series of perceptual, intellectual, and projective tests; and most of
them and their mothers were interviewed as well. Our expectation in
these studies was that there would be considerable stability in relative
extent of differentiation in adulthood; and that there would be some
stability in the growth years as well, even though children tend to
become more differentiated as they grow older.

4

ANALYTICAL FUNCTIONING
IN PERCEPTION

The present chapter and the four that follow are concerned with differences among people in extent of articulation of experience. The first three deal particularly with experience in special perceptual and intellectual situations, the remaining ones particularly with experience of the self.

Articulation implies that experience is both analyzed and structured. We start in this chapter with the analytical component, as encountered in perception.

Individual differences in analytical functioning in perception have been investigated in our earlier work as part of the study of the field-dependence-independence dimension. Each of the tests of the perceptual battery devised in the course of this work requires the person to separate an item from the field or context of which it is a part and which therefore exerts a strong influence upon it; to "break up" a field or configuration. The person with a more field-independent way of perceiving tends to experience his surroundings analytically, with objects experienced as discrete from their backgrounds. The person with a more field-dependent way of perceiving tends to experience his surroundings in a relatively global fashion, passively conforming to the influence of the prevailing field or context.

We first describe some of the tests used to evaluate individual differences along the field-dependence-independence dimension of perceptual functioning. Then we review our earlier work on this dimension and the results of more recent studies which have contributed to its further delineation.

A. TESTS OF PERCEPTUAL FIELD DEPENDENCE

The tests used in the present studies were chosen on the basis of their simplicity and effectiveness from a larger group of tests of field dependence devised in the course of our earlier work. Descriptions of the tests, data on reliability, and procedures for computing an index of field dependence are given below.

1. Description of the Tests

a. The rod-and-frame test (RFT).[1] This test evaluates the individual's perception of the position in relation to the upright of an item within a limited visual field.

The apparatus used consists of a luminous square frame, pivoted at its center so that it may be tilted to left or right. Pivoted at the same center, but moving independently of the frame, is a luminous rod. Since the test is conducted in a completely darkened room, all the subject can see are the frame and rod. These are presented in tilted positions. With the frame remaining tilted, the subject is required, by his instructions to the examiner, to adjust the rod to a position he perceives as upright. For successful performance of this task the subject must "extract" the rod from the tilted frame through reference to body position. The subject is tested on some trials while sitting erect, so that it is relatively easy to refer to the body in establishing rod position, and on other trials while tilted, so that it is more difficult to refer to the body. On all trials a large tilt of the rod when it is reported to be straight indicates adherence to the visual field; a small tilt indicates independence of the field and reliance on the body.

When children are used as subjects, the test is presented as a "game" the rules of which are given before they enter the experimental room. The procedure is made concrete by actual demonstrations, and several practice trials are given. The concept "vertical" is carefully defined in terms of concrete and specific reference criteria, such as the flagpole outside the building.

Three series, each consisting of eight trials, comprise the standard test. *Series 1:* The subject is tilted to one side (at 28° left or at 28° right) and the frame is tilted to the same side (at 28° left or 28° right). The rod is to be adjusted to the upright from an initial tilt of 28° (at times to the same side as the frame, at other times to the opposite side).

---

[1] A fuller account of this test may be found elsewhere (Witkin, 1948; Witkin, et al., 1954). A study of the factors governing perception in this kind of situation has been reported by Witkin and Asch (1948b).

Series 2: Body and frame are tilted to opposite sides (both at 28°).
Series 3: The body is erect and the frame is tilted to left or right (at 28°).

The score for each of the three series of the test is the mean absolute error in degrees from the true upright for the eight trials of the series.[2] The raw scores for each series are converted into standard scores, using the mean and standard deviation of the sex-age group to which the subject belongs. The total RFT "index" is the mean of the standard scores for the three series, equally weighted; positive scores reflect relatively field-dependent, negative scores relatively field-independent performance.

b. The tilting-room–tilting-chair tests (TRTC).[3] Whereas the RFT evaluates the subject's perception of the position of an item within a field, these tests evaluate his perception of the position of his body and of the whole surrounding field in relation to the upright.

The apparatus for these tests consists of a boxlike room, 70 by 71 by 69 inches, suspended on ball-bearing pivots so that it can be tilted by any amount to left or right. Inside the room is a chair for the subject which also can be tilted to left or right independently of the room. The apparatus is shown in Figure 4-1.

The way in which the subject establishes the position of his body is determined by seating him in the tilted room and requiring him to bring his body to a position that he perceives as upright. If he tilts his body far in the direction of the tilted room in order to make himself straight, he is judging his position in terms of his apparent relation to the field. If, on the other hand, he brings himself close to the true upright, he is resisting the influence of the field and showing marked awareness of bodily sensations.

To determine the manner in which the subject establishes the position of the whole surrounding field, the room in which he is seated is tilted, and he is asked to bring it to an upright position. If he reports the room straight at its initial tilt, he is accepting its vertical axis, now tilted, as the true upright. If, on the other hand, he succeeds in mak-

---

[2] There are a number of possible alternative scoring methods for the RFT and for the other orientation tests. For example, the mean error in the direction of the tilt of the frame has been used by some workers instead of the absolute error. These alternatives may be useful for specific research problems, but we have not found a scoring method that has greater construct validity as a measure of field dependence than does the absolute error.

[3] A fuller account of these tests may be found in earlier reports (Witkin, 1948; Witkin, et al., 1954) and a report of the factors governing perception in this kind of situation in Witkin (1949a).

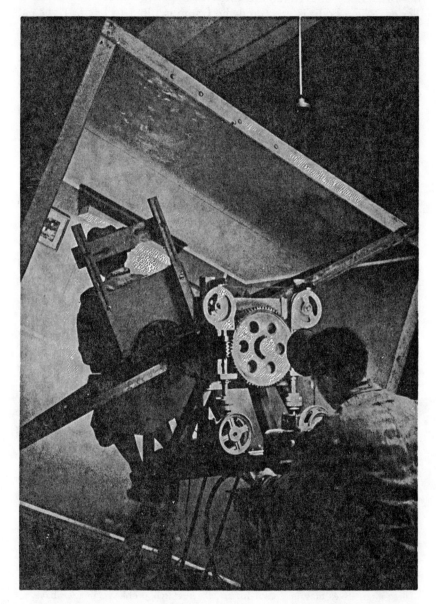

Figure 4-1. Tilting-room–tilting-chair test. (Photograph by David Linton.)

ing the room truly straight, he is perceiving its position in relation to the felt position of his body.

When children are used as subjects, advance demonstrations of the procedure of the test and of the working of the apparatus are given. The child is seated in the chair of the apparatus and the movement of room alone, chair alone, and both together are shown to him. He is then given, in simple language, the "rules of the game" which he and the examiner will "play."

The standard test is made up of two parts: *The room-adjustment test* (RAT) consists of eight trials, in four of which (Series 1a) room and chair are initially tilted to opposite sides and in four (Series 1b) to the same side. At the outset, the room is always tilted 56° and the chair 22°. On each trial, while his chair remains in its initial position of tilt, the subject instructs the examiner to move the room to a position in which he perceives it as upright.

The body-adjustment test (BAT) consists of six trials, in half of which (Series 2a) room and chair are initially tilted to the same side, and in half (Series 2b) to opposite sides. The initial tilt of the room is 35° and of the chair 22°. With the room remaining tilted, the subject directs the movement of the chair to a position in which he perceives it to be upright.

The raw score for each of the four series is the mean absolute error in degrees from the true upright for the several trials of the series. As with the RFT, each series score is converted to a standard score, using the mean and standard deviation of the subject's age-sex group. The total RAT index is the mean of the standard scores for Series 1a and 1b. For the BAT, the index is the mean of the standard scores for Series 2a and 2b. For both tests, a positive index reflects relatively field-dependent and a negative index relatively field-independent performance.

c. The embedded-figures test (EFT).[4] This test also requires the subject to separate an item from the field in which it is incorporated, but it involves neither orientation toward the upright nor body position.

The subject's task is to find a particular simple figure within a larger complex figure. The figures which make up the test were selected from those developed by Gottschaldt (1926) for his study of the role of past experience in perception. To make Gottschaldt's black-and-white outline complex figures more difficult, colored patterns were superimposed. The simple figure is "hidden" by being incorporated

[4] This test has been described in detail elsewhere (Witkin, 1950b).

into the pattern of the larger figure (e.g., its outlines may form the boundaries of several prominent subpatterns in the complex figure).

The standard test makes use of a series of twenty-four complex figures, in each of which a simple figure is to be located. A maximum of 5 minutes is allowed per trial. The subject's score is the mean amount of time taken to find the simple figures within the complex ones. This provides a measure of the extent to which his perception is influenced by the context in which an item occurs. As in the other tests, the raw score is also converted into a standard score, positive standard scores reflecting relatively field-dependent and negative standard scores relatively field-independent performance.

2. Reliability of the Perceptual Tests

All the tests in the perceptual battery have satisfactorily high reliabilities. For an interval of 3 years the following test-retest correlations have been obtained: for the rod-and-frame test (RFT), $r = .84$ (men) and .66 (women); for the body-adjustment test (BAT), $r = .77$ (men) and .74 (women); and for the embedded-figures test (EFT), $r = .89$ (men) and .89 (women) (Bauman, 1951). Dana and Goocher (1959) report a test-retest correlation for EFT of .92 after a one-week interval. Split-half reliabilities tend to run somewhat higher. Loeff (1961) has reported a corrected odd-even correlation of .84 for the BAT; Linton (1952) has obtained correlations of .90 and .86 for BAT Series 2a and 2b, respectively. Corrected odd-even correlations for the EFT of .90 (Linton, 1952), .92 (Longenecker, 1956), .95 (Gardner, Jackson, and Messick, 1960), and .88 (Loeff, 1961) have been found. For the RFT, corrected odd-even correlations of .92 (Gardner, Jackson, and Messick, 1960) and .89 (Loeff, 1961) were obtained.[5, 6]

These reliabilities are generally high enough to warrant a reduction in the length of the tests for many research purposes. Jackson (1956) has conducted an item analysis of the EFT and recommends the use of a 12-item test with a 3-minute instead of 5-minute time limit. He reports correlations in the mid-nineties between the shortened and full-scale EFT for several groups of subjects.

Our own data indicate that the first twelve items in the standard order of presentation provide about as reliable a measure as any twelve items drawn from the total set. The use of the first twelve items has

---

[5] Data on stability of children's test scores are reported in Chapter 23.

[6] A comparison of scores for tests conducted by different examiners showed no significant examiner differences.

the advantage that available data for the total test can be rescored and compared with short-form scores. Because of learning effects within the test series, data from the total test cannot be compared directly to data from Jackson's short form.

Our own data also suggest that scores for Series 3 of the RFT may be substituted for total RFT scores with no loss in validity. Since the tilting chair is not required for Series 3, this modification has the advantage of reducing equipment costs. In some of the studies reviewed, these or similar modifications have been made in the perceptual tests. However, in the work reported the full battery has been used since we were committed to the standard testing procedure by the design of our developmental studies.

3. The Perceptual Index

To evaluate the extent of a subject's field dependence, the mean of the separate indices for the RFT, BAT, and EFT is computed. This composite index gives comparable (but not exactly equal) weight to the three tests from which it is derived. The room-adjustment test (RAT) is not included in this index because, as shown later in this chapter, it seems to provide a much poorer measure of field dependence than the other tests. As for each of the separate tests, a positive perceptual index score reflects relatively field-dependent and a negative index score relatively field-independent performance.

B. EARLY WORK

The concept of field dependence emerged initially from our studies of perception of the upright in space.[7] Studies of RAT (room-adjustment test), BAT (body-adjustment test), and RFT (rod-and-frame test) performance demonstrated striking individual differences in the extent to which location of the perceived upright is determined with reference to the axes of the prevailing visual field. They also demonstrated that an individual tends to be consistent in his perceptual functioning from test to test. Thus, the person who is unable to maintain the "separateness" of his body from the surrounding field in the BAT also cannot determine the position of the rod independently of the tilted frame in the RFT.

Early in our work, we considered three hypotheses in an attempt to account for these consistent individual differences in perception.

[7] Witkin, 1948, 1949a, 1949b, 1949c, 1950a, 1950b, 1952; Witkin and Asch, 1948a, 1948b; Asch and Witkin, 1948a, 1948b.

One hypothesis interpreted the individual differences in terms of "accuracy" in perception of the upright. It soon became clear, however, that this hypothesis was not tenable.

The results of studies with the rotating-room test contributed particularly to the rejection of the "accuracy" hypothesis. In this test,[8] the direction of the force on the subject's body is changed by rotating him, while seated in a small, fully enclosed room, about a circular track. Under these circumstances, the effective force on his body is the resultant of the downward pull of gravity and the outward acting centrifugal force. The room within which the subject is seated—the surrounding visual field—remains upright throughout rotation. This is in contrast to the situation in the BAT, where the visual field is displaced from the upright, while the direction of the force on the body remains unchanged. The BAT and rotating-room tests are in other respects comparable.

If "accuracy" in perceiving the upright is the important determinant of individual differences in these tests, we would expect a person who is an accurate perceiver in the BAT (i.e., one who aligns his body with the upright indicated by the direction of the gravitational pull) also to be an accurate perceiver in the rotating-room test (i.e., one who aligns himself with the upright indicated by the visual field). In fact, however, just the opposite result was found. High *negative* correlations were obtained (.66 for men and .72 for women), indicating that the "accurate" perceivers in the BAT tended to be among the most "inaccurate" perceivers in the rotating-room test and vice versa.

Another hypothesis we considered was that individual differences in the orientation tests reflect differences in extent of body sensitivity. Early in our work, when only the results of the orientation tests were available, it appeared that some people determined the upright primarily with reference to bodily sensations and others primarily with reference to the visual field. Considered in these terms, it seemed possible that the field-dependent person might have little sensitivity and the field-independent person great sensitivity to body cues. However, it soon became clear that the "body-sensitivity" hypothesis also was untenable. Early findings with a series of tests involving body action and body perception contributed particularly to the rejection of the body-sensitivity hypothesis.

Two of the situations used in these earlier studies were the ataxiameter and stabilometer, tests of body steadiness and body balance, respectively (Wapner and Witkin, 1950; Witkin and Wapner, 1950). Performance in these tests involves the use of body cues very directly, but yet was

[8] Described in earlier reports (Witkin, 1950a, 1952).

found to have little relation to performance in the orientation tests. Moreover, accuracy in adjusting the body to the upright from an initially tilted position with body surrounded by a tilted visual field—the task in the BAT—had little relation to accuracy in carrying out the same task with eyes closed, i.e., in the absence of a visual field. Correlations of standard BAT scores with scores for the "eyes-closed" version were .23 for men and .20 for women, neither significant.[9] Since the "eyes-closed" BAT directly evaluates ability to utilize body cues of tilt in determining body position, these low and nonsignificant correlations suggest that body sensitivity, as such, cannot account for the striking differences among individuals in BAT performance.

The standard BAT conducted with eyes open (hence under the influence of the visual field) is more highly related to the EFT, which does not involve body position in any way, than to the BAT conducted with eyes closed. In contrast to the low correlations just cited between scores for the two kinds of body-adjustment tests, fairly high significant correlations were found between scores for the standard BAT and EFT (.54 for men and .58 for women).

This pattern of relations suggested rejection of the hypothesis that sheer alertness to cues of body tilt is a major determinant of individual differences in the ability to adjust the body to the upright when it is surrounded by a tilted visual field.

A third hypothesis accounted for the consistent individual differences in perception in terms of differences in ability to overcome an embedding context. At an early stage in our work it became clear that this hypothesis provided the most reasonable basis for interpreting the findings.

The embedded-figures test (EFT), which is now part of the standard battery of tests of field dependence, was developed to check the third hypothesis. This test features the ability to perceive an item independently of its context and does not involve body position. In our early studies, the EFT was found to be highly related to the BAT and RFT and only moderately related to the RAT. More recent studies, carried out with a variety of groups, have confirmed these findings (Linton, 1952; Gruen, 1955).[10] Intercorrelations among the perceptual tests

---

[9] These low correlations cannot be attributed to poor test reliability. We earlier cited evidence of the satisfactory reliability of the standard BAT. The uncorrected odd-even reliability coefficients for the BAT with eyes closed are .77 for men and .73 for women.

[10] Similar results were obtained in a number of other studies which compared performance in two of the four tests: Bound (1957), Gardner, Holzman, Klein, Linton, and Spence (1959), Young (1959), Gardner, Jackson, and Messick (1960).

reported by these authors are summarized in Table 4-1, along with our earlier results for college and hospital populations, and those of Epstein (1957) who used the BAT, RAT, and RFT. Table 4-2 summarizes the intercorrelations for six age groups used in our cross-sectional studies of perceptual development (Witkin, Goodenough, and Karp, 1959).

The correlations among scores for the BAT, RFT, and EFT are for the most part significant, giving a picture of substantial consistency in individual functioning in these situations. This finding supports the

Table 4-1. Intercorrelations among perceptual test scores for groups of adults [a]

Test	Group	Sex	RAT	N	RFT	N	EFT	N
BAT	College	M	.28 **	136	.43 **	136	.54 **	51
		F	.31	75	.39 **	75	.58 **	51
	Hospital	M	.22	38	.39 *	38	.26	35
		F	.02	39	.55 **	39	.15	35
	Gruen	M	.02	30	.14	30	.26	30
		F	−.30	30	.11	30	.52 **	30
	Linton	M	.26	53	—[b]		.61 **	53
	Epstein	M	.52 **	35	.32	35	—[b]	
RAT	College	M			.37 **	136	.56 **	51
		F			.44 **	75	.25	51
	Hospital	M			.28	38	.28	35
		F			.21	39	.12	35
	Gruen	M			.61 **	30	.44 *	30
		F			.13	30	−.16	30
	Linton	M			—		.06	53
	Epstein	M			.61 **	35	—	
RFT	College	M					.64 **	51
		F					.21	51
	Hospital	M					.63 **	35
		F					.30	35
	Gruen	M					.42 *	30
		F					.37 *	30

[a] Intercorrelations taken from or computed on data reported by Witkin, et al., 1954; Gruen, 1951, 1955; Linton, 1952; and Epstein, 1957.
[b] Linton's subjects did not receive the RFT, Epstein's did not receive the EFT.
* Significant at .05 level.
** Significant at .01 level.

Table 4-2. Intercorrelations among perceptual test scores for age groups from 8 to 17 years (cross-sectional study)

Test	Age	N [a]	RFT	TRTC BAT	RAT
EFT	10	60	.31 *	.36 **	.02
	12	50	.51 **	.45 **	−.11
	13	59	.55 **	.42 **	.24
	15	50	.31 *	.26	.35 *
	17	48	.42 **	.27	.38 **
RFT	8	53		.30	.24
	10	60		.30 **	.22
	12	50		.25	−.15
	13	59		.45 **	.45 **
	15	50		.41 **	.24
	17	48		.40 **	.26
BAT	8	53			.34 *
	10	60			−.09
	12	50			.19
	13	59			.43 **
	15	40			.25
	17	48			.33 *

[a] No systematic differences between sexes were present in the intercorrelation matrices. The data for the sexes were therefore combined by the use of Fisher's r to z technique.

* Significant at .05 level.
** Significant at .01 level.

hypothesis that the ability to overcome an embedding context is central to the field-dependence dimension.

Correlations with the RAT tend to be lower and, for the younger age groups (particularly those below 13 years), almost all are insignificant. These results for the RAT support the same hypothesis.

In our 1954 report we suggested that perception in the RAT has a rather complex basis and is, in important ways, different from perception in the EFT, BAT, and RFT. The RFT, BAT, and EFT all straightforwardly require separation of an item (rod, body, or geometric design) from the context or field in which it is embedded. They were therefore designated "part-of-a-field" perceptual situations. In effect, these situations involve the ability to overcome an embedding context directly. The

RAT, in contrast, requires the subject to evaluate the position of the field itself. In this "field-as-a-whole" task, as we designated it, there is no surrounding context against which the object of perception—the room—may be evaluated. The task of separating an item from context may enter RAT performance only indirectly, therefore.

The distinction between part-of-a-field and field-as-a-whole tasks was supported by matrices of intercorrelations then available. It was also supported by a number of other findings. In our earlier studies we observed that the developmental curves for the RAT differed markedly from those of the other three tests, the RAT being the only test in which no systematic changes occurred with age. The RAT also differed from the three other perceptual tests in the degree and pattern of relationships of scores derived from it with a series of personality variables used in those studies. Further, in a factor-analytic study, Linton (1952) found that the BAT and EFT had their major loadings on one factor and the RAT had its major loading on another factor.

The weight of the evidence leaves little doubt about the uniqueness of the RAT. Because of this we decided not to include it in computing the perceptual index. This decision was later supported by the results of a factor-analytic study (Goodenough and Karp, 1961) described in Chapter 5.

It is striking that the correlations between scores for the EFT, which does not involve perception of the upright, and for the BAT are generally much higher than the correlations between scores for the BAT and RAT (Tables 4-1 and 4-2), both of which are orientation tests given in the same apparatus. It seems impossible to account for these results in terms of a "body-sensitivity" or an "accuracy" hypothesis. On the other hand, they are readily and clearly interpreted if field dependence is defined in terms of ability to overcome an embedding context.

C. FURTHER CHARACTERIZATION OF THE FIELD-DEPENDENCE DIMENSION

Many recent studies have supported this interpretation of the field-dependence-independence dimension of perceiving, and have contributed further to the definition of the dimension. These studies bear mainly on the distinction between embedding and distracting contexts in perceptual functioning, and on the relation of field dependence to Thurstone's flexibility-of-closure (freedom-from-Gestaltbindung) factor, perceptual constancies, and the perception of reversible figures.

1. Distracting vs. Embedding Contexts as Determinants of Field Dependence

On the basis of the results of our early studies we defined the field-dependence dimension in terms of individual differences in ability to separate an item from its context. In all the situations we have used to evaluate this kind of ability, the field has been a highly structured one and its structure has been of such a nature as to embed the item within it. It is possible to devise test situations that are similar, but in which the field is relatively unorganized and distracting, rather than embedding. In fact, it may even be that an embedding field is a special category of the more general class of distracting fields. It seems important to establish whether individual differences in field dependence reflect the ability to overcome embedding contexts, specifically, or a more general ability to resist distraction in perceptual functioning.

Attention was directed to these alternative interpretations of the field-dependence concept by the studies of Longenecker (1956) and Jackson (1955).

Longenecker gave his subjects a battery of tests including the EFT and two versions of the Holtzman Form-Recognition Test (Holtzman, 1955). The achromatic version of this test requires the identification of incomplete line drawings of various animal and human figures and appears, on the surface, similar to Thurstone's Hidden Pictures Test. In the chromatic version, transparent colored inkblots are superimposed on the incomplete line drawings, serving as a source of distraction. Longenecker found the two versions of the Form-Recognition Test to be significantly related to each other ($r = .70$) and each, in turn, significantly related to the EFT ($r = .54$ for the achromatic version and .46 for the chromatic version).

Jackson (1955) has reported a significant relation ($r = .46, P < .05$) for men, and an insignificant relation for women ($r = .21$) between EFT scores and performance in an auditory situation which requires that words be identified against a background of noise. At least among men, subjects who had difficulty in locating the hidden figure in the EFT also experienced difficulty in identifying the hidden words.

The general description of the Form-Recognition Tests and the auditory test suggests, on the surface, that the fields employed in them may be distracting rather than embedding. If this is so, the results of the Longenecker and Jackson studies would suggest that individual differences in field dependence may reflect a general ability to resist distraction. However, without more intensive study of the test situations it is difficult to be certain that the fields employed do not involve embedding contexts. Loeff (1961), for example, concludes that the achromatic version of the Form-Recognition Test includes some figures which present embedding fields, despite the fact that the test figures were not specifically developed to maximize the embeddedness feature.

With the Longenecker and Jackson findings as background, Karp (1962) recently undertook a study which had the distracting-embedding issue as its focus.

Karp gave his subjects (150 college men) a battery of eighteen tests, including three which required separating items from embedding contexts (EFT, BAT, RFT) and four which were specifically designed to require the separation of items from distracting contexts. The latter tests were:

1. Distracting Contexts Test I. The subject must locate a series of simple geometric figures (similar to those used in the EFT), obscured by a field of irrelevant and distracting lines.

2. Distracting Contexts Test IIA. The subject must find each of a designated group of thirteen simple geometric figures in a matrix of fifty-two such simple figures within which the thirteen test figures are randomly distributed. The irrelevant simple figures serve as a potential source of distraction.

3. Distracting Contexts Test IIB. This test is the same as IIA, except that colored semitransparent designs are superimposed on the field of simple figures as an added source of distraction.

4. Arithmetic Operations Test. The subject must solve twenty-four simple arithmetic problems (addition or subtraction of one-digit numbers), spaced evenly on a single page; surrounding the problems are a series of totally irrelevant pictures, sayings, jokes, etc. The subject's score is the time taken to solve the twenty-four problems.

The achromatic Form-Recognition Test was included in the battery, in an attempt to evaluate it with regard to the distraction-embeddedness issue.

Correlations among scores for these tests and several others in the battery were factor analyzed.

The results suggest that there is little relationship between ability to separate an item from an embedding context and ability to separate an item from a distracting context. The three "embedding" tests, EFT, RFT, and BAT, clearly defined one factor (field dependence). Moreover, none of the distracting tests were loaded on the field-dependence factor, but instead emerged together on another factor.[11]

Taken together, the studies described above tend to support the view that tests of field dependence measure ability to overcome embedding contexts and that this ability is distinct from the ability to overcome the effects of distracting contexts.

2. Field Dependence and Flexibility of Closure

In his factor-analytic study of perception, Thurstone (1944) identified a dimension of perceiving which he called "freedom from Gestaltbindung" or "flexibility of closure." This dimension has also emerged in subsequent factor-analytic studies by Thurstone (1949), Botzum (1951), and Pemberton (1952a). Thurstone (1944) suggested that this dimension might involve the "ability to shake off one set in order to take a new one" (p. 111).

It was because of the similarity between this definition and our definition of field dependence that we first became interested in the flexibility-of-closure concept.

Three of the tests which best defined the flexibility-of-closure factor in Thurstone's 1944 study were the Gottschaldt Figures (or Thurstone Gottschaldt, as it has come to be called), Hidden Pictures, and Two-hand Coordination Tests. Performance in each of these has been found to relate significantly to performance in the tests of our perceptual battery.

The Thurstone Gottschaldt test and EFT both use modifications of Gottschaldt's original figures, with the subject required to locate a simple figure embedded in a complex one. A high relationship between these tests would therefore be expected. Such a relationship has been demonstrated in several studies.

In a study of 150 medical students (one complete class) we found a correlation of .46 ($P < .01$), in the expected direction, between EFT and Thurstone Gottschaldt scores. Similarly, correlations of .77 ($P < .01$) and .69 ($P < .01$) between EFT and Thurstone Gottschaldt scores were obtained by Phillips, et al. (1957), and Goodman (1960), respectively. Comparing the Gottschaldt and RFT, correlations in the expected direction of .55 ($P < .01$), .27 ($P < .05$), and .32 ($P < .01$) are reported by Rudin and Stagner (1958), Crutchfield, et al. (1958), and Goodman, in that

---

[11] It is interesting to note that Holtzman's achromatic Form-Recognition Test was loaded on the field-dependence factor, but not on the distracting factor, apparently supporting Loeff's suggestion that embedding fields are represented in this test.

order. Goodman also obtained an r of .42 ($P < .05$), in the expected direction, between Gottschaldt and BAT scores.

The second test defining Thurstone's flexibility-of-closure factor, the Hidden Pictures Test, requires that the subject discover faces or other familiar figures which are hidden in a complex scene (e.g., among trees and shrubbery). Although this test was highly loaded on flexibility of closure in Thurstone's factor analysis, subsequent studies by Bechtoldt (1947), Botzum (1951), and Pemberton (1952a) provide conflicting evidence on the relation between flexibility of closure and the Hidden Pictures Test. The weight of the evidence is probably in favor of the hypothesis that the Hidden Pictures Test is loaded on flexibility of closure. However, the test seems to be a relatively poor measure of this factor.

Performance in the Hidden Pictures Test is apparently not highly related to performance in our perceptual battery (Goodman, 1960). However, in our factor-analytic studies (reported in Chapter 5) this test was found to have its principal loading on the same factor as our tests of field dependence, although the loading was not high (.27).

The third test of flexibility of closure, the Two-hand Coordination Test, requires the subject to tap in each of four 90° segments of a circular plate in a prearranged sequence, and to repeat this sequence as rapidly as possible. One part of the test, most relevant to the present discussion, involves tapping with both hands simultaneously, each on a different plate, using a different sequence for each hand. Thurstone (1944) suggests that "the subject improves his performance if he can suppress the separate configurations for the two hands and combine them into a configuration involving the two plates in one configuration" (p. 110 f.). In a study by Podell and Phillips (1959), described below, performance on the Thurstone Two-hand Coordination Test was found to be significantly related to EFT performance, as might be expected.

Our 1954 study provided some additional related evidence. Measures of field dependence were compared to performance in another kind of two-hand coordination test, the SAM (School of Aviation Medicine) Two-hand Coordination Test (McFarland and Channell, 1944), which seems similar in its requirements to Thurstone's test. The SAM test involves tracking a target with a follower knob which is controlled by cranking movements of the two hands. However, the direction of movement of the cranks does not correspond to the direction of movement of the follower knob. Thus, for successful performance on the SAM test the subject must overcome or ignore firmly established expectancies regarding visual-motor coordination. A clockwise rotation of the left-hand crank, for example, moves the follower knob in an initially unexpected direction. In this sense, both types of two-hand coordination tests require the suppression of strong initially preferred ways of organizing the components of the task in order to perform effectively.

Correlations between SAM Two-hand Coordination Test scores and perceptual index scores of .48 ($P < .01$) for men and .33 ($P < .05$) for women, both in the expected direction, were obtained. Epstein (1957), using the SAM Two-hand Coordination Test and two measures of field dependence (BAT and RFT) with a group of 17-year-old boys, failed to substantiate this finding, however.

Other tests loading flexibility of closure in the Thurstone study included Color-form Memory Count, Block Designs, Shape Constancy, Hidden Digits, and PMA Space and Reasoning subtests. It has been shown that scores for several of these tests relate significantly to measures of field dependence.[12,13]

In general, the evidence suggests that the field-dependence and flexibility-of-closure dimensions are related. Even stronger evidence of such a relation comes from recent studies by Gardner, Jackson, and Messick (1960) and Podell and Phillips (1959).

Gardner, Jackson, and Messick factor analyzed a large battery of perceptual, intellectual, and personality tests. They included two tests to represent the field-dependence dimension, the EFT and RFT, and two tests to represent the flexibility-of-closure dimension, Concealed Figures and Designs. Both tests of flexibility of closure were taken from the Educational Testing Service Kit of Selected Tests for Reference Aptitude and Achievement Factors (French, 1954), which was developed on the basis of a comprehensive review of the relevant factor-analytic literature. All four tests were found to have their major loadings on the same factor.

Podell and Phillips have identified a cluster which includes tests of field dependence and flexibility of closure. In each of two studies, cluster analyses of correlations among a large battery of cognitive tests were conducted. Included among these tests was the EFT, to represent field dependence, and Thurstone's Gottschaldt Figures and Two-hand Coordination Tests, to represent flexibility of closure. Both studies revealed a cluster which the authors call "spatial decontextuali-

---

[12] For evidence on the relation between Block Designs and field dependence see, e.g., Goodenough and Karp (1961) and Karp (1962); for evidence on the relation between tests of the PMA Space and Reasoning factors and field dependence see, e.g., Young (1957), Podell and Phillips (1959), Gardner, Jackson, and Messick (1960), and Goodman (1960).

[13] Thurstone also found that the sex of the subject, included as one of the variables in his study, loaded the flexibility-of-closure factor, with women displaying greater flexibility than men. This finding would appear to contradict the Goodenough and Karp finding, with 12-year-olds (Chapter 5), that sex did not load the field-dependence factor, and the repeated finding with adults (see Chapter 13) that men are significantly more field independent than women.

zation." Scores for the three tests mentioned were among those most highly correlated with scores for this cluster.

Taken together, these studies provide impressive support for the view that flexibility of closure, spatial decontextualization, and field dependence may be different names for the same dimension. In view of this evidence we may appropriately consider results obtained with tests loaded on the flexibility-of-closure and spatial-decontextualization factors as bearing upon the field-dependence dimension.

3. Relation of Field Dependence to Perceptual Constancy and Perception of Reversible Figures

A "job analysis" of many classical perceptual phenomena suggests that they may involve the ability to break up a field or overcome an embedding context, in the same way as do our tests of perceptual field dependence. We shall consider two of these phenomena as illustrative: perceptual constancy and perception of reversible figures.

a. Perceptual constancy. Objects usually tend to be perceived in a stable fashion despite variations in their illumination, the position from which they are viewed, and their distance from the observer. Marked individual differences have been observed, however, in the extent to which perceptual constancy is maintained under given circumstances. For people at one extreme, perception tends to conform closely to the characteristics of the stimulus, as it is represented at the sensory surface. Perception seems to be "stimulus directed"; constancy is minimal. For people at the other extreme, perception corresponds more to stable characteristics of the object perceived; constancy is maximal.

These differences may be thought of in terms of the ability to overcome an embedding context or break up a perceptual field. People in whom the "stimulus-directed" approach predominates may be regarded as able to perceive an item independently of the context in which it occurs. In fact, they have been described in the literature as having an "analytical attitude" (Brunswik, 1933, 1944; Henneman, 1935). People who show a high degree of constancy may be considered to be strongly influenced by a context in their perception of an item within it; they passively accede to the influence of the surrounding field; their perception is relatively global in nature.

Viewing in this way the individual differences that have been observed in classical perceptual constancy situations, we may reasonably expect to find a relation between performance in our battery of tests of field dependence and performance in perceptual constancy situations.

There is now available a considerable body of literature bearing on the relationship between field dependence and performance in constancy situations (Thurstone, 1944; Witkin, et al., 1954; Perez, 1955; Holtzman and Bitterman, 1956; Podell and Phillips, 1959; Gardner, et al., 1959; Gardner, Jackson, and Messick, 1960). In some of these studies relationships in the expected direction have been reported; in other studies no significant relationships have been found.

In searching for an understanding of these diverse findings we considered the possibility that situational factors in the size constancy experiment might be crucial in determining the extent of the relationship between field dependence and constancy performance. Accordingly, a "job analysis" was conducted of the various constancy situations that have been used. This analysis was strongly influenced by the work of Perez (1955) described below, and was guided by our conceptual framework and particularly by the concept of levels of differentiation. The job analysis suggested two conditions for making judgments in the constancy experiment which may maximize, if not be essential for the occurrence of, the relationship with measures of field dependence. First, the constancy situation should be designed so that the cues for object judgments are not drastically reduced. For example, the use of reduction screens and monocular viewing conditions in the size constancy experiment should be avoided. In the extreme case, at least, the basis for this requirement is obvious. If all cues for depth perception are eliminated, then the retinal image of the object provides the only basis for making size judgments. Accurate judgments of the size of the retinal image do not require an analytical approach under these conditions.

The second condition is, perhaps, of greater general interest. Apparently the subject should be specifically required by the instructions to adopt a stimulus-directed or analytical attitude in making his judgments. The study by Perez is directly relevant here.

Using male psychiatric patients as subjects, Perez studied the relation between EFT performance and size constancy following "look" and "bet" instructions. The "look" instructions were designed to emphasize an analytical attitude; the subject was encouraged to base his estimate on the size of the retinal image of the object. The "bet" instructions were designed to emphasize a global attitude; the subject was encouraged to estimate the actual size of the object.

There was no significant relation between accuracy of estimate under the "bet" instructions and EFT performance. However, a measure of change in estimate toward the size of the retinal image under "look" instructions was significantly related to extent of field dependence in the EFT ($r =$

.37, $P < .01$). Field-dependent subjects were less able to adopt an analytical attitude when required to do so by the instructions.

We would not have predicted that stimulus-directed instructions would be necessary in the constancy studies for the relationship with field dependence to emerge. In fact, in our brightness constancy experiments (Witkin, et al., 1954) the instructions used for the constancy test were purposely left ambiguous with respect to the attitude required of the subject, in the expectation that an individual's personal style would emerge most clearly under such free conditions. Under these conditions we did not find clear-cut evidence of a relationship between field dependence and constancy measures.

Not all of the studies on the relationship between constancy performance and field dependence are reported in enough detail to be certain about the conditions under which constancy judgments were taken. In general, however, the literature suggests that when the appropriate constancy conditions have been met, the expected relationships with field dependence can be found.

Apparently field-independent perceivers may adopt either an analytical or a global attitude when the task requirements are left ambiguous.[14] When the situation requires an analytical approach for effective performance, they are able to adopt it; field-dependent people, on the other hand, cannot and so, enforcedly, use a global approach. Under these conditions a relationship is found between measures reflecting extent of field dependence and measures of perceptual constancy.

The same principle may be stated more generally, as follows: To say that a person is relatively differentiated means that he is *capable* of operating at a high level of differentiation. He may sometimes operate at a lower level, however. Whether or not he operates at his highest possible level may depend upon motivational factors and/or upon the demands of a particular situation.

b. Perception of reversible perspective. A figure may be so organized that it can be perceived in several alternative ways. A well-known illustration is Schroeder's stair figure. It is a stairway that may be seen in two perspectives, leading down from left to right, or from right to left. As this figure is viewed, it typically undergoes continuous reversals of perspective. Marked individual differences in rate of alternation have been observed. These have often been interpreted in terms of ability to restructure a field or overcome field forces. On the basis of such an interpretation we might expect performance in our

[14] The nature of the task presented by each of the tests in our perceptual battery does not permit such an option; the person is required to perform analytically, if he is able to do so.

perceptual tests to be related to the rate at which alternation of perspective occurs when viewing reversible figures. The evidence suggests that such a relation may exist, but again only when the instructions for the reversible perspective situation require the subject to alternate as rapidly as possible. As with perceptual constancy, there seems to be no relation when the instructions are left ambiguous.

In his early factor-analytic study of perception Thurstone (1944) included a number of reversible-figure tasks with instructions left ambiguous. Rate of alternation on these figures was generally not related to performance on his tests of flexibility of closure. On the other hand, Newbigging (1954), using instructions requiring rapid alternation, found a significant average correlation (r tau $= .35$, $P < .01$) between rate of alternation on three reversible figures and EFT scores. Subjects who were able to overcome the embedding context in the EFT were generally able to restructure the field when required to do so in tests of reversible perspective.

In another series of studies, Jackson (1955, 1958) approached the phenomenon of reversible perspective from a slightly different point of view. He measured the subject's ability to resist spontaneous alternations in perspective and interpreted such performance in terms of the ability to organize "perceptual and cognitive field forces, rather than submitting to them" (1958, p. 279). His results are consistent with the theoretical framework presented here.

The evidence that has been presented in this section indicates that a tendency toward a more field-dependent or -independent approach is a very general feature of an individual's functioning, characterizing his perception in a variety of situations.

D. FIELD DEPENDENCE IN RELATION TO SOME OTHER ASPECTS OF PERCEPTUAL FUNCTIONING

1. Field Dependence and Speed of Closure

In addition to the flexibility-of-closure factor, discussed above, Thurstone identified a "speed-of-closure" factor. Because these two factors are similar in some respects, it is of particular value to explore the relation between field dependence and speed of closure.

The speed-of-closure factor is most clearly defined by tasks which require immediate, spontaneous identification of an impoverished figure. For example, Thurstone found the Street Gestalt Completion Test, an adaptation of Street's (1931) test, to be loaded on this factor. In this test the subject must identify a series of familiar figures from which parts have been removed. His score is the number of figures he fails to identify correctly in 3 seconds.

In his 1944 study Thurstone also found the Gottschaldt test to be loaded on speed of closure (as well as on flexibility of closure). However, further studies by Thurstone (1949), Botzum (1951), and Pemberton (1952a) showed the Gottschaldt test to be loaded on flexibility of closure but not on speed of closure. The weight of the evidence suggests that the Thurstone Gottschaldt test—and we would presume the EFT as well—does not involve speed of closure.

There remains, however, the question of whether other tests of field dependence, i.e., the BAT and RFT, may involve speed of closure.

A study of the relationship between tests of field dependence and the Street Gestalt Completion Test, which provides a measure of speed of closure, offers pertinent evidence on this point. Crutchfield, et al. (1958), found scores for the RFT to be unrelated to scores for a modified version of the Street Gestalt test, but significantly related to scores for the Thurstone Gottschaldt. This result suggests that the RFT does not involve speed of closure.

In apparent contradiction to the Crutchfield findings are those obtained by Goodman (1960), who compared measures of field dependence with scores on the Mooney Closure Test (Mooney and Ferguson, 1951), a modification of the Street Gestalt test. She found that correlations of Mooney test scores with scores for the BAT, RFT, and EFT were all in the expected direction, and two of the three (BAT and RFT) were significant.[15] This result might raise doubts about our impression that tests of field dependence are not loaded on speed of closure. However, further comparison of the Mooney and Street Gestalt tests does much to reconcile the Crutchfield and Goodman findings.

Although in both the Mooney Closure and the Street Gestalt, the subject must identify a series of pictures of familiar objects which have been impoverished by the removal of segments of the figures, there is a major difference between the two tests. Whereas the Street Gestalt (Thurstone version) has a very short time limit for recognition (usually less than 3 seconds per figure), the Mooney version allows considerably more time (20 minutes for forty figures). Recognition after prolonged study may involve different processes than rapid recognition.

A factor-analytic study of closure by Mooney (1954) tends to support this view. Mooney obtained loadings for his Closure Test on both speed of closure and a factor called "cognitive rigidity," which he believes may be equivalent to flexibility of closure. The Mooney Closure Test may thus involve both speed of closure and flexibility of closure.

---

[15] Longenecker (1956) has reported a significant correlation between scores for the EFT and Mooney Closure Test. A similar relation has been found by Gump (1955) between Mooney Closure and Thurstone Gottschaldt test scores for two groups of subjects.

The relationship found by Goodman, Longenecker, and Gump between Mooney Closure Test scores and field-dependence measures may thus be accounted for in terms of the common involvement of the flexibility-of-closure—or the highly similar field-dependence—factor. On the basis of the available evidence, the Mooney Closure Test seems of doubtful value in testing the hypothesis that our orientation tests involve speed of closure. In contrast, the evidence seems clear in showing that the Street Gestalt Completion Test is not loaded on the flexibility-of-closure factor.

Although the problem requires further research, the evidence now available on the relation between field dependence and speed of closure suggests that these dimensions may refer to distinctly different aspects of perceptual functioning.

2. Field Dependence in Relation to Performance in Other Perceptual Tasks

Many studies have explored the relations between performance in our battery of perceptual tests and performance in a variety of other perceptual situations.

One group of studies investigated susceptibility to illusions in relation to field dependence (Miller, 1953; Aronson, 1957; Crutchfield, et al., 1958; Gardner, 1957). Studies by Guskin (1955) and Konstadt (1961) have related extent of field dependence to performance in mirror-tracing tasks. A relation between the starting position effect, as defined by Werner and Wapner (1952), and field dependence has been established in studies by Wapner,[16] using RFT performance as a measure of field dependence, by Levine (1957), using RFT and BAT performance as measures, and by Friedman (1960), using EFT performance as a measure. Sinclair (1956) has related field-dependence-independence to the color-form-dominance dimension. Finally, field dependence has been studied in relation to performance in an auditory-visual conflict situation (Witkin, Wapner, and Leventhal, 1952), and in relation to eye torsion (Greenberg, 1960). Because the relationships investigated in these and other studies do not directly contribute at this time to our task of clarifying the field-dependence concept, we do not consider them here.

E. SUMMARY

An analytical, in contrast to a global, way of perceiving entails a tendency to experience items as discrete from their backgrounds, and

[16] Personal communication from Seymour Wapner.

reflects ability to overcome the influence of an embedding context. People differ in the extent to which their perception is analytical. This dimension of individual differences has been called field-dependence-independence. A tendency toward an analytical or global way of perceiving characterizes a person's perception in a wide variety of situations, making for marked individual self-consistency.

A comparison was made of performance in perceptual situations employing structured, embedding fields, on the one hand, and unstructured, distracting fields, on the other; in both kinds of situations the task was to discover an item within the field. A factor analysis showed that scores for these two kinds of perceptual situations loaded on different factors. This finding provides further support for the view that the field-dependence-independence dimension refers quite specifically to the ability to overcome an embedding context, which appears distinct from the ability to overcome the effects of distracting fields.

The results of several studies suggest that the field-dependence-independence dimension is very similar to dimensions of perceptual functioning (flexibility of closure and spatial decontextualization) identified by other investigators. It may be that these refer to the same dimension, called by different names.

5

ANALYTICAL FUNCTIONING
IN INTELLECTUAL ACTIVITIES

Early in our work we considered the possibility that the individual differences we had identified in the area of perception might have their counterpart in intellectual functioning.

"Intellectual problems that call for a high degree of creative activity, but do not involve perception directly, often also require that 'parts' be separated from the context in which they are embedded and brought into new relationships (Wertheimer, 1945). It is likely—and this is of course subject to experimental test—that if a person has this basic ability to 'break up' a configuration it will be manifested not only in straightforward perceptual situations, but in problem-solving situations as well" (Witkin, et al., 1954, p. 477).

There was some early evidence which seemed consistent with this expectation. Woerner and Levine (1950), working in our laboratory with a small group of 12-year-old children, found a significant relation between scores on our perceptual battery and scores on the Wechsler Intelligence Scale for Children (WISC). This result raised the possibility that field independence might be associated with superior general intelligence. However, their further finding that perceptual measures were more highly related to WISC performance scores than to WISC verbal scores suggested that such a view was too simple. The particularly high relationship obtained between perceptual scores and scores on such WISC performance subtests as Block Design indicated that aspects of intelligence which involve analytical ability might be contributing heavily to the over-all relation found between full-scale intelligence and perception.

Our first studies of children (1954) provided an additional early source of interest in comparing intellectual and perceptual performance. The impression from informal contacts was that relatively field-independent youngsters, in contrast to more field-dependent ones, have more penetrating awareness of people and situations, more developed interests, and more crystallized views of the future. Although this impression was not systematically documented, it pointed to differences in quality of intellect among children with contrasting modes of perception.

Our studies of the relation between perceptual and intellectual functioning were guided at the outset by the hypothesis that the ability to separate an item from its context expresses itself in an individual's intellectual activities as well as in his perception. This hypothesis was refined and supplemented by other more specific hypotheses as our investigations progressed.

Our first step was to explore further the relation observed between perceptual field dependence and general intelligence as expressed in performance on a standard intelligence test. The 1937 Revised Stanford-Binet (Form L) was given to the Group-II 10-year-olds (24 of each sex). A significant relation, in the expected direction, was found between IQs and perceptual index scores for both boys ($r = .57$, $P < .01$) and girls ($r = .76$, $P < .01$),[1] thus confirming the results of Woerner and Levine with the WISC.

In an attempt to "go beyond the IQ," and explore the basis of this relation, we next compared performances on individual Binet items of children differing in extent of field dependence. Particular attention was given to items which seemed to involve overcoming embeddedness. Although inspection of the data suggested some hypotheses which were subsequently tested, the fact that all subjects, even within a restricted age range, do not receive the same test items in the Binet precluded systematic analyses.

Accordingly, the WISC, the subtests of which are consistently given to each subject, was administered to the next groups studied: 25 boys and 25 girls of age 12 and the 30 Group-III boys of age 10. Significant relations were found between total IQ and perceptual index scores for boys at 10 and 12, as anticipated ($r = .55$ at 10, $r = .73$ at 12, $P < .01$ for both); for girls at 12 the relation was in the expected direction but not significant ($r = .36$).

A comparison of relations between perceptual scores with WISC verbal and performance scale scores separately gave results consistent with those reported by Woerner and Levine. The relation with per-

---

[1] Many other studies have since been reported on the relation between perceptual field dependence and performance on standard tests of intelligence and achievement: Miller (1953), Bell (1955), Jackson (1955, 1957), Bound (1957), Podell and Phillips (1959), Seder (1957), Carden (1958), Crutchfield, et al. (1958), Fenchel (1958), Rosenfeld (1958).

ception tended to be somewhat higher with the performance than with the verbal scale.[2] For the 12-year-old girls, in fact, only the relation with the performance scale was significant.

In view of the apparent importance of analytical ability for successful performance on some of the subtests in the performance scale of the WISC, the consistently higher relation between perceptual and performance scale scores seemed to lend support to the idea of a common component in perceptual and intellectual functioning.

A. THE FACTOR-ANALYTIC STUDIES [3]

To determine more definitely whether the relation observed between full-scale IQs and extent of perceptual field dependence is "carried" by certain types of subtests of the WISC, we did a factor analysis of the matrix of intercorrelations among WISC subtests and the various perceptual tests for the 12-year-old boys and girls and the 10-year-old boys of Group III. This approach appeared particularly promising since factor analyses of the Wechsler-Bellevue (and subsequently of the WISC and WAIS) had identified a distinct factor, often called a "perceptual-organization" or "closure" factor, which seemed in some ways similar to the field-dependence dimension.[4]

For the factor analysis of the 10-year Group-III boys we had, in addition to the WISC and the standard battery of perceptual tests, data from a number of perceptual and problem-solving situations which had been given to most of the children. These situations are described below. The first two are perceptual tasks which require that an item be separated from its context. The remaining situations were designed to test specific hypotheses concerning the nature of the field-dependence dimension and the basis of the relation between perceptual and intellectual functioning.

1. The children's embedded-figures test (CHEF). This test, described in detail elsewhere (Goodenough and Eagle, in press), was developed to provide an EFT-like situation particularly suitable for young children. An attempt was made to make the task intrinsically interesting to children, to avoid any requirement for sustained attention, to reduce frustration due to failure, and to insure understanding of the task. As in the EFT, the sub-

---

[2] For 10-year boys, r with performance scale = .54 $(P < .01)$, r with verbal scale = .37 $(P < .05)$; for 12-year boys, r with performance scale = .71 $(P < .01)$, r with performance scale = .60 $(P < .01)$; for 12-year girls, r with performance scale = .70 $(P < .01)$, r with verbal scale = −.06 (not significant).

[3] A more detailed account of the factor analyses for the 10- and 12-year groups is presented elsewhere (Goodenough and Karp, 1961).

[4] See, e.g., Cohen (1957, 1959).

ject is required to locate a simple form embedded in a complex figure. In the CHEF, however, the complex figures are representations of meaningful figures. Such figures were used both to make the task more interesting and to insure initial perception of the complex figure as an organized whole. In contrast to the EFT, the CHEF is more of an action than a spectator situation. Each of the complex figures is mounted on a 21-inch square board in the form of a multicolored jigsaw puzzle. Knobs are attached to several of the pieces, but only the correct simple form can be removed from the board by pulling at the appropriate knob. The subject is seated across the room from the board and is required to identify the simple form among the constituent pieces of the puzzle. He then goes over to the board and indicates his choice by pulling a knob. The subject's score is the number of correct first choices in a series of complex figures.

2. Thurstone's (1944) Hidden Pictures Test. As described in the previous chapter, the subject must discover a familiar object or figure hidden in a complex scene, a task similar to that presented by the EFT.

3. Recognition-efficiency test. This test was developed by Gump (1955). The rationale for its use in our study is described in Chapter 6. To anticipate briefly, the subject is presented tachistoscopically with meaningful stimuli shown in varying degrees of clarity. In the "serial" version of the test, the same stimulus is presented in increasingly sharp focus. In the "nonserial" version, stimuli are presented only once in a moderately out-of-focus setting. For both versions, we hypothesized, field-independent children would be more likely to recognize relatively unclear stimuli correctly, whereas more field-dependent children would require that the stimulus itself be relatively clear—that is, better organized—in order to recognize it.

4. Incidental learning. This situation and the hypothesis which led us to include it in our battery of tests are described in detail in Chapter 8. Briefly, the incidental learning test was designed to check the hypothesis that children with a relatively global field approach are apt to preoccupy themselves with the particular aspects of a situation to which their attention is directed, whereas children with an analytical approach are more apt to deal with broader aspects of their surroundings. An incidental learning situation seemed to provide an effective means of checking this expectation. A modification of a situation employed by Gardner, et al. (1959) was used. The experimental situation had two parts:

a. Incidental learning. Each of a series of eight words was printed in one of four colors and projected on a screen for 1 second. The child's task was to call out the *color* of the word as it was presented. After a practice period, the series was exposed once, following which the child was asked to recall as many of the *words* as he could. The number of words recalled was taken as a measure of the degree of learning incidental to the task which the child had been assigned.

b. Intentional learning. Following the incidental learning test, the child was given a second series of words-in-color, with the instructions that he call out and try to learn the *words* themselves. He was then tested for recall of the words. The number of words recalled provided a measure of degree of learning with intent to learn.

5. Reconciliation of opposites. This situation was patterned after a subtest of the Stanford-Binet, modified to make it suitable for younger children. The child was given thirteen pairs of opposites (as "black"—"white") and asked to indicate how they are the same. Answers were evaluated according to Binet-like criteria, the child's score being the number of correct responses.

This situation was used to test the hypothesis that the child who shows a capacity for overcoming a context in perceptual situations would display such capacity in dealing with verbal material as well. In the reconciliation-of-opposites test a pair of words is presented in a context (i.e., opposition) which the subject has to overcome to find similarities between the words. In this regard, it seemed essentially similar to the task presented by our perceptual tests.

6. Cancellation. As we discuss more fully in Chapter 8, this situation was used to test the hypothesis that the tendency of field-dependent children to conform to the demands of authority would lead them to persist at an assigned routine task longer than more field-independent children. We would therefore expect a relation between perceptual performance and persistence (and, by implication, success) at such a task.

The materials for this test consisted of four sheets filled with lines of letters in random order. The child was given these sheets, one at a time, and asked to cross out all the "t's" on the page as rapidly as possible. The first and fourth pages were scored for both time taken to finish and for errors (i.e., the number of "t's" missed plus the number of other letters cancelled). Time-drop and error-drop scores were obtained, based on the differences in speed and accuracy between the first and last pages. These scores were converted into standard scores which were then combined with equal weight to provide a change score for each subject.

The matrix of intercorrelations among test scores for the Group-III 10-year boys (who received the six tests just listed, the four tests of perceptual field dependence, and the WISC) was factor analyzed, as was the matrix of intercorrelations for the 12-year group (who received only the perceptual tests and the WISC).

The factor analysis of the matrix for the 12-year-old group was carried out first. Each of the two subtests of the RAT, the two subtests of the BAT, and the three subtests of the RFT was treated as a separate variable. However, it soon became apparent that the subtests of a given test were quite similar in factor composition. Hence, for the factor analysis of the 10-year-old group, RAT and BAT were each treated as single variables and RFT as two (body-tilted and body-erect conditions).

The analyses for both groups used the methods of centroid factor extraction and rotation to oblique simple structure described by Cattell (1952). The hyperplanes were reasonably well defined in both analyses, over 60% of the loadings falling within ±.10. In all, eight factors were extracted in the analysis of the 12-year group and nine in the analysis of the 10-year group.

The first three factors to emerge were well matched in the two analyses. Moreover, they were consistent with the three major factors repeatedly found in other analyses of Wechsler Scales.[5] The remaining factors were not well matched. Some of the discrepancies were apparently a function of differences in the variables for the two groups. It is also likely that several factors were residuals.

The three major factors which emerged from both factor analyses are summarized in Tables 5-1 through 5-3. Intercorrelations among these factors are presented in Table 5-4.

Table 5-1. Factor I—verbal comprehension [a]

Variable	10-year-old group loading	12-year-old group loading
WISC Vocabulary	.73	.63
WISC Information	.67	.65
WISC Similarities	.57	.44
WISC Arithmetic	.53	.39
WISC Comprehension	.46	.38
Reconciliation of opposites	.64	— [b]
Intentional Learning	.37	—
Sex	—	.42
WISC Digit Span	.25	−.06
WISC Picture Completion	−.07	.35
WISC Picture Arrangement	−.01	.35
(−) [c] RAT (Series 1a)	−.59	−.06
(Series 1b)		−.05

[a] Loadings greater than .25 were used in defining factors. Variables whose loadings on the factor were less than .25 for both age groups are not included. When only one of two loadings reaches .25, the variable is presented below the dotted line (e.g., WISC Digit Span).

[b] In this table and in Tables 5-2 and 5-3 a dash, "—," indicates that the variable was not included in the analysis.

[c] (−) These variables were reflected, with the result that high scores indicate field-independent performance.

[5] See, for example, Davis (1956), Cohen (1957, 1959).

Table 5-2. Factor II—attention-concentration

Variable	10-year-old group loading	12-year-old group loading
WISC Digit Span	.53	.62
WISC Arithmetic	.46	.41
WISC Coding	.43	.39
Recognition-efficiency: nonserial	.52	—
Intentional Learning	.31	—
CHEF	.29	—
Cancellation	−.38	—
Sex	—	−.44
WISC Block Design	.42	.00
WISC Comprehension	.01	.29
WISC Picture Completion	−.07	−.39
(−) RFT—Body erect (Series 3)	.03	−.30

Table 5-3. Factor III—analytical field approach

Variable		10-year-old group loading	12-year-old group loading
(−) RFT—Body tilted	(Series 1)	.74	.68
	(Series 2)		.50
(−) RFT—Body erect	(Series 3)	.69	.58
(−) EFT		.69	.50
CHEF		.61	—
WISC—Picture Completion		.52	.38
WISC—Block Design		.50	.42
(−) BAT	(Series 2a)	.43	.39
	(Series 2b)		.44
WISC—Object Assembly		.33	.57
WISC—Comprehension		−.32	−.24
(−) RAT	(Series 1a)	.37	.06
	(Series 1b)		−.03
Incidental Learning		.29	—
Hidden Pictures		.27	—
Recognition-efficiency: serial		−.40	—
WISC Mazes		−.10	.57

Table 5-4. Factor intercorrelations

Age Group	Factor II		Factor III	
	10	12	10	12
Factor I	.25	.36	.30	.34
(Verbal comprehension)				
Factor II			.17	−.11
(Attention-concentration)				
Factor III				
(Analytical field approach)				

1. Factor I. Verbal Comprehension

The first factor is clearly the verbal comprehension factor found in many factor-analytic studies of intellectual functioning. In our study it is best defined by the WISC Vocabulary, Information, Comprehension, and Similarities subtests. It is not surprising to find that for children the Arithmetic subtest also has a high loading on this factor. Cohen (1959) found a similar result at age 10½ in his factor analysis of the WISC.

We have chosen three WISC subtests to represent Factor I: Vocabulary, Information, and Comprehension. Two criteria were used in the selection: size of loading on this factor and lack of relation with other factors. Thus, Arithmetic and Similarities, more highly loaded on the verbal factor than Comprehension, were not included because of the presence of Arithmetic on Factor II and the high degree of relationship between Similarities scores and perceptual index scores.

A verbal index score is computed by summing the scaled scores for Vocabulary, Information, and Comprehension.

2. Factor II. Attention-Concentration

Factor II is apparently the "attention-concentration" factor previously isolated in factorial studies of the WISC. As in those studies, we find that WISC Digit Span and Arithmetic best define this factor. A third WISC subtest, Coding, is also highly loaded on Factor II. Since performance on this subtest is likely to suffer from lack of ability to concentrate, it is not surprising that it should appear on this factor.

It seems surprising, however, that the EFT, which apparently requires focused attention is absent from the factor. This is especially true since the CHEF, which is a modification of the EFT designed to minimize attention and concentration, receives some loading. In the absence of more conclusive evidence we are inclined to think that EFT performance requires some kind of attention-concentration ability.

If this assumption is correct, it provides a reasonable basis for interpreting the results of certain other studies. In an unpublished investigation we found that ingestion of alcohol impairs EFT, but not RFT or BAT performance. Similarly, in our 1954 study we found that the EFT was the only one of our perceptual tests on which a sample of patients drawn from a psychiatric ward was significantly more field dependent than normal comparison groups. It seems reasonable to suppose that people under the influence of alcohol and hospitalized psychiatric patients would generally be handicapped in maintaining the focused, sustained attention which performance on the EFT requires. The relation between EFT performance and scores on tests of the ability to carry out straightforward arithmetical operations, reported by Bieri, et al. (1958), and Rosenfeld (1958) may also have its basis in the attention-concentration ability presumably required by both kinds of situations. On the other hand, the pattern of relations reported by Rosenfeld among perceptual, personality, and arithmetical test scores suggests a linkage between field independence and effectiveness in *complex* operations requiring mathematical reasoning. Such a relation might be expected on the basis of a common requirement for overcoming embedding contexts.

To compute an index score for Factor II, the scaled scores for Digit Span, Arithmetic, and Coding subtests are summed.

3. Factor III. Analytical Field Approach

The three tests of perceptual field dependence, RFT, EFT, and BAT, have their highest loadings on this factor,[6] as do two other perceptual tests, CHEF and Hidden Pictures, which we had reason to consider as very similar to the tests in our standard battery.

Three subtests of the WISC are also heavily loaded on this factor for both age groups: Block Design, Picture Completion, and Object Assembly. A "job analysis" of these subtests suggests that effective performance in all of them requires the overcoming of an embedding context.

In the Picture Completion subtest the child is shown a meaningful picture which has something missing. If the missing element is to be found, he must not limit himself to an overview of the well-organized

[6] The RAT had a moderate loading on this factor in the analysis for the 10-year-olds but did not appear on this factor in the 12-year-old analysis. These inconsistent results support our decision to omit the RAT from the standard battery of tests of field dependence.

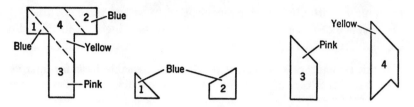

Figure 5-1. Example of object-assembly type of item.

figure but, disregarding the organization, must give his attention successively to one part at a time.

In the Block Design subtest the child is given a reference design
which he is asked to reproduce by the appropriate arrangement of
blocks. The reference design has an organization which must be
"broken up" into component blocks if it is to be reproduced.

The Object Assembly subtest is similar in many ways to a jigsaw
puzzle. The child is presented with parts of a meaningful picture
and asked to assemble these parts. Of the four items making up this
subtest, the subject is told what the completed puzzle will be for the
first two but not for the last two items. To the extent that the child
must assemble parts of a known or imagined whole, Object Assembly
seems similar to Block Design in its requirements.

The way in which Object Assembly, and Block Design as well, may
require that an embedding context be overcome is best illustrated by
reference to an object assembly item sometimes encountered in children's puzzle kits. As shown in Figure 5-1, the task is to assemble four
pieces of cardboard into a T-figure, in the manner shown.

Even adults find it difficult to solve this problem. The imagined
"T" seems to "break up" most naturally into a vertical base and a hori-
zontal crossbar and there is a strong tendency to use the long piece "4"
in Figure 5-1 as one of these two parts. Even when it becomes clear
that because of the notch in piece 4 it cannot be used as a base or
crossbar, it is extremely difficult to overcome the "natural" organization of the imagined "T," which is required if piece 4 is to be used
correctly in the assembly.[7]

Though this kind of analysis cannot be applied quite as clearly to the
items which make up Object Assembly, it seems likely that all but the

[7] In "assembly" tasks of this kind the context to be overcome may also represent
a wrong assumption about the identity of the object to be assembled. Such a
wrong assumption may, for example, result from an incorrect interpretation of one
of the pieces.

very simplest Object Assembly items must to some extent involve the process of overcoming a context. When the subject has a "key" or hypothesis as to what the completed puzzle represents, the organization of this imagined "key" provides a context which governs the assembly of the pieces. For optimal performance this context must be dealt with analytically.[8]

The high loadings of Block Design, Picture Completion, and Object Assembly subtests of the WISC on the same factor as the perceptual tests lends strong support to the hypothesis that there is a general cognitive style which runs through perceptual and intellectual functioning. This finding also suggests that this common cognitive style underlies the observed relation between extent of field dependence and performance on standard tests of intelligence.

The high loading of Block Design on Factor III provides further evidence of overlap among field dependence, spatial decontextualization, and flexibility of closure. In Thurstone's study (1944) the Kohs blocks situation, from which the WISC Block Design subtest was adapted, was highly loaded on the flexibility-of-closure factor. In a study by Podell and Phillips (1959) the Wechsler Block Design subtest correlated highly with their spatial-decontextualization cluster.

The Mazes subtest of the WISC is loaded on Factor III at 12 years, but not at 10. In the study by Podell and Phillips, the very similar Porteus Maze Test was consistently found related to their spatial-decontextualization cluster. It seems likely, therefore, that the small loading of Mazes in our study of 10-year-olds may be a chance occurrence. A possible explanation that may account for the presence of Mazes is presented in Chapter 9.

There remains the question of an appropriate label for Factor III. Even though all our tests of field dependence are heavily loaded on this factor, the designation "field dependence" is not adequate. Such a label has a very specific perceptual connotation and thus is too limited to encompass the intellectual tasks which also appear on this factor. All the tests loaded on Factor III appear to evaluate extent of ability to overcome an embedding context. This ability, when developed, makes possible an analytical way of experiencing; inability to overcome a context results in a global way of experiencing. The dimension of individual differences with which we are dealing thus represents, at its extremes, contrasting ways of approaching a field, whether the field is immediately present or represented symbolically.

---

[8] Our interpretation is focused on the way in which a "key" may impede solution of an Object Assembly item. This in no way implies that a trial-and-error approach to the task is most effective.

It may therefore best be described as an analytical vs. global field approach. What we have been calling "field dependence" is in effect the perceptual component of this more general cognitive style.

The analytical field approach in intellectual activities is best represented at this point by performance in the three WISC subtests which have their highest loading on Factor III: Picture Completion, Block Design, and Object Assembly. In our further studies we have summed the weighted scores for these three tests to constitute an intellectual index, paralleling the perceptual index. The perceptual and intellectual indices in turn have been combined with equal weight to form what we shall call the cognitive index. Hereafter, when reporting studies on the relation between mode of field approach and other variables we shall, wherever the data are available, present results for all three indices.

The results of our factor-analytic study enable us to understand more clearly the relation between field dependence and intellectual functioning. The many significant relations reported between perceptual measures and full-scale intelligence test scores cannot be interpreted to mean that field-independent children are of generally superior intelligence. The finding of striking differences in the extent to which various IQ subtests contribute to these relations rules out such an interpretation.

The differences in contribution of various subtests revealed by the factor-analytic studies are also shown by correlational results. If we consider the relation of perceptual index scores to the three factor scores derived by combining WISC subtests, we obtain the following results for the 10-year group: perceptual index vs. intellectual index (Block Design + Picture Completion + Object Assembly), $r = .66$ ($P < .01$); perceptual index vs. verbal index (Information + Comprehension + Vocabulary), $r = .26$ (not significant); perceptual index vs. attention-concentration index (Arithmetic + Digit Span + Coding), $r = .18$ (not significant). It is clear that the relation between extent of field dependence and full-scale IQ scores is "carried" specifically by portions of intelligence tests which, like the perceptual tests themselves, involve the capacity for analytical functioning. The relationship in performance of perceptual and intellectual tasks which have the common requirement of overcoming embeddedness provides clear-cut evidence of a general cognitive style. The relation between full-scale IQ scores and field dependence measures is best explained on the basis of the expression of this general cognitive style in both.

The factor-analytic study by Karp (1962), cited in another context in Chapter 4, provides considerable support for these conclusions. He gave the BAT, RFT (Series 3 only), EFT (short form), six subtests of the Wechsler Adult Intelligence Scale (Block Design, Object Assembly, Vocabulary, Comprehension, Arithmetic, and Digit Span), and a modified version of a seventh subtest (Digit Symbol) to a group of 150 male college students. These tests loaded three factors which correspond very closely to the three main factors obtained from our studies of 10- and 12-year-olds with the WISC: an attention (or memory) factor, loading Arithmetic, Digit Span, and Digit Symbol; a verbal comprehension factor, loading Vocabulary and Comprehension; and an analytical ability factor, loading BAT, RFT, EFT, Block Design, and Object Assembly.

The conclusions from these studies are supported by the results of a number of other studies, reviewed below.

B. FURTHER EVIDENCE ON THE RELATION BETWEEN PERCEPTUAL AND INTELLECTUAL FUNCTIONING

1. Guilford's Adaptive-Flexibility Factor

One of the most impressive demonstrations that the capacity to overcome an embedding context can be identified in both the perceptual and intellectual functioning of an individual comes from a series of factor analyses conducted by Guilford and his associates (1952, 1955a, 1955b, 1957). These workers identified a factor, designated "adaptive flexibility," which appears similar to our Factor III. In one of the most recent studies of Guilford, et al. (1957), the tests reported to be highly loaded on the adaptive-flexibility factor are:

1. Insight Problems, which are similar to those used by Duncker (1945) in his classical studies. There are twelve such problems, of which the following one is illustrative: A man went out to hunt a bear one day. He left his camp and hiked due south for 10 miles, and then went due west for 10 miles. At this point he killed a bear. He then dragged the bear back to his camp, a distance of exactly 10 miles. Problem: What was the color of the bear he killed? Why? The correct answer is: White or polar bear. Only near the poles are these distances possible.

2. Match Problems, in which the subject is shown a set of matches (or diagrams representing matches) arranged in the form of a lattice and asked to remove a specified number of triangles or squares. Three solutions are required for each problem. In order to solve this problem, the subject must overcome the organization of the presented lattice work and discover within it a subsidiary organization which meets particular requirements. What may be especially important is the requirement of repeated restructuring, with the matches used in different ways for subsequent solutions.

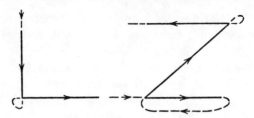

Figure 5-2. A sample Planning Air Maneuvers problem (after Guilford, et al., 1957).

3. Penetration of Camouflage, adapted from Thurstone's Hidden Pictures Test.

4. The Squares Test requires the subject to place a specified number of X's on a checkerboard so that no two are in the same row, column, or diagonal. Several different solutions are required to the same problem. As with the Match Problems Test, the material must be restructured repeatedly, with the same materials used in new ways.

5. Planning Air Maneuvers, a test in which the subject is asked to "plan the construction of two consecutive letters, as in skywriting, by the most economical path." Certain restrictions are imposed as to the way in which the maneuver is to be carried out, for example, the sharpness of the turn. The achievement of a solution to this problem requires that the organization of familiar letters be overcome. Thus, in the letters "L" and "Z" (see Figure 5-2) the base of the "L" and the base of the "Z" need to be considered a functional unit, so that they can be written without change in flight direction. If each base is considered in the usual way, as part of a familiar letter, solution of the problem is impeded.

6. Hidden Figures, which is an adaptation of Thurstone's Gottschaldt test.

Each of these tests requires that a predominant organization or context be overcome. The intellectual tasks show this characteristic quite clearly, having been chosen by Guilford and his associates on the basis of specific hypotheses about the nature of adaptive flexibility. The presence of the Gottschaldt test on this factor makes it reasonable to consider the cognitive dimension involved analogous to the one we have identified. In fact, Guilford (1957) has called attention to the similarity between adaptive flexibility and Thurstone's flexibility-of-closure factor, although he suggests that these two dimensions may be distinguished in further factor-analytic studies.[9]

[9] The other major factors in Guilford's study were: verbal comprehension, general reasoning, logical evaluation (based on tests requiring "careful evaluation of interpretations of problems"), originality, spontaneous flexibility or perseveration, ideational fluency, and structural redefinition. It is noteworthy that a number

In order to check more directly on the indicated linkage between adaptive flexibility and analytical field approach (Factor III), we gave each of 31 college men a series of nine cognitive tests:

1. BAT
2. RFT (Series 3, subject seated erect)
3. EFT (a shortened form consisting of the first eight pairs of simple and complex figures)
4. Block Design subtest of the Wechsler Adult Intelligence Scale (WAIS)
5. Picture Completion subtest of the WAIS
6. Guilford's Match Problems (eighteen were used)
7. Guilford's Insight Problems (twelve were used, including the example given above)
8. Vocabulary subtest of the WAIS
9. Comprehension subtest of the WAIS

The first three of these represent the perceptual tests and the next two the intellectual tests which appeared on our Factor III. The two tests that follow (Match and Insight Problems) represent two of Guilford's measures of adaptive flexibility. The last two tests listed were loaded on Factor I, the verbal factor, in our study.

On the basis of Guilford's findings, we anticipated that measures from tests representing mode of field approach (tests 1 through 5) and adaptive flexibility (6 and 7) would be interrelated, but they would tend not to be related to measures of the verbal factor (8 and 9). The pattern of intercorrelations among measures for the nine tests, shown in Table 5-5, offers strong support for this hypothesis. Of twenty-one correlations among measures of analytical field approach and adaptive flexibility, twenty are significant. In contrast, only four of fifteen correlations between verbal measures and measures of these two dimensions are significant.

These findings are supported by the factor-analytic study of Karp (1962), which used the nine tests described above, as part of a larger battery of tests. The results were consistent with those cited. Measures of analytical field approach and adaptive flexibility emerged on the same factor (analytical ability) and, as already noted, Vocabulary and Comprehension defined a different factor (verbal comprehension).

The evidence indicates a high degree of overlap between Guilford's adaptive flexibility and our analytical field approach, and shows once

of other studies also suggest no relation between field dependence and common measures of perseveration: Sangiuliano (1951), Jeffreys (1953), Bieri, et al. (1958), Fenchel (1958).

Table 5-5. Intercorrelations among measures of analytical field approach, adaptive flexibility, and verbal comprehension

Test ($N = 31$)	2	3	4	5	6	7	8	9
1. BAT	.75 **	.74 **	.27	.37 *	.49 **	.53 **	.23	.32
2. RFT		.86 **	.40 *	.55 **	.67 **	.65 **	.13	.27
3. EFT			.58 **	.60 **	.72 **	.80 **	.15	.39 *
4. Insight Problems				.51 **	.59 **	.74 **	.06	.40 *
5. Match Problems					.39 *	.60 **	.06	.36 *
6. Picture Completion (WAIS)						.69 **	.22	.40 *
7. Block Design (WAIS)							.16	.34
8. Vocabulary (WAIS)								.34
9. Comprehension (WAIS)								—

* Significant at .05 level.
** Significant at .01 level.

again a close connection between perceptual and intellectual functioning. The low relation between verbal measures and measures of analytical field approach, found here for adults, are consistent with the results of our factor analyses, based on data for children.

2. Insight Problems

Among the tests which define adaptive flexibility in Guilford's factor analysis, the Insight Problems Test attracts the most interest because of the close parallel between the problems on this test and tests of field dependence.

Insight problems commonly require the subject to restructure the problem material. A particularly clear illustration is found in the problems employed by Duncker (1945) in his studies of "functional fixedness." To solve these problems the subject needs to use familiar objects in new ways. For example, in one problem a pair of pliers must be made to serve as a shelf support rather than as a tool. Functional fixedness refers to the marked difficulty that is often encountered in identifying the possible uses of objects outside their familiar function. It thus implies difficulty in overcoming embedding contexts.

A study by Harris [10] provides substantial support for the hypothesis

[10] Personal communication from Frances Harris.

that the ability to solve problems of this nature is related to field dependence. Harris administered two such problems, taken from Duncker, as well as the EFT and the Kohs' Block Design Test to adult subjects. The two insight problems, as described by Duncker (1945), were:

1. The "box problem." The subject is given three small candles with instructions to affix them, side by side, to a (vertical) door at eye level. He is allowed to use anything in the room for this task. On a table, in the test room, is a variety of small items, including a few thumbtacks and three small pasteboard boxes (about the size of small matchboxes). Each of the boxes is filled with objects, some of which are irrelevant to the task (e.g., matches). To solve the problem the subject must empty each of the three boxes and affix them to the door with thumbtacks to serve as platforms for the candles.

2. The "pliers problem." The subject must construct a stand (or shelf) consisting of a board resting on two supports. In the room are a number of objects, including the board, one support, and a pair of pliers. The support is nailed to the board in such a way as to require the subject to use the pliers in a conventional manner to remove the nail. To solve the problem, the pliers must also be used as a second support for the shelf.

The results reported by Harris are quite striking. If subjects who solve *both* problems are compared with subjects who solve *neither* problem, there is almost no overlap between the two groups in either EFT or Block Design performance. The data on the relation between EFT performance and solution of the Duncker problems are presented in Table 5-6.[11] According to our computations, using Fisher's exact method, this relation is significant ($P < .01$).

Table 5-6. Success on two Duncker problems as related to EFT performance (after Harris)

EFT	Solved both problems	Failed both problems
Thirteen most field-independent subjects	12	1
Thirteen most field-dependent subjects	2	11

[11] Correlations between insight problems and Gottschaldt scores are also reported by Pollack (1955). Some of these data are difficult to interpret for our purposes, however, since his subjects all had spinal, skull, or brain injuries.

3. Overcoming Set

a. The Einstellung test. Studies with Einstellung problems also provide evidence that ability to overcome contexts is expressed in both the perceptual and intellectual functioning of an individual.

The Einstellung situation has often been used to study the effect of set upon problem solving. In the typical Einstellung problem the subject is given (or told about) three jars of known capacity and required to obtain a given quantity of water in one of them by appropriate manipulation of the contents of these jars. The only measures available to him are the known maximum capacities of the jars. The first few problems can be solved by one method only. For example, designating the jars A, B, and C, the only possible solution may take the form A-C-2B. (That is, if A is filled, and from its contents C is filled once, then B twice, the residue in A will correspond to the amount required.) The repetition of this solution induces a set. The effect of this set is measured by performance on two kinds of problems. The first, designated the "critical" problem, may be solved by the method used in the set-inducing problems (A-C-2B) or by a shorter method (for example, $A - B$ or $A + B$). The second or "extinction" problem may be solved by the shorter method only.

There has been a tendency in the recent literature (Levitt and Zuckerman, 1959; Levitt, 1956) to minimize the distinction between the critical and extinction problems, pointed out by Luchins (1951) and Guetzkow (1951). For our purposes there may be important differences in the meaning to be attributed to abandonment of the long (set) method in the critical and the extinction problems. Persistence in the set method on the critical problem cannot be taken as evidence of inability to break the set since the set method may offer as rapid and successful a solution as the short method (Levitt and Zelen, 1953). On the other hand, the time required for solution of the extinction problem, given immediately afterwards, may be taken as a measure of ability to break the set.

Adamson and Taylor (1954) have shown that failure to break the set on extinction problems is significantly related to "functional fixedness," while failure to adopt the set on critical problems is not. They conclude that "continuing to use an effective indirect method, even though a more direct method is available, does not have the same significance psychologically as does continued use when the method is inappropriate" (p. 125).

The set-breaking process may be conceptualized in terms of ability to overcome embeddedness. The elements A, B, C are used repetitively in a given pattern, for example A-C-2B, during induction of the set. For the set to be broken, the elements must be considered apart from this previously adopted organization and arranged into a new organization. The findings of Adamson and Taylor, just cited, support this interpretation.

Viewing the set-breaking process in this way, we would expect that persons who tend to show an analytical field approach would display greater capacity for breaking the set in the Einstellung situation. Since only the extinction problem provides an effective test of set-breaking ability, we would further anticipate that the expected relation would be found with performance on the extinction problem and not necessarily with performance on the critical problem. These expectations have received support in a number of studies.

Fenchel (1958) gave the Einstellung test (using an extinction problem only) and the EFT to a group of 63 outpatients in a VA Clinic. He found a significant relation ($r = .36$, $P < .01$), in the expected direction, between relative speed of solving the extinction problem and EFT performance. In another study, Zaks (1954) found a relation in the same direction, although not significant, using a Gottschaldt-type test.

Guetzkow (1951) carried out a series of studies in which he used a form of the Einstellung situation containing two critical problems followed by an extinction problem. He divided his subjects into two groups according to their set-breaking ability. The set-breakers were those who adopted the set, as shown by their use of the long method of solution on the critical problems, but who were able to break the set on the extinction problem, and who, in addition, were able to achieve the pendulum solution on Maier's two-string problem.[12] The nonset-breakers were subjects who were unable to break the set on the extinction problem and who also failed to achieve the pendulum solution in the Maier situation.

Guetzkow reasoned that set-breaking ability should be related to Thurstone's flexibility-of-closure factor. His finding that set-breakers did significantly better than nonset-breakers on the Thurstone Gottschaldt and Hidden Pictures Tests tends to confirm this expectation.

Guetzkow also divided his subjects on the basis of another dimension, which he called "susceptivity to set." Subjects who used the set solution on the critical Einstellung problem and who also gave many stereotyped solutions to the two-string problem were designated as set-susceptible; those who used the short method on the critical Einstellung problem and gave few stereotyped solutions to the two-string problem he designated nonset-susceptible. The performance of the set-susceptible group was significantly poorer on the Thurstone Gottschaldt, but no significant differences were found in performance on the Hidden Pictures Test.

[12] Maier (1940) and Guetzkow consider achievement of the pendulum solution as reflecting the ability to overcome stereotyped solution approaches.

Zaks (1954) also found that set-susceptible subjects scored significantly lower on the Thurstone Gottschaldt. However, Jeffreys (1953) failed to find a significant relation between Thurstone Gottschaldt performance and method of solution on the critical Einstellung problem; and Guilford, et al. (1957) report performance on Einstellung problems reflecting susceptivity to set to be loaded significantly on two reasoning factors, but not on adaptive flexibility. Miller (1953), on the other hand, found that male subjects who used the short solution method on the critical problem did significantly more poorly on the EFT. No significant differences were found for women. Although these findings are contradictory and their basis is at this time unclear, the trend of the evidence suggests that performance on the critical Einstellung problem may not be related to mode of field approach. In contrast, performance on the extinction problem is related to capacity for analytical functioning.[13]

Additional evidence for these conclusions comes from a study performed in our laboratory by Goodman (1960). Most of the college students who served as subjects in that study received the EFT, BAT, RFT, the Hidden Pictures Test, the Thurstone Gottschaldt, and the Einstellung Test.

No significant differences in performance on any of the perceptual tests were found between subjects who solved the critical Einstellung problem by the short method and those who solved it by the long method. In contrast, time required to solve the extinction problem showed some tendency to be related to perceptual performance. Significant correlations were found between extinction problem solution time and EFT and Thurstone Gottschaldt performance. The correlations with RFT and BAT were in the expected direction, but not significant.[14,15]

These results, confirming and extending the findings of Fenchel and Guetzkow, indicate that set-breaking ability in the Einstellung situation tends to be related to mode of field approach, as expected.

If we consider that set-breaking in the Einstellung involves the ability to overcome an established mode of organizing elements, as a condition for combining them into a new pattern, we have further

---

[13] Consistent with our finding that women are more field dependent than men is that of Guetzkow that women show less set-breaking ability than men on the Einstellung extinction problem. However, in performance on the critical problem, which it appears may not be related to field dependence, sex differences were not observed.

[14] The findings for the BAT may be complicated by the fact that some of the subjects had received the RAT on the same apparatus, prior to taking the BAT, whereas other subjects had not.

[15] The subjects in this study also received the Vigotsky Test. Nonsignificant correlations were obtained between this test and RFT, BAT, and EFT. In a previous study by Goodman (1955), Vigotsky Test performance did relate significantly to a measure of perceptual field dependence. In another study by Rodgin (1955) no relation was found with the EFT, however.

evidence in these results that the capacity to overcome an embedding context extends through an individual's perceptual and intellectual functioning.

b. Overcoming a "personal" set. The Einstellung procedure seeks to induce a particular set in the subject. Other studies have made use of the already established sets which subjects bring to the experimental situation with them. An investigation by Linton (1952) illustrates this approach.

Linton first assessed the attitudes of each of a group of college students toward several social issues. She then administered a series of syllogistic reasoning problems, all of the same logical form. The correct conclusion—that is, the one which formally followed from the premises—sometimes coincided with and sometimes contradicted the subject's known social attitudes. In addition, neutral problems were used, involving conclusions which did not bear upon the subject's attitudes.

For the neutral problems, no relation was found between syllogistic reasoning ability and measures of field dependence.[16] For problems where the correct conclusion conflicted with their social attitudes, field-dependent subjects made significantly more errors than did field-independent subjects.[17] Field-dependent subjects thus tended to use the "atmosphere effect" created by their attitudes as the context for interpreting or organizing the material, with the result that they did violence to the inherent structure of the syllogistic form. Field-independent subjects, in contrast, were able to overcome the "atmosphere effect" and to organize the material more in accordance with the requirement of the syllogistic form itself.

4. Overcoming an Embedding Context in Humor Appreciation

Overlade (1954, 1955) developed a multiple-choice sense of humor test in which several punch-line choices were offered to each of a number of joke stems. The "humorous" choice was determined by consensus of a sample of college students. Overlade hypothesized that the essence of humor experience is the discovery of a hidden meaning, only alluded to in the joke. From this hypothesis, it may be expected that sense of humor would be related to capacity for overcoming an embedding context. Overlade's data are consistent with this expec-

---

[16] See also Rodgin (1955).

[17] A significant relation was found as well between extent of field dependence and an index of reduction in problem-solving effectiveness under conflict conditions.

tation. Number of "right" answers on the sense of humor test correlated significantly with scores on the Thurstone Gottschaldt.

C. SUMMARY

A tendency toward an analytical or global way of experiencing characterizes a person's problem-solving activities as well as his perception. We have adopted the term "analytical field approach" for the style of functioning represented in both the perceptual and intellectual behavior of an individual, which involves the ready ability to overcome an embedding context and to experience items as discrete from the field in which they are contained. The term "global field approach" has been suggested to describe the style of functioning that involves submission to the dominant organization of the field and the tendency to experience items as "fused" with their background. Field-dependence-independence represents the perceptual component of this broader dimension. Individual performances are represented continuously along the analytical-global dimension of experiencing, rather than constituting distinct "types." When we say that a person shows an analytical or global field approach, we mean only that he falls above or below the mean of his group on this dimension.

The pervasive self-consistency in cognitive functioning that has now been demonstrated suggests that the classical division into the perceptual and intellectual is of limited value in the study of cognitive styles.

The significant relation frequently reported between measures of field dependence and total standard intelligence test scores is "carried" largely by those portions of intelligence tests which require analytical functioning. In other words, the relation is based on the expression of a particular style of field approach in both.

A number of cognitive dimensions, identified by different investigators, may tap the same core of individual functioning. Field dependence, Thurstone's flexibility of closure, Guilford's adaptive flexibility, Phillips' spatial decontextualization, Duncker's functional fixedness, and "perceptual organization" on the Wechsler scale all appear to involve the ability to overcome an embedding context. In a period of extensive research on cognitive styles it is not surprising that there should be overlap or even identity among the cognitive styles established by different investigators. There is clearly a need for studies aimed at codifying these cognitive styles.

6

STRUCTURING AND ARTICULATION
OF EXPERIENCE

We hypothesized on grounds set forth in Chapter 2 that children with an analytical field approach would be able to impose structure on a field which lacks it. On the other hand, children who in their global field approach show adherence to the prevailing organization of the field would tend to leave "as is" stimulus material that is unorganized, and so experience it as poorly structured. In the first section of the present chapter we consider studies bearing on this hypothesis.

Several approaches have been used in the assessment of children's ability to structure experience: an evaluation of perception of Rorschach inkblots and other vague stimulus material; a study of the organization of ideas stimulated by TAT pictures; tests of memory, conducted with the view that experience which registers in a relatively organized way is more likely to persist in memory.

The separation of the analytical from the structuring aspect of experience is, in practice, inordinately difficult. At best we can attempt through specially designed situations to feature one or the other aspect. Our battery of perceptual tests emphasized the analytical aspect; the situations considered in this chapter have emphasized the structuring aspect. The studies of structuring are at a relatively preliminary stage, compared to the studies of analysis of experience.

In the second section of the chapter we report a study in which, as a first step toward exploring experience in "real life," an examination was made of the quality of children's experience in everyday situations, as described in an interview. The study was undertaken with the hypothesis that children with a relatively analytical field approach in the laboratory tests would tend to show greater articulation in their experience under "real-life" circumstances.

A. STRUCTURING OF EXPERIENCE

1. Analysis of Rorschach Percepts

Because the Rorschach requires the person to deal with essentially unorganized stimulus material, it lends itself to exploration of ability to structure experience. We undertook a study of the nature of children's perception of Rorschach inkblots, with the following hypothesis: Children with a relatively global field approach would have limited ability to impose organization on the stimulus material; the material would therefore tend to "register" as unstructured and vague for them, and they would find the task of interpreting it perplexing, confusing, or overwhelming. In contrast, children with a relatively analytical field approach would be better able to organize the stimulus material; it would therefore "register" in structured fashion and they would feel neither confused nor overwhelmed by the task.

The extent to which a child's experience of the inkblots is vague and confusing or structured and clear for him may be deduced from a series of definable manifestations or cues, even though the experience is a private one for him. For example, is he willing to leave his percepts diffuse, ill-defined, indefinite, or does he achieve, or strive to achieve structure in his percepts? Is he able to respond differentially to the succession of stimuli presented to him, or do they tend to "look alike" and to fuse with one another? Is his "hold" on his percepts sufficiently secure so that, in the inquiry, he can recall and specify what he saw? Or are his percepts unstable, so that he forgets what he has seen? Is he able to impose an organization, eliminating or otherwise actively handling distracting aspects of the stimulus material that do not fit in with his percept? Or does he become confused, allowing distracting aspects of the material to interfere with his thought process? What does the quality of his verbalizations suggest about the extent to which the whole experience is vague or structured for him?

It was possible to pinpoint ten specific facets of the test productions which might serve as inferential cues in identifying a child's experience as relatively structured or unstructured. These cues were established through a study of the Rorschach records of the Group-I boys. They were then used to formulate a rating scale. The boys of Group II, whose performance in other tests was not known to the investigator, served as a trial group for application and further modification of the scale. The investigator ascertained the perceptual standing of each child of Group II after a blind prediction of his mode of field approach had been made, and before the judgment of the Rorschach record of the next child was undertaken. Finally, Group III was used in a cross-validation study of the scale.

Standard procedure, essentially following Klopfer, et al. (1954), was used in obtaining all Rorschach records, with certain modifications for Group III. In this group, a child who gave only one response for Card I was told, "Some boys see only one thing in a blot, some see more than one. Was there anything else you saw?" In conducting the inquiry, spontaneous recall was asked for, the examiner supplying only the responses which the child had not recalled. This procedure was adopted since "stability of percepts," from main performance to inquiry, had emerged as one of the cues on which the final rating was based.

In Group III, both Rorschach administration and application of the rating scheme were done by the same investigator. She administered no other tests to this group, and had no other contact with or knowledge of the individual children. All the Rorschachs of Group I and some of Group II were administered by other staff members.[1]

The final evaluation of each Rorschach record was based on a five-point rating scale, in which the ten cues previously identified were used as definitional guides to an over-all clinical evaluation. A rating of 5 was assigned to children whose Rorschachs were judged to show a high level of structuring and a rating of 1 to children at the opposite extreme. Intermediate ratings were assigned to children who were judged to be genuinely intermediate on the majority of cues, and to children for whom the separate cues pointed in opposite directions.

The definitions of the ten cues used in assigning ratings, the rationale underlying them, and examples in instances where the definition is not self-explanatory, are presented in detail below. Although, for the most part, single responses are cited as examples, in applying the scale the evaluations must necessarily be based on a child's total Rorschach record.

Table 6-1. Rating scheme for judging Rorschach percepts

Low level of structuring   High level of structuring

1. DEFINITENESS OF PERCEPTS

Accepts indefinite and vague per-   Impression is that whatever the child
cepts. The content of the response   sees, he sees clearly, knows what he
may be by definition vague (e.g.,   sees, can anchor it to blot, and de-

[1] For Group III approximately a year elapsed between administration of the test and rating of the records. This would tend to minimize the examiner's memory of the individual children as seen during the test administration.

Table 6-1. Rating scheme for judging Rorschach percepts—(*Continued*)

Low level of structuring	High level of structuring
"clouds"), or it may be by implication specific (e.g., "bat"). But even if the referent of the percept is specific in structure, the impression is that the child does not know what it is he sees, is not sure where he sees it, is not able to describe it in appropriate detail, or anchor it to the blot. There is little interest in structuring or clarifying what is seen. Blot characteristics tend to be passively registered.	scribe it in appropriate detail. There is a clear *intent* to structure the material. Blot characteristics are actively handled rather than passively registered.

Rationale: Willingness to leave percepts vague and indefinite suggests a low level of structuring.

Examples [2,3]

Card VII. (W) Looks like some people dancing around. [(?) (Specific questions elicited only the information that there are "six people"; hesitantly points to top *d*'s as "heads." Comments that it is "a little hard" to describe what he sees.)]	*Card II.* 2. (W) Looks a little bit like a clock this way, the frame. [That's right, I found the shape of a clock, looks like the shape of a clock, and this (thin protruding red strips) looks like the things you push down (on an) alarm clock, and—the face of the clock (center S). (Points out frame in whole black area.)]

2. PASSIVE ACCEPTANCE OF VS. ACTIVE DEALING WITH SPECIFIC BLOT
CHARACTERISTICS

Passive acceptance of physiognomic characteristics of the blot. The attitude is: "The card does it. I only report what is there." The "thing seen" implies definite structure, but, in the process of elaboration, the	Ability actively to use, eliminate, or otherwise rationalize or deal with the characteristics of the blot, or blot features that do not fit in with the intended organization. The attitude is one of active coping with

[2] In citing sample responses, the inquiry, sometimes in abbreviated form, is given in brackets immediately following each response. The examiner's questions, indications of location, and comments, if any, are set off by parentheses. The usual symbols $\vee$ $>$ $<$ are used when the card is held in other than the standard position. The sequential number of the response is indicated, unless the response was the only one given to a card.

[3] When material is quoted, whether from the Rorschach or other sources, omissions are indicated by three dots (. . .) and pauses by a dash (−).

Table 6-1. Rating scheme for judging Rorschach percepts—(*Continued*)

Low level of structuring	High level of structuring

"perceptual intrusion" of some specific feature of the blot distorts the percept. The child seems unable to resist the impact or "pull" of the stimulus material.

rather than passive submission to what the card "says." Absence of "perceptual intrusions" as defined on the left.

Rationale: This cue deals with a somewhat different aspect of passive acceptance of vs. active dealing with blot characteristics from that considered in cue 1 above. Inability to resist the impact of a specific blot feature, usually leading to confusion in elaboration of the percept, reflects inability to impose structure. An intended organization is disrupted in the very process of being imposed.

Examples

Card IV. (W) A dog—a little like a French poodle. [(In describing the dog's feet in lower side *D*'s, suddenly exclaims) "His feet—got high heels—must be a girl."]

(The absence of "perceptual intrusion" does not require specific illustration. The example given below illustrates active handling of blot features which, in its explicitness, represents an extreme of structuring ability.)
Card II. 1. (W) . . . looks like two people, sort of doing a dance. . . . 3. And where the hands go together, looks something like a torch . . . [3. And the middle (top center *d*) looks like a torch. 1. (People?) Not counting this (lower center red) and counting this (top center *d* which was the torch originally) looks like hands, but in my other idea, it was separate . . . (A child given to "perceptual intrusions" might perhaps have concluded that the hands are on fire.)]

3. STABILITY OF PERCEPTS

Percepts unstable, in flux, ideas shift and change, as if child was unable to hold on to them or separate them. Percepts tend to fuse. In inquiry, child may characteristically forget

Percepts are stable, ideas clearly separate from each other. Ideas and percepts "stay put," both in main performance and in inquiry. If a new idea is given in inquiry, or

Table 6-1. Rating scheme for judging Rorschach percepts—(*Continued*)

Low level of structuring	High level of structuring
his original responses, change responses without being aware of it, or confuse cards.	if percept is changed, child is aware that change has occurred, recognizes new idea as new. Does not confuse cards in inquiry.

Rationale: Instability of percepts is inconsistent with ability to impose clear effective structure. It suggests a world which is confused and confusing to the child, and in which he is not able to get his bearings.

Examples

Card VIII. 3. (W) Reminds me of a sad face, no, a mad face, two eyes here, also reminds me of—no, doesn't remind me any more—back to the sad face—he has a mad face. *Card VIII.* (Probably W) This looks like a—bird, and it's a male bird, and it has very beautiful colors. IX. This is a—a dress of a girl. [VIII. I believe it was a dress. (Bird?) Not here, must have been someplace else. IX. (Child does not remember original response) (Dress?) No, I don't remember this one, I don't think I used two dresses.]	*Card V.* 1. A butterfly. [(This way ∨, like a butterfly. (?) The wings, and the head up here, pretty small head. (Area?) I left off this (lower center *d*) . . . and the feelers here (top center *d*) that most insects have.)] 2. And another way ∧ it could look like a bat. Upside down ∧ be a bat [(?) The wings, and the body, and if you use your imagination, could make (lower center *d*) that the head. And I left out this (top center *d*). And the feelers, I think—I am not sure if a bat has feelers . . . I've never really seen a live one.]

4. HANDLING OF ALTERNATIVES

Indiscriminate alternatives. Two or more responses given to the same blot area, with implication that the blot might just as well look like one as the other, without differentially anchoring alternative response to blot. This is qualitatively different from "precision alternatives." Indiscriminate alternatives may occur in the context of a fluid or of a relatively "stable" record.	Absence of indiscriminate alternatives, or presence of "precision alternatives." The latter implies that the child has a clear standard of accuracy in mind, and strives to improve the "fit" between percept and blot area.

Rationale: If a blot area can indiscriminately "look like" two or more different things in the manner described, the inference is that none of the things named by the child are seen in the blot in a structured manner.

Table 6-1. Rating scheme for judging Rorschach percepts—(*Continued*)

Low level of structuring	High level of structuring

Examples

Card VIII. 2. Looks like two animals crawling, like a beaver. [Two animals, two octopus climbing up, just write two animals because it isn't very definite . . . (Beaver?) can say that, write down beaver.]

Card IV. (W) Well, this looks something like a giant, a giant ape, or dinosaur, with his big tail. [Like a giant monster, and I got the idea from its funny shaped head, and big feet, and the arms, and the big tail. (?) More like a giant dinosaur, because of the tail. Apes don't have so much tail.]

5. ABILITY TO RESPOND DIFFERENTIALLY TO CHANGING STIMULATION

Perseveration [4] or perseverative attitude. As used here, perseveration includes (a) giving the same response to three or more blots, exclusive of populars, such as "bat" on I and V; (b) helpless comments that blots "look the same," even though no actual perseveration occurs; (c) repetitive, enumerative elaboration, on several cards, of percepts that are roughly similar in general structure.

Absence of perseveration or of perseverative attitude.

Rationale: Lack of ability to respond differentially to changing stimulation seems a direct manifestation of inability to experience the world in a structured manner. When objectively different stimulus configurations "look the same," it is unlikely that they should be experienced as structured.

Examples

Example of (c) above: Wolf's face on I, man's face on II, and clown's face on III, all W's, are described in an essentially interchangeable way; on inquiry, repetitively mentions on each "mouth, eyes, ears, nose."

"Lack of perseveration" does not require illustration.

[4] For readers unfamiliar with Rorschach terminology, it may be noted that the term "perseveration" is used here in its conventional Rorschach sense. This meaning is different from the sense the term has in general psychological usage which is followed in Chapter 8.

Table 6-1.   Rating scheme for judging Rorschach percepts—(*Continued*)

Low level of structuring	High level of structuring

6. CONFUSION IN ELABORATING PERCEPTS

Confusion in elaborating percepts. This necessarily implies that the child attempts some structure, but gets "mixed up" in the course of elaborating it. The child may or may not express his awareness of being confused. Confusion may overlap "perceptual intrusion."

No confusion in elaborating percepts. Responses of F— form quality need not reflect confusion, provided that whatever is seen, is seen clearly.

Rationale: Confusion, as specified here, suggests inability to experience the world as structured.

Examples

Card VIII. (Location uncertain.) Looks like a moth got caught in a spider web . . . a moth, a big white thing (apparently means "rib" area). [Now points to side red *D*'s "as . . . moth . . . because the face, the feet . . . the whole web . . ." (What made it look like a web?) Because this (points to side *D*'s) is the moth.]

Card II. (W) Looks like a man with red eyes and black mouth and red beard, mouth is open. [Points out parts without hesitation.]

7. SPECIAL ASPECTS OF VERBALIZATION

Verbalization suggestive of "approximations" and lack of precision, primitive verbalizations, hesitations in verbalization that suggest child is not sure what he sees. (The last point must be distinguished from searching for the "mot juste" that the child feels he needs in order to convey his meaning exactly.)

Verbalization suggestive of precision in use of language reflects clarity in the child's experience.

Rationale: The assumption is that the quality of the verbalization will, to some extent at least, reflect the way in which the stimulus is experienced. A problem in applying this cue is that an ververbal child will be overrated, and the verbally inarticulate child underrated.[5]

---

[5] See discussion of verbal skills in Chapter 11.

Table 6-1. Rating scheme for judging Rorschach percepts—(*Continued*)

Low level of structuring	High level of structuring

Examples

Card VI. (W) . . . It has something to do with the Indians . . . [That's the one with the Indian thing . . . with something coming down here . . . something coming out of it . . . let's see—fire or smoke . . .]

Card III. (*dr*) Looks like a skeleton. [I think it was—somebody's—looks like a skeleton (?) Over here, it has things like skeleton bones. (Location indefinite, apparently including bottom center and parts of adjacent black.)]

Card VI. (Small side lower details in top side "wings.") This could be two awkward-looking faces, something like the type you see, those imaginary witches they draw, with long noses, narrow chin.

8. HANDLING OF W's

No evidence of interest in giving of W responses, or of pulling D responses into a W organization. Such an approach may result in a high W%, but not in a high proportion of structured W's.

Marked interest in, or striving for, W organizations. This interest may or may not result in a high W%, or in a high proportion of W+ organizations. It may result in combinatorial W's scored only additionally, in W's of poor quality (F−, M−, etc.), or of arbitrary character, but not in a high proportion of vague W's.[6]

Rationale: The relevance of this item to ability to impose structure on the blots is obvious.

In contrast to Items 1 through 7 which are most obviously manifested and most clearly definable in records of children who show a low level of structuring, W striving is most naturally defined in terms of the presence of this characteristic in records of children who show a high level of structuring. Children who are uninterested in and unable to impose structure on the blot material may produce a high W% on the basis of passive compliance with the task. In such cases, the W's are likely to be predominantly vague (e.g., "an island," "a mountain," "a design") or at best at the level of easy populars.

[6] In 10-year-olds, in a period of rapid development, W's of F− or arbitrary quality result when a child's striving to organize the stimulus material outstrips his ability to produce such organizations successfully.

Table 6-1. Rating scheme for judging Rorschach percepts—(*Continued*)

Low level of structuring   High level of structuring

Examples

Card III. 1. This could be two ani-mals. 2. And this could be a butter-fly. [. . . 1. Animals . . . but this (points to part of body to which usual "leg" is attached) is too high—2. (Butterfly?) . . . Shaped like a butterfly.]

Card IX. Flowers—plants. (Points to whole card.) [Still looks some-thing like flowers and bushes . . . this (points to pink) could be flowers.]

Card III. 1. Looks like two birds talking to each other. 2. A bow tie in the middle. 1. They are sitting on a branch (usual "leg" for branch). 3. Two flares behind them (outer red). [Two little ducks holding a bow tie . . . sitting on a tree, top of it (top of tree in bottom center). (Note that this example also illus-trates "interest in card coverage" on item 9 below.)]

Card IX. (W) Looks like a Navy emblem . . . there's the top of the world on top ("dome" at top) . . . and the wings on top (in orange) represent Navy planes, the green represents green trees . . . and the pink . . . all the dry and dusty parts. The white line in the center represents the water.

9. INTEREST IN CARD COVERAGE

Little interest in accounting for, or in "getting an answer for" the total blot area. When this occurs, it is likely to be in the context of little interest in *W*'s also.

Marked interest in accounting for, or "getting an answer for" all the parts of the blot, whether these are organized into combinatorial *W*'s or not.

Rationale: A high or low degree of interest in card coverage may be con-sidered, along with *W* striving, as a manifestation of active interest in struc-turing one's experience. The emphasis may be on *D*'s rather than on over-all structure. It should be noted that card coverage may reflect an attitude of passive compliance with instructions, encountered in an occa-sional child judged to show a low level of structuring. On the other hand, it may reflect an attitude of actively taking up the challenge presented by the task. Only card coverage accompanied by the latter attitude is under consideration here. When such an attitude is present, the evidence for it is usually unmistakable in the child's explicit comments.

Table 6-1.   Rating scheme for judging Rorschach percepts—(*Continued*)

Low level of structuring	High level of structuring

Examples

Card VII. ∨ (top *d*'s) Looks like . . . Indian's hair [. . . Indian has long braids sticking down and these two look like it. (No other responses or comments about the rest of the blot.)]	*Card VII.* Could be two rabbits, one on each side, just this part (upper two-thirds). [But I didn't say anything for this (lower third). Could be a butterfly.]

10. GENERAL IMPRESSION OF COMPETENCE AND ADEQUACY OF RESOURCES
IN DEALING WITH TASK

Inference that child is overwhelmed with task, based on impression of incapacity, helplessness, and perplexity in dealing with it.	Inference that child is "in the saddle" in dealing with task, based on impression of competence, and lack of evidence of helplessness or perplexity.

Rationale: A summary impression that a child is helpless or is master of the situation ordinarily overlaps specific cues 1 through 9. It is, however, included as a separate cue since an impression of helplessness or its opposite may manifest itself in ways not previously specified. Because such an impression is gleaned from a total record, and may result from a variety of indications, it is not practicable to cite examples.

It should be evident that the cues differ in the extent to which they are separable from the total flow of the test production, and in the extent to which they may be illustrated by means of specific examples. Thus, while perseveration may be fairly specifically located in a record and illustrated, the impression of incapacity to deal with the task must necessarily be inferred from the quality of the total record. It should also be evident that an example given to illustrate one cue may not be a "pure" example of that cue alone: a vague and indefinite percept may also be forgotten in inquiry, and may be verbalized in a helpless manner. Such overlap is inevitable when considering a complex process which, by its very nature, cannot be fragmented. Finally, cues formulated in terms of one extreme of the structuring continuum may not have a clearly definable opposite at the other extreme. In such instances, the absence of a given feature was considered as synonymous with its opposite. Thus, the opposite of perseveration could only be defined as absence of perseveration, and the opposite of W striving as absence of such striving.[7]

As an aid to making ratings, the judge wrote out capsule comments about each Rorschach record. The following are examples of such comments, recorded before knowledge of their standing on the perceptual test battery, for two children rated at opposite extremes of the structuring continuum:

Rated 1 (lowest level of structuring): Very little interest in structuring. Impression of real incapacity in coping perceptually. His world seems to be a blur, and he seems willing to leave it so. Repeated impression that he doesn't know what it is that he sees, even when the content of the percept is definite (e.g., "six people" on VII). Perseveration of "design" response on II, VIII, IX, and additionally on X. Helpless verbalization. Elaborations and specifications of percepts have a literal, enumerative quality.

Rated 5 (highest level of structuring): There is never any doubt in his mind about what it is that he sees. His world is clearly perceived, his ability to structure situations is high. Bold organizations, which are characteristically cut-off W's in which he clearly eliminates parts of the blot he is not using (e.g., giant on IV is described in detail; he comments "and I didn't use this part," omitting lower center D). Is never vague or confused, spontaneously locates and describes in inquiry, percepts remain stable.

An attempt to check on the reproducibility of this rating scheme by another judge was made under the following conditions. The second judge evaluated for another purpose the Rorschach, TAT, and figure drawings of the Group-III boys for a number of variables. She had no contact with the subjects themselves, and had no other information about them. For each variable, she was given a number of specific cues as aids to judgment. Included among the variables to be rated was one based on the cues given above.[8] The correlation between Rorschach percept ratings made by the two judges was .73 ($P < .01$).

For validation purposes, the ratings of the thirty Group-III Rorschach records made by the first judge according to the rating scheme

[7] The cues listed above were formulated in order to assess a particular aspect of cognitive functioning, the capacity to structure ambiguous stimulus material. However, a survey of the definitions of the contrasting ends of the continua (e.g., fluid vs. stable, vague vs. precise perception) suggests that the cues constitute aspects of Rorschach records recognizable, clinically, as those of performance expected from hysterical vs. obsessive-compulsive personalities. A specific investigation of the hysterical-obsessive polarity as related to mode of field approach is reported in Chapter 9.

[8] With the exception of minor editorial changes, the cue definitions were the same as the definitions given the second rater.

described above were correlated with the various indices of mode of field approach, with the following results: with perceptual index scores, $r = .41$ ($P < .05$); with intellectual index scores, $r = .26$ (not significant); with cognitive index scores, $r = .37$ ($P < .05$). Our hypothesis is thus essentially confirmed.

These relationships are further substantiated when the ratings of the second judge are considered. Correlations of these ratings with perceptual, intellectual, and cognitive index scores were .41 ($P < .05$), .35 ($P < .05$), and .42 ($P < .05$), respectively. Since two other projective tests were available to the second judge, these results provide suggestive rather than conclusive evidence of the objectivity of the scale.

Thus, the nature of children's experience in interpreting Rorschach inkblots is related to their mode of field approach. As expected, children who are able to impose structure on the amorphous Rorschach stimulus material and therefore experience it in clear, definite fashion, also tend to be able to overcome an embedding context in perceptual and intellectual situations so that their experience tends to be analytical. Children who cannot readily structure the Rorschach inkblots, with the result that their experience of this material is vague, are strongly influenced by an embedding context, so that their experience tends to be global.

2. Related Studies

a. Recognition efficiency. The use of the Rorschach in the study of perceptual clarity limited us to a fixed set of stimuli; moreover, complex judgments of structuring ability were required. In a subsequent study we sought a technique which would make possible more precise manipulation of the degree of ambiguity or structure of the stimulus material and which would permit direct, objective evaluation of structuring ability. The Recognition-efficiency test developed by Gump (1955) suggested itself as particularly suitable for this purpose.

In our modification of the Recognition-efficiency test, referred to as the nonserial version in Chapter 5, blurred, meaningful stimuli (pictures) were presented tachistoscopically. Ten pictures were projected on a screen, one at a time, for 3 seconds each. The degree of clarity of each picture was controlled by appropriate settings of the projector focusing system. Settings which led to adequate difficulty for each picture were determined in an exploratory study. The subject's score was the number of pictures correctly identified. This test was given to 29 of the boys of Group III.

At face value it would seem that individual differences in performance on this test would reflect differences in ability to structure one's
experience.   We considered that a subject who recognizes the stimulus, even when it is vague, must actively organize the material.   In
contrast, a subject who cannot recognize the stimulus would seem to be
approaching the task more passively, requiring that organization be
provided by the figure itself.   Accordingly, it was our hypothesis that
subjects with a relatively global field approach would tend to have difficulty in recognition.

However, this expectation was not confirmed.   No relationship
($r = -.03$) was found between perceptual index and Recognition-
efficiency scores.   Nor, as we have seen, was this version of Gump's
test loaded on the analytical-field-approach factor isolated in the factor analysis reported in Chapter 5.

A possible interpretation of these negative results is that the version
of the Recognition-efficiency test provides a measure of Thurstone's
speed-of-closure factor, described in Chapter 4, rather than of structuring ability.   Admittedly, this is an ad hoc interpretation, but it is one
that is amenable to experimental test.

There is an important similarity between the Recognition-efficiency test
we used and the Street Gestalt test.   Both require immediate recognition of
an impoverished meaningful figure.   The difference in method of impover-
ishing the stimuli may not be important.

We have already seen (Chapter 4) that the speed-of-closure dimension
of perceptual functioning must be distinguished from the analytical-field-
approach dimension.   Apparently, a distinction also needs to be made between recognition efficiency and capacity to organize an unstructured field.
This distinction can be further illustrated by the findings with Gump's original or serial version of the Recognition-efficiency test, which was also given
to the children of Group III.

In the serial version, described briefly in Chapter 5 and in more detail
by Gump (1955), the pictures are presented in increasingly sharp focus until correct recognition is achieved.   As in the nonserial version of the test,
scores reflect the capacity to recognize the pictures when out of focus.   However, the difference between the two versions is important.   In fact, in the
serial version it is difficult to predict what the relationship will be with
measures of field dependence, since the ability to structure may hinder
recognition and the ability to overcome embedding contexts may aid recognition.

In the serial version the subject must discard incorrect prerecognition hypotheses elicited by the extreme out-of-focus presentations.   In our terms,
the initial structure which the subject imposes upon the material must be
overcome.

It seems reasonable to suppose that organized and well-integrated pre-recognition hypotheses would be more difficult to overcome than vague prerecognition hypotheses. For example, if a subject's earliest hypothesis is "fog," there is little if any structuring of the picture to interfere with subsequent recognition. Furthermore, such vague prerecognition percepts are precisely the kind we would expect of a person with little capacity to impose organization. In contrast, the person who is able to organize the amorphous stimulus, using whatever features of the stimulus are present, should have greater difficulty in subsequent recognition.

Recognition efficiency in the serial version of the test should therefore reflect the capacity to impose organization. On this basis we would expect recognition efficiency to be *poorer* among subjects who have the ability to impose an organization and, by implication, among subjects with an analytical field approach. Consistent with this line of reasoning we found that among our 10-year-olds, children with an analytical field approach actually did less well in the serial version of the Recognition-efficiency test than children with a global approach (Chapter 5). This result could not have been predicted from the information we had available.

If overcoming prerecognition hypotheses is considered an expression of an analytical field approach, we would expect subjects with such an approach to discard prerecognition hypotheses more easily. The person who forms the most definite prerecognition hypothesis, with the greatest potential for interference with subsequent recognition, is therefore also the person who is most able to discard the hypothesis as more information becomes available. In other words, the person who experiences articulately may be helped at one point and hindered at another point on the serial version. The precise relationship between field dependence and recognition efficiency cannot, therefore, be predicted without additional information.

In contrast to our results with 10-year-olds, Gump (1955) found that adult subjects who are field dependent on the Thurstone-Gottschaldt do less well on the serial version of the Recognition-efficiency test than field-independent subjects. The difference in findings may reflect a difference between adults and children in manner of performing this task.

b. Other studies of ability to structure experience. The Rorschach "W sign," developed by Hertzman for our 1954 study of young adults, may be interpreted as bearing on structuring of experience.

In determining the W sign, three ways of handling the impact of the blot were considered:

1. "The subject can produce an appropriate response to the blot as a whole, with well-articulated forms and adequate use of the blot's structural features." 2. "The subject can try to cope with the blot as a whole, but produces an inadequate concept through arbitrary manipulation and distortion of the blot (F-)." 3. "The subject's whole response can be determined primarily by a single impressive feature of the blot . . . This kind

of 'blot-determined' whole response represents little organizing activity on the part of the subject, but is representative of a passive acceptance of a relatively unstructured feature of the blot" (p. 207).

A subject received the W sign on an all-or-none basis if his Rorschach record showed a dearth of adequate whole responses or a large proportion (50%) of inadequate or blot-determined whole responses. A significant relation was found for both men and women between W-sign ratings and index scores based on a composite of TRTC, RFT, and rotating-room scores. Field-dependent subjects were assigned the W sign significantly more often than field-independent subjects. This finding has been substantiated in several independent studies with adults.[9] Capacity for overcoming an embedding context is thus shown to be associated with capacity to impose structure on unorganized stimuli.

This relation was not found, however, for the 10-year-old children in our 1954 study, even when the standards for scoring were modified for application to children's Rorschach records.[10] The reasons for this negative result are not entirely clear. The likelihood that the ability to impose structure successfully is not as highly developed in 10-year-olds as in adults may be important. Developmental studies of the W response (e.g., Hemmendinger, 1953), and of Beck's z, described as "an index to the organizational aspect of intellectual functioning" (Thetford, Molish, and Beck, 1951), point to the existence of age trends in "organizing ability."

Still another approach to the structuring aspect of perception of Rorschach inkblots is found in the work of Phillips and his collaborators, who have reported findings similar to our own.

In the most recent and comprehensive of these studies (Phillips et al., 1957), the Rorschach was administered to two groups of subjects who had also been given a large battery of cognitive tests. Cluster analyses of correlations among various Rorschach indices were conducted for both groups, in addition to the analyses of the cognitive battery itself to which we have already referred. The Rorschach clusters were then correlated with a composite measure of spatial

[9] It has been confirmed by Linton (personal communication) for her group of college men ($r = .36, P < .01, N = 47$) and by us in our study of hospitalized psychiatric patients (for men, point biserial $r = .30, P < .05, N = 35$; for women, .63, $P < .01, N = 31$). [Data for these hospital groups were presented in our 1954 report (p. 344) in terms of frequency of the W sign among low-, intermediate-, and high-index perceptual performers.] The relation was further confirmed by Gardner, et al. (1959), for women ($r = .63, P < .01, N = 30$), but not for men ($r = .28, N = 30$).

[10] In the 1954 report results for the W sign for children were not reported separately.

decontextualization, which included EFT scores as one component. The Rorschach cluster, which was significantly related to spatial decontextualization in both studies, was defined by four indices: (1) $D\text{-}\% = 100\dfrac{D\text{-}}{D}$, where $D\text{-}$ is the number of detail responses with inadequate form level and D is the total number of detail responses. (2) Di = number of integrative detail responses. (3) Wi = number of integrative whole responses. (4) M = number of human-movement responses.

Inspection of the criteria for scoring $D\text{-}\%$, Di, and Wi, leaves little doubt that the capacity actively to organize the blots is featured in this Rorschach cluster.[11] To the extent that the spatial-decontextualization and field-approach dimensions are similar (Chapter 5), the Phillips study provides further evidence that ability to impose organization on an unstructured field is related to mode of field approach. This confirmation is of particular interest since Phillips approached the problem with a different conceptual framework.

3. Structuring Ability as Evaluated in TAT Productions

In another study of structuring ability the organization of TAT stories created by the 10-year-old children was considered.

Productivity and effectiveness of integration of ideas were the main criteria used in judging organizational level. Productivity—reflected, for example, in interpretation of features of the picture, endowment of figures shown on the card with thoughts and feelings, addition of characters needed to make sense of the picture, development of a theme—implies an attempt to give some structure rather than leave "as is" scenes which in varying degrees are vague. ·Composition of the thoughts generated by the TAT pictures into an orderly, logical sequence may also be considered to reflect ability to impose structure on this ideational material. The rationale for using organization as an indication of structuring ability is in many ways similar to the rationale which guided the Rorschach percepts analysis.

The procedure for evaluating stories according to organizational level made use of four categories of classification:

Level A. Stories involving no organization at all are included here. They are, in a literal sense, not stories but simply descriptions of objects,

11 Phillips scored the Rorschach of the college group from our 1954 study with an earlier version of his scoring system. The correlation of these scores with index scores for our perceptual test battery was in the expected direction, but not significant.

people, scenes, usually very briefly stated, with no attempt at interpretation of what is going on, or what people in the picture are feeling. Omission of important parts of cards may occur. Also included here are highly illogical stories. Such stories usually have a plot, but the material is contradictory and the sequence of ideas is chaotic.

Level B. Stories are placed in this category if there is some attempt to give direction to the material and to go beyond sheer description. However, the relation of characters to each other, or the feelings of characters is barely touched upon in such stories. Stories at this level are primarily impressionistic and descriptive, but differ from A-level stories in that they contain a small amount of interpretation. Also included are stories with characteristics of Level C which contain slightly illogical elements, or of Level D which contain some seriously illogical elements.

Level C. These stories involve greater elaboration of the motives or feelings of characters in the story, of the relationships between people, and of some sort of theme. Popular stories and their variations (e.g., current movies) are placed here as are stories with characteristics of Level D which contain some slightly illogical elements.

Level D. These stories involve elaborate but consistent plots, or extensive consideration of inner motives of characters, or a high level of awareness and productive use of most of the outstanding features of the card, or of the creation of characters not pictured on the card who played an important role in the story.

This rating scheme was developed on the TAT stories of the boys of Groups I and II, and cross-validated on the stories of the Group-III boys. As was our practice in evaluating TAT material, each story was removed from the original record, and all the stories for a given card rated separately, without any indication of their source. A value of "1" was assigned to each story rated "A," a value of "2" to stories rated "B," and so on. A total level-of-organization score was computed for each child by adding the scores for all his stories. The correlation between total scores derived from the ratings of two independent judges was .98 ($P < .01$), reflecting good interjudge reliability.

It was, of course, our expectation that children with a relatively analytical field approach would tend to achieve higher organizational ratings. For the Group-I and -II children, a correlation of .63 ($P < .01$), in the expected direction, was obtained between organization-level ratings and perceptual index scores. The relation did not hold up, however, in the cross-validation study. Organizational-level ratings did not relate significantly to perceptual index ($r = .12$), intellectual index ($r = .21$), or cognitive index scores ($r = .18$). Our starting hypothesis must be rejected.

The negative outcome of this analysis of structuring ability in the medium of verbal material may relate to the finding to be reported in

Chapter 11 that the ability to overcome an embedding context in a verbal medium is apparently unrelated to such ability in the medium of stimulus configurations. It is noteworthy, in this connection, that whereas organizational-level ratings did not relate significantly to perceptual, intellectual, or cognitive index scores, they were significantly correlated ($r = .37$, $P < .05$) with verbal index scores. The issues raised by these differences in performance of verbal and nonverbal tasks are considered in Chapter 11.

4. Memory as Indirect Evidence of Nature of Experience

The degree of organization of learned material helps determine its fate in memory. Poorly organized material is less apt to "survive" than well-organized material (see, for example, Katona, 1940, Rieff and Scheerer, 1959). From this we might expect that children whose experiences characteristically register in clearly structured fashion would tend to remember past events better than children whose experiences tend to be unstructured. We might further anticipate that if the experiences of children with an analytical field approach are relatively structured, they would tend to have better memory for earlier events than children with a global approach. Impressions formed in the course of many varied contacts with our children were in line with this expectation. On interview, for example, boys with an analytical approach often seemed to recall earlier events with greater precision and certainty than boys with a more global approach.

We accordingly undertook studies of memory of children with different modes of field approach. In one, susceptibility to retroactive inhibition of intrinsically unorganized material was investigated. In the second, a test was made of long-range memory for an earlier experience (taking the TAT in the laboratory). We hypothesized, on the grounds already considered, that in both situations memory would be poorer among children with a global field approach than among children with an analytical approach. Confirmation of this hypothesis, we reasoned, would provide indirect evidence of differences between such children in extent of structure of experience on initial registration.[12]

[12] In the case of the TAT the child is dealing with emotionally significant material. The possibility may be raised that children with a global field approach might show poorer memory for the TAT because they are likely to repress such material. If this is so the characteristics which make the material subject to repression are also likely, for protective reasons, to make the initial experience of the material diffuse. This would heighten the difference in extent of structure of the initial experience between children with relatively global and relatively analytical approaches.

a. Retroactive inhibition. Material which is organized during original learning is less subject to the "corrosive effects" of retroactive inhibition than unorganized material (Newman, 1939). With unstructured material, as nonsense syllables, subjects with contrasting modes of field approach may be expected to differ in their ability to organize the material in a fashion necessary for learning, resulting in differences in susceptibility of the material to retroactive inhibition.

Just such a result was obtained by Gollin and Baron (1954), with college men as subjects. Nonsense syllables were used for both original and interpolated learning. Mode of field approach was evaluated by the Gottschaldt. As anticipated, field-dependent subjects suffered greater retroactive inhibition than field-independent subjects. There were no significant differences in speed of original learning. However, in a similar unpublished study by Miller (1953), which came to our attention after our own study had been completed, the findings on the effects of retroactive inhibition were not confirmed. In fact, field-dependent subjects demonstrated significantly less retroactive inhibition than field-independent subjects.

The study we did with Group-III boys employed a standard retroactive inhibition situation, adapted for use with children.

Both nonsense syllables and words were employed as learning materials. In the first part of the study, each subject learned a list of seven nonsense syllables, to the point where he could reproduce all the items in correct order on two successive trials. The subject's learning score was the number of trials taken to learn the list to this criterion. A second list of nonsense syllables was then learned, by the same procedure, following which the subject was tested for recall of the first list. Then he was required to relearn the first list to the original criterion. Subsequently, the entire study was repeated in the same fashion, using lists of words, instead of nonsense syllables as learning material.

Significantly more trials were needed to learn nonsense than meaningful material, but extent of recall or savings in relearning did not differ with type of material used.

Measures of retroactive inhibition were in no instance significantly related to measures of mode of field approach. Moreover, relearning and recall measures for nonsense syllables were not significantly related to comparable measures for words.

The lack of consistency in individual performance with different types of learning material points to the operation of as yet unidentified situational factors. These must be better understood before the retroactive inhibition situation may be used in the investigation of individual styles of functioning in learning and memory. An effective test of the hypothesis we undertook to evaluate must thus await further work.[13,14]

We believe that an approach to classical learning situations, in terms of individual differences in ability to structure experiences, will prove fruitful.

b. Long-range recall. An unusual opportunity to study memory phenomena was provided by our longitudinal studies. The children in these studies were seen repeatedly over a period of years, making it possible to conduct tests of recall after extremely long intervals. The finding of Katona that the better retention of organized than unorganized material is especially apparent after long-term periods made it particularly desirable to use conditions of long-range recall for a test of our hypothesis.

As already described, the Group-I boys used in the longitudinal studies were first tested when they were 10 years old. At that time, half of them received a series of personality tests, including the TAT, in addition to the perceptual tests given to the whole group. At age 14, and again at 17, the entire group received both the perceptual and personality tests. In all, 27 boys and 21 girls were studied over the 7-year interval: all of them received the TAT at 14 and 17 years; 14 of the boys and 11 of the girls had also received it at 10 years.

The test of memory used was recall at age 17 of the TAT situation encountered at age 14.[15] An interval of 3 years had thus elapsed between the two test occasions. Since the TAT situation is not encountered by children under everyday circumstances, the possibility was ruled out that differential recall at age 17 might be a function of

---

[13] In comparing the Gollin-Baron and Miller findings to our own, it must also be considered that the retroactive inhibition situation may be different in important ways for adults and children. As one possibility, we had the impression in conducting this study that the children generally did not try to organize the material through imposition of meaning (as using reference words which the nonsense syllables suggested) or structure (as using mnemonic devices), procedures commonly followed by adults.

[14] Since this report went to press, there has been another study, by Gardner and Long (1961), which apparently confirms the work of Gollin and Baron on the relation between field dependence and retroactive inhibition in adult subjects.

[15] It may be more appropriate to think of experience of the TAT situation in terms of degree of articulation, rather than degree of structure alone. Taking a TAT is a complex, "real-life" situation, and, as in any such situation, the analytical aspect of experience is emphasized along with the structural aspect. On this basis, differences in memory for a situation like the TAT would reflect differences in extent to which experience of the situation is articulated.

differences in amount of interpolated experience with the material.[16]

The procedure used to evaluate memory for the TAT was as follows: After the subject had been given the TAT instructions during the 17-year test session, he was asked whether he had ever encountered the test before. Of the subjects who did not recognize it at first, some came to do so as the test proceeded. Those who did not recognize the test by the time it was completed were again asked whether they recognized it. One measure of memory for the TAT was thus simply whether or not the child at any point recalled having taken the test before.

Those subjects who did recall the test were shown each card after the test was over and asked to indicate whether it had been included in the series given at age 14. The number of cards recognized provided a second measure of recall.[17] A third measure of recall reflected the point at which the subject remembered having taken the test. To provide a rough measure of "point-of-recall" a score of "3" was assigned if the test was remembered at the very beginning, a score of "2" if it was remembered somewhere after the beginning but before the end of the test, a score of "1" if it was remembered at the end, and a score of "0" if it was not remembered at all.

In relating memory scores to perceptual index scores, the results for boys and girls were treated separately. Moreover, within each sex, separate analyses were carried out for the 17-year group that had been given the TAT both at 10 and 14 years and the group that had been given it at 14 only. Separate correlations were computed for subjects who had taken the test at age 10, and those who had not. A composite r was obtained by combining the two separate correlations by the "r to z, z to r" method. Using the chi-square model for combining results of several studies (Jones and Fisk, 1953), the "P" values obtained for the two within-sex groups from separate t-tests were combined.

For boys the results confirm our expectation. Boys with a relatively analytical field approach, as compared to boys with a global approach, were more likely to remember having taken the TAT before, to recall more cards, and to recognize the test more quickly. Thus, boys who recalled the TAT achieved significantly lower perceptual index scores (were more analytical) than boys who failed to recall it ($P < .01$);

[16] Only one subject reported having seen the TAT outside the laboratory. This subject had had the TAT a short time before she was retested at age 17, as part of a diagnostic work-up. She was excluded from the study.

[17] Subjects who failed to recall ever having taken the test were given a score of "zero."

and number of cards recalled related significantly to perceptual index scores ($r = .54$, $P < .01$), as did "point-of-recall" scores ($r = .85$,
$P < .01$).

There is evidence that the observed relation between mode of perceiving and memory occurs only under conditions of delayed recall. In
another study, each of the 30 Group-III 10-year-old boys was asked
at the conclusion of the TAT to recall as many pictures as he could.
No relation was found between number of cards remembered and
perceptual index scores ($r = .02$).

For girls, we find no significant relations between mode of field approach and the various measures of recall. For two of the measures
(number of cards recalled and the point at which recall occurred),
although not for the third (sheer memory of having seen the test before), the relatively restricted range of the measures may have contributed to the outcome.

There is a significant sex difference for two of the memory measures—
number of cards recalled and memory for having seen the test before.[18]
Boys more often recalled having taken the test, and remembered a
greater number of cards. These sex differences in memory parallel
the sex differences observed in mode of field approach (see Chapter
13).

B. ARTICULATENESS OF EXPERIENCE UNDER
EVERYDAY CONDITIONS

The studies considered thus far investigated the nature of children's
experiences under special "made-up" conditions. As a next step we
sought to determine whether differences in quality of experience similar to those we had observed in the laboratory are manifested under
circumstances which come closer to life. An assessment of the nature
of experience under "real-life" conditions is of course difficult to make.
As a first step, we sought to make such an assessment on the basis of
the child's account of his impressions of everyday events and activities. An interview with the child seemed to offer a possible way of
obtaining such an account. In this approach the structuring and

---

[18] The series of TAT cards used was not entirely the same for boys and girls.
(Of the 9 cards given girls and 10 cards given boys, there were 7 cards in common.)
The results for the number-of-cards-recalled measure do not therefore provide
clear-cut evidence on sex differences in memory; specifically, the sex differences
observed may be a consequence of the difference in the particular cards used. It
does not seem likely, however, that the relatively slight difference in test material
could account for the sex differences found in sheer recall for the TAT situation.

analytical aspects of the child's experience, hitherto considered separately, are of course intimately and inseparably linked, as are his experiences of himself and his surroundings. In effect, what we sought to explore in this preliminary way was the extent of articulation of the child's experience of himself and his world.

We have adopted the term "cognitive clarity" to describe the very broad dimension evaluated in the study of children's interviews. This dimension is a continuous one and reflects the extent to which information and impressions are discrete, structured and assimilated, or blurred, confused, and unassimilated. We considered that a high level of cognitive clarity may be manifested by a child in the following ways: he tends to experience the world and himself in a relatively clear and organized way, rather than as blurred and poorly structured; he is likely to be aware of the discreteness of events, as well as their connections, and to be aware of people both in their separate roles and in their interrelationships; his view is not limited to the immediate present, but includes past, present, and future in a continuous association; he tends to be aware that people, including himself, have reasons for the things they do; he is apt to define people in terms of attributes that go deeper than their actions or physical characteristics. Amount of knowledge is not as important in cognitive clarity as is the degree of assimilation of knowledge. Even though circumstances and interests may have limited a child's fund of information, the information he does have may be well assimilated. In contrast, a child may have a very large fund of facts; yet because he has failed to achieve appropriate assimilation of these facts his account of them may be confused, circumstantial, overspecific and overconcrete, and have a generally "out-of-focus" quality.

In undertaking to study extent of cognitive clarity in relation to mode of field approach in laboratory situations, we hypothesized that children with a relatively analytical field approach would tend to show greater cognitive clarity than children with a global approach.

The concept of cognitive clarity emerged gradually in the course of studying the accumulated data for the boys of Groups I and II, especially the interviews with the Group-II boys. These interviews had not, however, been oriented toward an analysis of cognitive clarity. In the interviews with Group-III boys, cognitive clarity was made the focus; included were many specific questions designed to explore the child's awareness of persons and events and relationships among them. As a means of obtaining comparable information from child to child, all the Group-III interviews were conducted by one staff member.

The general method of interview was a compromise between a direct questionnaire approach and a "free-wheeling" approach. Particular questions were asked and particular areas covered with all children, the child's responses guiding further exploration of a given issue. An attempt was made to achieve fairly uniform coverage of a number of areas, enumerated in the outline below. Each area was introduced by a standard question and additional questions were uniformly asked in the course of covering that area. Two "projective" questions were also included. Differences among children in interests, expressiveness, and cooperation naturally made for some variation in procedure, depth of probing, and extent of coverage.

The interview was conducted in a single session lasting 1 to 2 hours and was recorded on tape. The transcriptions were used in carrying out the cognitive clarity analysis.

The areas covered in the interview (including examples of standard questions asked each child) were as follows:

Areas Covered	Examples of Specific Questions Routinely Asked
I. Introduction and free-time activities	Q: Could you begin by telling me a bit about yourself?
A. Sports	
B. Hobbies	Q: Do you have any hobbies?
C. Books, music, newspapers	Q: Do you read the newspapers?
	Q: Can you tell me about something you've read lately?
D. Television and movies	
E. Clubs	
F. Vacations	Q: What do you generally do when you are on vacation from school?
1. Weekends	
2. Christmas and Easter recess	
3. Summers	
II. School	Q: How are things going in school this term?
A. Grades	Q: What kind of marks have you been getting?
B. Best and worst subjects	Q: What are your best subjects?
C. Best and worst teachers	Q: What is your teacher like?
	Q: Who is the very best teacher you've ever had?
D. Earlier school experiences	Q: Do you remember the very first day you ever went to school? Tell me about it.

Areas Covered	Examples of Specific Questions Routinely Asked
E. Future schools and courses anticipated	Q: Where do you expect to go after you finish P.S. 152?
III. Career	
A. Vocational choice or preference	Q: What do you expect to be when you're older?
B. Background to vocational choice	
1. How to achieve	Q: How do you become a _____ (doctor, etc.)?
2. Why this choice	Q: Why would you like to be a _____?
3. Familiarity with field	Q: Do you know anyone who is a _____?
4. Parental attitudes toward choice	
IV. Current events	Q: Do you discuss current events (in school or with your family)?
A. 1956 presidential campaign	Q: Do you ever discuss the coming elections?
1. Likely candidates	Q: Who do you think is going to win?
2. Own preferences	Q: Who are you for? Why?
3. Family discussion, preferences	
4. Details of elections	
5. Issues in the election	
B. Juvenile delinquency	Q: Do you ever talk about juvenile delinquency?
1. Causes	
2. Possible remedies	Q: What do you think could be done about it?
V. Health	Q: How's your health been lately?
A. Recent illnesses	
B. Major past illnesses	
C. Activities during illness	Q: What do you do to amuse yourself when you are sick?
D. Current state of vision, hearing, teeth	Q: How's your eyesight?
E. Food habits and preference	Q: How's your appetite?
F. Sleep habits	Q: Do you like to sleep?
G. Height, weight	
VI. Self	Q: What are you like?
A. Earliest memories	Q: What kind of a baby were you? What's the very first thing you

Areas Covered	Examples of Specific Questions Routinely Asked
	ever remember? What's the first birthday party you remember?
B. Projective questions	Q: Suppose you had a magic wand and you could get anything you wanted with it, what would you want to get most of all?
	Q: Suppose you could use this wand to change yourself in any way. How would you want to change yourself?
VII. Family	Q: Tell me about your family.
A. Constellation of family	
B. Living quarters and arrangements	
C. Father—description, occupation, important events in life	Q: What's your father like?
D. Mother—same	Q: What is your mother like?
E. Siblings—description, relationship with	
F. Issues	
1. Choice of clothing	Q: Who buys your clothing? Who picks it out?
2. Bedtime hours	
3. Punishment	Q: Do your parents ever punish you?
4. Allowance	Q: What do you do for spending money?
5. Pets	
6. Chores, duties	
7. Religion—type and degree of observance	

The staff member who conducted the interviews also devised and applied the cognitive-clarity rating procedure. At the time of the interview and the analysis of the interview records he had no knowledge of any other test results for the children.

In preparation for the development of a rating scale of cognitive clarity, the interview records were studied with the aim of establishing criteria that might serve as the basis for such a rating scale. This study led to the identification of six kinds of general manifestations which provided such criteria. These manifestations are described below, with examples of responses which reflect the extremes of developed cognitive clarity and lack of cognitive clarity.

1. Awareness of means-end relationships. This refers to an understanding of the methods and steps by which one arrives at goals; grasp of interrelationships between events; awareness of continuity between past, present, and future or anticipated events; and, in general, the possession of "hypotheses" as to how things come about.

a. *Example of a response suggestive of cognitive clarity:*

Examiner (E): How do you become a doctor?

Subject (S): It's a very long feature —you have to go first to a college and then a special university.

E: And after you finish the special university?

S: Then you get an office and the equipment you need for your work—but you start working in hospitals so you'll get patients to know you.

b. *Examples of responses suggestive of lack of clarity:*

E: How do you become an accountant (which subject now plans to be)?

S: Well, that I don't know—I'll have to ask my father.

E: How do you become a doctor?

S: You go to doctor school and learn to be a doctor.

E: How long does it take?

S: I dunno, maybe 14 or 15 years— but I figure it could take me one year (can give no explanation of this).

2. Clarity with regard to time and space. This refers to the understanding of: geographic relationships between places (e.g., cities, countries, rooms in an apartment, etc.); where people (e.g., relatives, friends) live, work, and perform various functions; temporal relationships between events; concepts of time and space.

a. *Example of a response suggestive of clarity:*

E: How long a distance do you run?

S: 2½ miles—it's six times around the block.

b. *Examples of responses suggestive of lack of clarity:*

E: . . . .

S: Got the time?

E: Well, it's 5 after 3:00.

S: I leave at 4:30.

E: That's right.

S: So how many more hours I got, half an hour?

| E: When was that? | S: About three years ago, when I was three years old. (Subject is now 10.) |

E: How long has he (your father) been a lawyer? S: About two years or a year.

E: What was he before that? S: I don't know. I don't remember.

3. Awareness of motives of self and others. This refers to understanding why people do things, why the subject himself does things or acts in certain ways, how to get people to do things; in general, what motivates people.

a. *Example of a response suggestive of clarity:*

E: Do you remember the very first day that you ever went to school? S: Yes, I was scared.

E: How come? S: I didn't know what it was going to be like.

b. *Examples of responses suggestive of lack of clarity:*

E: Do you remember the very first day you ever went to school? S: Yes.

E: Tell me about it. S: I was crying.
E: Why? S: I don't know.

E: How is he (best friend) like you? S: Well, he weighs the same as I do, he's about as tall as I am . . . that's all.

4. Evidence of interest in and activity directed at filling in gaps in one's fund of information. This refers to any evidence which would suggest that the subject has made some effort, on his own, to learn about things or gather information other than that presented by such sources as parents, television, teachers, etc.

a. *Example of a response suggestive of clarity:*

E: How did you know that it (a rock found by subject) was granite? S: I looked it up in a book.

b. *Example of a response suggestive of lack of clarity:*

E: How much have you saved (toward a new bike)? S: Twenty-one dollars.

E: How much do you need for a new bike? S: I don't know . . .

5. Clarity of expression and relevance of responses. Questions are answered clearly and relevantly, with few digressions.

a. *Example of a response suggestive of clarity:*

E: What kind of book is it (that you save match book covers in)?

S: Well it's an album and it has slots for the match covers, and on the back it has places for larger match covers that won't fit into the slots.

b. *Example of a response suggestive of lack of clarity:*

E: Tell me about it (your first day of school).

S: Well—my friend went to school longer than me 'cause I was—I'm older than him—he's in kindergarten when I went in—'cause my birthday's in June—that's the end of the season for school. First day I went in I was a little nervous—then I saw my friend there—I—you know—I was playing around—we played—and we went outside and then sang songs and all.

6. Ability to abstract or generalize. This refers to the ability to form abstractions and generalizations rather than being limited to the very concrete and specific.

a. *Examples of responses suggestive of clarity:*

E: How often (do you go to the movies with your friends)?

S: About once a month.

E: What are you like?

S: Well, I'm usually very agreeable—(and) very cheerful.

b. *Examples of responses suggestive of lack of clarity:*

E: Do you ever go out with your family?

S: Yes.

E: About how often?

S: Well, let's see, we go out Saturdays, Sundays, Fridays, and Tuesdays.

E: What is it (juvenile delinquency)?

S: Well, it's when boys join together in a gang and they rob stores.

E: Do you ever discuss juvenile   S: Yes.
    delinquency?
E: What do you think about it?   S: I don't believe I could get caught.

Using these six areas, a 5-point rating scale was devised for characterizing extent of cognitive clarity as expressed in the interview as a whole. A rating of 5, representing developed cognitive clarity, was assigned to interview records containing statements by the child which, both qualitatively and quantitatively, were suggestive of cognitive clarity, with relatively little evidence of lack of clarity. Conversely, a rating of 1 was given to records which gave considerable evidence of lack of cognitive clarity with only little evidence of clarity. Where the evidence was more ambiguous, but still pointed in one direction or the other (e.g., a few lapses in an otherwise consistent picture of clarity) a rating of 4 (relative clarity) or 2 (relative lack of clarity) was assigned. A rating of 3 was given to cases which presented too mixed or too sparse a picture to allow a rating to be made with any degree of certainty.

In evaluating a subject's record no attempt was made to assign separate ratings for each of the six areas considered. Rather, the rating represented a judgment of all the evidence available in the record, with a rough weighting of various aspects of this evidence. Thus, a rating of 5 might in one case be based mainly on the child's awareness of means-ends relationships, whereas in another case it might be based on evidence drawn in equal degree from all six areas considered. It was also possible for similar responses to the same question to be evaluated differently depending on the context in which these responses occurred. Thus, if two subjects expressed interest in becoming doctors and both replied, "a couple of years," when asked how long it takes to become a doctor, these answers would be interpreted quite differently if one of the children was a doctor's son and the other the son of an electrician.

To test the hypothesis that children with an analytical approach in laboratory tests would show greater cognitive clarity than children with a global approach, the cognitive clarity ratings of the 30 Group-III boys were correlated with their perceptual index scores. The resulting r of .77 ($P < .01$) serves to confirm the hypothesis. Significant correlations were also found between cognitive clarity ratings and intellectual index ($r = .53, P < .01$) and cognitive index ($r = .71, P < .01$) scores. Repetition of this study and a check on interjudge reliability remain to be carried out.

The nature of the main characteristics considered in the ratings made suggests that children who show an analytical field approach in laboratory situations are likely to experience the world and themselves in relatively clear and structured fashion under everyday circumstances.

The limitations of this study must be emphasized, however. In designing the interview and analyzing its results the emphasis was on the quality of the child's experience, considered from the standpoint of extent of articulation. At the same time it is obvious that the interview yielded a great deal of information about the child, some of which went beyond the articulateness-of-experience dimension with which we were especially concerned. We cannot therefore be sure that the ratings made reflect this dimension alone. The need now is for studies which, while keeping the aim of exploring experience in natural life settings, seek to delimit and identify the information on which ratings of quality of experience are based. This aim is an important one, and the results of the first step we have taken in this preliminary study suggest that there exists here a profitable direction for further research.

Partial confirmation of one aspect of these findings comes from a recent study by Bieri, Bradburn, and Galinsky (1958). The analysis made in that study bears upon one of the areas of experience considered in rating cognitive clarity, "awareness of nature of self and others" (area 3). Following a method developed by Kelly (1955), each subject was asked to consider three people known to him and to indicate important personal characteristics with regard to which two of these people resembled one another and differed from the third. The personal attributes selected by the subject in his comparisons were considered to involve the use of "external constructs" if they were based upon one of the following: physical characteristics (dark hair), relationships (married), interests (interested in the ballet), similarities (similar tastes), activities (drives a car) or likes (likes science). Contrasted to these were "internal" constructs which emphasized motivation, emotional expression, or social behavior. The subject's score was the number of external constructs used in twenty-five sorts. Bieri, Bradburn, and Galinsky found that women who were relatively field dependent on the EFT used external constructs in characterizing others significantly more often than field-independent women. For men, the relation was in the expected direction, though not significant.

An analysis patterned after the procedure used by Bieri, Bradburn, and Galinsky, carried out for our 10-year boys, yielded similar results. In this analysis, the answers to four of the questions routinely asked each of 30 Group-III boys in the interview on which the evaluation of cognitive clarity was based, were rated from the standpoint of the use of internal or external constructs. (The questions were: What is your teacher like? What are you like? What is your father like? What is your mother like?) A significant relation, in the expected direction, was found between these ratings and perceptual index scores. Since the internal-external-constructs analysis overlaps with the broader cognitive clarity analysis, both in underlying conceptualization and information used, these analyses cannot be considered independent.

The use of internal constructs does not necessarily imply greater accuracy in the perception of people. A study by Taft (1956) does suggest, however, that people with a more analytical field approach (as determined by Gottschaldt performance) may in fact be more accurate in their perception of others than people with a global approach, although his evidence is not conclusive.

C. SUMMARY

Whereas studies in the preceding chapters were concerned with differences among children in the analytical aspect of articulated experience, the studies in this chapter focused on differences in the structuring aspect, and, in a preliminary way, dealt as well with differences in articulation of experience in "real life."

The evidence suggests that children who tend to experience analytically are also better able to structure their experiences. In the main study of the relation between ability to analyze and ability to structure experience, structuring ability was evaluated through an analysis of children's Rorschach percepts. It was found that children with a relatively analytical field approach are more likely than children with a global approach to impose organization upon the ambiguous stimulus material of the Rorschach. This finding was confirmed in several other studies in which Rorschach inkblots were used as stimuli. As an indirect approach to the study of structuring of experiences investigations of memory were conducted. The rationale of these investigations was that experiences which are structured on initial registration are more likely to survive in memory than vague experiences; if, as postulated, children with an analytical field approach are better able to structure their experiences, they should show better memory for earlier events. This expectation was confirmed for boys (but not for girls) in one study which showed that recall for a test situation encountered three years before was significantly better among boys with a relatively analytical field approach than among boys with a relatively global approach. The expectation was not confirmed, however, in a retroactive-inhibition study, although because of methodological difficulties the situation used may not have permitted an adequate test of the starting hypothesis. The results of a study of level of organization of TAT stories of children differing in mode of field approach were also not in accord with expectations.

A first step was taken to explore differences among children in quality of experience under conditions which come close to life. In this preliminary study an interview was used to obtain from children accounts of their everyday experiences. In designing the interview emphasis was placed on eliciting information which would be useful in evaluating articulateness of experience, in both its analytical and structuring aspects; this was also the emphasis in the dimension (labeled "cognitive clarity") considered in rating the interview records. Children with a relatively analytical field approach in laboratory situations showed greater cognitive clarity, as expected. The impressions reported by these children of their social and physical surroundings, of other people and themselves, tended to be relatively discrete, structured, and assimilated, as compared to the impressions of children with a more global approach.

The studies of the structuring dimension are at an early stage, relative to studies of the analytical dimension, and need to be extended. It is already indicated, however, that, considering analysis and structuring as complementary aspects of articulation, there are identifiable differences among children in the extent to which their experience is articulated.

7

ARTICULATION OF THE
BODY CONCEPT

The studies thus far focused mainly on children's experience of situations external to themselves. Some of the studies, however—as perception of body position and cognitive clarity—considered children's experience of themselves as well. Experience under these conditions could not easily be divided into "experience of external situations" and "experience of the self," emphasizing that ordinarily these two aspects are complexly interwoven and inseparable. The evidence from the studies mentioned suggested similarity in a child's manner of experiencing himself and the world around him. The child who could not readily perceive his body as separate from the field had difficulty identifying a simple figure embedded in a complex design; the child who had a clear sense of the relations among important people around him also had a definite sense of his own role in the family and in various social groups.

We now extend our analysis of self-consistency in nature of experience by considering studies which focused particularly on the nature of children's experience of themselves. The conceptual framework offered in Chapter 2 would lead us to expect that greater or more limited articulation is manifested as much whether the experience has its primary source in one's own actions and attributes or in objects and events outside.

In the explorations concerned with nature of experience of the self, two approaches have been used. One, considered in the present chapter, was concerned with the individual's concept of his body. These explorations in effect extend the studies of perception of body position considered in Chapter 4. The second, considered in the next chapter, focused on what we have labeled "sense of separate identity."

A person's conception of his body arises out of the full gamut of his experiences, in the course of growing up, with his own body and the bodies of others. Though the body concept (or body image, as it is often called) is based on knowledge about the body, it does not fully correspond to the body as a physical entity; the discrepancy may be small or very marked.

The body concept obviously involves much more than factual information about the body. Through experiencing pleasure or pain, success or failure, pride or shame in connection with the body, by incorporating the social values which the environment attaches to the body and its parts, the person's body concept comes to be heavily invested with a variety of special and highly personal meanings, feelings, and values. While the body concept no doubt changes in the course of development, and may undergo alterations in adulthood as well, it also shows stability, remaining at various stages "my body," with unique attributes.

The nature of a person's body concept may be considered from a variety of standpoints. In the literature, perhaps the greatest attention has been given to the disturbances to which it is subject. (See, for example, Schilder, 1935; Kolb, 1959.) Our special interest, dictated by our research objectives, is in the degree of articulation of the body concept, that is, the extent to which the body is experienced as having definite limits or "boundaries," and the "parts" within these boundaries experienced as discrete, yet joined into a definite structure.

Early in life the formation of body boundaries is an essential aspect of the emerging sense of separation of the body from the environment. This process of segregation is a continuing one during development. Even in adult life, as William James (1908) pointed out long ago, ". . . between what a man calls *me* and what he simply calls *mine* the line is difficult to draw" (p. 291). The development of awareness of the "separateness" of the body has its beginnings in the active exploration of the body and the experiences of being handled, with the attendant kinesthetic, tactual, and visual sensations. It depends as much on the exploration of objects other than the body; such exploration, by providing quite different sensations from those generated by handling the body itself, helps sharpen the difference between the "me" and "not-me."

Along with the emergence of a sense of the boundaries of the body, there develops awareness of individual parts of the body and their interrelations. For example, in the developing child we find a progression in use of the hand from gross actions, such as pounding or scooping, to skilled movements, as building, greeting, fighting, writing, playing ball. Through engaging in these specialized activities and through the consequences which follow upon them, a more definite image of the hand, invested with special symbolic meaning, emerges, in the context of the developing broader concept of the body as a whole.

As a guide to the study of the body concept, we considered that articulated experience is expressed in the person's impressions of his body as well as in his impressions of a field. We hypothesized that children with an analytical field approach would tend to have a more articulated body concept than children with a global approach.

A. ARTICULATENESS OF BODY CONCEPT AS REFLECTED IN HUMAN FIGURE DRAWINGS

Direct evidence of the nature of an individual's body concept is difficult to obtain. One useful medium for obtaining evidence is the drawing of the human figure. Such drawings, like any other projective expression, are obviously multidetermined. The final product may represent, in addition to the body concept itself, aspects of the broader self-concept, a projection of the idealized self-image, an expression of the concept of others in the environment; and it is influenced by cultural factors and by drawing skill as well. In the last analysis, all of these are organized about the concept of the body as the person has experienced it, consciously and unconsciously. With this rationale, drawings of the human figure have been used as an index of body concept in several of the studies reported below.

The hypothesis that nature of body concept as expressed in human figure drawings is related to mode of field approach was first explored in our earlier study of young adults (1954). A special scale was developed by K. Machover, consisting of a variety of specific items based on graphic features. While this scale included a cluster of items referring directly to the body concept (the "lack-of-body-esteem" cluster), it also included clusters bearing on other areas (uncontrolled or primitive expression of anxiety, lack of self-assurance, lack of struggle for sexual identification, and lack of drive or drive modification). The scale, used in both a long and a shortened version, successfully distinguished individuals differing in extent of perceptual field dependence, among college men and women as well as boys and girls of 8, 10, and 13 years. More recently the short form of this scale was applied by Machover to the figure drawings of 22 of our Group-II 10-year-old boys. A correlation of .41 ($P < .05$) between figure-drawing scale scores and perceptual index scores was found, confirming the previously obtained relations. Others have also obtained significant relations between scores on this scale, sometimes in abbreviated form, and scores on tests of perceptual field dependence (Epstein, 1957; Fliegel, 1955; Gruen, 1955; Linton, 1952; Rosenfeld, 1958; and Young, 1959). Dubno (1954), Rosenfeld (1958), and Young (1959) have reported satisfactory interjudge agreement for the scale.

Epstein, in a study described in detail below, selected twenty-one items from the original figure-drawing scale which he interpreted as reflecting distortion of the body image. Scores on this cluster of items related significantly to perceptual index scores for a group of high school boys. Fliegel obtained significant correlations between perceptual index and short-scale figure-drawing scores for women but not for men age 20. Gruen reported a significant relation between short-scale figure-drawing and perceptual-index scores for a group of male dancers. This relation did not reach significance for a group of female dancers. Linton selected fourteen items from the figure-drawing scale which she considered to reflect self-image problems, immature sex attitudes, and need for external support. In her group of college men, thirteen of these fourteen graphic items distinguished significantly between field-dependent and -independent subjects, as determined by TRTC and EFT performance. Rosenfeld applied the short-form of the figure-drawing scale to the drawings of 100 boys between 13 and 15 years of age. Scores for this scale were significantly related to EFT performance. Young studied 49 college men and 48 college women with the RFT, EFT, and a modified short-form figure-drawing scale. He obtained significant relations between figure-drawing and perceptual performance for men, but not for women.

Dubno found agreement of 80%, 83%, and 78% between each of three pairs of judges ($P < .01$ in each instance) in rating drawings from a group of 195 college men on the short scale. Rosenfeld, in the study just cited, obtained 85% agreement between judges in rating the short-form scale. Young reports satisfactory agreement in ratings of figure drawings by two independent judges ($r = .82, P < .01$).

As already indicated, the Machover scale included items specifically related to body concept, along with a variety of other discriminating items. To check on the hypothesized relation between mode of field approach and articulation of body concept, a figure-drawing scale limited to the articulation issue was required. Such a scale, developed by Marlens, was designed to reflect degree of primitivity or sophistication of the figures represented by subjects in their drawings. We accordingly call it the "sophistication-of-body-concept" scale. In contrast to the previous scale, which consisted of discrete items, the sophistication scale involves a single global rating based on a number of specific criteria. These criteria are based on directly observable characteristics of the figures drawn rather than on the usual projective interpretations of drawings.

The sophistication scale was developed on the basis of the drawings made by 23 of the 24 boys of Group II. The procedure followed in obtaining these drawings was to ask the child to draw a person, and, when he had finished, to draw a person of the opposite sex. The test had been administered by other staff members and when making her analyses the rater had no other information about the subjects. Although associations to the drawings had been obtained, they were not made available to the rater for the present analysis.

The first step in formulating the sophistication-of-body-concept scale was to group together sets of drawings of different levels of sophistication on the basis of an over-all global impression. The drawings were then studied intensively in order to identify the specific graphic features that provided the basis for the global impressions of degree of primitivity or sophistication. This process resulted in a detailed definition of three categories of characteristics, presented in Table 7-1. The three categories are the form level of the drawings,

Table 7-1. Characteristics of drawings reflecting level of sophistication

A. Form level
  1. Primitive features
    a. Circles or ovals for body and limbs
    b. Triangular or rectangular body with limbs stuck on
    c. Other forms lacking attempt at human shape (e.g., absence of waist, shoulders, etc.)
    d. Limbs in form of sticks or ovals, shapeless, ending in pronglike or clawlike fingers; no shaping of hands; pronglike or clawlike toes
    e. Contact point of limbs to trunk involving overlapping or transparent joining; limbs stuck on or detached (as opposed to integrated body parts)
    f. Grossly unequally sized arms, legs, ears, fingers, etc., combined with primitive form, uncontrolled lines
    g. Indiscriminately attached or misplaced body parts (e.g., arms attached at center of trunk)
  2. Sophisticated features
    a. Definite, shaped body outline; head, neck, shoulders well integrated into body outline and lead into trunk and appendages
    b. Attempt at humanlike shape, proportioning
    c. Adequate profiling (e.g., trunk and legs facing in same direction, etc.)

Table 7-1.   Characteristics of drawings reflecting level of sophistication—
(*Continued*)

B. Identity and sex differentiation
1. Primitive features
    a. Objectively interchangeable male and female figures
    b. Difference between figures only in hair and/or hat treatment
    c. Minimal inadequate trunk differentiation (i.e., triangle trunk for
        female, oval for male, but otherwise identical; or belt for male
        and buttons for female as only difference)
2. Sophisticated features—marked and adequate role assignment, ex-
    pressed in clothing and/or shape (also expressed in hair, features,
    appropriate accessories, uniforms, etc.)
C. Level of detailing
1. Primitive features
    a. Body parts omitted (e.g., absence of neck, nose, ears, or eye-
        brows; fingers attached directly to arms with hands omitted)
    b. No clothing indicated
    c. Facial features expressed by dots or ovals
    d. Inadequate or inconsistent clothing (e.g., buttons but no neck-
        line, cuffs or hemline; hat, but no other clothing; toes shown in
        otherwise clothed figure; tie, but no neckline, etc.)
2. Sophisticated features
    a. Consistent, well-rationalized detailing; clothing; facial expression;
        shoes
    b. Figure cast in role with good attempt at presentation of action
    c. Figure cast in role with presentation of accessories consistent
        with this role (e.g., cowboy with smoking gun, etc.)

the extent of identity and sex differentiation of the figures, and the
level of detailing.   The final step was to formulate a five-point rating
scale based on the detailed definition of these characteristics.   The
rating scale is described in Table 7-2.   A single rating based upon

Table 7-2.   Sophistication-of-body-concept scale ratings

1. Most sophisticated drawings: These manifest high form level (e.g.,
    waistline, hips, shoulders, chest or breasts, shaped or clothed limbs,
    etc.); appendages and details represented in proper relation to body
    outline, with some sophistication in mode of presentation; appropriate,
    even imaginative, detailing (e.g., successful profiling, as young girl in
    evening clothes, well-dressed man with cigarette, etc.)
2. Moderately sophisticated drawings: Drawings which show a definite
    attempt at role assignment (with regard to age, activity, occupation,

Table 7-2.   Sophistication-of-body-concept scale ratings—(*Continued*)

---

etc.) through adequate detailing, shaping, clothing; with continuity of outline (i.e., integration of parts) attempted.

3. Drawings intermediate in level of sophistication: Drawings in which identification of sex is evident, attempts at shaping and a fair level of integration of parts are manifest and a minimum of detailing is present.

4. Moderately primitive drawings: Drawings which essentially still lack features of differentiation through form, identity, or detailing; however, these drawings show slightly more complexity in some respect (e.g., presence of one body part that is unusual in most primitive drawings, such as the neck).

5. Most primitive and infantile drawings: These manifest a very low level of form (ovals, rectangles, sticks stuck on to each other); no evidence of role or sex identity (same treatment of male and female with, at most, difference in hair treatment, no facial expression, little shaping or clothing).

---

both drawings was assigned to each child.

To illustrate the rating scale, Figures 7-1 through 7-8 reproduce the male and female drawings made by each of 8 of our 10-year-old boys. The first four sets of drawings were rated 1 (most sophisticated), the last four were rated 5 (least sophisticated). These were selected from a larger group rated 1 and 5 to illustrate features of drawings found in the two extreme rating categories.

Figure 7-1 shows the drawings of Keith, who is discussed in some detail as Case #1 in Chapter 15, the most analytical perceiver of the 68 10-year boys. The rating of 1 was based on the following graphic features: high form level, realistic representation of human shape, well-proportioned and integrated body-parts; successful profiling; definite and adequate assignment of roles, expressed in general configuration, clothing, hair treatment, accessories; consistent and well-rationalized detailing, especially imaginative in the representation of the male figure.

With some modifications, similar descriptions apply to the drawings in Figures 7-2 (Case #2, Chris, in Chapter 15), 7-3, and 7-4, all rated 1. Profiling is not attempted in the drawings in Figures 7-2 or 7-3. The level of skill varies from set to set, and, in the case of the drawings in Figure 7-2, is somewhat higher in the female than the male. The drawings in Figures 7-1 and 7-4 represent the most consistently adult figures. In all four cases, sex identification and general role identification are clearly delineated. Detailing is also abundant and appropriate in all four sets of "sophisticated" drawings, as if these four youngsters had a good deal to say about "what people are like."

The drawings in Figure 7-6 were made by Phil, Case #6 of Chapter 15. This boy's performance on perceptual tests places him close to the extreme global end of the distribution. Drawings are of consistently low form level, with poor integration of parts; parts are "stuck" on to each other and overlap in attachment; poor attempts at representation of persons, with rectangularlike trunks, circular heads, omission of neck and shoulders, primitive arms, with omission of hands, though with some attempt at representation of fingers; minimal sex differentiation, with hat on male and hair on female as only difference; facial features have evolved slightly beyond the dot or circle level, but attempt is not successful; no indication of clothing; drawings almost totally lacking in detailing.

Again, with some variations, similar comments may be made about the other three sets of "primitive" drawings. Thus, the drawings in Figure 7-8 are tiny, compared to the more "normal" size of the other three. None of the three sets has realistically shaped bodies; proportion and integration is generally poor and detailing sparse, with only hats and buttons to represent clothing. Sex differentiation is either minimal or absent.

The sophistication scale was applied by the staff member who developed it to the drawings of 23 boys of Group II for whom the scale was devised. Scores for the scale correlated .71 ($P < .01$) with perceptual index scores.

Figure 7-1. Drawings rated 1 (most sophisticated).
(Reduced to ⅔ of original size.)

Figure 7-2. Drawings rated 1 (most sophisticated). (Reduced to ⅔ of original size.)

For purposes of cross-validation, as well as to check interjudge agreement, the sophistication scale was applied to the drawings of the 30 Group-III boys both by the original rater and by a second independent judge. A correlation of .84 ($P < .01$) between ratings of the two judges suggests satisfactory interjudge reliability. The original relation was substantiated on cross-validation as shown by a correlation of .57 ($P < .01$) between sophistication-scale scores, based upon ratings of the second judge, and perceptual index scores.[1,2] Correlations of .54 ($P < .01$) and .61 ($P < .01$) were obtained between sophistication ratings and intellectual and cognitive index scores, respectively. These

---

[1] In a second cross-validation study, using the drawings of the 14 Group-I boys, a correlation of .67 ($P < .01$) was obtained between sophistication-scale and perceptual index scores.

[2] Silberman (1961), in a study of two groups of 12-year-old boys, obtained correlations of .76 ($P < .01$) and .44 ($P < .05$) between sophistication-scale and EFT scores.

Figure 7-3. Drawings rated 1 (most sophisticated).
(Reduced to ⅗ of original size.)

findings together show, as expected, that children with an analytical
field approach tend to have an articulated body concept.

The magnitude of the correlations suggests considerable correspondence
between mode of field approach and extent of articulation of body concept. In some cases, the correspondence was very high. The children
whose drawings are shown in Figures 7-1 through 7-8 are examples. Other
children presented a more discrepant picture. One such child provides
especially interesting case material.

This boy, Neal (Case #3 of Chapter 15), was an overintellectual child
of superior intelligence with a strong scientific bent. His high level of
differentiation was apparent on all the techniques of investigation except
the figure drawings, and it was especially evident in the intellectual sphere.
As reported in Chapter 15, it was said of him in a blind interpretation

of the three projective tests that "he will not permit himself to enjoy impulse life . . . the problems of human relations are seen by him as intrusions. . . ." His problems lie in the areas of self-acceptance and identity. He gives an impression of an obsessivelike split between the intellectual and the emotional-instinctual spheres. It is not surprising that, of the three projective tests, the one which focuses on the body concept should show a relatively low level of differentiation.

The relationship found for 10-year-olds between extent of sophistication of body concept and mode of field approach has been observed with older groups as well. For these groups an adaptation of the scale, specifically developed for use with adult subjects, was employed. The adaptation consisted of several minor modifications, which had the effect of raising the standard for each of the scoring intervals.

In one study this "adult" version of the scale was applied by the psychologist who developed it to drawings of a group of 41 college men. The resulting correlation with perceptual index scores was .50

Figure 7-4. Drawings rated 1 (most sophisticated).
(Reduced to ½ of original size.)

Figure 7-5. Drawings rated 5 (least sophisticated).
(Reduced to ⅔ of original size.)

($P < .01$). In a recent application of the adult scale to drawings of 24 of the hospitalized male psychiatric patients of our 1954 study, the sophistication ratings correlated .53 ($P < .01$) with perceptual index scores. A third study, with 16 college men, provides evidence on the communicability, scoring reliability, and validity of the scale. Four psychiatrists independently scored the sixteen sets of drawings, with interjudge correlations ranging between .83 and .92. A correlation of .64 ($P < .01$) was obtained between pooled ratings of these four judges and perceptual index scores.

Although on first view the drawings of children and adults with a global field approach appear impoverished, they do not seem to reflect general intellectual inferiority. The correlation of sophistication-scale scores with full-scale WISC IQs for the Group-III boys is .55 ($P < .01$). However, when the WISC intellectual and verbal indices are considered separately, we find that figure-drawing sophistication-scale scores correlate .54 ($P < .01$) with the former and .33 (not significant) with the latter. An even more marked difference in the relation of sophistication-scale scores to intellectual and verbal index scores was found by Silberman, in the study cited above. For one group of 12-

year-old boys, Silberman found that sophistication-scale scores correlated .79 ($P < .01$) with intellectual index scores and only .17 (not significant) with verbal index scores. For a second group of 12-year-old boys the corresponding values were .53 ($P < .01$) and $-.10$ (not significant). It seems that the relations with total IQ may be particularly a function of performance on those WISC subtests which require analytical competence and which identify a child's mode of field approach in the area of intellectual functioning.

The sophistication-of-body-concept scale considers features of figure drawings also considered in the Goodenough Draw-a-Man Scale (Goodenough, 1926). The Goodenough scale was developed as a test of nonverbal intelligence. It is interesting to compare results for these two scales, developed for quite different purposes.

The male drawings of our Group-III boys were scored according to the Goodenough scale. The Goodenough point scores and the sophistication-scale ratings correlated .74 ($P < .01$). To a considerable extent, then, the two scales address themselves to similar aspects of figure drawings. The two scales relate similarly to perceptual index scores (.53 for the Goodenough scale, .57 for the sophistication scale) and to total WISC IQ (.55 in both instances). The relationships of Goodenough scores to the intellectual in-

Figure 7-6. Drawings rated 5 (least sophisticated).
(Reduced to ¾ of original size.)

Figure 7-7. Drawings rated 5 (least sophisticated). (Reduced to ½ of original size.)

dex and the verbal index scores, previously defined on the basis of factor analysis (Chapter 5), are very similar (.45 and .41, respectively). It is interesting to note, however, that the sophistication-scale ratings show a somewhat higher relation to intellectual index scores (.54) than to verbal

Figure 7-8. Drawings rated 5 (least sophisticated). (Original size.)

index scores (.33) in our sample. The differences involved in the patterns of relations for the two figure-drawing scales are not large and may well be a chance occurrence, but the possibility raised by these findings that sophistication-scale scores may relate particularly to performance in those intellectual tests which feature analytical ability receives support from the results of the Silberman study. By comparison, the Goodenough scale may provide a measure of effectiveness of functioning in diverse areas of intellectual activity, as it set out to do. It would be interesting to pursue this possibility in future research.

The sophistication scale focuses particularly on aspects of figure drawings which reflect extent of articulation of body concept. It does not deal with problems of adjustment or pathology as expressed in drawings. An articulated body concept may be helpful in adaptation. But, as our studies of drawings of hospitalized patients show, various levels of articulation of body concept may be found in a pathological population. However, the nature of maladaptation or pathology is likely to be different at high and low levels of articulation of body concept. The higher level of skill shown in more sophisticated drawings may reflect "a high level of interest in and respect for" the body, as suggested in our earlier report (1954, p. 518). However, when carried to extremes, the "loving elaboration" of the body portrayed in great detail may imply a high degree of narcissistic self-absorption. On the other hand, drawings with a low level of sophistication, lacking in detail, may reflect too little interest in and respect for the body. Consideration of effectiveness of adjustment takes us well beyond aspects of drawings important for evaluating articulateness of body concept.

The results considered thus far strongly support the hypothesis that extent of articulation of body concept, as reflected in figure drawings, is related to style of field approach. Children—and adults as well—who in their drawings project an articulated conception of the body are likely to show an analytical field approach. Those whose drawings reflect a relatively unarticulated body concept are likely to show a global field approach.

B. OTHER APPROACHES TO STUDY OF BODY CONCEPT

A quite different approach from ours was used by Epstein (1957) in his studies with high school boys. Epstein employed the Finger Apposition Test in which the subject is shown pictures of pairs of hands in various positions, with fingers touching. The subject's task is to reproduce with his own hands the finger positions shown in the pictures. A common error is for the subject to respond as if he were looking into a mirror rather than at another pair of hands. The score for this test is the time taken to reproduce the finger appositions in a series of fourteen pictures. Ability to "maneuver" the hands vicariously in one's imagination in order to achieve a particular relationship between them would appear to require a relatively developed conception of the body. Piaget (1952) considers responses made on a mirror-image basis to be less differentiated and more primitive.

Among other tests in Epstein's battery were the BAT and RFT and, as mentioned, a special modification of the original figure-drawing scale consisting of items reflecting distortions of the body image. When the data from these tests were subjected to a factor analysis, three factors emerged. Factor 1 is particularly relevant to the present discussion. Loadings on this factor included the following: BAT, Series 2b, .70, Series 2a, .68; RFT, .59, .40, and .60 for Series 1, 2, and 3 respectively; figure-drawing scale, .50; Finger Apposition Test, .42.

Thus, distortion of body image (as evaluated by figure-drawing scale scores) and ability to manipulate the body vicariously (as reflected in performance on the Finger Apposition Test) are loaded on a factor which includes tests of field dependence.[3]

Two studies, using still different approaches, have investigated the body concept problem with reference to body boundaries. One, by Silverman, Cohen, Shmavonian, and Greenberg (1961), investigated body boundaries quite literally, in terms of the subject's manner of experiencing stimuli on the surface of his body.[4] Using RFT performance

---

[3] In another part of the study, Epstein explored the accuracy with which his subjects estimated their height. The subject's task was to adjust a luminous vertical rod in a dark room to his own height. As a group, these adolescent boys almost invariably made the rod shorter than their own height. Field-dependent boys, however, underestimated their height significantly more than the field-independent boys. For a group of 35 boys, the correlation between perceptual index scores, based on RFT and TRTC combined, and scores reflecting amount of underestimation of height was .53 ($P < .01$). The height estimation variable was loaded .68 on Factor 1, described above.

Field-dependent adolescents, experiencing themselves as shorter than they are, appear to undervalue their bodies to a far greater extent than field-independent adolescents.

The finding by Crutchfield and Starkweather (1953) that field-dependent men tend, significantly, to identify themselves with the weak and handicapped seems consistent with this result.

[4] This study was carried out as part of a larger investigation of the relation between neurophysiological characteristics and field dependence (see also Cohen, Silverman, and Shmavonian, 1959, 1961; Cohen and Silverman, 1961; Silverman, Cohen, and Shmavonian, 1961).

as a measure, these workers found that field-independent men show finer 2-point discrimination than field-dependent men. Field-independent men also tend to show more accurate identification of letters written with a dull rod on the forehead and dorsum of the hand. In other words, they are better able to experience separate stimuli on the surface of the body as discrete, and to apprehend the relation among these stimuli. Such characteristics are consistent with what might be expected if experience of body boundaries is relatively articulated.

It must be emphasized that these results speak on articulateness of body concept, rather than sheer awareness of body sensations. That there is an important distinction between these is suggested by some of the studies with the BAT, reported in Chapter 4. The person who readily brings his body to the true upright in the BAT, we may infer, experiences his body as a separate entity, segregated from the field, an important aspect of an articulated body concept. We found that accuracy of adjustment of the body to the upright in the BAT is not significantly related to accuracy in performing the same task with eyes closed. Thus sheer sensitivity to sensations from the body, implied by accurate performance of the latter task, does not relate to capacity to experience the body as a segregated entity. This is reasonable when we consider that alertness to body stimulation of the gross sort involved in experiencing the body as tipped over may very well occur in persons who experience the body in a relatively unarticulated fashion.

The nature of body boundaries as an aspect of body concept has also been investigated by Fisher and Cleveland (1958). As an index of the degree to which the body boundaries serve as an effective barrier separating body from environment, these workers developed a "barrier index," based on Rorschach content. They applied their barrier-index rating method to a set of Holtzman Inkblot Tests (1956) obtained by Young (1957, 1959) from a group of college men and women whose mode of field approach had been determined on the basis of RFT and EFT performance.[5] Women with high barrier scores were found to be significantly more field independent on both perceptual tests. There was a corresponding difference between low- and high-barrier score women in a third test, the Chair-Window Test. (Performance in this test related significantly to performance in both the RFT and EFT.) For men, on the other hand, these relations were not maintained, although there was a trend in the same direction as for women for both the RFT and EFT. When the figure drawings of

---

[5] Personal communication from Seymour Fisher.

these subjects were scored according to Machover's short scale, a significant relation, in the expected direction, was found between measures for this scale and barrier scores for men, although not for women.

Finally, Fisher and Cleveland scored sets of Rorschachs we had obtained from groups of college men and male psychiatric patients. No relation was found between barrier scores and perceptual performance. It is noteworthy that here again male subjects were used. It is possible that, for reasons not now apparent, relationships between barrier index and perceptual performance do not show the same pattern in women and men.

In another pair of investigations, "naturemade" situations which involve alterations of the body concept were utilized. Bennett (1956) studied a group of psychiatric patients characterized clinically as having a distorted body image, in the absence of organic findings. In RFT performance, patients with such disturbances were significantly different from control subjects. Perceptual functioning of hemiplegics, a group suffering drastic physical impairment of the body, has been extensively investigated by Bruell, Peszczynski, and Albee (1956), Bruell, Peszczynski, and Volk (1957) and by Bruell and Peszczynski (1958). Hemiplegics were found to be more field dependent on the RFT than controls. Moreover, hemiplegics who were relatively field independent on the RFT benefited more from rehabilitation training than hemiplegics who were relatively field dependent.

C. SUMMARY

Our investigation of individual differences in manner of experiencing has been extended through studies of the way in which the body itself is experienced. As anticipated, children who experience their surroundings in relatively analytical fashion tend to have an articulated concept of their bodies.

Figure drawings were used to infer the nature of a child's concept of his body. Measures on a sophistication-of-body-concept scale, developed to evaluate children's figure drawings, were significantly related to mode of field approach, children with an analytical approach tending to have a more articulated body concept. Studies with normal adults and with hospitalized psychiatric patients showed a similar relation. Confirming evidence has also come from studies by others, in which the nature of the body concept was investigated by methods often quite different from the ones we used.

A more articulated or less articulated body concept carries no necessary implication about effectiveness of adjustment.

Earlier we saw that an individual who can readily separate his body from the field (in the BAT) can also keep any item apart from its surroundings (in the RFT and EFT). Now we find that capacity to experience an object as discrete from its context (rather than fused with it) is particularly characteristic of people who experience their bodies as articulated (rather than as a vague "mass," not clearly segregated from its surroundings). If the "outside" is experienced as articulated the "inside" tends to be so experienced as well.

The relationship observed between articulation of body concept and capacity to analyze experience has enlarged the picture of self-consistency in manner of experiencing. The existence of such a relation lends support to the differentiation hypothesis which led us to expect it.

8

SENSE OF
SEPARATE IDENTITY

The study of experience having its main source "within the person" has focused thus far on the way in which the body is experienced. We turn now to studies of experience of the self more broadly conceived.

Our discussion of differentiation in Chapter 2 suggested a relation between the child's growing awareness of his body and of his characteristics and activities in general. We proposed there that just as a child's experience of his body may be conceived as more or less articulated, so may the experience of the self.

The term "sense of separate identity" was applied to the outcome of a person's development of awareness of his own needs, feelings, and attributes, and his identification of these as distinct from the needs, feelings, and attributes of others. A sense of separate identity implies experience of the self as segregated. It implies as well a self that is structured; internal frames of reference have been formed and are available as guides for definition of the self and for viewing, interpreting, and reacting to the world. To the extent that inner frames of reference fail to develop, definition of attributes of the self is subject to determination from without, and the ability to function independently of external forces is greatly limited.

In what observable ways may we expect a sense of separate identity to manifest itself? We have considered three categories of behavior manifestations from which extent of development of a sense of separate identity may be inferred. First, we might anticipate that, on the basis of his better developed inner frames of reference, a person with a developed sense of separate identity would be capable of functioning with relatively little need for guidance and support from others. In contrast, lack of a developed sense of separate identity would foster a need for guidance from others in many situations. Second, within limits, we would expect a person with a developed sense of separate identity to maintain more firmly his own direction in the face of contradicting attitudes, judgments, and values of others. In contrast, the person with a limited sense of separate identity, lacking developed frames of reference of his own, and so forced to use the attitudes, judgments, and values of others to define his own, would be more susceptible to external influences and pressures. Third, we would expect a person with a well-developed sense of separate identity to have a relatively stable view of himself in varying social contexts, since he needs these contexts less for self-definition. In contrast, instability of self-view would be expected in persons with an underdeveloped sense of identity, precisely because their self-definition is more dependent on these external contexts.

These three categories of behavior manifestations, on the basis of which a sense of separate identity may be inferred, have been formulated in part on conceptual grounds, and in part in relation to existing evidence. They vary in scope and in the amount of supporting evidence available. To the extent that they refer to a single construct—separate identity—there is inevitable overlap among them. The first category—reliance on guidance and support from others—is the broadest conceptually, and the richest in supporting evidence. The third category—stability of self-view—refers to an important aspect of behavior which has as yet been little explored.

A. RELIANCE ON OTHERS FOR GUIDANCE AND SUPPORT

In the studies cited, many diverse manifestations of reliance on others are represented. Some of these were observed in everyday life, others in special test situations; some provide direct evidence of reliance on others for guidance and support, others permit only an inference about this characteristic.

For ease of presentation, the studies considered have been grouped according to the particular conditions under which reliance on others was investigated. Furthermore, some of the studies by other investigators were carried out with a primary interest in different issues than the ones with which we are here concerned. Consequently, the data relevant to our problem often had to be taken from the context in which they were presented and interpreted in the light of our own conceptual framework.

1. As Shown in Performance of Special Tasks

a. Task-attitude in the TAT. This study was based on the child's behavior while taking the TAT, rather than on the content of the stories themselves. We hypothesized that under conditions where a task is defined in very general terms, and the role of the examiner is left deliberately vague, children with contrasting modes of field approach would react in characteristically different ways. Children with a relatively global field approach, being less able to define their own role in relation to the task, would seek guidance from the examiner as to how to proceed; they would lack confidence in their ability to perform the task and, consequently, would react with tension and anxiety during the test. Children with a relatively analytical field approach, on the other hand, would define their role for themselves and would not need to seek guidance from the examiner; they would proceed with greater confidence and would tend to show less tension and anxiety.

The data necessary for evaluating the child's attitudes and feelings consisted of the remarks he made during the test, supplemented by the examiner's extensive notes, made as the test was going on. An accurate account of the child's remarks was provided in most cases by verbatim transcriptions of the recorded sessions.[1] The content of the stories was not used in judging the child's attitudes and feelings. In order that the material available for making judgments might be viewed in its sequence in the total flow of the child's test production (e.g., whether a given comment was made by the child right after the initial instructions or prior to his last story), and the content of the stories yet avoided, another staff member prepared the records for analysis by underlining parts of the record that were relevant to the analysis.

A study of the 38 TAT records of the 10-year-old boys of Groups I and II suggested four criteria that could be used in making over-all judgments of the child's task approach. These criteria, dynamically interrelated, represented identifiable areas of evidence to which to anchor final global ratings of children's task approach.

(1) EXTENT OF RELIANCE ON THE EXAMINER FOR TASK DEFINITION

The behavior of some children while taking the TAT suggested that they were characteristically unsure of how to react to the situation and looked to the examiner for support and direction. They tended to

---

[1] The test session was tape recorded for Groups II and III. For Group I, the stories were taken down by the examiner in longhand.

view the examiner as an authority who insisted on certain ways of behaving and, through their questions, sought to determine his wishes, in order that they might comply with them, or obtain his permission for something they wanted to do.

Examples of questions such children asked are: [2] "How long does this story have to be? . . . Do I have to say anymore?" "You mean I have to make a story out of this . . . What else should I say? . . . Well, what's he supposed to be doing?" "How can I tell what people are feeling and thinking? . . . Shall I sit back? . . . Should I put it down? . . . Should I say what's in the forest, things like that?" "A story or just a phrase? . . . How long do they have to be? . . . Should I start with once upon a time? . . . Does this have to be a happy ending all the time or could it end up to be a sad ending?"

Other children, in contrast, were generally able to establish their own procedures for dealing with the task. The assistance they sought from the examiner tended to be on quite specific points, such as requests for clarification of particular portions of a card.[3]

(2) THE CHILD'S ATTITUDE TOWARD HIS COMPETENCE

Some children tended to be self-deprecating and to assume blame for the difficulties they encountered. Other children characteristically expressed positive feelings about their story-telling abilities, and/or cast blame for whatever difficulties they encountered onto shortcomings in the cards or the examiner.

Illustrative of feelings of inadequacy are comments such as these: "I'm not good at saying what is a story . . . I'm not good at really making up stories." "I'm not a good story maker-upper . . . I don't think I can make up a story about it." "I never have no ideas of anyone . . . This one I'm sure I couldn't make anything up about . . . This one I don't have any idea. I don't know what's going to happen to him, and I don't know what's happening now." "How do I know what kind of story to tell?"

A more self-confident approach to the task was reflected in such statements as: "I tell long ones—for—just one look at one picture . . . Oh, I got a dilly for this one." "This is a hard one but I guess I can do it." "These are easy . . . I have a good imagination . . . I make up a lot of whoppers." "Oh, this is a very easy one. I think . . . I can explain this very easily . . . This is a little difficult . . . I'll still try to make it out."

Statements suggesting that the child directed the blame for difficulty he experienced at the card or examiner, rather than toward himself, included

[2] Statements within the same set of quotes were made by the same child, but are not necessarily contiguous within the test record.

[3] The need for specificity found among some compulsive children would be included here.

the following: "How can you make up pictures like these, phew." "You sound just like Dragnet (repeating the examiner's 'uh huh') . . . You must write in a foreign language . . ." "Gee, when you write it looks like a straight line. I can't understand it, I can't even read it. Can you?" "At least you should have a wire recorder . . . You should pick an easy one (TAT card) like a boy reading Tom Sawyer." "You drew these? Why couldn't it be Donald Duck or Mickey Mouse? . . . You ought to make these (cards) pictures, not in silhouettes."

(3) QUALITY OF THE CHILD'S FEELINGS DURING TEST SESSION

Some children were relaxed and evidently enjoyed the test, telling their stories with animation, gusto, and humor and often commenting that it was "fun." Others appeared anxious and tense, seemed to feel helpless and overwhelmed by the test, and in general found the task trying and unpleasant. Such children sometimes gave evidence of being preoccupied with how well they were doing. This concern was reflected in such comments as: "Am I doing good . . . Did I really do good, tell the truth." "Do they tell us how many marks we get?" "Do you think I'll make a good story-teller?"

(4) "EVIDENCE OF AN I"

Comments of some children while taking the TAT gave a strong impression of a story-teller behind the scenes, going about his task of developing and organizing a sequence of ideas. This feeling of a "story-teller in action" came from a variety of specific manifestations. For example, a child might comment on the problems he encountered in developing a story, on the alternatives he was considering, or on the use he was making of particular aspects of the card; he might state in advance his general plan for the story. The sense of a story-teller in action also emerged from remarks which suggested his ability to stand aside from the product he had created and to offer an evaluation. Another manifestation was the interpolation, in relevant and appropriate fashion, of references to his own experiences, indicating the manner in which he was drawing on these experiences in constructing his story. Because these comments so frequently involved first-person references, the descriptive term "evidence of an I" has been used for this criterion.

Not all comments which included the first-person pronoun could be considered as giving "evidence of an I." In some records, the first-person references occurred in the context of incoherent intrusions, reflecting the child's inability to maintain an appropriate separation between his own feelings, needs, and experiences, and those of the character in his story. First-person references also occurred in the context of complaints about inability to perform the task. Such comments were not considered as "evidence of an I." Neither were the numerous side comments of a talkative child, unless they showed the qualities cited.

The following excerpts illustrate the kind of material that provided "evidence of an I."

"I play the violin, so I think I can make one up . . . So I'll guess we'll forget about her . . . I didn't see at first how they could be leaning on the outside of the railing." ". . . it proves crime doesn't pay . . . An emotional love scene . . . It won't turn out that lovey-dovey so much." "I know how he feels (about practicing music) . . . All those things are about love." "This, of course, is like a fairy tale." "Boy, I've been watching too many mysteries." "What should I tell about? (to self). Let me see, this one . . . This is going to be a short story with no ending . . . This is a happy story . . . Oh, McCarthy and Cohen . . . I'll . . . we'll call him Tommy the Thief." "Oh, this picture is up to no good . . . This (picture) might have a connection to the other picture . . . I know how he feels, I'm glad I never had it . . . I never saw a man do that . . . I always see women in this . . . I don't see what the paper's got to do with it . . . You know, the old screwy things . . . Nobody is holding it, I'll bet."

Children whose records did not show "evidence of an I" could not necessarily be regarded as lacking the characteristics which such evidence implies. The record of a reserved or taciturn child, whatever other qualities he showed, might simply be lacking in data necessary for judging "evidence of an I" positively.[4]

A 5-point rating scale was developed to evaluate the child's attitude toward task and examiner, using these four areas of evidence as a basis for judgment. Cases were put in category 1 if the material in the record gave strong evidence of many or all of these four characteristics: reliance on examiner for task definition, lack of self-confidence, anxiety, and absence of "evidence of an I." Conversely, cases were put in category 5 if the record showed a strong predominance of

[4] The material on "evidence of an I," considered here impressionistically in making global ratings of task approach, seemed to provide so promising a basis for distinguishing among children that we subsequently made it the object of a separate, systematic analysis. In a cross-validation study, ratings of "evidence of an I," based on a dichotomous classification, correlated significantly with perceptual, intellectual, and cognitive index scores. As anticipated, there was a tendency for a sense of a story-teller in action, of a person functioning on his own, to be conveyed more strongly in the test behavior of children with an analytical field approach than children with a global approach. Since the data used in the "evidence-of-an-I" scale are also considered in the more comprehensive task-approach scale, we cannot consider the two independent.

the following characteristics: ability to define standards and procedures for performing the task independently of the examiner, a positive attitude toward one's own competence, enjoyment of the task,
and "evidence of an I." The intervening points on the scale were
defined with reference to these two extreme categories. In applying
the scale the individual criteria were not separately rated, but an over-
all judgment was formed, with evidence bearing on the four criteria
combined and weighted in a manner that seemed appropriate to the
individual case.

Two judges applied the scale to the TAT records of the 38 Group-I
and -II boys. The correlation between the two sets of ratings was .82
($P < .01$), indicating good interjudge agreement.

For these same children the TAT ratings related significantly to
perceptual index scores ($r = .70$, $P < .01$), in the expected direction.
When the scale was applied, for validation purposes, to the records of
the 30 Group-III boys, the TAT ratings again showed a significant relation with perceptual index scores ($r = .33$, $P < .05$), as well as with
intellectual ($r = .44$, $P < .01$) and cognitive index scores ($r = .42$,
$P < .01$). Our starting hypothesis was that children with a relatively
global field approach, being less able to define the task and their role
in it, would tend to seek guidance from the examiner as to how to
carry it out, would show a lack of confidence in their own ability, and
would react to the test with feelings of anxiety and tension. This
hypothesis has been confirmed.

Observations by other investigators of subjects' behavior during tests are
consistent with these results. Linton [5] found that field-independent subjects
were likely to be active and task-oriented in a testing situation, and field-
dependent subjects to display an anxious, driven, talkativeness during testing. Sangiuliano (1951) reports for her hospitalized psychiatric women
patients that, during the tests, "the field-oriented group showed diffuse
anxiety reactions, a great deal of emotional display, and more active seeking of the examiner's acceptance, concomitant with greater passivity and
compliance in accepting the testing session in toto" (p. 90).

b. Performance of a routinized task. In another study we used a
different approach to evaluate children's readiness to follow the guidance of an authority figure. It was hypothesized that in a task which
is well-defined, mechanical, and highly monotonous, so that satiation
is easily achieved, and where continuing is seen by the child as conforming to the wishes of an authority figure, children with a global

[5] Personal communication from Harriet Linton.

way of experiencing would be more apt to persist at the task than children with an analytical approach.[6,7]

A conventional letter-cancellation test, already considered in Chapter 5, was given to 29 of the 30 Group-III boys. The subject was given four sheets (one at a time) filled with lines of randomly ordered letters and requested to cross out every "t" on the page, working as quickly as possible. The first and last pages were scored for both time taken to finish and for errors, that is, the number of "t's" missed plus the number of other letters incorrectly crossed out. Time-drop and error-drop scores were obtained, based, respectively, on the difference in speed and accuracy between the first and last pages. These scores were converted into standard scores which were then combined, with equal weight, to provide an improvement score for each subject.

When improvement scores were compared to perceptual index scores, a correlation of .26 was obtained, in the expected direction, although not significant.

There is some indication that the task was not long enough to permit an adequate test of our hypothesis. Analysis of changes in performance from the first to the fourth pages showed significant improvement with practice for the group. Only 2 subjects took more time and made more errors on the fourth page than the first. There is no evidence, therefore, that the children were satiated by the task. Lengthening the test, in future studies, might provide more clear-cut results.

c. Incidental learning. Another indication that children with a global field approach are apt to follow the guidance of an authority figure is provided by the finding that their attention, and therefore their learning, is likely to be limited to those aspects of a situation to which they are directed by the task put to them by the examiner. Children with an analytical approach are more likely to attend to and learn about aspects peripheral to the immediately given task.

Evidence of such a relation comes from a study with our 10-year-olds, using an incidental learning situation briefly described in Chapter 5, and carried out to test the hypothesis that children with a global field approach show relatively little incidental learning.

The situation employed was based on a test used by Gardner, et al. (1959) in a study of incidental learning.

Two lists of eight three-letter words, each word printed in one of four

[6] We would make this prediction for simple, routinized tasks only.

[7] Impulse-ridden children in the global group would be an exception.

different colors, were presented to the subject tachistoscopically, one word at a time. In the incidental learning condition, the subject was instructed to call out the *color* of the word, without any indication that this was a learning task. He was subsequently tested for recall of the words. In the intentional learning condition, the subject was instructed to call out the *words*, and was told to "try to remember them." He was subsequently tested for the number of words recalled. One presentation of the list was used for each condition. The two lists were not significantly different in difficulty under either condition of learning.

The subjects were the 30 Group-III boys. Half the group received one list for incidental learning, and the second list for intentional learning. For the remaining subjects, the order of the lists was reversed.

Each subject was assigned two scores: an incidental-learning score, which was the total number of words correctly recalled under the incidental-learning condition; and an intentional-learning score, which was the total number of words recalled under the intentional-learning condition.

As might be expected, more words were remembered under the intentional- than under the incidental-learning condition. To test the hypothesis that children with a global field approach would tend to show relatively little incidental learning, the children's incidental-learning scores were compared to their perceptual, intellectual, and cognitive index scores. Correlations of .37 ($P < .05$), .31 (not significant), .37 ($P < .05$) respectively, tend to support the hypothesis.

The picture for the intentional-learning situation is quite different than for the incidental-learning situation. Measures for these two tests appeared in different factors in the factor-analytic study reported in Chapter 5; incidental learning was loaded, along with measures of field dependence, on Factor III (analytical field approach), and intentional learning on Factor II (verbal comprehension). Moreover, intentional-learning scores do not relate significantly to incidental-learning scores ($r = .17$), suggesting little overlap between the kinds of abilities involved; nor do they relate significantly to perceptual index scores ($r = .22$).

2. As Shown in Expressions of Dependent Attitudes [8]

In all the studies to be considered here rating scales were used to evaluate attitudes of dependence and independence.

A study by Gordon (1953) has shown that field-dependent persons tend both to view themselves, and to be viewed by others, as socially dependent. As a measure of social dependence, Gordon used a modified Thurstone-type scale. In the development of the scale ten psy-

[8] Although a limited sense of separate identity is likely to foster dependent attitudes, and so make them more characteristic of persons with a global approach, other factors (as trust or lack of trust in people) may also influence their development. The same may be said of socially dependent behavior.

chiatrists were asked to place along a dependence-independence continuum a large number of adjectives and phrases culled from the psychiatric literature as descriptive of this dimension of behavior. The final scale consisted of items on which there was substantial agreement among the ten judges. Examples of items at the dependent extreme of the scale are: I attach myself to some other patients in the group in a dependent manner; I consider myself completely at the mercy and direction of others in the group; infantile; whiny; submissive. Examples of items at the independent extreme are: The group usually accepts anything I express; I take responsibility to draw others into the conversation; self-assertive; daring; adventurous; individualistic; strong.

Self-ratings of dependence, based on this scale, were significantly related to measures of field dependence from the RFT, both in normal subjects and in neurotic patients.[9] The relationships were, however, different in a group of ulcer patients. As we see further in Chapter 12, this last finding was in accord with Gordon's expectations, based on the common view that ulcer patients tend to deny their dependency.

In the same study Gordon found that subjects who were field dependent on the RFT were also judged by others to be dependent. The physician in charge of each neuropsychiatric and ulcer patient was asked to rate his patient on the dependence scale described above. For both the neuropsychiatric and ulcer patients, extent of field dependence in the RFT related significantly to dependence-scale ratings.[10]

This last finding is consistent with certain results of the study by Crutchfield, et al. (1958) with Army Air Force captains, cited previously. Some of the check list and Q-sort items which were significantly related to mode of field approach on the RFT were: *field dependent*—concerned with good impression, gregarious, affectionate, considerate, tactful; *intermediate*—energetic, adventurous, social poise and presence, nonconforming; *moderately field independent*—demanding, effective leader, takes ascendant role, manipulates people, self-

[9] With a more sophisticated "test-wise" group we found an insignificant relation between perceptual index scores and scores for a short form of Gordon's scale.

[10] The "succorance" variable from Edwards Personal Preference Schedule is described by Edwards (1954) as reflecting the need for passive dependence. Several studies have investigated the relation of this variable to perceptual field dependence, with inconsistent results (Marlowe, 1958; Gardner, Jackson, and Messick, 1960; and Dana and Goocher, 1959). Study of the items which constitute the variable suggests, however, that the passive dependence implied in the trait name, succorance, may be quite different from the social dependence evaluated by Gordon.

reliant; *extremely field independent*—cold and distant with others, unaware of social stimulus value, concerned with philosophical problems, individualistic, strong.[11]

The characterization of the field-dependent group is consistent with the hypothesized need of such people to rely on others for guidance and support; the terms other persons use to describe them add up to an interest in earning the good will of those on whom they rely. In contrast, subjects in the extremely field-independent group impress others with their lack of interest in people.

The characterization of the two extreme perceptual groups suggests a difference between them in the "warm-cold" dimension. From the point of view of human relations, the field-dependent subjects are experienced by others as having assets which the extremely field-independent subjects conspicuously lack; they are perceived as "affectionate, considerate, tactful."

Judging from the scores reported, the Air Force captains, as a group, perhaps by virtue of occupational selection, are perceptually more field independent than the adult subjects we have studied. The characterization of this extremely field-independent subgroup suggests that, as we go far out to the field-independent extreme, we are more likely to encounter persons who are "cold, distant," and markedly overintellectual. As we will see in Chapter 15, such characteristics appear only occasionally among 10-year-old boys (those we designated emotionally "hard"), and then in a milder form. When they do occur, it is among children who are field independent.

Pemberton (1952b), in a factor-analytic study, also found measures reflecting dependent attitudes to be related to perceptual performance. She administered tests loading on Thurstone's flexibility-of-closure factor, including the Thurstone Gottschaldt, to college students. Responses made by these subjects to a large number of personality inventory items and self-descriptive adjectives and phrases were grouped into eleven categories. Scores for five of these categories related significantly to measures of flexibility of closure. Individuals who, in our terminology, were field independent tended to be "ambitious and persevering" and "logical and theoretical." Field-dependent subjects tended to be "dependent on the good opinion of others," "socially outgoing," and "systematic." "Systematic" is defined by Pemberton as a tendency toward tidiness and a need for routine or, more generally, dependence on superficial, rigid rules. Pemberton's results are thus quite consistent with those of Crutchfield, et al.

---

[11] Personal communication from John Starkweather.

Another approach to attitudes toward dependence was used by Bell (1955). On the basis of the concept of inner-directed and other-directed attitudes, proposed by Riesman (1950), she developed a scale of four related clusters of attitudes, one pole of each cluster reflecting the inner-directed (ID), the other the other-directed (OD) orientation. The other-directed pole, with its emphasis on need for security, approval, and contact with people, corresponds to some extent to "need for guidance and support," the inner-directed pole to the relative freedom from such need. The clusters are:

A. Hard-headed practical orientation (ID) vs. a rather global, unrealistic interest in warmth and sincerity (OD).

B. Work-oriented values such as efficiency, control, competence, and especially excelling over others (ID) vs. needs for friendships, popularity, intimacy, group adjustment and cooperation, and responsiveness to social pressures toward conformity on the basis of these needs (OD).

C. Concern with the self, inner drives and preferences which may be unconventional, with strivings toward creative achievement and personal recognition and with independence from social restrictions (ID) vs. needs for security, social approval, participation in the community, and a responsiveness toward conformity pressures on the basis of these needs (OD).

D. Concern with ideas and principles rather than people, and an intellectual approach to human problems (ID) vs. concern for people and for adjustment in concrete, short-run situations (OD).

The scale and a battery of perceptual tests (EFT, RAT, BAT) were given to a group of college students. Bell's hypothesis that field-dependent subjects would tend to score toward the other-directed and field-independent subjects toward the inner-directed pole of the scale was confirmed. The correlation of total attitude–scale scores with composite perceptual index scores was .49 $(P < .01)$. Also significantly related were measures of field dependence and scores for each of the first three subscales.[12]

Indirectly relevant here are studies of the relation between mode of field approach and authoritarianism. The existence of such a relationship might be expected on several grounds. First, aspects of the authoritarian syndrome, adherence to external values and great respect for authority, are suggestive of what we have been calling "reliance on others for guidance and support." Second, Frenkel-Brunswik (1949) has reported that people with authoritarian attitudes tend to show intolerance of ambiguity in

[12] These findings have demonstrated a relation only between field dependence and the particular characteristics evaluated by Bell's scale. They cannot be used to equate the field-dependence dimension with the inner-other directed dimension, which has a highly complex rationale.

perception.[13] The situation used to evaluate this characteristic may well require the breaking of a particular set, which we have seen to be related to mode of field approach. In view of these and other similarities, it is not surprising to find some evidence of a relationship between measures of authoritarianism and field dependence. Because of the scope and complexity of the authoritarianism concept, however, these relationships need to be explored further before their basis can be adequately understood.

A number of studies have used the F-scale, sometimes in abbreviated or modified form, to evaluate authoritarianism in relation to mode of field approach (see, for example, Rudin and Stagner, 1958; Pollack, et al., 1960; Jackson, 1955; Linton, 1952). In most of these a significant relation, in the expected direction, was found. There is some evidence, however, that the relation between the two types of variables may be nonlinear (Mednick).[14]

Two studies utilized attitude scales which are closely related to the F-scale.[15]

Fenchel (1958) investigated the relation between mode of field approach, as reflected in EFT performance, and extent of "social rigidity," as measured by the RAPH scale (Meresko, et al., 1954). For descriptive purposes, RAPH–scale items may be grouped into five categories: traditionalism (the belief in tradition for tradition's sake), rule-riddenness (the belief in rules for rules' sake), opposition to change in judgment, opposition to change in plans, intolerance of ambiguity. For a group of 63 VA psychiatric outpatients, a correlation of .26 ($P < .05$), in the expected direction, was obtained between RAPH scores and EFT performance.[16]

In a similar study, Bieri (1960) used his scale of "acceptance of authority" (Bieri and Lobeck, 1959), based on items from an earlier study of attitudes (Bales and Couch, 1956). Men who showed a tendency to accept authority were significantly more field dependent in EFT performance than men who did not. The results for women were in the same direction, but not significant.

The hypothesis that people with a global field approach require greater support and guidance from others than people with an analytical approach is further confirmed by the evidence in this section.

---

[13] See Titus and Hollander (1957), however, for a review of more recent efforts to replicate the study.

[14] Personal communication from Sarnoff Mednick.

[15] Rokeach (1960) found no relation between EFT performance and measures for his dogmatism scale, a result anticipated on the basis of his conceptual framework.

[16] We prefer not to use the term "rigidity" because of the many different ways in which it has been employed in the literature. Performance in a number of tests that purport to measure rigidity is not related to field dependence.

3. As Shown in "Real-Life" Situations

Although it is important to extend the study of reliance on others into everyday life situations, there is thus far only one investigation in which this has been attempted.

Fliegel (1955) restudied, after a 3-year interval, subjects we had originally studied at age 17. In one analysis she found that the women who were still living at home at the time of retest were significantly more field dependent on initial testing, three years before, than women who had left or were about to leave home, because of working out of town, being married, living at school, etc. (biserial $r = .59$, $P < .01$, $N = 25$). In another analysis, women who were single and not engaged were found to be significantly more field dependent than women who were married or engaged (biserial $r = .54$, $P < .02$, $N = 25$). The "real-life" actions considered in these analyses may be interpreted, in general, as reflecting ability to separate from one's family. As a reservation, in the instance of marriage the possibility must be considered that a woman who gets married may be transferring her dependence from parents to husband.

4. Attentiveness to Others

The need for support and guidance felt by people who lack a developed sense of identity, and their reliance on others for a definition of their judgments and self-view, may make such people especially alert to the moods and attitudes of those around them. A study by Beller (1958) has shown that dependency correlated positively with greater attention to those on whom a subject was dependent. In that study measures of dependency were based on repeated ratings of children in nursery school situations by participant observers. Observations were made of where these children directed their attention—literally, where they looked—under highly structured (a meal session), moderately structured (a work situation), and relatively unstructured conditions (a free-play situation). It was found that the more dependent the child the more did he focus his gaze on the human environment, particularly the teacher, and the less oriented was he to the physical environment. Beller also found a tendency for girls to be visually more oriented toward the human environment and less toward the physical environment than boys. This difference is particularly interesting in view of the parallel finding of consistent sex differences in field approach.

The results of several studies suggest, as we might have expected, that people with a global field approach are particularly attentive to others, especially to facial characteristics and expressions which provide ready cues to another person's moods and attitudes.

In the previously cited study by Crutchfield, et al. (1958), each of the group of Air Force captains was given a series of pictures of people, among which were included pictures of the officers with whom he had spent several days at the assessment center. The subject's task was to identify the men in the pictures. The number correctly identified was significantly related to extent of perceptual field dependence as measured by RFT performance. The ability to recognize or recall faces was greater for subjects with a global field approach.[17]

Such people also appear more aware of characteristics of their own faces. De Varis (1955) found that 12-year-old field-dependent boys were significantly more accurate in identifying cut-out photographs of their own noses, eyes, ears, etc., among a set of similar part-photographs of others.

The De Varis results raise an interesting problem. If persons with a global field approach have a less articulated concept of their bodies, why are they more accurate in recognizing their own faces? Two considerations are relevant. First, if such persons are particularly concerned with how they are regarded by others, and how others literally look at them, greater attention to their own faces might be the result. Second, we noted in Chapter 6 a tendency for persons with a global field approach to describe themselves and others in terms of "external constructs." Physical characteristics are one kind of external construct. Reference to one's own face ("I have a big nose," or "I have big brown eyes") might well be stressed by such persons when asked for a self-description.

Thus, attention to one's own face need not necessarily indicate an articulated body concept. This problem merits further investigation.

The studies in this section and several others presented previously are concerned with "perception of others." Their results together suggest that, as compared to people with a global field approach, people with an analytical approach tend to experience others in terms of deeper attributes (Chapter 6), reflecting their more developed awareness and greater ability to maintain the kind of distance from people necessary for objective evaluation. They also seem less alert to the facial characteristics of others, as a result, perhaps, of not needing to rely on others for self-definition. There thus appear to be character-

[17] Again we find parallel sex differences. Witryol and Kaess (1957) have reported that women are superior to men in memory for names and faces.

istic patterns of perceiving others associated with contrasting modes of field approach.

B. SUSCEPTIBILITY TO INFLUENCE BY EXTERNAL STANDARDS IN FORMATION AND MAINTENANCE OF ATTITUDES AND JUDGMENTS

A second postulated manifestation of a sense of separate identity is the ability, within limits, to establish and maintain attitudes and judgments, with relative independence of expressions offered by others. This ability is a reflection of the availability of developed inner frames of reference. The person who lacks inner frames of reference is apt to use attitudes and judgments of others to define his own. We presume no sharp division between this manifestation of sense of separate identity and the one considered in the preceding section. One difference lies in the emphasis on direct emotional dependence in interpersonal relations in the first, and on social influences in cognitive operations in the second.

Our hypothesis was that persons with a global field approach would be relatively more influenced by the frames of reference which the attitudes and judgments of others provide.

The studies to be considered in relation to this hypothesis bear upon the large, complex area of research on formation and change of attitudes and judgments. Our particular interest is in individual consistency in manner of forming and changing attitudes.

1. Conformance to Group Pressure [18]

The most comprehensive study in this area is one by Linton (1952), already cited in Chapter 5 and earlier in this chapter. Linton gave a group of college men the BAT, RAT, EFT, and a syllogisms test. Also included were the following tests, designed to evaluate the subjects' reactions to social pressure:

1. The autokinetic situation. This well-known procedure was used to determine the extent to which the subject's judgments of the amount and direction of movement of a stationary pinpoint of light conformed with the judgments of a planted confederate. At the end of the test, each subject was interviewed, and, on the basis of the account he gave, various aspects of his functioning in the test situation were rated according to spe-

[18] This heading and the one for the next section (suggestibility) are the labels by which these areas have come to be known in the literature. In terms of essential dynamic processes involved the areas really belong together.

cially devised scales. Four of these scales are particularly relevant to our present problem:

a. Coping—based on spontaneous statements indicating active attempts at achieving a stable basis for his judgments.

b. Resisting confederate—based on statements indicating a conscious effort to resist the influence of the confederate.

c. Prestige effect—based on statements to the effect that the confederate's responses were likely to have been more correct than his own.

d. Report of influence—based on stated beliefs that the confederate had influenced him.

2. Attitude change. The subject's attitudes on several issues were measured before and after reading articles presumably written by authorities in fields relevant to the issues in question. For example, one issue involved the advisability of selling anti-histamines without a doctor's prescription. The authoritative article was attributed to the New England Journal of Biology and Medicine.

Finally, in another test the subject was required to solve a set of syllogisms. In some, the logical conclusion conflicted with his existing attitudes, in others it did not. A measure of impairment in function as a result of conflict was developed, as well as a measure of ability to solve neutral problems.

A factor analysis yielded four factors, two of which involved both social and cognitive variables. The nature of tests with high loadings on one of these latter two factors, Factor A, clearly supports the hypothesis that people with a global field approach tend to adapt their views to conform with the views held by others. Appearing on this factor, in order of magnitude of loading, were:

1. Autokinetic situation: Change of judgments in the direction of conformity with a confederate's judgment.

2. EFT (long solution time).

3. BAT (large deviations of body from upright).

4. Syllogisms: Impairment in syllogistic reasoning as a function of conflict between the logical conclusion and the subject's attitude.

5. Autokinetic situation: Ratings of "resisting confederate" (lack of).

6. Autokinetic situation: Ratings of "coping" (lack of).

7. RAT (Series 1a only, in which room and body are initially tilted to the same side) (large deviations of room from upright).

Of the situations which we might have expected to be loaded on Factor A only the attitude-change test failed to appear. However, in a reanalysis of the data, Linton and Graham (1959) found that subjects whose attitudes changed toward conformance with the opinions attributed to an authority were significantly more field dependent than subjects who showed no change ($P < .01$). In this reanalysis Linton and Graham considered in a separate category cases in which the judgment went contrary to the opinion of the authority.

The statements made by subjects in the interviews following the autokinetic test make it clear that the field-independent subjects were more likely to make active, planful attempts to arrive at their own judgments. Some of them reported that they tried to make up their minds before the confederate offered his judgment so as to avoid being influenced by him. Others used a plan, even if ineffective, such as basing their judgments on "feeling the motion of the eyeball following the light." In contrast, field-dependent subjects made fewer active attempts to cope with the situation.

Many other studies tend to confirm Linton's findings. The relationships found are invariably in the expected direction, and in most instances are significant.

A study by Mednick and Shaffer [19] used the "autokinetic word" technique of Rechtschaffen and Mednick (1955). As in the standard autokinetic situation, the subject is shown a stationary point of light in a completely darkened room but is told that the light will move so as to write messages. Many subjects actually report seeing words being written under these conditions. Field-dependent subjects, as established by performance in the EFT, tended to see more "words" than independent subjects, as expected ($r = .30$, $P < .05$).

Studies of group influence on individual judgment also tend to confirm the relation between extent of field dependence and ability to function independently of the frame of reference provided by a group. Rosner (1956, 1957) administered the EFT to 20 conforming and 20 nonconforming subjects, selected on the basis of performance in an Asch-type group pressure situation (Asch, 1956). Conforming subjects tended to be more field dependent. Crutchfield (1957) found a significant relation between extent of field dependence, as measured by Gottschaldt performance, although not as measured by RFT performance, and degree of conformity in his group-pressure situation.[20]

Jackson (1955) has reported a significant relation for men (but not for women) between a perceptual index of "stability in resistance to field forces" and a measure of changes in judgments of line length in conformance with an announced class average ($r = .53$, $P < .01$). The perceptual index was a composite of the subject's scores on the EFT, and measures of his ability

[19] Personal communication from Sarnoff Mednick.

[20] Paralleling the finding of consistent sex differences in perceptual field dependence, laboratory studies of conformity to group pressure have repeatedly found that women show significantly greater conformity than men (Feinberg, 1951; Crutchfield, 1955; Nakamura, 1955, 1958).

to recognize words against a background of noise and to "hold" one of the two alternative ways of perceiving a reversible cube or a reversible cross. However, the correlation between EFT scores and conformity measures was not significant for men or women.

In still another study, Nakamura (1958) investigated the relation between capacity to overcome embeddedness in problem solving and susceptibility to influence by the frame of reference proferred by a group. He found for college men (but not women) a significant correlation ($r = .38$, $P < .01$) between extent of conformity in Crutchfield's group pressure situation and ability to solve insight problems requiring restructuring.

2. Suggestibility

Suggestibility, as investigated by traditional laboratory methods, provides another index of readiness to accept external standards in determining one's own attitudes and judgments.

A study which has related suggestibility to mode of field approach was carried out by Sangiuliano (1951), with 85 female psychiatric ward patients as subjects. Mode of field approach was evaluated by means of the BAT and RAT. The following tests of "secondary suggestibility," taken from the study by Eysenck and Furneaux (1945) were used:

a. Inkblot suggestion. Two Rorschach cards are shown to the subject and, as in the standard "testing the limits" phase, a number of responses are suggested to him. The list of suggested responses begins with two populars and is followed by seven inapplicable responses. The suggestibility score is the number of inapplicable responses accepted.

b. Odor suggestion. The subject is given a series of bottles containing liquids. Each bottle is labeled with the name of an odor, such as coffee, rose, etc. The subject is told that he is being given a test of smell. The first few bottles contain the odors indicated on the label, but later in the series the bottles contain odorless water only. The suggestibility score is the number of odors attributed by the subject to bottles containing only water.

c. Binet's Progressive Weights. The subject is given a series of twelve boxes and told they are of different weights. His task is to lift two boxes at a time, progressing through the series, and to judge which of the two is heavier. The first five boxes are arranged in order of increasing weight, but the last seven are all of the same weight. The suggestibility score is the number of times the subject judges one of two objectively equivalent weights as heavier.

Scores for the three tests were combined to form a composite measure of secondary suggestibility. These scores agreed significantly with extent of field dependence as measured by the BAT ($r = .30, P < .01$).

As expected, field-dependent subjects responded more to suggestion.[21]

The trend of the data in this section suggests that the use of external standards in the definition of attitudes and judgments tends to be relatively great in persons with a global field approach, permitting an inference that they have a less well-developed sense of separate identity.

It must be emphasized that the dynamics of the conforming behavior observed in some of these studies require deeper exploration. In particular, attention needs to be given to the possibility that conformity, or the lack of it, may occur with different underlying motivations. This point has been emphasized by Asch (1952, 1956). In a group-discussion situation some subjects may "go along" with the group on the basis of acceptance of its judgment. Others may consider the group judgment wrong, but may outwardly conform because of an aloof attitude to the group and a disinclination to engage in argument with it. Dynamically, blanket acceptance and blanket rejection of authoritative judgments may not represent opposite attitudes; both may be rigidly directed by externally imposed standards. The person with a stable inner basis for making judgments is able to react more selectively, accepting others' judgments or rejecting them. As Erikson (1959) has observed, ". . . whoever is not sure of his 'point of view' cannot repudiate judiciously" (p. 125). Such distinctions are necessarily lost when a purely behavioral criterion of acceptance or rejection is employed. In this connection, it is noteworthy that Linton and Graham, in the study cited above, identified a group of subjects who consistently changed their attitudes in a direction opposite to those of a presumed authority. These subjects tended to be perceptually intermediate rather than field independent. The study of Mednick, also cited above, suggests that though field-dependent people may tend to show greater authoritarianism on the F-Scale than field-independent people, both groups may score higher for authoritarianism than people with intermediate perceptual performances.

Also insufficiently considered in the studies described is the possibly different effect of external standards on attitudes which are relatively peripheral or central in the person's attitudinal system—or as Jahoda (1959) has put it, attitudes in which the person has limited or considerable personal investment. A particular individual may readily formulate or adapt his judgment to conform with that of another person when the issue is one in which his interest (and relevant information) are very limited—as the direction of movement of a pinpoint of light in a dark room. The same person's stand may be most difficult to alter on an issue of great personal moment. Again, a given attitude in one person (as a strong preference for a particular political party), taken over, for example, from his father

[21] RAT scores were not significantly related ($r = .18$), again showing this test to be different from those we have included in our battery of tests of field dependence.

in the course of an early, strong identification, may be as resistant to change in the face of external influence as a similar attitude in another person, formed out of his own extended experience and deliberation. The reasons for lack of readiness to change are obviously greatly different. Also, the kind of external influence that may conceivably produce change is apt to be quite different in the two cases.

It is possible that more clear-cut and substantial relationships might have been found in some of the studies reported if instead of considering presence or absence of conforming behavior alone, the bases of the conforming behavior had been explored.

C. STABILITY OF SELF-VIEW

A sense of separate identity implies a relatively stable conception of oneself. The view of himself held by a person whose developed inner frames of reference provide a guide for self-definition and self-evaluation is less at the mercy of situational determinants and of evaluations others make of him. At the opposite extreme might be found persons exemplified by one of our 10-year-olds who, when asked in an interview, "What are you like?" replied: "Other people say I am nice," as if unable to make such a judgment on his own. It would be expected that persons with an analytical field approach would tend to have more stable impressions of themselves than persons with a global approach.

Rudin and Stagner (1958) developed several ingenious situations ideally suited to the study of stability of self-view. In their Self Contextual Influence Test the subject is required to imagine himself in each of four situations and to describe himself in each on rating scales taken from Osgood's (1952) Semantic Differential. The scoring reflects the extent of similarity among a subject's self-descriptions for the four situations. The similarity scores correlated significantly with measures of perceptual field dependence derived from the RFT and Thurstone Gottschaldt. Relatively field-dependent subjects showed greater fluctuation in their views of themselves in different contexts. Field-independent subjects tended to be less influenced by changes in the imaginary contexts, suggesting that they were able to maintain a more consistent view of themselves.

Rudin and Stagner also developed a Picture Contextual Influence Test. In this test subjects were given four pictures showing the same person in different settings. They were required to describe the person in each setting in terms of Osgood's rating procedure. As in the Self Contextual Influence Test, a score reflecting similarity in description of the person from setting to setting was developed for each subject. These scores were also significantly related to measures of field dependence, in the expected direction.

Results reported by Stark, Parker, and Iverson (1959) may also be interpreted in terms of the concept of stability of self-view. These investigators studied changes in performance in a relatively simple task (the Stroop Color Naming Test) as a function of "ego-enhancing" and "ego-threatening" instructions. The absolute amount of change in performance as a function of variations in the examiner's attitude toward the subject was significantly related to mode of field approach, as evaluated by the EFT. Subjects with a global field approach tended to be influenced by the examiner's attitude toward them, while subjects with an analytical approach were relatively immune to such influence.

D. SUMMARY

Through studies of "sense of separate identity," performed by ourselves and others, the exploration of differences among people in nature of experience which has its apparent source within the person has been extended.

A "sense of separate identity" is the result of development of awareness of one's own needs and characteristics as distinct from those of others. The self is experienced as segregated and structured; stable internal frames of reference are available for self-definition and for interpreting and reacting to the world. In the absence of such inner frames of reference, definition of characteristics of the self is likely to be determined from without and ability to function independently of external standards limited. The following observable ways in which a developed sense of separate identity might manifest itself were considered in explorations of sense of separate identity: limited need for guidance and support from others; ability to establish and, within limits, maintain attitudes, judgments, sentiments without continuous reference to external standards; a stable self-view, despite variations in social context.

It was our hypothesis that persons with an analytical field approach would be more apt to show these characteristics than persons with a global approach, reflecting their more developed sense of separate identity. Some of the studies bearing upon this hypothesis we performed ourselves; most are by others; these studies have used a great variety of situations and methods. Their results give strong, consistent support to our hypothesis.

The range and diversity of activities found to be related to mode of field approach in the course of these studies is particularly impressive. To illustrate, individuals with an analytical field approach, in contrast to people with a global approach, tend to be less dependent on the examiner in test situations for definition both of the task and their role in it; they are regarded by others as socially more independent; they show less interest in and need for people and a relatively intellectual and impersonal approach to problems; they are usually less influenced by authority, tending to be guided by values, standards, needs of their own; they are apt to have a stable self-view; and they are less attentive to subtle social cues given by others. Using the terminology employed earlier in another context, we may say that in general their attitudes, feelings, and needs are developed and discrete and do not easily become fused with the matrix of attitudes, feelings, and needs of others.

The evidence thus suggests that people with a relatively analytical field approach tend to experience themselves as articulated; body and self are experienced as segregated from the field, with their "parts" discrete and structured. If we consider that self-differentiation involves segregation of what is experienced as "inner" from what is experienced as "outer," and involves, further, the mutually determined articulation of each area of experience, it is indicated that people with an analytical field approach tend to show greater self-differentiation than people with a global approach. This relationship was anticipated from the differentiation hypothesis; its confirmation accordingly lends support to this hypothesis.

9

NATURE OF
CONTROLS AND DEFENSES

Guided by the differentiation hypothesis we have carried out several studies with the expectation that children with a relatively analytical field approach, as one indicator of their developed differentiation, would use more complex, specialized forms of defense (as intellectualization, isolation) than children with a global field approach (who would tend to use massive repression, primitive denial), and would have relatively structured controls and defenses.[1] In the first section below we present studies by ourselves and others concerned with the relation between field approach and defensive structure. The studies in the second section deal particularly with the specific kinds of defenses used by people with contrasting modes of field approach. The division between these closely related aspects of an individual's defense system is to an extent an arbitrary one, adopted for ease of data presentation.

In expecting a relation between mode of field approach and nature of defensive structure we assume a degree of correspondence in extent of development of differentiation in the two areas. The functional interrelations between defensive structure and articulation of experience

[1] Though neither conceptually nor in practice do we find clearly drawn distinctions between "defenses" and "controls," most often the term "controls" is used to refer to the adaptive techniques governing the discharge of impulse, and the term "defenses" to the array of devices which provides protection against the experience of anxiety. The controls and defenses used determine an individual's characteristic way of handling his impulses. In the analyses reported in the first section controls and defenses are considered together; the focus is on the extent to which they are structured, as judged particularly from ability to regulate impulse. In the analyses of the second section, the concern is with particular kinds of defenses.

during development seem to justify such an assumption, even though the complexity of these linkages allows for exceptions to the correspondence postulated.

To begin with, structured controls make possible the regulation of attention, which in turn is important if the ability to analyze and structure experience is to develop. Again, "how things go" in the development of controls and defenses is related to the kind of self that is formed. Continued easy spilling over of impulse through failure to develop structured controls may hamper the development of self-differentiation. In contrast, developed control of feelings is likely to aid, although not necessarily guarantee, differentiation of the self and articulation of experience in general. Again, if standards taken over from parents are not assimilated during growth, and remain as raw intruding proscriptions, the achievement of a structured self may be made inordinately difficult.

In considering the relation between development of articulation of experience and choice of defenses, it is interesting to note an analogy between the vagueness of impressions which primitive denial presupposes and the globality implied by poor articulation of experience. A congruence is also apparent between an articulated way of experiencing, on the one hand, and the splitting off of ideas from feelings, or ideas from each other, involved in intellectualization and isolation, or in the sharpened attention to detail which so often seems to defend the obsessive person against feelings. Pursuing the connection between articulation of experience and choice of defenses during growth, we may consider that the rapid early development of an articulated way of experiencing, constitutionally aided perhaps, may foster the use of intellectualization and isolation, although this would be only one possible factor in choice of defenses. On the other hand, once a tendency to favor intellectualization or repression has developed, the articulation of experience may be fostered in the case of intellectualization and hindered in the case of repression. The consistent relation between differentiation of the self and form of controls and defenses is apparent when we consider that on the basis of clinical experience it is not easy to conceive of a highly differentiated self in a person who uses massive repression and primitive denial as major preferred defenses or, conversely, of a relatively undifferentiated self in a highly intellectualized person.

The status of a person's defensive structure is often inferred from the quality of his actions. Chaotic activity, for example, suggests less structured controls and defenses; specific and directed activity suggests structured controls and defenses. To the extent that a high level of differentiation involves a developed control structure, it is apt to be manifested in and inferred from a quality of "directedness" in activity. Obviously, the determinants of this quality of behavior are multiple and complex, and not limited to the formation of controls alone; growth in other areas contributes to the development of directedness in behavior and is in turn affected by this development. Thus, clear awareness of one's needs, implied by a developed sense of separate identity, and articulated experience of the surroundings facilitate directedness in activity by aiding identification both of goal objects and means to a goal. The formation of internal frames of reference, also implied by a sense of separate identity, provides necessary guides to action. In contrast, the determination and maintenance of a course of action is apt to be greatly hampered in persons with a limitedly articulated self who, from moment to moment, lack clear awareness of self-field relations. Conversely, the extension of experience, made possible by an increase in activity which is directed, plays an important role in the development of self-differentiation and articulation of experience.

Obviously, impairment of integration may affect the directed quality of activity, and impulse expression more generally. It may be supposed, however, that the particular ways in which these are affected may be quite different in the kinds of disintegration that occur in relatively differentiated and relatively undifferentiated persons. In line with the suggestion in Chapter 2 that the weakly developed boundaries between subsystems, characteristic of less differentiated persons, may suffer further dissolution with impairment of integration, we may expect that impairment in these people may lead to such disturbances as direct affective discharge. Intellectual control over impulse, which is weak to begin with, is further diminished; the initially limited separation of the ideational from the affective is further reduced. Again following the proposal in Chapter 2 that the developed boundaries between subsystems found in highly differentiated individuals may be enhanced with impaired integration, disturbances in these persons may be expected to take such forms as overintellectualization, for example. Intellectual control is too severe, the ideational and affective too sharply separated. Pathology involving very easy spilling over of impulse and/or chaotic behavior betokens both limited differentiation and impaired integration. Pathology in the form of marked overintellectualization is suggestive of developed differentiation and impaired integration. Within more moderate limits, with integration more or less effective, variations in control over impulse expression may be taken to reflect primarily differences in extent of development of differentiation.

A. STRUCTURE OF CONTROLS AND DEFENSES

The approaches we used in studying capacity for impulse control consisted, in one analysis, of a clinical evaluation of structure of controls and defenses as manifested in the three projective tests considered together; and in another, of an evaluation of handling of aggression in the TAT.

1. Clinical Evaluation of Structure of Controls and Defenses

The primary interest in this analysis was in the degree of structure of the child's system of controls and defenses. Since a highly developed defensive system is likely to be characterized by the use of such defenses as intellectualization and isolation and a less developed system by the use of such defenses as primitive denial and massive repression, preferred mode of defense was necessarily considered in evaluating structure.

The analysis was based on the three projective tests given to 23 of the 24 boys of Group II—the Rorschach, TAT, and figure-drawing test (including drawing associations).[2] The psychologist, Meta Steiner, who carried out this analysis was not told of the hypothesized relation between structure of controls and defenses and mode of field approach, nor was she aware of the analyses made of these tests by other staff members, or of the performance of the children on any other test.

The psychologist was asked to classify the children according to degree of structure of controls and defenses indicated by their projective test records. She was given very general instructions, in order to leave her free to use the test material as she usually did in her clinical work. Only the extremes of degree of defensive structure were defined for her, as follows: Boys at one extreme of the scale would be characterized by a well-organized defensive structure; controls might be adaptive and fairly easily carried, or they might be tight and rigid. Boys at the opposite extreme would be characterized by a relatively

[2] These records were also used for other analyses, presented elsewhere in this book. Though the aims of these analyses, and the aspects or portions of the records therefore considered, were quite different, the possibility of overlap between them and the present analysis, as a function of use of common data, must be kept in mind.

less well-developed and organized defensive structure, perhaps to the point of fluidity and diffusion, and/or easily penetrable defenses; they might present a picture of poorly controlled impulses or chaos and disorganization; or, on the other hand, of "emptiness," lack of resources, and a low level of energy requiring control. Using these two extreme categories as anchoring points, she was instructed to formulate additional intermediate categories as the data indicated. She was also asked to write a brief summary of each child's over-all structure, commenting particularly on types and effectiveness of defenses used.

In the scale that finally emerged, a rating of 1 was assigned to children whose test material suggested the least structured defenses and a rating of 5 the most structured defenses. Ratings of 2 and 4 were used when the test material pointed more clearly in one direction than the other, but in a less extreme or less clear way. Finally a rating of 3 was given to three kinds of children: those who, on all three tests, seemed consistently moderate or "in-between" in development of defensive structure; those who presented a different picture from test to test; and those who showed ambiguous, inconsistent, and contradictory trends within each of the three test productions.

As an aid to making her ratings, the psychologist recorded for each child the evidence in his test material, at the level of both raw data and interpretative comments, which pointed toward either of the extremes defined by the scale. As might be expected, the evidence typically went in both directions. The balance of the evidence in each case, with regard both to quantity and "impressiveness," did, however, permit the ordering of the 23 boys along the 5-point scale.

Examples of the way in which children were described by the rater in notations made prior to the final assignment of ratings are given below:

Rating of 1 (relatively low degree of structure). He is easily overwhelmed by both the demands of reality and by inner experiences; (his) experiences are "fleeting" and in flux; (he) is restless and overactive. Some evidence of attempted controls, but these are not well developed and are mechanically applied.

Rating of 3 (intermediate). This boy was placed in the intermediate category because of the impression that, while in behavior he might easily be mistaken for a child with poorly "structured" defenses, with overt and poorly compensated manifestations of insecurity, and over-all self-dissatisfaction, with the use of denial and repression as favored defenses, and with shifting and labile moods, underneath these manifestations one could discern persistent struggles for better structuring and organization. There was a quality of persistence; frequent though at present not always successful attempts to maintain distance; an interest in maintaining high standards.

Rating of 3 (intermediate). This boy was put in category 3 for reasons almost opposite to the ones given for the preceding case. He may perhaps be described as "an amoeba with a shell on." He appears to be a submissive "good boy" with evasion and repression as favored defenses; in behavior, nonspontaneous and sterile, with general poverty of resources. He has managed to work out an orderly but constricted mode of operation, without having attained a highly developed structure. Nor is there evidence of struggle for better structure.

Rating of 5 (relatively high degree of structure). Thinking is exact, often to the point of meticulousness; aloof, overdefended against feeling; maintains detachment; appropriate use of sense of humor; over-all impression of strong, well-functioning regulative capacity; appears to lean over backwards to compensate for residual childishness. Some naive bragging, that seems like an effort at simple denial of anxiety.

Although not intended as an account of the full process followed in arriving at judgments, the following examples of kinds of "test indicators" and interpretative comments utilized in part in making the judgments may be cited:

Evidence pointing to relatively less structure *at the level of test indicators*: Rorschach—predominance of vague or "sloppy" forms, high color with *CF* predominating. Drawings—generally poorly integrated drawings with lines not meeting, parts omitted or unrealistically attached, transparencies, diffuse shading. TAT—misinterpretation or omission of significant parts of the picture, rambling, poorly structured stories, frequent emotional shifts, stress on bewilderment and helplessness in description of characters. *At the level of interpretative comments:* reactions are characteristically unreflective, highly personalized and subjective, defenses seem to be extremely unstable, frequent use of simple denial, pervasive, poorly channeled anxiety.

Evidence pointing to relatively more structure *at the level of test indicators*: Rorschach—high form level, with interest in accuracy; comments about symmetry; emphasis on *dr, Hd, Ad*. Drawings—exactness of organization and detailing; neat erasures and corrections; symmetry. TAT—adaptive and realistic use of features of card; close attention to details of picture, perhaps with description, attention to their shape and size; story may be modified when meaning of an object is reinterpreted. *At the level of interpretative comments:* formalistic attitudes, meticulous and exact, haughty attitude towards authority, critical of self and others, uses variety of defenses, use of intellectualization and humor as defense, overdefended against feelings.

Comparing the ratings of defensive structure with perceptual index scores, a correlation of .61 ($P < .01$), in the expected direction, was obtained, thus confirming the hypothesis.

We have not repeated this study since the results of the study by Zukmann (1957) cited below have confirmed our hypothesis.

Although our subjects were drawn from a "normal" population, the differences in defensive structure described in the scale above correspond clinically to differences between obsessive-compulsive trends on the one hand and hysterical trends on the other.[3] It is therefore of special interest that Zukmann found a group of obsessive-compulsives to be significantly more field independent on the EFT than a group of hysterics. In contrast to our group, Zukmann's subjects were adult patients in private psychiatric treatment, both men and women. On the basis of the Rorschach, a psychologist, working without knowledge of psychiatric data, classified the majority of Zukmann's subjects as predominantly obsessive-compulsive or predominantly hysterical. These contrasting groups differed significantly in their EFT scores ($P < .01$), the obsessive-compulsives tending to locate the hidden figures more rapidly. In a subsample of 28 patients for whom the psychiatric and Rorschach diagnoses coincided, the difference between obsessive-compulsives and hysterics in ability to solve EFT problems was even more marked ($P < .001$), in spite of the smaller number of cases.

The results of Zukmann's study and our own highlight several points which are of concern to us in Chapter 12. First, though complexity of defensive structure is related to mode of field approach, it is not necessarily associated with good or poor adjustment or presence or absence of pathology. A developed defensive structure which very severely limits the awareness and expression of impulse may be as damaging as too little structure. Each may be associated with pathology of the contrasting kinds found among Zukmann's patients. The scale we used in evaluating children's defensive structure was not concerned with effectiveness of adjustment. Second, both global and analytical field approaches are to be found among psychiatric patients; however, mode of field approach is related to *direction* of pathology. Finally, the view in psychiatric thinking that the defenses typically used by hysterical personalities are more primitive than the defenses

[3] As noted in Chapter 6, the cues used in the Rorschach percept ratings correspond to some extent to the manner of approach to this test found in obsessive-compulsive and hysterical personalities. Our Rorschach ratings, however, were based on the nature of the child's experience, rather than on the character of his defensive structure.

of obsessive-compulsive personalities is consistent with the differentiation framework.

The finding of significant relations between mode of field approach and degree of structure of defenses among both normal children and adult psychiatric patients confirms our expectation.

2. Handling of Themes of Aggression in the TAT

This analysis was undertaken with the view that degree of structure of controls and defenses is reflected in extent of ability to manage strong impulses.

One of the TAT cards, 18GF, is especially appropriate for an analysis of controls. The picture on this card is described by Murray, et al. (1943) as: "A woman has her hands squeezed around the throat of another woman whom she appears to be pushing backward across the banister of a stairway" (p. 20). This picture, more than any other of the series used, evoked ideas and feelings of aggression; in their stories for it 36 of the 38 boys in Groups I and II made some reference to physical aggression or physical injury.

The question asked in analyzing each child's story for card 18GF was whether the aggression took the form of a direct, uncontrolled, unrationalized, impulsive outburst or whether some effort was made to modulate or attenuate the aggression. With this question as a reference, three categories were devised for classifying the stories obtained for card 18GF.

Category 1 included stories which suggested poor control over aggression. In such stories there was characteristically direct aggression from one figure on the card against the other. The aggression took the extreme form of choking, killing, or some other kind of physical assault. No attempt was made by the child to provide a rational context for the aggression; or if the attempt was made, it was not effective—for example, the aggression was inappropriate or excessive in relation to the cause given (as, "She's killing the boy because he isn't nice"). Also included in this category was the occasional story which omitted any reference to aggression or to physical injury. Such complete denial of the strong aggressive implications of the card was interpreted as inability to acknowledge aggression and express it in controlled fashion.

Category 2 included stories which manifested some attempt at control over the expression of aggression. Placed in this category were stories in which strong, direct aggression occurred, but the aggression was attenuated through offering a milder alternative (e.g., "She's scratching his eyes out or maybe she's caressing him"). Also included were stories in which the aggression was placed in a playful or humorous context. Such handling of aggression was taken to represent a modified form of avoidance.

Category 3 included stories in which genuine control seemed to be exercised over the expression of the aggressive ideas evoked by the card, without reliance on any form of avoidance. For example, the aggression rather than involving a direct outburst from one figure on the card against the other, was somehow mediated; the aggression or physical injury came about through an outside agency, such as another person, or an impersonal force as, for example, an injury through accident. Another kind of story placed in this category involved control through effective rationalization of the aggression. Such stories might also show mediation of aggression. Rationalization sometimes took the form of providing a realistic basis for the aggression; of placing the aggression in the context of a mystery story; or of giving the aggressor a role which makes the aggression socially acceptable (e.g., "She is a policewoman"). In such stories, the aggression may actually be directed from one person on the card against the other, but compared with the stories in the first category, an effective rational context is provided.

Each child's story for card 18GF was separated from the rest of his TAT record, and rated according to this classification.

The rating scale was developed for the 38 boys of Groups I and II. To check on interjudge reliability, it was applied independently by a second judge. A correlation of .84 ($P < .01$) was obtained between the ratings of the two judges, indicating satisfactory interjudge agreement.

The ratings for the 38 boys were then compared to their perceptual index scores, with the expectation that children with an analytical field approach would show greater capacity for impulse control, according to the criteria used. A correlation of .54 ($P < .01$) was obtained.

For validation purposes the rating scale was applied to the card 18GF stories of the 30 Group-III boys. Again a significant relation, in the expected direction, was found between TAT ratings and perceptual index scores ($r = .33, P < .05$). The relation was not significant, however, when these ratings were compared to intellectual index scores and cognitive index scores ($r = -.08$ and .23, respectively).

Thus, in part, the evidence suggests that children with a global field approach tend to be less able to contain, modulate, and channelize aggressive ideas and feelings than children with an analytical field approach.

3. Other Studies

A number of additional studies, many from other laboratories and using methods different from ours, tend to confirm the view that people with a global field approach have less capacity for the management of impulse than people with an analytical field approach.

In our 1954 studies of young adults, capacity for impulse control was investigated by means of the Rorschach. One of the Rorschach scores, derived by Hertzman, was the "color-balance" score, or "C sign," assigned on the basis of the relative frequency of responses indicating controlled emotional reaction (FC) and responses showing predominantly uncontrolled color reaction (CF + C). The "C sign" was given to records in which uncontrolled color reactions predominated. A significant correlation, in the expected direction, between C-sign scores and perceptual index scores was found for men although not for women. When the study was repeated with a group of hospitalized psychiatric patients, a significant relation was again found for men but not women.[4,5]

In our 1954 study miniature-toys-play productions were used to evaluate children's capacity for impulse control. Two 5-point scales were devised by Meissner. One, "method of handling impulse problems," drew on evidence from the entire play record. The other, the "animal-use" scale, was based specifically on the kinds of animals the child used and his manner of dealing with them. Ratings for both scales related significantly[4] to mode of field approach in groups of 8-, 10-, and 13-year-olds, although the relation was not confirmed when the scales were applied by a new rater to the plays of the 24 Group-II boys.

Crutchfield and Starkweather (1953), in the previously cited study of 100 Air Force captains, identified clusters of related characteristics of subjects with contrasting modes of field approach. The 20 most field-dependent subjects on the RFT were described as follows on the basis of an adjective check list and various Q-sorts: "undercontrols impulses," "confused, disorganized, and unadaptive under stress," "acts with insufficient thinking and deliberation." In contrast, a group of extremely field-independent subjects —more extreme than those we have encountered among college students— was described as overcontrolled. An item which significantly distinguished Crutchfield's 20 most field-dependent subjects from the remainder of the group was "emphasizes oral pleasure; self-indulgent." This characteristic is in striking contrast to the quality of overcontrol found among the field-independent subjects.

Among items found by Crutchfield to distinguish his extremely field-dependent subjects was "acts with insufficient thinking and deliberation." This characteristic reflects a lack of what earlier in this chapter we called "directedness" in behavior. Though, as noted there, the linkages are complex, we would, on the basis of the differentiation hypothesis, expect some relation between mode of field approach and the quality of directedness in activity. The evidence is sparse, but the results of three studies, in

[4] The correlations were computed from data on which our 1954 report was based.
[5] This relation was confirmed by Guskin (1955), but not by Gardner, et al. (1959).

addition to those reported by Crutchfield, et al., suggests that this view may be correct.

One set of results comes from studies of the mazes subtest of the WISC. According to the usual clinical interpretation, successful performance on this test, and on the Porteus Mazes on which it is based, depends in part on the ability to plan ahead. In the factor-analytic studies reported in Chapter 5, this subtest was significantly loaded on the same factor as the three perceptual tests at age 12 but not at age 10. Podell and Phillips (1959) found Porteus Mazes to be loaded on their spatial-decontextualization factor which, it will be recalled, is similar to our analytical field approach factor. There is thus evidence that ability to plan ahead, as shown in performance on mazes, is related to mode of field approach.

Persistence with a difficult task may be considered another manifestation of directedness. Sangiuliano, in a study already cited, reports that a composite score on three tests of persistence on difficult, sometimes virtually insoluble, tasks was significantly related to BAT scores.[6]

The greater ability of more field-independent people to maintain direction in these difficult tasks and in the maze tests we interpret as partly a function of their better developed controls, and their greater freedom from disruptive impulse expression.

A unique study which links mode of field approach and the characteristics associated with it to GSR reactivity has been reported by Block (1957). Using two groups, selected from medical school applicants on the basis of high and low GSR responsiveness, he found the GSR-labile (responsive) group to be more field dependent on the RFT [7] and "sometimes radically subject to their moods and impulses." The GSR-labile group was further characterized as dependent, suggestible, and markedly oriented toward appropriate behavior in their social contexts. The GSR-stable group, on the other hand, was significantly more field independent and was characterized as showing "self-control of their behavior," and as independent, practical, and realistic.

An indirect method of studying the problem of controls and de-

[6] Sangiuliano (1951) distinguished between persistence in the face of difficulties and sheer perseveration (as expressed, for example, in the task of writing numbers forward and then backwards for one minute). Measures of perseveration did not relate to perceptual field dependence. Guilford, et al. (1957) have also distinguished between persistence and perseveration. Whereas measures from tests of persistence occurred on the adaptive-flexibility factor, measures of perseverance did not, appearing instead on the spontaneous-flexibility factor (see Chapter 5).

[7] This relation between field dependence and GSR lability has been confirmed in the study by Cohen, Silverman, and Shmavonian (1959).

fenses was used in a group of studies concerned with the relation between field approach and manifest anxiety. With a less structured defensive system, a greater amount of anxiety is apt to be expressed, so that extent of open anxiety may reflect indirectly on nature of defensive structure.

In our 1954 study a rating was made of the extent of each subject's self-assurance or anxiety and tension during a clinical interview. This rating was based on the subject's behavior rather than on interview content. A significant relation in the expected direction was found, for both men and women, between these ratings and perceptual index scores. Other investigators have also commented on the greater self-assurance and self-confidence of field-independent perceivers. Sangiuliano (1951) determined the extent of each of her subject's confidence in the judgments made in the TRTC, using a special self-rating check list. Field-independent subjects expressed significantly greater confidence in their judgments. Gross (1959) tested a group of subjects on the RFT with a plate of plain glass placed in front of the apparatus. The subjects were told that the glass was a specially ground lens which distorts vision in unknown ways. At the end of the test, after being told about the supposed distorting effect of the lens, they were asked to check terms on an adjective check list which best expressed their feelings. The two most commonly checked adjectives were "uncertainty" and "expectancy." The very field-dependent subjects most often checked "uncertainty," and very field-independent subjects most often checked "expectancy." The difference was highly significant.

Linton (1952), using a very different approach, has reported evidence of a similar sort. In leading her blindfolded subjects into the autokinetic situation, she noted differences among them in the ease and comfort with which they moved. One group of subjects she characterized as especially self-confident, their movements approaching normal walking behavior despite being blindfolded. Another group showed an especially fumbling gait, clinging to the examiner for support. Comparison of the perceptual performances of these two groups showed the first to be significantly more field independent than the second.

Gump (1955), using a "freedom from aversions" scale consisting of items dealing with fears and disgust selected from the GAMIN, found among college students a significant relation between scores on this scale and Thurstone Gottschaldt scores, with a greater tendency toward aversions among field-dependent subjects. Verbally expressed fears and aversions may be interpreted as open expressions of anxiety.

Finally, differences in anxiety-proneness in relation to mode of field approach were demonstrated by Cohen, Silverman, and Shmavonian (1959) in their study of sensory isolation. Field-dependent subjects tended to react to this extreme condition with manifest anxiety, field-independent subjects with either anger or a combination of anger and anxiety.

The results of this group of studies suggest that persons with a relatively global field approach are more apt than analytical people to show open anxiety reflecting, presumably, less effective controls.

B. TYPES OF DEFENSES

Our expectation was that people with a global field approach would be more apt to use primitive denial and massive repression as characteristic modes of defense and people with an analytical approach to use intellectualization.[8] We characterized the former kinds of defense as less specialized, and thus reflecting less developed differentiation.

Denial is one of the earliest mechanisms of defense. Fenichel (1945) speaks of "a wish-fulfilling denial of unpleasant realities" as very common among little children. Anna Freud (1946) refers to denial as "a preliminary stage of defense" and describes intellectualization as showing a special spurt during adolescence, i.e., as associated with a much later stage of development. Repression (or massive repression as we designated it in Chapter 2) is another relatively primitive form of defense.

Denial and repression are not the only defenses we may expect to find among those who are less differentiated, nor are they abandoned when more complex defenses are developed. We can only postulate that persons who are less differentiated are more likely to use denial and repression than highly differentiated persons. People who are relatively differentiated also use denial, but only as part of their more varied defensive repertoire. They would be expected to use some of the more sophisticated forms of defense, as intellectualization and rationalization, more often than less differentiated people.[9]

1. Use of Denial

a. Manifestations of denial in the TAT. The specific form of denial considered in this study was the exclusion from awareness of environmental stimuli which are threatening or provocative of unacceptable impulses. It is likely to be effective only when these stimuli are relatively mild. Except in severe pathological states, denial of a very insistent stimulus, whatever its implications, is less likely to occur.

[8] Only the defenses cited have been studied thus far.

[9] It has already been suggested that the types of defense used are intimately related to the nature of over-all defensive structure. Thus, in the evaluation of children's defensive structure reported at the beginning of the chapter the specific modes of defense used were necessarily considered.

Primitive denial must be distinguished from "active avoidance," a relatively specialized form of defense. Denial involves failure to apprehend a stimulus. Active avoidance is a form of evasiveness, an effort to maintain distance, often in a planful and deliberate manner. In the TAT, it may be shown in a wary, noncommittal attitude, such as an "either-or" formulation which avoids taking a stand. Active avoidance may be accompanied by awareness of the maneuver that is being used; denial is not. By putting the designation "primitive" before denial we mean to emphasize its difference from "active avoidance."

The TAT was used to check the hypothesis that children with a global field approach are more likely than children with an analytical approach to use primitive denial as a defense. In the TAT denial is apt to take the form of failure to identify and deal with features of a picture associated with feelings and ideas that are difficult to handle. The finding that children with a relatively global field approach are likely to be limited in their ability to manage strong impulses led us to choose for this analysis cards which commonly lead to stories involving aggression, severe conflict, and strong feelings of being overwhelmed. It was our specific expectation that children with a global field approach would be more likely than children with an analytical approach to deny features of the card which are particularly provocative of such issues.

No attempt was made to use all manifestations of denial in the TAT records; as far as possible we relied on quite specifically defined manifestations. Decisions both as to selection of cards and methods of rating were guided by experience gained in working with children's TAT material.

The specific manifestations of denial considered were:

1. Omission of the violin in the story for card 1, with or without the substitution of some other object for it.

Card 1 shows a boy alone looking at a violin. Among our 10-year boys the figure on the card is usually said to be around that age, so that he is an obvious identification figure. Most commonly card 1 elicits some version of the theme "practicing the violin at mother's insistence but against one's own wishes." The violin is thus often a symbol of conflict with mother. For the 10-year boys of Groups I and II this card led to more parent-child stories than any of the other cards used, although no figure is shown who might represent a parent.

Analysis of the card-1 stories for the boys of Group II revealed two converging trends. While some children allowed themselves to become involved in the "conflict-with-parent-over-practicing" issue, both by introducing the parent and utilizing the violin in their stories, other children avoided the conflict, by omitting the parent, the violin, or both. Since the violin commonly leads to the association, "parent-makes-practice," failure to deal with the violin may be one means of blocking the line of association to the parental-coercion issue at its perceptual source. The violin is a very prominent part of the picture; its omission can therefore hardly be considered accidental. These results seemed related to another finding, considered in Chapter 21, that in their TAT stories, children with a global field approach commonly cast parental figures in coercive, nonsupporting, punitive roles. Both types of evidence together suggested that if children with a global approach do in fact use denial as a mode of defense, they would in this instance show the denial by omitting the violin.

2. Failure to refer to the object on the floor, commonly seen as a "gun," in the story for card 3BM; or if it is referred to, failure to identify its aggressive implications.

3. Failure to note the commonly seen sad implications of card 3BM. Crying, the emotional state frequently assigned to the figure shown on the card, is a state of extreme, primitive helplessness, usually produced by overwhelming environmental forces.

4. Omission in the story for card 18GF of the issue of aggression, so compellingly suggested by the picture.

For each of the 38 boys of Groups I and II a total score, ranging from 0 to 4, based on these four specific "signs" of denial was computed.[10] A significant correlation of .42 ($P < .01$), in the expected direction, was found between these scores and perceptual index scores.

The rating method was then applied to the TAT stories of the 30 Group-III boys. The correlations between these ratings and perceptual, intellectual, and cognitive index scores were not significant (.17, .08, and .14, respectively).

A further check on the relation between TAT denial-scale scores and perceptual performance was made with a group of 14 14-year-old boys. For this group the relation did prove significant ($r = .52$, $P < .05$).

Though these findings are not clear-cut, other studies have yielded results showing the same trend.

b. Other studies of denial. On the basis of a clinical interview, Lewis, in our 1954 study, rated each subject as showing a predominant tendency toward either denial or self-awareness. The concern was primarily with extent of denial of one's own feelings and impulses, rather than with denial of external stimuli, as in our study of children. A subject was judged to show self-awareness if the interview data

---

[10] Interjudge agreement was not checked since no judgment is required in determining the presence or absence of each of the four indicators.

revealed either full, mature insight; frankness in describing personal problems, even in the absence of awareness of the correct solution; or simply introspectiveness or concern with inner life, even if this concern was realistically unproductive. The subject was rated as showing denial if symptoms were unrecognized, except perhaps as generalized anxiety; if childhood experiences tended to be "forgotten"; if he experienced difficulty in identifying anything about himself that might be criticized or changed. The correlation of these ratings with perceptual index scores proved significant for both men and women.

Further evidence that people with a global field approach tend to use denial comes from the previously cited study by Linton (1952). She set up groups of "conformers" and "nonconformers" among her college students, based in part on extent of field dependence in the BAT and EFT. Fewer conforming than nonconforming subjects reported conflicting feelings of love and hate toward members of their family, and wished they had been born into a different family or in a different time or place. Conformers also more commonly agreed with the statement: "There is hardly anything lower than a person who does not feel a great love, gratitude and respect for his parents." Conformers thus seem to deny possible negative or conflict features in their present situations.

2. Nature of Defenses as Expressed in Dream Recall

Infrequent dream recall has often been attributed to the use of massive repression as a defense against threatening dream content. The finding, in three separate studies, of a relation between frequency of dream recall and extent of field dependence is therefore of interest for our present concern with the defenses of people with contrasting modes of field approach. The differentiation hypothesis would lead us to expect that persons with a global field approach would tend to report fewer dreams than persons with an analytical approach. The evidence tends to confirm this expectation, though the basis of the relation is complex.

Linton was the first to relate the frequency of dreaming to perceptual performance. On the basis of a questionnaire administered to each of her 53 college men, she found that the 15 most field-dependent subjects reported a mean of 6.2 dreams per month, and the 16 most field-independent subjects a mean of 13.5 dreams.[11]

---

[11] These data are from a personal communication from Harriet Linton. They were not included in her 1952 report.

These results have been confirmed in studies by Eagle [12] with our 10-year-old Group-II boys and with the 17-year-old boys and girls of our longitudinal study. The 10-year-olds were asked about their dream experiences in the course of the interview conducted with them. Dividing the children into three subgroups, on the basis of perceptual performance, Eagle found that the 7 most field-independent boys reported a mean of 1.3 dreams and the 5 most field-dependent boys a mean of 0.6 dreams. The 17-year-old subjects were asked to keep a "dream diary" over a 15-day period, writing out their dreams, if any, immediately on waking each day. The 6 most field-independent of the 18 subjects who cooperated in the study reported a mean of 2.8 dreams during this period, the 6 most field-dependent a mean of 1.0 dreams.

In all three studies, each using a different method of dream collection, field-independent subjects (those in approximately the bottom third of the distribution) reported about twice as many dreams as field-dependent subjects (those in approximately the top third of the distribution).

If we accept the common assumption that failure to recall dreams is a function of massive repression, these results would support the hypothesis that repression is a common defense among persons with a global field approach and, in more general terms, would support the differentiation hypothesis. Recent evidence on dream recall suggests, however, that individual differences in frequency of dream reporting may have a more complex basis.

Goodenough, et al. (1959) recently carried out a study of people who claim they never or rarely dream, using the eye-movement criteria of Dement and Kleitman (1957) to identify a dream state. When awakened during an eye-movement period, these subjects were often able to report a dream. In instances where no dream experience occurred, some subjects typically said they had been in a dreamless sleep or they had dreamed, but could not recall the content of the dream, responses that the clinical literature commonly accounts for in terms of repression. Other subjects typically said that they were "thinking" or "imagining," rather than dreaming. These "thinking" reports were usually associated with a sense of being only partially asleep during the experience and with a feeling of some control over the content.

There were thus two kinds of nonreporters, those who failed to recall their dreams, and those who attached a "thought" rather than a

[12] Personal communication from Carol Johnson Eagle.

"dream" label to their experience. It seems reasonable to suppose that the failure to report dreams may have a different basis in different kinds of people. The relation between dream reporting and field dependence may therefore be complex.

3. Use of Intellectualization as a Defense

We hypothesized that children with a global field approach would tend to use relatively unspecialized defenses, as denial and repression, and children with an analytical approach relatively specialized defenses, as intellectualization. We have not carried out specific studies to check the second part of this hypothesis, although the analysis of degree of structure of defenses and controls described earlier in this chapter did provide some evidence for such an hypothesis.

Additional suggestive evidence comes from case studies of children with different modes of field approach, given in Chapter 15. Of particular interest are those children in the analytical group who, as we shall see, show distance from others and a lack of interest in and empathy for people. The isolation, which distinguishes these emotionally "hard" children, as we call them, from other children in the analytical group, appears to be a function of intellectualization carried to an extreme.

More systematic support for the hypothesis that field-independent persons tend to use intellectualization as a defense comes from the work of Crutchfield and Starkweather (1953). Their Q-sort analysis showed that the following characteristics most effectively distinguished field-independent from field-dependent subjects: "Cold and distant with others," "unaware of their social stimulus value," "concerned with philosophical problems, e.g., religion, values, the meaning of life." Another item which characterized the most field-independent group and distinguished it from the most field-dependent group was "highly cathects intellectual activity; values cognitive pursuits."

This characterization roughly fits the emotionally "hard" boys in our analytical group. As noted earlier, the field-independent subjects in Crutchfield's group of Army captains were more extreme in their perception than the field-independent subjects among the college students we have studied and certainly more than the field-independent children on whom the present report is in part based. It may be for this reason that overintellectualization and isolation are so much more prominent in their field-independent group than in any of ours.

Results similar to those of Crutchfield and Starkweather, but obtained by a very different method, have been reported by Bertini

(1960). Bertini's study started from an interest in the nature of defense mechanisms, rather than in perception. He considered that "the capacity to separate and isolate an idea from its emotional content or to separate two ideas that belong together," involved in the mechanism of isolation, parallels the capacity in analytical perceiving to "separate several elements from the phenomenal field, in isolating them from a context" (p. 4). This concept led Bertini to hypothesize that people who use isolation as a characteristic defense would tend to perceive analytically. In the study carried out to test this hypothesis, 80 Italian college students were given the Rorschach and the Gottschaldt test. The Rorschach was employed to evaluate extent of use of isolation as a defense, following suggestions made by Schafer (1954), and the Gottschaldt test to evaluate capacity for analytical perception. A significant relation was found between measures for the two tests. Subjects who employed isolation as a defense tended, in our terms, to be field independent in their Gottschaldt performance.

The results of a recent study by Kalis (1957) are also in line with our hypothesis. Kalis evaluated people's views of the world through their perception of size and distance, in a "periscope tracing" test which required the subject to reproduce a periscopically viewed outline square seen in a setting of reduced constancy cues. She postulated that for persons with an inadequately differentiated ego the psychological world would be close and objects large and for persons with a highly differentiated or overdifferentiated ego the psychological world would be distant and objects small. Field-independent subjects—especially those who are very extreme—should therefore tend to see the square as distant, and reproduce it as relatively small. Scores on the periscope-tracing test correlated significantly with RFT scores, in the predicted direction. In Kalis' view this suggests that very field-independent people are overdifferentiated and maintain distance between themselves and the world.

The evidence suggests, in keeping with our hypothesis, that persons with an analytical field approach are particularly apt to use intellectualization and isolation as modes of defense. This relation needs to be confirmed for the age levels we have been studying.

C. SUMMARY

Children and adults with an analytical field approach tend to have a relatively developed defensive structure and to use relatively specialized complex defenses (as isolation and intellectualization, rather than primitive denial and massive repression). The existence of such a relation was hypothesized on the premise that both an analytical field approach and structured defenses and controls are aspects of a relatively high level of differentiation.

Evidence concerning controls and defenses of children with different modes of field approach has come from a number of studies, employing a variety of methods. To illustrate, in one study, which used a clinical evaluation of the three projective test records for each of a group of 10-year-old boys, it was found that children with an analytical field approach tended to have a more developed defensive structure. In another study children with an analytical approach were shown to be better able to modulate and mediate the ideas and feelings of aggression set off by a TAT picture with strong aggressive implications. As to types of defenses favored by children with different modes of field approach, the expected tendency for children with a global approach to use primitive denial in their manner of dealing with aspects of TAT pictures was investigated but the evidence is not clear. Studies using adult subjects showed that people with a global field approach, in giving an account of their life situation, are likely to deny conflict material. The hypothesis that people with an analytical approach, as a sign of their more developed differentiation, would use intellectualization and isolation as modes of defense was confirmed for adult subjects. Such a relation was also suggested by our intensive study of relatively differentiated individual children.

Taken together the findings in this chapter lend further support to the differentiation hypothesis which guided these studies.

10

ACTIVITY

The preceding six chapters have been devoted to an exploration of several areas of psychological functioning, considered from the standpoint of individual differences in extent of differentiation. The areas were those examined in Chapter 2 in delineating some of the ways in which more developed or less developed differentiation may manifest itself. The usefulness of the differentiation framework is not limited to the particular areas considered. Although we have not attempted to apply it as systematically to other areas, either conceptually or by specific investigations, evidence bearing on differentiation in several other areas is available from preliminary explorations or as a "byproduct" of our general studies. In the next chapters we consider four of these areas: activity, verbal skills, sex differences, and psychopathology. The picture in these areas, both conceptually and with regard to evidence, is obviously at a preliminary stage, compared to the areas already considered; the "interim report" given may be useful, however, in suggesting directions for further research.

At an earlier stage of our work (1954) we believed that a tendency toward "active coping" or "passive submission" was the dimension of personal functioning most closely associated with field-dependence-independence. The studies we performed had been guided by the view that ability readily to separate item from context, involved in analytical perception, represents an active way of dealing with a field, as compared to acceptance of the dominant organization of the field, involved in global perception. The expectation that persons with an analytical approach would show active coping in dealing with the environment in fact appeared to be confirmed by the results of these studies. We now believe that the concept of active coping is too inclusive to be meaningful in describing individual differences.

Since our earlier studies, work on the problem of activity by ourselves and others has continued, and from its results it has become clear that not all facets of activity are related to mode of field approach. This work contributed to the delineation of the differentiation concept, which was evolving in our general program of research during the same period; and as the definition of the differentiation concept became clearer, it in turn contributed to sharper distinctions among the various facets of activity.

A. CONCEPTS OF ACTIVITY

Of the several different senses in which the term "active" may be used, one refers to sheer quantity of motorically expressed energy expenditure. An active child is, in this sense, one who shows considerable motoric output. This usage of "active" is broad enough to describe children showing marked restlessness, hyperkinesis, and impulse control problems, although not limited to them.

"Active" has also been used in a broader, more psychological sense to describe a quality of interest in being active, in striving, in being assertive. This quality may be manifested not only in behavior of a physical kind, but in social and intellectual pursuits as well. It may be evident in many areas of behavior or concentrated in a particular area. We may use the term "active attitude" to refer to the quality of interest in activity, striving, assertiveness shown by an individual in one or many areas.

A further distinction may be drawn between active attitude and the "directedness" aspect of activity. The latter has already been considered in the preceding chapter. A child whose preference is to deal actively with situations may yet lack the techniques necessary to give actions a specific, purposeful, goal-directed character. The concept of directed activity is neutral with regard to such questions as the area or areas—intellectual, physical, social—of behavior in which the activity is invested; the particular goals that are being pursued; or the success of the activity.

Finally, we must distinguish between an active attitude and a developed sense of separate identity. A person with a developed sense of separate identity need not be particularly interested in being active, even though a clear sense of identity may help foster an active approach to the world. On the other hand, a person with an active attitude may put his activity into the service of winning and maintaining dependent relations with others, which a limitedly developed sense of separate identity is apt to make necessary.

Our conceptual framework gives us more adequate grounds for speculating about the relation of mode of field approach to some of the facets of activity considered than to others.

First, we have no clear grounds for anticipating that activity, in the sense of high motoric output, will be related to mode of field approach. Only one very limited basis for expecting a connection is evident. In cases where such activity is a function of severe difficulty in impulse control we may reasonably anticipate a global field approach.

With regard to the quality of directedness in activity, for reasons considered in the preceding chapter, we would expect a relation between this characteristic and mode of field approach. The results of studies considered in that chapter are consistent with this expectation, although further supporting evidence is needed.

There are clear grounds (Chapters 2 and 8) for conceiving of sense of separate identity, as we have called it, to be related to mode of field approach. The results of many studies reviewed in Chapter 8 offer clear consistent evidence of such a relation.

Finally, our conceptual framework offers only a very limited basis for speculating about the relation between mode of field approach and what we have called an active attitude. One basis for expecting a relation has already been mentioned. Attempting to "break up a configuration," as contrasted to accepting its dominant organization, would seem to require an active attitude. Second, the tendency of people with a global approach to use primitive denial and massive repression as characteristic defenses would work against the development and maintenance of an active attitude. The constriction which continued reliance on such defenses provides might manifest itself in the area of activity in reduced readiness to participate in various kinds of experience.

On these limited grounds we might expect an active attitude to be relatively common among persons with an analytical field approach. Obviously we do not presume the relation to be an inevitable one. The sources of an active attitude are multiple and complex and not well understood; and many of them derive from aspects of individual psychological economy not directly related to differentiation. One source, for example, is a constitutional predisposition toward a low or a high energy level. Another is the individual's characteristic manner of resolving conflict about aggressive impulses. On the one hand, there may be a masochistic resolution, leading to abdication of self-assertion, and to the assumption of passivity. On the other hand, the resolution may take the form of intensification of overt aggressive behavior, the necessity of maintaining aggressive supremacy making for a high level of activity. Numerous other pathways may be sketched to suggest the varied sources of active or passive attitudes, and, therefore, the complex basis on which predictions in this area must rest.

To this point, evidence on the relation between active attitude and mode of field approach has not been considered. The available evidence is reviewed in the next section.

B. STUDIES OF ACTIVE ATTITUDE IN RELATION TO MODE OF FIELD APPROACH

1. TAT Studies

Two analyses were made of the TAT productions of our 10-year boys, both based on the hypothesis that children with a relatively analytical field approach would be more likely to create active, assertive characters in their stories.

a. Assertiveness. The stories for card 17BM, which shows a male figure on a rope, were found to be particularly useful for evaluating the assertiveness of the central characters created by the child. The question asked in assessing these stories was whether the child projected onto the central character feelings of "being in the saddle," of being the initiator, of being willing to struggle with challenging environmental forces; or, on the other hand, whether the central character was portrayed as being at the intersect of strong forces, from within or without, over which he has no control and which determine his fate.

A fourfold grouping of stories for card 17BM was made with regard to the degree of assertiveness of the central character in the story.[1] One group included stories in which the central character appears outstandingly assertive; takes command of a difficult situation; is an enterprising, strong, courageous person; enters a challenging situation and masters it; is an effective, competent person who performs well. Another group of stories, at the opposite extreme, portrayed the central character as in the grip of strong and/or hostile environmental forces which he cannot control and which may overwhelm him or from which he may somehow escape (as by running away or by someone else's intervention); or the central character is swept by strong, diffuse impulses which overwhelm him ("he's so mad he doesn't know what he's doing"). In the two middle groups of stories the central character is described as a fairly effective, assertive person, who performs well; or he is cast in a basically assertive role, though

---

[1] Here, as in the next analysis, the story to be evaluated was separated from the child's total test record by a staff member other than the rater.

also showing weakness; or he is characterized as preparing himself for a more assertive role in the future.

Ratings made by two independent judges of the 17BM stories from the 38 boys of Groups I and II, according to this fourfold classification, correlated .92 $(P < .01)$.

The assertiveness scores for these children correlated .50 $(P < .01)$ with their perceptual index scores. The relation did not hold on cross-validation, however; for the 30 Group-III boys, the correlation between assertiveness and perceptual index scores was −.07.

b. Counteraction. This analysis, in which an evaluation was made of the central character's response to adversity, was based on the "counteraction" concept of Murray, et al. (1943).

The stories for card 3BM were found particularly useful for this analysis. The solitary, bent-over figure shown on the card was seen as crying by the great majority of our children. The stories were evaluated from the standpoint of what the child conceives to be the outcome of a situation in which a person finds himself helpless or despondent, has suffered loss, separation, physical injury, etc. Is the central character left in this state, with no possibility seen of overcoming it, by whatever means? Or is he somehow pulled out of this state? Does he rise above the adversity? Is the situation changed so he can go on functioning?

Stories for card 3BM of the Groups I and II boys, which started with the central character in a "negative" state, were categorized on a twofold basis: as showing no counteraction; or as showing some form of counteraction, whether achieved by the central character's own effort, by the help of an outside agency (the intervention of another person or a change in the environment), by a combination of both, or by "fiat" (the situation being restored suddenly and without any preparation).

Ratings by two independent judges of the 3BM stories for the Groups I and II boys correlated .88 $(P < .01)$.

The point-biserial correlation between perceptual index scores and counteraction measures was .56 $(P < .01)$. Again, in a cross-validation study with the Group-III boys the difference proved not to be significant $(r = .30)$.

For neither the "assertiveness" nor "counteraction" analysis is our hypothesis confirmed.

An analysis of extent of self-assertiveness, also based on the TAT, did yield positive results in our earlier study of young adults (1954). According to the method devised by Hertzman a story was rated as showing a lack of self-assertiveness when the central character appeared ruled by circumstances, or unable to do anything about them, or abrogated or rejected his own needs. Conversely, a story was rated as showing self-assertiveness when the central character was portrayed as capable of coping with difficulties created by the environment and of maintaining the integrity of his own drives. A total rating was computed for each subject based on his fifteen TAT stories. These ratings related significantly to perceptual index scores, based on RFT and TRTC, for both men and women, and to EFT scores for men only, field-dependent subjects tending to create central characters less capable of self-assertive behavior. This rating procedure was subsequently applied to the TAT records for groups of male and female hospitalized psychiatric patients. The relationship was confirmed. For male patients, the correlation of these ratings with perceptual index scores (based on the RFT and TRTC) was .40 ($P < .05$), and with EFT scores .34 ($P < .05$). For women, the corresponding values were .51 ($P < .01$) and .45 ($P < .01$).[2] When the study was repeated with children, for three age groups of boys (8, 10, and 13 years) no significant relations were found between TAT self-assertiveness ratings and perceptual index scores, although in all instances the relation was in the expected direction.[3] The relation was significant for two of three age groups of girls (8- and 10-year-olds). In viewing the difference in results for adults and children in this earlier study, it must be considered that the TAT rating procedure had originally been developed for use with adults.

2. Active Attitude as Expressed in Posture

Common experience suggests that a tendency toward an active or passive attitude is directly apparent in the characteristic posture of the body. On this premise we made a study of the posture spontaneously assumed by children while being photographed.

Full-length front-view photographs were taken of 26 of the 30 10-year-old Group-III boys. The child was asked to stand toward the end of a corridor, away from the wall, in order that his picture might be taken for our records. No instruction was given as to pose to be assumed.

The photographs were then given to a judge who had never seen the

[2] The results for the hospital groups were presented in our previous report (1954, pp. 365–371) in terms of mean scores for low-, intermediate-, and high-index perceptual groups.

[3] Rosenfeld (1958) also found no significant relation between TAT assertiveness and EFT scores for a group of boys in the 13 to 15 year age range.

subjects. To insure that facial expressions would not enter into judgments, the face on each photograph was blotted out. The judge, Hanna Marlens, was asked to devise a scale for grouping these photographs according to characteristics of the posture the child had assumed. A 4-point scale was developed.

A rating of 1 (active-assertive stance) was given to photographs which showed the following characteristics: good body balance with weight evenly distributed; secure stance with feet slightly apart or active, challenging pose; body and head generally erect, yet without obvious tension; relaxed or purposeful, intentional positioning of arms and hands (e.g., on hips, in pockets, crossed). A rating of 4 (passive stance) was given to photographs which showed the following characteristics: slouching; tight unbalanced stance; feet turned in or twisted; rigidity, tension of posture; head drooping; hands hidden; tense extending of arms from body; twisting, curling, or extending of fingers. The intermediate points on the scale were defined with reference to these extremes.

One major criterion for ratings in this scale is the extent of assertiveness apparent in the stance assumed. A second is the degree of observable relaxation or tenseness. Tenseness is conceived not as a state of alertness, but as strain, discomfort, "nervousness," uncertainty as to what stance to assume; it is thus a deterrent to action. Both criteria thus refer to the person's "readiness for action," as expressed in posture.

Ratings of photographs according to this scale were found to correlate .43 ($P < .05$) with perceptual index scores. The correlation with intellectual index scores was .40 ($P < .05$) and with cognitive index scores .45 ($P < .05$). These findings suggest that in the stance they spontaneously assume children with an analytical field approach tend to give evidence of greater "readiness for action" than children with a global approach.

This study is yet to be repeated, but its results point to a promising line of research.

3. Other Studies

The results of several investigations, carried out mainly in other laboratories and using a variety of methods, are for the most part consistent with the thesis that people with an analytical field approach tend to have a greater interest in activity, striving, and assertiveness.

Linton [4] has investigated assertiveness of human movement re-

[4] Personal communication from Harriet Linton.

sponses on the Rorschach in relation to mode of field approach. Dividing the distribution of perceptual index scores (based on TRTC and EFT performance) for her group of college men into quartiles, she found that predominantly assertive movement responses were given most frequently by subjects in the highest (most field-independent) quartile.

Eagle (1959) investigated activity in the medium of manifest dream content. This was done as part of a more general study of differences in dreams of persons with contrasting modes of field approach. The dreams used in this general analysis were collected from 18 boys and 17 girls in one of our longitudinal groups when these subjects were 17 years old. Eight boys and 10 girls reported dreams which were sufficiently complete for analysis. Ratings of dream reports were significantly related to perceptual index scores. For boys, the Spearman rank-order correlation was .78 ($P < .05$), for girls it was .76 ($P < .05$).

The general ratings were based on evidence in ten content categories. Analysis of the data suggested that activity in the dream was the characteristic that most clearly distinguished persons with contrasting modes of field approach. Field-independent subjects tended to be active participants in their dreams, engaging in interaction with other characters, whereas field-dependent subjects tended to be passive observers.[5]

These findings enlarge the picture of differences in dream processes between persons with contrasting modes of field approach considered in the last chapter, where results on dream recall were presented.

Need-achievement, as reflected in TAT stories, provides still another kind of index of attitude toward activity. Wertheim and Mednick (1958), using college students, found a significant tendency for

[5] Other features of dream content may be related to mode of field approach. Thus, a study by Linton (personal communication) suggests that nightmares of falling are more common among field-dependent than among field-independent persons. In this connection, the description Harris (1948, 1951) has given of persons who typically report nightmares in which the dreamer has the sensation of falling through space is very similar to our characterization of relatively undifferentiated persons. People with nightmares of falling have personality attributes which are "outcroppings of a stage in ego maturation in which the infant has not fully individuated itself from the mother and consequently in which the psychic controls reside externally rather than internally. Thus, there is a tendency in falling persons, because of this particular type of maturation or failure of maturation, to rely on external controls and objects" (1951, p. 294). As shown in Chapters 17 through 22, children with a global field approach and other characteristics of limited differentiation have had relations with their mothers similar to those which Harris ascribes to persons with nightmares of falling.

subjects who were more field independent in EFT performance to score higher on need-achievement (determined according to the method developed by McClelland, et al., 1953), as expected. In this study results for men and women were combined. A recent repetition of this study (Honigfeld and Spigel, 1960), in which results for men and women were treated separately, confirmed the relation for women, although not for men.

Several studies have investigated the relation between achievement scores on the Edwards Personal Preference Schedule and extent of field dependence (Marlowe, 1958; Gardner, Jackson, and Messick, 1960; Dana and Goocher, 1959). The study of Gardner, Jackson, and Messick showed a significant relation between EPPS achievement measures and RFT scores, although the relationship did not hold for EFT scores. In the other two studies the achievement measure did not relate to EFT scores. As Marlowe has suggested, the differences between these results and the finding on need-achievement in the TAT may be a function of differences in the measuring instruments involved.

The more striving quality of persons with an analytical field approach may be reflected even in their grammatical style. In a study of career essays written by subjects with contrasting modes of field approach Doob (1958) found that subjects with an analytical approach were significantly more likely to use verbs indicating action (e.g., "I took"), while subjects with a global field approach favored passive verbs (e.g., "I was given").

The studies considered show some tendency for an active attitude to be more characteristic of persons with an analytical field approach, although the evidence is not very substantial.

These results certainly cannot be taken to mean that persons with an analytical field approach are likely to appear active in their behavior and persons with a global approach to be found sitting quietly in a corner. Not only may an active attitude be found in people with a global approach, but also such an attitude may be expressed in many forms other than directly observable behavior. Particularly among adults, we have encountered persons with a global approach who, in many aspects of their daily lives, appear aggressive, energetic, and interested in dominating people and situations. On the other hand, we have encountered adults and children with an analytical approach whose lack of interest in physical pursuits or in mastery over people made them seem passive as far as apparent behavior is concerned.

That being active, in a behavioral sense, is not necessarily distinguishing with regard to mode of field approach has been shown in several studies.

League and Jackson (1961), for example, have found the degree of participation in a small leaderless discussion group to be unrelated to the extent of field dependence, as measured by EFT performance. This result appears reasonable when viewed against our earlier observation that some people with an analytical field approach may show isolation from others. If activity-oriented, such people are apt to be interested in mastery over the environment, rather than interaction with others. They may therefore purposefully avoid leadership or even participation in social groups.

Another study, by Eskin (1960), shows in a dramatic way that persons with a global field approach need not be passive in their behavior. Using the RFT, Eskin evaluated extent of perceptual field dependence of several prisoner groups in a state penitentiary, each group constituted on the basis of a particular kind of criminal act. What is of interest for our present purpose is that this prisoner population was markedly field dependent. Yet their criminal acts identify them as behaviorally aggressive and rebellious rather than passive.[6]

That overt behavior toward others has a complex basis and is therefore not related to mode of field approach in simple, direct fashion is also apparent when we consider behavior ordinarily characterized as socially dependent.[7] A child with a global field approach, whose limitedly developed sense of separate identity leaves him without a sufficient inner directive for coping with a given problem, is likely to seek help from an adult. He is, however, more likely to seek help if he has a relatively active attitude and a trusting feeling toward people; on the other hand, if he has a passive attitude and is fearful of people, he may give up and withdraw instead of seeking help. The dimensions of active-vs-passive attitude and nature of emotional involvement with others,[8] knowledge of which is needed for effective prediction of behavior in the example cited, are only indirectly, and at most limitedly related to mode of field approach and level of differentiation. Prediction of overt social behavior from mode of field

[6] Of course, the forces that lead a person to criminal behavior are inordinately complex. Criminals cannot be characterized in a single, simple way, nor can they be thought of as a psychologically homogeneous group. It is possible to speculate that among criminals would be found many who seek to hide their passivity and inadequacy in exaggeratedly aggressive behavior.

[7] This particular issue was touched upon in Chapter 8.

[8] The latter dimension is considered further in relation to differentiation in Chapter 15.

approach is further complicated by the inevitable fact that outwardly similar behavior may have different motivational sources. For example, in children recognition-seeking may signify primarily a need for support from others and so be interpreted as socially dependent behavior, or it may signify primarily a strong interest in mastery. In the conceptualization of socially dependent behavior it seems useful to delineate the contributions of extent of sense of separate identity, active-vs-passive attitude, nature of emotional involvement with others, and kinds of motivation.

C. SUMMARY

In considering the relation between mode of field approach and activity it is necessary to distinguish among several different facets of what is ordinarily called activity.

The term activity has sometimes been used to refer to independence or, as we have called it, a sense of separate identity. As we saw in an earlier chapter, both on conceptual grounds and in evidence, sense of separate identity is closely linked to mode of field approach. Another meaning of the concept of activity is level of motorically expressed energy expenditure. There are no conceptual grounds for expecting a relation between activity in this sense and field approach. Concerning a third facet of activity, a quality of directedness, we considered in the previous chapter reasons for expecting a relation to mode of field approach and presented results of studies consistent with such an expectation.

In the present chapter we have given particular attention to still another facet of activity—assertiveness, striving, an interest in being active, or, as we labeled it, an "active attitude." Though on some limited conceptual grounds a relation between an active attitude and field approach may be anticipated, the sources of such an attitude are complex and not adequately understood. The weight of the evidence from the studies presented is that people with an analytical approach are more likely to show an active attitude than people with a global approach. The evidence is not conclusive, however.

The relation between active attitude and sense of separate identity was considered. As shown in an earlier chapter, the latter is closely linked, both on conceptual grounds and in evidence, to mode of field approach. Though a developed sense of separate identity may foster an active approach to the world, it by no means guarantees it; nor does it directly determine the area of investment of an active attitude when present.

11

VERBAL SKILLS

We have not performed studies expressly concerned with the relation between mode of field approach and verbal functioning, nor had we considered this relation in our conceptual framework. Evidence bearing on it has, however, accumulated in the course of analyses in which aspects of what may collectively be called "verbal skills" entered, although the particular kind of verbal skill at issue could not always be precisely identified. A definition of the relation between field approach and verbal skills must await studies in which various components of verbal skills are identified and considered separately. The evidence now on hand does, however, permit some tentative generalizations and suggests useful lines of research.

In the following sections we review and interpret this evidence, and consider directions for further research to which it points.

A. STUDIES OF VERBAL SKILLS

1. "Verbal Comprehension"

In our factor-analytic studies (Chapter 5) a verbal factor was identified, best defined by three WISC subtests: Vocabulary, Comprehension, and Information. Verbal index scores, based on scaled scores for these three tests, were not significantly correlated with measures of mode of field approach. This finding was of course anticipated on the basis of the extensive factor-analytic literature on the Wechsler scales.

The designation commonly used for this factor, which appears not closely related to mode of field approach, is "verbal comprehension."

2. "Verbal Expressiveness"

We have applied this term to the ability to give extended fluent verbal accounts.

We became interested in this aspect of verbal functioning in the course of two analyses of data for our 10-year-old boys. One was an analysis of children's interviews, the other the analysis of organization level in the TAT described in Chapter 6. Both analyses depended on verbal expressiveness to a greater extent than any other we have used, and in each case measures for the resulting scales were unrelated to mode of field approach. It was in the course of seeking to understand the basis of these findings that we explored the relation between verbal expressiveness and differentiation.

a. General clinical evaluations of interviews. Early in our work we attempted a broad clinical evaluation of our 10-year boys by means of interviews. Group-II boys were used in this study; the interview conducted with them was fairly unstructured and geared to eliciting attitudes and emotional reactions.

Transcripts of the interviews were given to a psychologist, Hanna Marlens, who had had no contact with the children. She was asked to classify the children on the most salient dimension of individual functioning suggested by the interview material itself.

"Level of maturity-adequacy" suggested itself to her in the course of studying the interview records, as a meaningful concept for classification of the children. With continued study of the records five categories along the maturity-adequacy-immaturity-inadequacy continuum emerged. In Category 1 were placed boys whose interviews gave evidence of most or many of the following characteristics: general immaturity, poorly developed self-concept, little sense of awareness, lack of insight, low critical abilities, underdeveloped expressive powers, passivity, overdependence, relative lack of orientation as to past events, little comprehension of relationships between events. In contrast, in Category 5 were placed boys showing the highest development of self-esteem, positive abilities for interpersonal relationships, active interests, vitality, good expressive and analytical abilities, greater insight, clear general orientation. The intervening points on the rating scale were established with reference to these two extremes.

When the interview ratings for the 24 Group-II children were compared to their perceptual index scores, a significant correlation of .49 ($P < .05$) was obtained. To validate this finding, the study was repeated with 29 of the 30 Group-III boys. The transcribed interview records [1] were evaluated by a second psychologist, Jane Schick, using an extensive written statement of the rating procedure devised by the first rater. The new rater practiced on a large number of the original Group-II interviews, in consultation with the first rater. When the classification made by the second rater of Group-III interviews was compared to perceptual performance, the relationship did not prove significant ($r = .18$). Nor did the classifications relate significantly to intellectual index scores ($r = .07$) or cognitive index scores ($r = .14$).[2]

One of the reasons that suggested itself as a possible basis for the failure of the rating scale on cross-validation was its emphasis on verbal expressiveness. Not only was verbal expressiveness ("good expressive abilities vs. underdeveloped expressive powers") explicitly included among the rating criteria, but it undoubtedly entered into the rater's impressions of a number of the other characteristics to be rated, particularly awareness and insight. This emphasis on verbal expressiveness, though later found to be inappropriate, apparently did not interfere with the successful application of the scale to the Group-II boys, for in that group there was a high relation between mode of field approach and measures of verbal skills. Revised Stanford-Binet Vocabulary scores correlated .56, $P < .01$, with perceptual index scores. (Such a relationship was not found in Group III. Measures of mode of field approach and WISC Vocabulary scores correlated only .24, not significant.) Under these circumstances, reliance on evidence of verbal expressiveness, required by the scale, may have proved especially misleading in predicting mode of field approach. Moreover, the high relation for Group III of the interview general clinical ratings to various verbal measures, and the negligible relation to measures of field approach, suggested that verbal expressiveness was featured in making ratings, whereas characteristics indicative of differentiation were not featured. (In this group, the interview general ratings correlated .49, $P < .01$, with WISC Vocabulary scores and .61, $P < .01$, with WISC verbal index scores, but only .18

[1] These were the records used in the evaluation of "cognitive clarity," described in Chapter 6. The psychologist who made the general clinical evaluation of these Group-III records had no knowledge of the cognitive-clarity analysis or of its use with these records. Also, the method used in the general clinical evaluation of the Group-II interviews was originally devised and applied prior to the development of the cognitive-clarity analysis, and by a different staff member.

[2] The absence of significant relationships in this analysis provided one of the early suggestions that degree of maturity (in the sense of developed differentiation *and* effective integration) was not necessarily related to mode of field approach.

with perceptual index scores and .07 with WISC intellectual index scores.)

The lack of relation of the interview ratings with measures of mode of field approach was not a function of lack of information in the raw data for making ratings, but rather of the interview scale definition and of the manner in which the data were processed. This is shown by the outcome of the cognitive-clarity analysis based on the same Group-III interviews. Not only was verbal expressiveness not included as a criterion for judging cognitive clarity, but the criteria used specifically minimized the role of verbal expressiveness. The very high, significant correlation (.77, $P < .01$) between cognitive-clarity ratings and perceptual index scores suggests that the interview records, used for both the cognitive-clarity and interview general-clinical ratings, were not deficient in information for making ratings.

b. The TAT level-of-organization analysis. As described in Chapter 6, ratings of level of organization of TAT stories were based both on productivity and on organization of the stories. These ratings related significantly to perceptual index scores for Group-II boys, but not for Group-III boys. A post hoc study of the TAT records of individual children in Group III, for whom the organization ratings assigned were markedly "off," suggested that the lack of relation could in part be attributed to reliance on verbal expressiveness as a major source of evidence in making ratings.

On the one hand, there were two boys with a markedly global field approach who received a high rating for level of organization. These boys, with strikingly discrepant verbal and intellectual index scores, are described in Chapter 15. One of these is Case #8 of that chapter. Their TAT stories, on retrospective study, showed good vocabulary and general knowledge and a high level of productivity and organization (although it is probably not an accident that their stories reflected little of the problems and struggles common to 10-year boys). One of them, the most field-dependent boy in his group, received the fourth highest rating for organization level.

On the other hand, there were several boys with an analytical field approach who, because of their limited productivity and verbal expressiveness, received low ratings for level of organization. Retrospective study of their TAT records suggested that the lack of productivity reflected a cautious, even evasive, approach to the task, seemingly motivated by a desire to avoid overinvolvement.[3] Several

---

[3] The child with the highest frequency of card rejections in the total group of 68 was a boy with an analytical field approach (Case #3 in Chapter 15).

of these children limited themselves to an "interpretative description" of the picture, or a Talmudic-like commentary on it; or they presented alternative possibilities, without definite commitment, concerning the feelings and actions of the characters and the outcome of the stories. In view of the criteria used in evaluating the organizational aspects of the TAT record, it is understandable that some of the analytical children who were noninvolved, evasive, and cautious might receive a low rating on the level-of-organization scale.

These impressions, gained from our attempts to understand the failure of the interview general analysis and TAT level-of-organization analysis, suggested that verbal expressiveness, as we have defined it, and mode of field approach are not closely related.

3. Evidence from Patterns of Intercorrelations

Another indication that level of particular verbal skills and extent of differentiation may not be closely related came from an analysis of patterns of intercorrelations among variables we derived from a variety of test procedures. The patterns found could reasonably be interpreted on the basis of the hypothesis that they are not closely related.

Table 11-1 presents a matrix of intercorrelations for Group III. The nine variables represented include two measures of mode of field approach (the perceptual index and WISC intellectual index) and a verbal measure (the WISC verbal index). The remaining six variables are based on the interview and the three projective tests. In the case of the interview and TAT, for which more than one variable was developed, we selected the two which are most comprehensive from the point of view of utilization of the raw data. Using comprehensiveness as a criterion, the cognitive-clarity and general-clinical ratings were selected to represent the interview, the task-approach and organizational-level ratings to represent the TAT.

Table 11-1 shows a clear grouping of the variables into two clusters, which are distinct, though showing some overlap. Each cluster is defined by the relatively high intercorrelations among measures within it, and the relatively low correlations between these measures and those in the other cluster. The two clusters are "boxed" in the table, and are referred to as Cluster 1 (variables 1 through 6) and Cluster 2 (variables 4 through 9). Common to both clusters are variables 4, 5, and 6, which relate at approximately the same level to measures in both clusters. The perceptual index and intellectual index (variables 1 and 2) may be considered the "key" to Cluster 1, the verbal index (variable 9) the "key" to Cluster 2.

Table 11-1. Intercorrelations among variables for Group III [a,b]

	1	2	3	4	5	6	7	8	9
1. Perceptual index	—	.66 **	.57 **	.33 *	.41 *	.77 **	.18	.12	.26
2. Intellectual index	.66 **	—	.54 **	.44 **	.26	.53 **	.07	.21	.28
3. Sophistication of body concept (figure drawing)	.57 **	.54 **	—	.42 **	.37 *	.44 *	.11	.06	.33
4. Approach to task (TAT)	.33 *	.44 **	.42 **	—	.52 **	.51 **	.56 **	.54 **	.45 *
5. Rorschach percept analysis	.41 *	.26	.37 *	.52 **	—	.46 **	.39 *	.57 **	.46 **
6. Cognitive clarity (interview)	.77 **	.53 **	.44 *	.51 **	.46 **	—	.53 **	.37 *	.54 **
7. Interview general clinical analysis	.18	.07	.11	.56 **	.39 *	.53 **	—	.55 **	.61 **
8. Organization level (TAT)	.12	.21	.06	.54 **	.57 **	.37 *	.55 **	—	.37 *
9. Verbal index	.26	.28	.33	.45 *	.46 **	.54 **	.61 **	.37 *	—

Cluster 1

Cluster 2

* Significant at the .05 level (one-tail test used for r between any pair of the following variables: 1, 3, 4, 5, 8; two-tail tests used for all other correlations).

** Significant at the .01 level.

[a] $N = 30$ for all correlations except those involving variable 7, where $N = 29$.

[b] The boxed-in areas represent the two main clusters.

Cluster 1 may best be interpreted as a "differentiation cluster." Of the three variables (1, 2, and 3) which are unique to this cluster, none involves verbal test productions. The correlations between measures of mode of field approach (variables 1 and 2) and each of the other variables have been presented in previous chapters. The intercorrelations among these variables are now presented in Table 11-1 for the first time. As we might have expected on the basis of the differentiation hypothesis, the correlations are all in the expected direction and all but one are significant.

Cluster 2 is clearly distinguishable from Cluster 1 and, from the variables of which it is composed, must involve some kinds of verbal skills, although their nature cannot be precisely specified. We may therefore consider it a "verbal cluster." The three variables which are unique to Cluster 2 (7, 8, and 9) are interview general-clinical rating, TAT level-of-organization rating, and the verbal index score based on the WISC. These three measures are significantly interrelated and are not related to any of the measures unique to Cluster 1. In the context of the correlational matrix, the status of the interview general-clinical rating and TAT organization-rating scales as providing mainly measures of some kinds of verbal skill becomes clear.

The three variables common to both clusters (the TAT "approach-to-task," Rorschach percept-analysis, and cognitive-clarity ratings) are all based on verbal test productions. They therefore understandably relate significantly to all of the variables in Cluster 2, which is best defined by the verbal index. However, they also relate significantly to all the variables in Cluster 1, defined by the perceptual and intellectual indices. Thus, to the extent that they were developed for use with material which is verbal in nature, these three rating scales do involve some kinds of verbal skills. Apparently, though, the criteria for making ratings were so defined that the ratings succeed in reflecting extent of differentiation as well. This makes it clear that we are not dealing simply with a division between measures from verbal and nonverbal tests.

Several conclusions are suggested by the correlational matrix in Table 11-1. First, Cluster 1 clearly consists of measures bearing on differentiation. Second, Cluster 2 consists of variables which most of all reflect some kinds of verbal skills. Third, the measures derived from verbal productions were all influenced by aspects of verbal skills, but in instances where the rating scales took account of such influence, the resulting measures reflected extent of differentiation as well. The measures which relate to variables in both Clusters 1 and 2 are in this category. Finally, extent of differentiation and the particular kinds of verbal skills involved seem to bear little relation to each other.

It may be inferred from the high correlations of measures of field dependence with performance scores of the WISC and the low correlations of these measures with WISC verbal scores that field-dependent children tend to do better on the verbal than on the performance part of the WISC. Some of the children we studied illustrate this relation in a striking way. The two boys mentioned above in the discussion of TAT level-of-organization ratings, and considered further in Chapter 15, showed a discrepancy of over 40 points between their verbal and performance IQs on the WISC, in favor of the former. There was a corresponding difference between their verbal and intellectual index scores: one boy had the highest verbal index score in his group of 30, and was seventh lowest in the group on the intellectual index; the other was third highest on the verbal index and fifth from lowest on the intellectual index. Both boys were seriously "overrated" as to probable extent of differentiation on scales derived from verbal productions which in varying degree had made no special provision for minimizing the influence of verbal expressiveness, namely the interview general-analysis, TAT level-of-organization, and Rorschach percept-analysis scales. Both scored appropriately "low" on the cognitive-clarity scale (which to some extent circumvented the influence of verbal expressiveness), on the sophistication-of-body-concept scale (developed for the one completely nonverbal technique), and on the perceptual and intellectual indices. With both children the investigators responsible for the TAT and Rorschach analyses had recorded their impressions, in the course of assigning ratings, that they were probably "overrating" these highly verbal boys.

Two other boys, not members of our regular groups, showed an intelligence test discrepancy in a direction opposite to that of the youngsters just considered. They were 18-year-old twins, former inmates of a state school for mental defectives. One boy had a full-scale Wechsler-Bellevue IQ of 77, with a verbal IQ of 62 and performance IQ of 98. The corresponding values for the other boy were 69, 57, and 89, respectively. In both cases the performance IQ was more than 30 points above the verbal IQ. Their verbal index scores on this test were 10 and 11, respectively, their intellectual index scores 29 and 30.[4,5] No discrepancy of this magnitude, in favor of ana-

[4] As described in Chapter 5, the verbal index score is the sum of the weighted scores for the Vocabulary, Information, and Comprehension subtests; the intellectual index score is the sum of the weighted scores for the Object Assembly, Block Design, and Picture Completion subtests. The intellectual index scores of these two boys are about at the level of the average of the group used in the standardization of the Wechsler-Bellevue; the verbal index scores are well below the average level.

[5] Baroff (1959) found in a study of intellectual patterning of preadolescent and adolescent defectives that the highest WISC subtest scores were on the subtests represented in our intellectual index, namely Object Assembly, Block De-

lytical ability, has been encountered in any of our normal groups of children. Corresponding to the level of analytical ability manifested on the WISC, these boys gave an "intermediate" performance in our tests of perceptual field dependence. Moreover, their figure drawings showed a moderately sophisticated body concept. The suggestion from the available data is that these boys were severely limited in verbal skills, and relatively developed with regard to differentiation in the areas considered.

4. Overcoming Embedding Contexts in a Verbal Medium

It might be anticipated that the ability to overcome an embedding context in the realm of configurational stimuli (as in our tests of mode of field approach) would be related to ability to overcome a context when dealing with verbal materials. Contrary to expectations, the results of several studies suggest that there may be little or no relation between these abilities. The clearest evidence came from the study by Podell and Phillips (1959). In this study a word-decontextualization test developed by Podell (1957) was used. This test made use of anagram problems which require the subject to rearrange a number of letters so as to form a word. For one set of problems the letters were initially presented in word form; for a second set, in random order. Podell postulated that the meaningful arrangement of the letters in the first set would serve an embedding function. In keeping with this expectation he found that anagrams are more difficult to solve if the initial arrangement of the letters is meaningful. However, using as a score the ratio of time required to solve the problem under embedding conditions to the time required under random conditions, Podell and Phillips found that this test did not load the spatial-decontextualization cluster and, we would presume, is probably unrelated to mode of field approach as well.

In a factor-analytic study, described in Chapter 5, Guilford, et al. (1957) used a test, Camouflaged Words, similar to Podell's. This test did not appear on Guilford's adaptive-flexibility factor.[6]

The results for the reconciliation-of-opposites test (Chapter 5) were of a similar nature. In including this test in our factor-analytic study

sign, and Picture Completion. In general, high grade non-brain-damaged defectives are more likely than children represented in our normal samples to do relatively well on performance as compared to verbal tests.

[6] In a study of Forehand (1958) a correlation of .35 ($P < .05$) was found between Gottschaldt scores and ability to overcome a context in a verbal task (word spacing). This correlation is of about the magnitude to be expected from the relation found between the analytical and verbal factors in our factor-analytic study.

we considered that the discovery of similarities in pairs of words whose obvious meanings make them opposites requires overcoming the context of "opposition." Accordingly, we expected this test to load the same factor as our perceptual tests. This expectation was not fulfilled. Instead, the reconciliation-of-opposites test was loaded on the verbal factor, although scores for this test correlated significantly with perceptual index scores.

Though they appear similar in requiring the overcoming of an embedding context, in ways that cannot now be clearly specified, verbal tasks and tasks involving configurational stimuli seem to exploit different skills.

B. STATUS OF EVIDENCE ON VERBAL SKILLS

The results of the above studies permit no more than some tentative suggestions as to the relation between field approach and verbal skills.

The patterns of intercorrelations described in Section A3 indicate, in a general way, that characteristics indicative of a high level of differentiation need not be associated with at least *certain* aspects of verbal functioning. Evidence from the other studies provides some suggestion as to the nature of the aspects of verbal functioning involved, although we can only begin to describe them.

First, "verbal comprehension," as this concept is used in the factor-analytic literature, is one aspect of verbal functioning that seems not to be closely related to mode of field approach and to other characteristics of developed differentiation. Analysis of the tasks on Wechsler Scales from which measures of it are derived would not lead us to expect a consistent relation between proficiency in this function and extent of differentiation. There are no clear grounds for anticipating differences between more differentiated and less differentiated children in fund of words (Vocabulary), knowledge of the right and wrong thing to do in particular situations, usually of a social nature (Comprehension), or knowledge of facts and events (Information).

It is of interest here that one of our 10-year boys with a global field approach was the winner of a spelling bee in a schoolwide contest. He was clearly able to build up a large fund of words, with an effective knowledge of their spelling.

Verbal expressiveness appears to be another ingredient of the verbal-skills complex involved in some of the studies considered. We applied this term to the ability to elaborate verbally, to give extended verbal accounts. These accounts are apt to have a quality of fluency and convey the impression that the verbal medium is a congenial mode of expression. Communications of children who showed verbal expressiveness at times had an adultlike quality.

It appears from the evidence on hand that some children with a global field approach may show verbal expressiveness. We have the impression, yet to be documented systematically, that such children may be able to limit and give cohesiveness to their verbally expressed ideas under conditions which permit them to operate more or less "on their own" (as in making up TAT stories). However, they may not be able to do this under the pressure of reality conditions with which they cannot easily cope (as in dealing with the directed questions of an adult on interview). We already mentioned the two boys who were able to construct TAT stories of a high level of organization but whose ratings for cognitive clarity on the interview were low. We also have the impression, again to be documented, that the precision in use of words of which such children seem capable does not reflect corresponding clarity of experience. In both these regards, we feel, there may be differences between verbally expressive children with a global and analytical mode of field approach. On the other hand, there are occasional children with an analytical approach who give evidence of experiencing themselves and their surroundings in articulated fashion, who yet seem to have limited ability to communicate their experiences in correspondingly clear verbal form.

In view of the gross way in which verbal expressiveness has been explored in our studies thus far, we cannot be certain whether it involves to any extent capacity for articulation of experience in a verbal medium. We therefore cannot say whether this capacity is related to capacity for articulation in the realm of configurational stimuli, as we might expect from our conceptual framework. It may be that it is not. Such a possibility receives some support from the evidence cited, particularly the findings of Podell and Phillips. However, further evidence would be desirable before rejecting the hypothesis to which our conceptual framework would lead, that persons with an analytical field approach will tend to show articulateness in their use of language.

Though numerous questions are left unanswered by the findings reported, the evidence does indicate that the development of at least some kinds of verbal skills may follow a different pathway than the development of mode of field approach and other characteristics of developed differentiation. Furthermore, our individual case studies show that some children who show limited differentiation in many areas of functioning give evidence of particularly marked development of some verbal skills. Such skills constitute a very real asset, both in the contribution they may make to a variety of specific activities and in the role they may play in interpersonal relations. The fact that children with a global field approach may have such assets shows once again that their limited capacity for articulation of experience does not imply a uniformly lower level of functioning. The results for the two retarded boys mentioned above also argue against the uniformity idea. Though having an intermediate status with regard to several of the indicators of differentiation for which evidence was available, their impoverishment in other areas (particularly those requiring verbal-social-communication abilities) was severe.

How can we account for the marked development of some verbal skills among particular children who show limited differentiation in many areas? Several possibilities may be considered in seeking to understand such a picture of uneven development.

Children whose limited self-differentiation and poorly developed capacity for control and direction of energy make the handling of many ordinary life situations difficult may substitute "talking about" for active coping with situations. This is illustrated by one of the two 10-year boys mentioned, who showed a global field approach and well-developed verbal expressiveness.

A "good conversationalist," as he was described by one examiner, he succeeded in impressing a group of adults (members of our staff); but as we watched him with other children it became obvious that his peers were not impressed with his verbal flow, in the absence of skills and interests appropriate to their age which they valued more. This same boy, who had moved away from the city, returned briefly for a visit several years later. He was more than willing to come in for another test series, because he had "nothing to do"; and again talked at length to all who would listen, painting a glowing picture of his life in the other city, his school work, and his friends. We knew from another source that his school work was going badly, that he had no friends, that he had "gotten into trouble" with school and civic authorities because of solitary "pranks," and was considered a behavior problem and a near-delinquent. What is of interest here is that, when talking with adults who were appreciative and interested, he made full use of his verbal skills in giving accounts of life situations with which he was apparently unable to cope.

In talking about experiences and feelings children such as this one can somehow "gloss over" things with which they cannot easily deal in real life encounters. By "talking nicely" they may win adult approval which they are not able to gain in other ways. The conversational efforts of some of them with laboratory personnel seemed clearly designed to "make an impression."

The adaptive value of language as a "security operation" was dramatically described by Sullivan (1947), who wrote:

The infant has as perhaps his mightiest tool the cry . . . From this cry is evolved a great collection of most powerful tools which man uses in the development of his security with his fellow man. I refer to language behavior . . . Originally the infant's magical tool for all sorts of purposes, all too many of us still use vocal behavior as our principal adaptive device . . . some people . . . can do in words practically anything and . . . have a curious faith that having said the right thing, all else is forgiven them. In other words, they are a little more like the infant than we are; they figure that a series of articulate noises turns any trick. We have, of course, learned that many other acts, performances, and foresights are necessary for success in living. None the less, denied our language behavior . . . we would be terribly reduced in our competence and materially diminished in our security in dealing with other people (p. 7).

Another possible reason for particular investment in some kinds of verbal skills on the part of individual children with a global field approach may lie in their greater need for guidance and support from others. Verbal communication serves to elicit suggestions and directions from other persons.

Still another related basis for disproportionate development of language is suggested by the results of a study by Haggard (1957).

Haggard's subjects were school children of superior intelligence and over-all academic achievement. Within this group, he identified three subgroups whose achievements were highest in spelling and language, reading, and arithmetic. Characteristics of the group of high achievers in spelling and language, identified on personality study, included among others marked passivity and dependence upon outside sources for direction of their thoughts and actions and reliance on conformance and social techniques to gain acceptance.[7] Haggard considered that such characteristics make understandable these children's interest in language and spelling which require the obedient carrying out of rules learned by rote. High achievers in reading showed a general picture of more independent functioning. Though reading, like spelling and language, involves verbal skills, it places more emphasis on relations and abstractions and an intellectually more active approach is required.[8] Finally, of high achievers in arithmetic

---

[7] These characteristics are similar to those shown by our relatively global children. The attitudes of high spelling achievers toward their parents were also characteristically different from those of children in the high reading and high arithmetic groups in ways that resemble the differences we found between global and analytical children (see Chapters 17–22).

[8] Carden (1958) and Iscoe and Carden (1961) have reported for boys a significant relation ($r = .69, N = 16$) between reading ability and perceptual field independence, as measured by EFT performance. For girls, the correlation was in the expected direction, but did not reach significance.

Haggard says, "they viewed it (the environment) with curiosity and felt capable of mastering any problems they might encounter . . . (They) were emotionally controlled and flexible . . . In their relations with authority figures and peers, they were more assertive, independent, and self-confident than were the children in the other subgroups" (p. 397). Many of these characteristics are similar to those we find to be common among children with an analytical field approach. This is understandable in view of the need for well-developed analytical abilities in many kinds of arithmetic operations.[9]

The results of this study by Haggard suggest that particular proficiency in spelling and language of some children with a global field approach may reflect their preference for tasks requiring obedient rote learning and application of mechanical rules toward which their need for external guidance directs them.

Finally, ways in which the home experiences of some global children may have contributed to their special interest in particular verbal skills are discussed in Chapter 22.

C. DIRECTIONS FOR FURTHER RESEARCH

The material considered thus far has been more useful in suggesting further research steps than in defining relationships.

First, it is necessary to repeat these studies with other groups. The presence in a group (Group III) as small as 30 of 2 cases with extraordinarily large discrepancies between WISC verbal and performance scores—larger than any we have encountered in our work with children—may have resulted in underestimating the relation between proficiency in the particular verbal skills evaluated and mode of field approach. Studies of groups drawn from other cultural backgrounds than the one from which our samples have come are also necessary to check the possibility that the relations we observed may be unusual because of the common emphasis on verbal skills in the culture from which the groups we studied were drawn.[10]

---

[9] We suggested in Chapter 5 that a distinction must be drawn between the requirements of different kinds of arithmetical tasks. The evidence suggests that in general only performance in relatively complex arithmetical tasks, requiring a fairly high level of reasoning, relates to mode of field approach.

[10] Since this book went to press such an investigation has been carried out by Silberman (1961). He found that a group of culturally impoverished 12-year-old boys showed patterns of intercorrelations among WISC subtests and EFT scores similar to those for our sample of the same age and sex but of much higher cultural status.

Another important research step is the more precise identification of components of the inadequately defined cluster of verbal skills involved in the studies described, and the investigation of these in relation to mode of field approach. Particularly important is the development of tasks which would permit a specific evaluation of extent of articulation in the medium of language.[11] It would be our expectation that this particular aspect of linguistic functioning would be related to mode of field approach and other characteristics of developed differentiation. Comparison of various aspects of verbal functioning in children with a relatively global or analytical field approach is also needed. A first step in this area might be a check on the differences postulated above between such children in considering verbal expressiveness.

Still another potentially profitable area of research is the study of differences in the relation of verbal skills and field approach to sex and aging. As described in our earlier report (1954), and as further considered in Chapter 13, men as a group tend to show a relatively analytical field approach and women a relatively global approach. At the same time, it is well known (see, for example, Tyler, 1956) that women are more proficient than men in many kinds of verbal skills. With regard to age trends, it has been found (Schwartz and Karp, 1960), that in old age there is a rapid change toward a more global field approach. In contrast, many kinds of verbal skills change relatively little with advancing age. The fact that verbal skills and mode of field approach seem to relate differently to sex and aging is consistent with the view that they may follow different paths of development. A deeper study of these patterns may help clarify the relation

[11] An example is the extent to which the child has developed a speech medium which is relatively differentiated from the sphere of action and perception. As Werner, Piaget, and others have pointed out, language is first intimately fused with action and perception and only gradually becomes separated from the realm of concrete activity. The young child first uses speech in conjunction with his ongoing activity and in time uses it to refer to such activity. Later on language is employed for the statement of relations among concepts and can be radically divorced from actual events. At this point, where the child defines words in terms of other words, where he creates through language objects which have no existence in his perceptual world, he may be considered to have reached the level of differentiation of linguistic behavior from the sphere of action and perception. Findings bearing on the relation of this aspect of linguistic behavior to mode of field approach might come from a test of "definitions." Such a test would need to use material which can evoke either a response involving the fusion of language with concrete context or a response which permits the distancing of language from such contexts. It is questionable whether the Vocabulary subtest of the WISC has this characteristic.

between verbal skills and mode of field approach as well as other characteristics of developed differentiation.

D. SUMMARY

Although neither our conceptual framework nor the design of the studies we performed considered the relation between verbal functioning and mode of field approach, some evidence on this problem emerged as a byproduct of our investigations. This evidence suggests that some "verbal skills"—the collective term for various kinds of verbal ability—show little or only a limited relation to mode of field approach and other characteristics of differentiation.

One kind of unrelated verbal skill has been designated "verbal comprehension" in factor-analytic studies of the Wechsler Scales. It is best defined by the Vocabulary, Information, and Comprehension subtests of the WISC and WAIS. Neither on conceptual grounds nor from the existing factor-analytic literature would we expect a relation to exist. A second kind of verbal skill which appears unrelated to mode of field approach has been designated "verbal expressiveness." It refers to the ability to give extended, fluent verbal accounts. This quality was explored through the medium of children's test productions, particularly such verbal tests as the TAT and interview. Verbal expressiveness was found in children with a relatively global and a relatively analytical field approach. There is the impression, however, that this quality is not encountered among children with a global approach under the pressure of reality conditions with which they cannot easily cope. Finally, there is some suggestion that ability to overcome an embedding context in the medium of language may not be related to the ability to do so in the medium of stimulus configurations. More evidence is needed, however, before finally deciding whether such a relation, which might reasonably be expected from our conceptual framework, exists or not.

It is clear that the growth of some kinds of verbal skills may follow a different path than the development of differentiation. Possible bases of the particularly marked divergence of these areas of development found in particular cases were considered.

Finally, some directions were sketched for further research which might help clarify the relation between verbal skills and mode of field approach and other characteristics of developed differentiation.

12

ADJUSTMENT AND PATHOLOGY

The evidence which is considered further documents the thesis, already mentioned in several contexts, that adequacy of adjustment and presence or absence of pathology are not related to mode of field approach. The evidence also shows that disturbances and pathology assume different forms among people with relatively analytical and relatively global field approaches. These findings support the view that differentiation and effectiveness of integration are not closely related and in several ways lend support to the differentiation framework.

Our main evidence comes from studies with pathological groups. Analyses of behavioral disturbances and difficulties in some of our "normal" children provide another source of evidence.

A. STUDIES OF PATHOLOGICAL GROUPS

Among adult hospitalized psychiatric patients we found (1954) performances ranging over the entire perceptual continuum. Sangiuliano (1951) obtained a similar result with hospitalized psychiatric women patients, and Pollack and Goldfarb [1] with disturbed children in a residential treatment center. Persons who are psychologically ill to the point of requiring institutional care, whatever their disturbance, are patently suffering difficulties in integration. That people in such a state may show either a global or an analytical field approach provides prima facie evidence that there is no direct linkage between mode of field approach and effectiveness of integration.

The finding that an analytical approach may be found among patients in a psychiatric hospital should put at rest in a final way any idea that persons with such an approach are paragons of psychological

---

[1] Personal communication from Max Pollack.

virtue. Among patients with an analytical approach we have studied there were those who were actively delusional, even at the moment of taking the perceptual tests; some of these were later sent to state hospitals, perhaps for the remainder of their lives. Sangiuliano reports that one of the most disturbed patients in her group was a field-independent woman who complained that the perceptual tests were "crooked" and "Wall Street stuff." Such observations argue strongly against the idea that an analytical field approach bespeaks good adjustment.

A noteworthy finding both of our own previous study and that of Pollack and Goldfarb is that perceptual performances in the groups used tended to cluster toward the extremes of the distribution, although no such clustering was reported by Sangiuliano. The possibility that pathology is less likely to develop among "intermediates" than among the extremes merits further investigation.

The field-approach dimension does not seem to relate to some of the commonly used nosological categories. Among our psychiatric patients we found cases diagnosed "schizophrenic" by the hospital staff scattered throughout the distribution of perceptual performances. Studies by Bennet (1956) and Bailey, Hustmyer, and Kristofferson (1961) showed no significant difference in RFT scores between schizophrenics and normals. No relation was found by Bound (1957) between perceptual field dependence and an index of "neuroticism," based on performance in three of Eysenck's primary suggestibility tests. Franks (1956) reports low, positive, but nonsignificant relations between RFT scores and neuroticism measures derived from the Maudsley Personality Inventory.[2] Of the 30 male dancers in the previously cited study by Gruen (1951), 22 were homosexuals. Despite the homogeneity of the group in this regard, these subjects gave performances ranging over the whole continuum of perceptual scores.

Although a particular mode of field approach does not seem to characterize patients in some of the major conventional diagnostic categories, there is a tendency, as we see later in this chapter, for persons who have certain specific symptoms in common to be similar in perceptual performance. There is no contradiction here. Nosological categories are, in varying degree, based on manifest symptoms, dynamics, and etiology. Moreover, the lack of correspondence between nosological classifications and the nature of the disease has

---

[2] Taft and Coventry (1958) found no relation between neuroticism measures derived from Cattel's 16PF battery and magnitude of errors in adjusting a luminous rod to the upright in a completely darkened room. The task of adjusting a rod in the absence of a visual field cannot, however, be considered to provide a measure of field dependence.

206   PSYCHOLOGICAL DIFFERENTIATION

frequently been pointed out (see, for example, Kruse, 1957). The situation is further complicated by the lack of consistency with which nosological categories are applied in diagnosis. On the other hand, to the extent that a given symptom is an end-product of particular dynamic processes, it may serve to identify these processes. Classification in terms of particular symptom pictures is therefore likely to bring together persons with common underlying dynamic processes. Although symptoms are the main basis of classification in some diagnostic categories, in many instances classification on the basis of symptoms may transcend common diagnostic categories. For example, depression may appear as a major symptom regardless of whether the over-all diagnosis is neurosis, schizophrenia, reactive depression, etc.

The finding that mode of field approach, which mirrors deep aspects of psychological make-up, cuts across some of the conventional nosological categories is consistent with the growing shift in clinical classification from an emphasis on behavioral to an emphasis on dynamic characterization. Mode of field approach may thus offer one potentially useful basis for clarifying nosological problems.

Several studies have compared *kinds* of problems and symptoms encountered in people with a relatively analytical or relatively global field approach. The differences found may perhaps be understood on the basis of the differentiation framework.

In our 1954 study we found that the disturbances of psychiatric patients with a relatively global field approach often involved severe identity problems without evidence of struggle for clearer self-definition; poorly developed controls, resulting in chaotic functioning; strong uncompensated feelings of inadequacy; passivity; and helplessness. In contrast, patients with an analytical field approach tended to show expansive and euphoric delusions, self-aggrandizement, outward direction of aggression, isolation, overideation, and continuing struggle for the maintenance of identity, however bizarre the attempt.

Several studies have demonstrated marked field dependence in clinical groups with symptoms commonly regarded as rooted in severe dependency problems or in what we earlier called a lack of developed sense of separate identity. The groups covered by these studies were ulcer patients (Gordon, 1953), alcoholics (Witkin, Karp, and Goodenough, 1959; Bailey, Hustmyer, and Kristofferson, 1961; Karp, Poster, and Goodman, 1960), obese people (Pardes and Karp, 1958), asthmatic children (Fishbein, 1958).[3]

[3] These findings do not contradict the view that there is no difference in mode of field approach between some nosological categories. The groups considered here were all constituted on the basis of having a symptom or problem in com-

The results of the study by Gordon (1953), discussed in part in Chapter 8, suggest that dependent attitudes are reflected in field-dependent perception even in people who seek to cope with them by means of defensive striving. Gordon found no differences among groups of ulcer patients, neurotics, and normal controls in self-ratings on his dependency scale. In RFT performance, however, the ulcer patients were markedly more field dependent than the other two groups. In evaluations made of them by physicians, the ulcer patients were rated significantly more dependent than the neurotics. For the neurotics, the measures of dependency provided by self-ratings, RFT performance, and physicians' ratings were significantly interrelated. For the normal controls, the first two measures—the only ones available for them [4]—were also significantly related. For the ulcer patients, on the other hand, RFT performance and physicians' ratings were related, but RFT scores did not agree with self-ratings. As a group, the ulcer patients judged themselves to be more independent than their RFT performance and physicians' ratings indicated.

The discrepancy between self-ratings of dependency and RFT performance of ulcer patients is of particular interest.[5] The direction of the discrepancy suggests that, although tending to be very field dependent in their perception, these patients view themselves as relatively independent. A common clinical view of the ulcer patient is that of an overstriving person who through his striving is seeking to compensate for deep-seated passivity and persistent dependency needs (see, for example, Alexander, 1950). He seeks to make himself appear, both to himself and others, more active than he is, and capable of functioning independently of external support. Such an interpretation would be consistent with Gordon's results. It is possible that an individual's perceptual performance may "penetrate" the apparent assertiveness and reflect the strong underlying passivity and need for external support.

The study by Zukmann (1957), cited in Chapter 9, is relevant here in showing that people with contrasting field approaches tend to de-

mon, although members of a group might have a variety of psychiatric diagnoses. Thus, the group that had alcoholism as a common problem included individuals diagnosed as schizophrenic, character disorders, various types of neurosis, etc.

[4] The normal controls were not rated by physicians.

[5] It is possible that ulcer patients were rated by physicians as more dependent than anxiety neurotics because of a methodological artifact. To the extent that there is a prevailing view of ulcer patients as dependent, the physicians who rated them might have been guided by this general view, rather than by the particular characteristics of the patient. Self-ratings, however, do not suffer from this methodological difficulty.

velop different kinds of pathology, as anticipated. Patients in private psychiatric treatment, diagnosed as hysterics, were significantly more field dependent than obsessive-compulsive patients.

Taylor (1956) found differences in perceptual performance between delusional and hallucinatory psychotics. He postulated that hallucinatory states imply the dissolution of ego-boundaries whereas delusional states represent attempts to maintain separate identity and ego-integrity. Compared to hallucinations, delusions have a more logical structure and they do not represent as gross a fusion between self and nonself. In hallucinations, inner states often become indistinguishable from reality, reflecting reduction of ego-integrity and of sense of individuality to an infantile stage. From these premises, Taylor hypothesized that hallucinatory psychotics would tend to be more field dependent than delusional psychotics. He predicted, too, that psychotics who showed neither delusions nor hallucinations, and who might therefore be regarded as better able to maintain separation from the field on the basis of adequate ego-boundaries, would be less field dependent than the hallucinatory group, but not different from the delusional group. Results with a scale devised by Lorr (1953),[6] as well as data gathered from ward personnel, were used to set up groups of hallucinatory, delusional, and nondelusional-nonhallucinatory male psychotic patients. Cases showing both hallucinations and delusions were not used. To evaluate field dependence, Taylor employed the EFT. As hypothesized, the delusional group was significantly less field dependent on the EFT than the hallucinatory group; and the nondelusional-nonhallucinatory group was significantly less field dependent than the hallucinatory group, but not significantly different from the delusional group.[7]

The most direct application of the differentiation dimension to the study of types of psychopathology is found in an unpublished investiga-

[6] The indicators of delusional symptoms in this scale reflect the patient's use of self-aggrandizing mechanisms and self-preserving projection; for example, people are talking about him and watching him; he is endowed with special powers; he has great wealth; his mission is to spread new ideas in the world.

[7] Cohen, Silverman, and Shmavonian (1959) report interesting preliminary findings on the relation between mode of field approach and type of imagery induced by sensory isolation. According to these authors (and according to findings by Holt and Goldberger, 1959) the frequency of imagery has no apparent relation to extent of field dependence, but field-dependent subjects more often believe that their images have an "outside" source. The suggestion that hallucinatory-like experiences are more often encountered in normal, field-dependent people under conditions of sensory isolation points to a promising line of work which makes contact with Taylor's finding on symptomatology in schizophrenics.

tion by Korchin.[8] Subjects in the study were 62 patients (26 men and 36 women), successive admissions, except for patients too grossly psychotic or uncooperative for testing, to an out-patient psychiatric clinic in Genoa, Italy. These patients were classified into two major groups. One group consisted of patients who presented clinical pictures conceived to represent a relatively high level of differentiation. Included in this group were borderline and ambulatory schizophrenics with a reasonably well-developed defensive structure, and neurotics with organized symptoms. The second group consisted of patients whose clinical pictures were conceived to reflect a relatively low level of differentiation. In this group were placed patients with character disorders (generally inadequate personalities who had been unable to manage the ordinary problems of living); patients who somatised their complaints and denied any psychological problems; and patients whose primary symptom was direct affective discharge rather than defensive symptom organization. Each patient was given the EFT. Analysis of variance showed the less differentiated group to be significantly more field dependent than the more differentiated group, as expected. Once again, significant sex differences were found, women being more field dependent than men; and the sex-clinical group interaction was not significant.

The evidence considered thus far suggests that when they become psychologically ill persons with contrasting modes of field approach are apt to develop different kinds of pathology. From the relationships reported in previous chapters one might reasonably expect that pathological groups showing a relatively analytical or relatively global field approach would show other manifestations of more developed or less developed differentiation. The evidence now available is consistent with this expectation. Some of the characteristics given above of psychiatric patients in our 1954 study and patient groups in other studies suggest that patients with a more analytical approach are generally more likely to have a relatively developed sense of separate identity, however pathological its form. The study of alcoholics by Karp, Poster, and Goodman, already cited, provides evidence on another manifestation of differentiation, articulateness of body concept. The figure drawings obtained from their alcoholic women were compared to drawings from a nonalcoholic control group, according to the sophistication-of-body-concept scale. The mean rating for alcoholic women was significantly lower than for the control women, suggesting a tendency for the body concept to be less articulated in

[8] Personal communication from S. Korchin.

this group. Finally, the Korchin study and the study by Zukmann, cited above, suggest that patient groups with a more analytical field approach give evidence of a relatively developed defensive structure, in comparison to patients with a more global approach. The systematic study of pathological groups with contrasting modes of field approach, according to various indicators of more developed or less developed differentiation, would appear to be a useful direction for further research.

It seems possible to conceive of the disturbances observed among patients with a global field approach as of the kind likely to follow from impaired integration in limitedly differentiated persons; the disturbances found in patients with an analytical approach may be considered to reflect impaired integration in relatively differentiated persons.[9] The linkages between extent of differentiation and preferred forms of pathology are not easily worked out. For one thing, the pathways by which particular kinds of pathology may emerge in particular personality settings are inordinately complex and difficult to trace; for another, level of differentiation is only one determinant, though an important one, of the course that pathological development may take. Moreover, present knowledge of the dynamics of various kinds of pathology is limited. Even with these difficulties, it seems possible to see, for at least some of the pathological states considered above, why they may be expected to arise in a setting of relatively developed differentiation, on the one hand, or limited differentiation, on the other.

We already considered (Chapter 9) how it is that symptoms such as direct affective discharge are more likely to develop in less differentiated persons and symptoms such as overintellectualization in more differentiated persons.

As another illustration, we may speculate about some of the ways in which the characteristics of limitedly differentiated persons make the development of obesity more likely among them. Their inadequately developed sense of separate identity makes it plausible that under stress they would seek comfort in oral activities that had been an important source of satisfaction in the period of close unity with mother. As a technique of defense for dealing with anxiety, eating is a nonspecialized defense. It is applied indiscriminately in a wide range of stressful situations, and it does not act in a specific, directed fashion

[9] Lewis (1958) has given a very rich account of alternative directions of pathological development similar to these in her characterizations of "over-differentiated" and "under-individuated" people.

upon the source of stress. In particular kinds of persons, it may suffuse the organism with an animal pleasure which blurs anxiety.

We may think along similar lines about alcoholism, a condition which, in its dynamic aspects, is often considered equivalent to obesity. The nonspecialized character of the defense which the use of alcohol represents is particularly clear. Alcohol is resorted to when stress becomes too great, regardless of the source of the stress, and it seems to affect experience in general, not only the part responsible for the anxiety. If the drinking is carried far enough, the self, which to begin with is limitedly differentiated, may be temporarily obliterated.

Obviously, a symptom like alcoholism is only one of many possible "choices" of pathology open to the relatively undifferentiated person when integration becomes impaired. Reflecting the possibility that the same symptom may be achieved by different dynamic routes, we must recognize that alcoholism may also be the choice of relatively differentiated persons. Although we have found in our work that alcoholics who perform in a field-independent fashion are quite rare, their very existence points to the need for seeking other routes to the development of alcoholism than the one considered.

A final illustration may be found in patients in whom paranoid reactions are central in the symptom picture. In this patient group, an analytical field approach is frequently found. Projection, a characteristic defense of the paranoid, is quite specialized in comparison to such generalized tension-reducing techniques as eating and drinking. The paranoid projects his own system of ideas upon the world, and does so in a highly selective fashion—particular people, particular situations may be especially implicated. Such selectivity requires that experience of the world be articulated. In this connection, the paranoid is noted for the detailed, articulated system of ideas he develops. As an attempt at preservation of the self, projection contrasts with the alcoholic's preferred way of dealing with stress, which in extreme cases results in the dissolution of the self in drink. The use of projection as a device for self-preservation, however bizarre, presupposes a self that has achieved some degree of differentiation.

These illustrations, though sketchy, suggest that the characteristics of relatively greater or more limited differentiation may play a role in channeling pathological development.

The differentiation concept seems to provide a useful approach to the study of differences among people in directions of pathological development and in choice of symptoms. At the present time, however, it is most useful in considering the basis of differences in general classes of pathology and symptom-formation. For an understanding of "choices" within a general class it is very likely necessary to consider individual patterns of integration and impairment of integration, as well as specific content aspects of individual personality and prevailing life circumstances. For example, we have found that both alcoholics and obese people tend to be extremely field dependent. However, the question remains as to why some limitedly differentiated people choose drinking as their main symptom while others choose overeating. To answer this question intensive study of individual cases showing such symptoms is required, with attention given to specific patterns of integration, to particular content aspects of personality, and to nature of life circumstances. As an illustration of how these may be important, the suggestion has been made that an individual's personal values, derived from his cultural group, may place a taboo on drinking and so make overeating a more likely symptom choice. The specific values an individual holds represent a content aspect of his personality. As a natural extension of our work we are planning to carry out intensive studies of individual pathological cases in which evidence of development of differentiation is considered along with nature of integration and specific content aspects of personality.

B. DISTURBANCES IN "NORMAL" CHILDREN

Because they were infrequent, disturbances sufficiently severe to be considered pathological could not be studied systematically in our group of school children. There were, however, 6 boys among our 68 10-year-olds who stood out as seriously disturbed. Four of these 6 boys fell in the field-dependent group, when the perceptual distribution was divided into three segments, and one each in the field-independent and intermediate groups. In all 4 seriously disturbed field-dependent children the outstanding feature of the disturbance was impulse disorder. (Case #7, Arthur, in Chapter 15, is one of these.) The severely disturbed boy in the field-independent group (Nick, Case #5 in Chapter 15) showed marked paranoid trends. This is consistent with the finding for adults, noted earlier in our 1954 study, that paranoid and delusional patients are likely to be relatively analytical in their field approach. The sixth seriously disturbed boy, with an intermediate perceptual performance, showed marked grandiosity, near-delusional trends, and impaired reality testing.

Also relevant here are the adjustment difficulties, reviewed in Chapter 15, found in children with different modes of field approach. Among children with a relatively global approach the difficulties stemmed largely from impulse control problems, a poorly developed sense of responsibility, and lack of resources and initiative. Among children with an analytical approach problems were more likely to stem from too rigid controls, too great emotional distance, too great an investment in intellectualization and intellectual life, sometimes with corresponding circumscription of interpersonal relations. Though, as we shall see, children with an analytical approach had their share of fears, these fears, whatever their dynamic significance as symptoms, were of a circumscribed nature, and some countermeasures against incapacitation had been developed.

The trend of the differences between children with a relatively global and relatively analytical approach in problems of adjustment and methods of dealing with these problems appears consistent with the view that they differ in extent of differentiation.

C. SUMMARY

The global-analytical dimension of cognitive functioning appears not to relate to presence or absence of pathology, adequacy of adjustment, or some of the conventional psychiatric nosological categories. However, the *kinds* of problems, symptoms, and maladaptations found in children and adults with contrasting modes of field approach appear to be different. Among persons with a global field approach we find severe identity problems, with little struggle for maintenance of identity; symptoms often considered suggestive of deep-seated, unresolved problems of dependence, as alcoholism, obesity, ulcers, and asthma; and inadequately developed controls, resulting in chaotic functioning and passivity and helplessness. When such persons develop severe pathology, they are more likely to show hallucinations as part of their symptom picture. In contrast, disturbances in persons with an analytical field approach are apt to involve overcontrol, overideation, and isolation. In severe pathological states, such persons are likely to develop delusions, to have expansive and euphoric ideas of grandeur, and to engage in attempts at maintenance of identity, however unrealistic.

Persons with a relatively global or relatively analytical approach in a pathological state may apparently be distinguished according to most of the postulated indicators of differentiation. The differentiation concept may be useful in understanding the differences in disturbances and pathology found among adults and children with contrasting modes of field approach.

13

SEX DIFFERENCES

An early consistent finding of our investigation of individual differences in perception was that women tend to be more field dependent than men (Witkin, 1949b). A number of studies have substantially confirmed this finding for a variety of groups. Other studies, of a developmental nature, have demonstrated sex differences in perception at different age levels. Sex differences have also been reported in the performance of intellectual tasks which, in common with our perceptual tests, require the overcoming of an embedding context.

The results of these studies contribute to a picture of small but persistent sex differences in style of field approach. They also raise interesting questions concerning sex differences in differentiation, as well as the role of cultural and constitutional factors in the origins of sex differences.

A. SEX DIFFERENCES IN MODE OF FIELD APPROACH

1. Sex Differences in Perception

A number of studies with the RFT and EFT (or Thurstone Gottschaldt) have been reported, many of them confirming, for both adults and children, our original finding of sex differences in extent of field dependence (Newbigging, 1952, 1954; Miller, 1953; Wit, 1955; Gump, 1955; Andrieux, 1955; Franks, 1956; Bennet, 1956; Zukmann, 1957; Seder, 1957; Young, 1957; Pollack;[1] Carden, 1958; Bieri, Bradburn, and Galinsky, 1958; Chateau, 1959; Gross, 1959; Fink, 1959; Korchin;[2] Goodnow[3]). Our studies of perceptual development (Witkin, Good-

---

[1] Personal communication from Max Pollack.
[2] Personal communication from Sheldon Korchin.
[3] Personal communication from Robert Goodnow.

enough, and Karp, 1959) have demonstrated sex differences down to the 8-year level. Analyses of variance, based on cross-sectional data, showed significant sex differences for both tests. At ages younger than 8 the sex differences problem cannot be easily investigated, since these tests are not well suited for children below that level. However, studies of children in the 5- to 8-year range, with perceptual tests similar to the EFT and RFT, suggest that there may be no significant sex differences in field dependence at these younger ages (Crudden, 1941; Goodenough and Eagle, in press). There is also evidence suggesting an absence of sex differences in geriatric groups (Schwartz and Karp, 1960).

The picture for the BAT is less clear-cut. We found in our 1954 study that in the period of young adulthood women are more field dependent than men in this situation, as they are in the EFT and RFT. However, our cross-sectional and longitudinal studies of perceptual development showed no significant sex differences at earlier ages (Witkin, Goodenough, and Karp, 1959). At the present stage of evidence, we cannot interpret this finding with confidence. It is to be noted, however, that, in contrast to both the EFT and RFT, the BAT requires elaborate equipment. The BAT has therefore not been used in studies outside our laboratory so that there has not accumulated as much information about it. A possibility to be checked in further research is that sex differences emerge at a later age in the BAT than in the EFT or RFT.

Sex differences in extent of field dependence have been reported for diverse groups. In this country sex differences have been observed in groups of various educational and socio-economic backgrounds. They have also been observed in a number of Western European countries. Newbigging (1952, 1954) has reported significant sex differences, in the expected direction, for a group of English subjects tested with the EFT. Again with English subjects Bennet (1956) found significant sex differences on the RFT, and Franks (1956) found differences in the expected direction, although not significant, for a modified version of the same test. Wit (1955), using a modified version of the RFT and the EFT, has confirmed our sex differences finding for a group of Dutch subjects. Andrieux (1955) has observed similar sex differences among French adults tested with a modified group-administered EFT, and Chateau (1959) among French children and young adults in a Gottschaldt-like test. Korchin found significant sex differences in EFT performance in a group of Italian psychiatric patients. Finally, sex differences in the EFT performance have been reported by Goodnow for Hong Kong subjects. It is clear that the sex differences in field dependence we first observed in a group of college students exist in quite different groups as well; and they even "survive" the variations in culture among the geographic areas mentioned.

There is also evidence that *within each sex* mode of field approach is related to measures of masculinity and femininity. Miller (1953) reports a significant relation for men, although not for women, between scores on the masculinity-femininity scale of the MMPI and scores for the EFT. Fink (1959) has found a significant relation between these measures for both men and women. Crutchfield, et al. (1958) also found a significant relation for their group of Army captains between MMPI masculinity-femininity scores and RFT but not Thurstone Gottschaldt performance. Holtzman and Bitterman (1956) failed to find a significant relation between these same measures, but there is some question whether their modification of the RFT provides a valid measure of field dependence. Gump (1955) reports correlations for four different groups (two of each sex) between masculinity scale scores of the GAMIN and Thurstone Gottschaldt scores. All are in the expected direction, although only one is significant.

Indirect evidence of sex differences in the articulation of experience is provided by the finding already considered (Chapter 6) that girls showed poorer memory than boys for the TAT, taken 3 years before. The concept used to account for individual differences in memory would suggest, as an interpretation of this finding, that boys experienced the initial situation in more articulated fashion.[4]

2. Sex Differences in Intellectual Functioning

A tendency toward an analytical or a global field approach has been shown to manifest itself pervasively throughout an individual's perceptual and intellectual functioning. From the finding of consistent sex differences in the perceptual area, we may reasonably expect parallel sex differences in the intellectual area. There is ample evidence to support such an hypothesis.

Before reviewing particular investigations, a special difficulty in the study of sex differences in intellectual functioning should be noted. In the construction of standard tests of intelligence, items which consistently favor one sex are often excluded; data from standard intelligence tests are therefore of very limited use for the problem of sex differences. Even with test content that has not been subject to pre-

---

[4] The sex difference in favor of boys for long-range memory is particularly interesting in view of the well-established finding that girls are superior in short-range memory (Tyler, 1956).

selection on this basis, there is the problem of differences between the sexes in educational background and interests. Such differences may well make for differences in amount and kind of specific knowledge available to the two sexes for the solution of particular kinds of problems, thereby confounding the interpretation of data.

Nevertheless, in studies using a variety of problems the anticipated sex differences in intellectual functioning have been observed.

Of particular relevance is the study by Guetzkow (1951) of the Einstellung situation, referred to in Chapter 5. Guetzkow found men to be superior to women in set-breaking capacity, but not in susceptibility to set. As we would anticipate, sex differences occur when the task requires overcoming a context, which, as suggested in Chapter 6, is involved in set-breaking. They do not occur when this requirement is lacking, as in the set-inducing conditions.[5] In a similar study, Harris (1950) did not find significant sex differences in set-breaking capacity; the number of cases was much larger, however, in Guetzkow's study. Guetzkow's results would seem to warrant a repeat study with particular focus on the sex differences problem.

The most comprehensive investigation of sex differences in problem solving has been conducted by Sweeney (1953). Sweeney's hypothesis was that men are more effective than women in solving problems which require restructuring. Using a wide variety of types of problems he was able to confirm this hypothesis, even when the groups of men and women compared had been matched with respect to general intelligence, relevant special abilities, and level of specific information. Sex differences in performance on similar problems which did not require what we have called ability to overcome embedding contexts were generally not significant with these variables controlled.

This survey is by no means exhaustive.[6] The studies cited are, however, illustrative of a large number which have demonstrated sex differences in performance of intellectual tasks which require the overcoming of an embedding context, paralleling the sex differences observed in perceptual situations.

As in perception, significant relations have been found within each sex between masculinity-femininity measures and problem-solving behavior. Thus, Milton (1957) has reported significant relations between scores on various masculinity-femininity scales and skill in solving problems requiring restructuring.

Taken together the evidence demonstrates pervasive sex differences

---

[5] It does not seem likely that these findings could be interpreted on the basis of sex differences in availability of information.

[6] See, for example, Maier (1933) and Saugstad (1951).

in mode of field approach. Women as a group tend toward a global field approach in their perceptual and intellectual functioning, men toward an analytical approach. The differences between the sexes, though clear-cut and consistent, tend to be small compared to the range of individual differences within each sex. Sex differences are found through much of the life span, although below 8 years and above 60 they may be slight or not exist at all.

B. SEX DIFFERENCES IN OTHER ASPECTS OF DIFFERENTIATION

If, as considered in Chapter 2, mode of field approach is in fact one of a larger constellation of characteristics reflecting extent of differentiation, we would also expect a tendency toward sex differences in such areas as sophistication of body concept, sense of separate identity, and structure of defenses and controls.

Our own work has not been specifically directed toward investigating sex differences in these areas. In our studies of children we have used mainly boys, and our rating procedures were not developed with the sex differences problem in view. Unless such an interest is specifically present, it is likely that raters, in evaluating qualitative data, will adapt their standards to the sex of the subject, and so obscure sex differences. A systematic check of the hypothesis concerning sex differences in differentiation requires studies which seek specifically to evaluate sex differences in the various areas indicated. We may, however, look for leads in the comprehensive surveys of sex differences available in recent works on individual differences (Tyler, 1956; Anastasi, 1958). The evidence in these surveys suggests that sex differences may in fact exist, as expected, in several of the areas. There is the impression too that some of the diverse, well-documented sex differences that have been described in the literature may be interpreted and related on the assumption that men tend to be more differentiated than women.

The evidence is particularly suggestive in the area we have been calling "sense of separate identity." In accord with expectations, many studies have found sex differences in some behavior manifestations suggestive of a developed sense of separate identity. Some of the evidence may be cited as illustrative.

Women as a group have repeatedly been described as more dependent on others than men. They are apt to be more concerned with people and with the impressions they make. In line with this, they tend to be better in such specific activities as guessing ages and distinguishing between types of appearance (Tyler, 1956). Women are also superior to men in memory for names and faces (Witryol and Kaess, 1957). Concern for facial expressions of others, it was suggested in Chapter 8, is apt to be a characteristic of people with a relatively undeveloped sense of separate identity and is common among persons with a global field approach.

Women as a group also seem more likely than men to use external standards for definition of their attitudes and judgments. Janis, et al. (1959) have reported that high school girls are more susceptible to persuasion than high school boys. Laboratory studies of conformity to group pressure (Feinberg, 1951; Crutchfield, 1955, 1957; Nakamura, 1955) have demonstrated significantly greater adherence of women to the group standard. Patel and Gordon (1961) found that "planted" suggestions on a test paper had a greater effect on test responses of girls than on test responses of boys.

A study reported by McClelland, et al. (1953) showed that n-achievement is increased for women, but not for men, when withdrawal of social acceptability is threatened. Under stress of intellectual failure, however, n-achievement is increased for men but not for women. McClelland, et al. have suggested that this difference may be based on the greater dependence of women on others.

In occupational preferences, women show significantly greater interest in certain service areas in their responses to the Strong Vocational Interest Blank (Strong, 1943). Within groups of men such interests tend to be more common among persons with a global field approach (Crutchfield, et al., 1958).[7]

In quite another area, that of verbal skills, sex differences take the direction we might expect on the basis of the evidence in Chapter 11. When differences between men and women in verbal functioning are found, it is women who appear to develop at a more rapid pace. Tyler (1956) has summarized the available evidence as follows: "From infancy to adulthood, females express themselves in words more readily and skillfully than males. Throughout the grades and high school, they obtain higher scores on verbal sections of intelligence tests and do better work in English courses" (p. 252). Although there may be other reasons for these sex differences, their occurrence is consistent with the suggestion in Chapter 11 that disproportionate investment in

---

[7] As a related finding, Linton (1952) has reported that the conforming subjects (as established in part by performance in our perceptual tests) in her group of college men were more likely to indicate a preference for conventional professions. Karp (1957) found a similar relation in a study of occupational preferences of boys.

verbal skills (as compared to analytical and related functions) is particularly apt to occur among people who show a global field approach and who are less differentiated.

The hypothesis that in our culture men and women as groups tend to be different in extent of differentiation in various areas of functioning clearly merits further investigation. The concepts and procedures that have emerged from our work suggest some of the research routes that may be followed in submitting this hypothesis to systematic test.

C. SOME SPECULATIONS ABOUT THE SOURCES OF SEX DIFFERENCES

The origin of the sex differences that have been described remains a problem for further investigation. Any speculation must presuppose a multiple basis.

One possibility, suggested in our earlier report (1954), is that differences between men and women in biological role and anatomic make-up may lead to differences in development of articulation of experience. The fact that the sex organs of women are "hidden" may make it more difficult for them to develop a clear conception of the body. This, in turn, may affect the further development of articulation of experience.

Another possible basis for the observed sex differences, also· considered in our 1954 report, may lie in the encouragement of a more dependent role for women in our culture. Barry, Bacon, and Child (1957) have called attention to differences in social roles of men and women in most societies. A survey they made of a number of cultures, mostly illiterate, showed that men more often engage in activities, as work and warfare, that place emphasis on self-reliance and achievement. Women, in contrast, more often have the nurturant role of homemaker and child-rearer. These differences are consistent with differences in training goals for the two sexes, with training for boys more often focused on independence. Some of the mother-child interaction patterns found to be associated with the development of a global field approach (Chapter 19) may well occur more often in relationships between parent and daughter than parent and son.

Also to be considered is the positive value our society apparently attaches to characteristics associated with developed differentiation for boys and limited differentiation for girls. There appear to be .well-defined views in our culture about personality differences between men and women (Tyler, 1956), most people believing that men tend to have characteristics indicative of independence. Tuddenham (1951,

1952) reports evidence suggesting that boys who are most popular with their peers tend to be independent and the most popular girls dependent. Carden (1958) and Iscoe and Carden (1961) have reported a study which links this evidence more closely to our own. Using sociometric techniques they found that girls more often chose field-dependent girls among their peers while boys tended to choose field-independent boys. For both sexes the difference in frequency of choice of field-dependent and field-independent children was significant.[8] Children who conform to their sex-role stereotypes thus tend to be more popular than children who do not. To the extent that these stereotypes include for boys characteristics associated with greater differentiation, the possibility needs to be considered that predominant social pressures in our society work in the direction of contributing to sex differences in differentiation.

D. SUMMARY

Extensive evidence now exists of sex differences in mode of field approach. Both in perceptual and intellectual situations men tend to be relatively more analytical than women. This difference has been observed in this country, in groups of different educational and socio-economic backgrounds, as well as in groups from a number of Western European countries and Hong Kong. Significant relations between mode of field approach and measures of masculinity-femininity have also been found within each sex. Finally, developmental studies have demonstrated that sex differences are present down to the 8-year level, but they may not exist in children below that age or in geriatric groups.

The sex differences that have been observed are clear-cut and pervasive, but they are relatively slight, compared to the range of individual differences within each sex.

The possible existence of sex differences in other areas of functioning, viewed from the standpoint of differentiation, was also considered, although no clear evidence on the problem is now available. Some of the possible sources of the observed sex differences were examined.

[8] Mednick, also using sociometric procedures, found that for some activities field-independent children were chosen more often than field-dependent children. Separate results for boys and girls are not reported, however (personal communication from Sarnoff Mednick).

14

SELF-CONSISTENCY
AS A FUNCTION OF
EXTENT OF DIFFERENTIATION:
A REVIEW

Chapters 4 through 13 have presented a large body of evidence bearing on the "differentiation hypothesis." We pause now to evaluate the status of the hypothesis.

At the outset, some of the main ways in which highly developed differentiation may manifest itself in various psychological areas were suggested. These were labeled "indicators of differentiation." Included were a tendency for the world to be experienced as analyzed and structured; an articulated body concept and sense of separate identity, which reflect a differentiated self; and specialized, structured defenses and controls. We anticipated that measures of these characteristics would tend to be significantly interrelated, even though in individual cases unevenness of growth may make for greater development in some areas than others. This expectation we have called the "differentiation hypothesis."

To test this hypothesis it was necessary to translate each of the postulated indicators into specific operational terms, and to analyze behavior in a wide variety of situations. Although many problems remain unresolved, the results of the studies now on hand give substantial support to the differentiation hypothesis.

Our research strategy was to study the relation between a tendency to experience analytically and each of the other postulated indicators of differentiation. Analytical experiencing was featured in this way because it had been very intensively studied in our earlier investigations and an effective test battery was available for its evaluation.

Each of the tests in this battery requires the subject to deal with a given field analytically, if he can.   It seems clear that individual differences in performance in these tests, ranged along what we earlier designated the field-dependence-independence dimension of perception, reflect differences in ability to apprehend an item as discrete from its background, to overcome an embedding context in perceiving an item within it.   Greater or more limited ability in this regard has now been shown to be a general characteristic of an individual's cognitive functioning—of his intellectual activity as well as of his perception. We have labeled the extremes of this broad cognitive dimension the "analytical field approach" and the "global field approach."   Persons whose perception is field dependent tend to have difficulty in solving problems which require that contexts be overcome.   The presence of such problems (Block Design, Picture Completion, and Object Assembly) in standard intelligence tests largely accounts for the relation frequently found between total IQ scores and performance on our tests of field dependence.   Ease of solution of "insight" problems, Einstellung problems, and problems which involve "functional fixedness," all of which require the overcoming of embedding contexts, also clearly relates to extent of field dependence.   In general, the evidence of characteristic individual approaches to perceptual and intellectual situations strongly supports the thesis that people are self-consistent in the extent to which they experience in analytical fashion.

A tendency to experience analytically was next shown to be related to ability to structure experience.   Thus, it was found that children with an analytical field approach tended to be better able to impose structure upon vague, amorphous stimuli, as Rorschach inkblots.   A tendency was also found for their long-range memory to be relatively good, a characteristic to be expected if the material to be remembered is initially experienced as well structured.   We have used the term "articulated" for experience which tends to be both analyzed and structured.   In contrast, in a "global" way of experiencing, a stimulus field that is highly structured is experienced as strongly cohesive, a stimulus field that is amorphous is experienced as vague.   Ordinarily, the analytical and structuring aspects of experience are difficult to separate, although, as we have done in our studies, situations may be devised which feature one or the other aspect.   A tendency toward a more or less articulated way of experiencing seems evident in lifelike circumstances as much as in specially devised laboratory tasks.   In a first study of experience in "real-life" situations we found that children with an analytical field approach in laboratory situations were more apt than children with a global field approach to have impressions of people and situations which are discrete, structured, and assimilated.

Further studies showed, as expected, that children with an analytical field approach tend to experience body and self as segregated and structured, which reflects more developed self-differentiation. The relatively articulated concept of the body of children and adults with an analytical field approach was evident both in their figure drawings and in their performance in experimental situations from which the person's view of his body could be inferred. The particular aspect of experience of the self featured in the studies presented was sense of separate identity. This entails, most of all, awareness by the person both of what he is like and of his distinctiveness from others. A sense of separate identity implies too that the person has formed stable internal frames of reference for self-definition and for viewing himself and the environment. Considering as presumptive evidence of a developed sense of separate identity the ability to establish and, within limits, to maintain attitudes, judgments, sentiments without continuous reference to external standards, and in the face of contradicting expressions from others, many studies have shown that children and adults with an analytical field approach are apt to have a relatively developed sense of separate identity.

Greater or less articulation thus appears to be a consistent characteristic of an individual's experience whether the source of the experience is an immediately present stimulus configuration or symbolically represented material, the self or the world outside.

Results of studies of the relation between mode of field approach and structure of defenses and controls, another postulated indicator of differentiation, were also in accord with expectations. Children and adults with an analytical field approach have relatively structured controls and are apt to use complex defenses, as intellectualization and isolation. Persons with a global approach are apt to have less well-structured controls and to use such defenses as primitive denial and massive repression.

The results in the preceding chapters thus make it clear that mode of field approach is related to many other characteristics assumed to reflect extent of differentiation.

This relation is highlighted when we pool the major measures of these other characteristics and compare the resulting composite scores to measures of field dependence. To compute composite scores we used for each of the four major personality-assessment techniques employed the measure which considered the record most comprehensively: the sophistication-of-body-concept measure from the figure-drawing test, the cognitive-clarity measure from the interview, the task-approach measure from the TAT, and the percept-analysis measure from the Rorschach. Since each of these measures was based on a 5-point rating scale, we averaged for each child the scores he achieved according to the four scales. The distribution of these composite scores is given in Table 14-1 for the Group-III boys, divided into three subgroups (field-dependent children, intermediate, and field-independent children), according to their scores on the battery of perceptual tests. In this distribution there is only one instance of overlap between the analytical and global groups, and the intermediate children fall clearly into the middle range of the distribution.

Table 14-1. Distribution of averages of major ratings for Rorschach, TAT, Figure-drawing Test and Interviews (Group III)

Composite scores	Field-independent children (N = 10)	Intermediate children (N = 10)	Field-dependent children (N = 10)
4.9–5.0			I
4.7–4.8			
4.5–4.6			I
4.3–4.4		I	
4.1–4.2			
3.9–4.0			I
3.7–3.8	I	I	III
3.5–3.6		I	II
3.3–3.4		II	II
3.1–3.2			
2.9–3.0	I	III	
2.7–2.8	II		
2.5–2.6		I	
2.3–2.4			
2.1–2.2			
1.9–2.0	I	I	
1.7–1.8	I		
1.5–1.6	I		
1.3–1.4	II		
1.1–1.2			
1.0	I		

To this point, our study of the relation among the various postulated indicators of differentiation has been limited to a comparison of measures of mode of field approach to measures of each of the other indicators. The relations have been generally significant, as anticipated. The differentiation hypothesis would lead us to expect that the relations among all these measures would be significant as well. The intercorrelations among these measures in Table 11-1 (Chapter 11) confirm this expectation.

Because of the criteria used in selecting variables for Table 11-1 none of our measures of controls and defenses were included. The evidence in Chapter 9 showed clearly that these measures tend to relate significantly to mode of field approach. However, our evidence on the relation of these measures to measures of indicators of differentiation other than mode of field approach is not clear. A problem exists in that some of the measures to be compared in exploring this relation were devised from the same test records. Even though different rating criteria and different aspects of the record were considered in their determination, the possibility exists of overlap in information used in determining the measures. This problem arises in the comparisons of measures of structure of defenses (based on all three projective tests) with Rorschach percept-analysis measures, sophistication-of-body-concept measures, and TAT task-approach measures (considered to reflect sense of separate identity). It arises as well in the comparison of the other two measures of defenses and controls (handling of aggression and denial, both based on specific TAT cards) with TAT task-approach measures.[1] Considering all pairs of measures from Groups I, II, and III, for which this kind of contamination problem does not exist, there are eight correlations between the handling-of-aggression and denial measures, on the one hand, and measures of differentiation other than mode of field approach, on the other hand. Of the four correlations involving the handling-of-aggression measure, two are significant; of the four including the denial measure, one is significant.[2]

The relations among the postulated indicators of differentiation are thus more firmly established in some instances than others. We consider the evidence on interrelatedness among the aspects of articulated experience considered to be particularly clear. The existence of continuity in an individual's manner of experiencing body, self, and field,

---

[1] It should be emphasized that nowhere in this book have correlations been reported where such contamination might exist.

[2] It will be recalled that the denial scale did not stand up on cross-validation.

from the standpoint of greater or more limited articulation, in fact represents to us the "hard core" of our findings. The relation of nature and structure of controls and defenses to other characteristics of differentiation, on the other hand, is not as well supported in evidence, and has not been studied as comprehensively.

Taken together, the evidence suggests that children, and adults as well, tend to be self-consistent in their psychological functioning in ways predictable on the basis of the differentiation hypothesis.

As already noted, the self-consistency that has been observed does not preclude the possibility of unevenness in development. The intercorrelations reported, though generally high, leave ample room for unevenness in individual cases. At various points we have given instances of uneven growth. Intensive study of children presenting a picture of unevenness in various areas of development would be most useful to the further refinement of our conceptual framework. Such studies are now in progress.

The differentiation hypothesis has received confirmation from a large body of evidence, obtained from numerous studies, using a wide variety of techniques and subject groups. Many of these studies have been conducted by investigators in other laboratories, often with a focus very different from our own. The diversity in source and nature of evidence is important not only because of the support it gives to our findings, but also because the conclusions that may be drawn are broader than if the evidence had been obtained with a particular technique, theoretical approach, or subject population.

A number of additional findings of interest emerged in the course of the studies concerned with the differentiation hypothesis. First, we found, as anticipated, that pathology reflecting severe impairment of integration tended to take different forms in people who, in various areas of functioning, gave evidence of relatively highly developed or limitedly developed differentiation. Second, the tendency observed in our earlier studies for women to be more field dependent than men has been substantially confirmed with a variety of subject groups drawn from a number of geographic areas both inside and outside the United States. Sex differences are also evident when the broader analytical-global cognitive dimension, of which field-dependence-independence is the perceptual component, is considered. And there is a suggestion in the evidence that sex differences may exist with regard to sense of separate identity as well. Third, some tendency was found for persons with an analytical approach to have a greater interest in activity, assertiveness, striving. This relation is by no means an inevitable one, however, and the linkages between active attitude, as we called it, and extent of differentiation are quite complex. Finally, we found that measures reflecting various characteristics of developed differentiation tended to show only a slight relation to measures of some kinds of verbal skill. Though this finding suggests that the growth of differentiation and of verbal skills may follow different developmental paths, it may not necessarily mean that a tendency for experience to be articulated in the realm of configurational stimuli is unrelated to a tendency toward articulation in the verbal sphere. On a priori grounds we would expect such a relationship to exist. A critical test on this point requires that the constituents of what we call "verbal skills" be carefully identified and situations which provide a measure of articulation in verbal experience be devised.

SUMMARY

The main findings bearing on the differentiation hypothesis, presented in preceding chapters, were brought together. The weight of the evidence clearly favors the hypothesis. A definite association is found, as anticipated, among such characteristics as a tendency for experience of the surroundings to be analyzed and structured; an articulated body concept and sense of separate identity, reflecting developed self-differentiation; and structured defenses and controls. Self-consistency in psychological functioning, in ways predictable from the differentiation hypothesis, is thus indicated.

15

CASE STUDIES

After the analyses described in the preceding chapters had been completed, we undertook intensive case studies of individual children who made up the groups used in these analyses. This step was taken with several objectives in mind.

First, we were interested in determining whether the pictures of more differentiated and less differentiated children, suggested by the patterns of interrelated characteristics, correspond to individual children as encountered in real life, or whether they are abstractions. This question may be answered by shifting the focus of study from ratings of separate, specific characteristics to consideration of the child as a functioning totality, with these characteristics viewed in their dynamic interplay.

Second, we were concerned with exploring further the kinds of diversity to be found among children who are similar in showing greater or more limited differentiation in many areas of their functioning. That diversity does exist has already been evident in the studies presented to this point. It seemed that individual case studies, focused on diversity as much as similarities, would help identify subgroups among more differentiated and less differentiated children, as in fact they did.

Third, we hoped that through the case studies other manifestations of more developed or less developed differentiation, not investigated systematically before, might come to light.

A final objective was to make a careful study of intermediate children. In all the analyses reported we of course used data for an entire group, rather than for extremes alone. We felt it important to determine whether children who fall in the middle of the performance range on tests of mode of field approach, used as our reference standard, are qualitatively different from children at the extremes or are "truly intermediate" in the characteristics associated with mode of field approach or other characteristics. A careful study of children in the middle range, we felt, would help us make a choice between these alternatives.

In the sections that follow we present, first of all, several case studies of children who are extremes with regard to mode of field approach. These cases illustrate the impression obtained from intensive study of all the material available for each of a sizeable group of children, namely, that the pictures presented by more differentiated and less differentiated children, as individual living personalities, are consistent with the impressions which emerged from the statistically based studies of them considered in preceding chapters.

One consideration in the selection of cases was to illustrate the variety of individual settings in which greater or more limited differentiation may occur. Exemplified in a particularly dramatic way is the possibility, already strongly supported by evidence given previously, that disturbed functioning may be found among highly differentiated as well as among limitedly differentiated children, though the disturbances are likely to take different forms. The cases chosen also illustrate the subgroups that emerged in the course of the studies of individual children.

Following the case reports an account is given of some further impressions gained from the case studies of children at the extremes beyond those suggested by the statistical studies already reported. These impressions of course need to be checked in further systematic investigations. They concern, first, specific manifestations of particular indicators of differentiation, somewhat different from the manifestations already considered; and second, some characteristics that had not been made evident by our previous methods of investigations. Case material illustrative of relationships earlier found in our statistical studies is given as well.

Finally, an account is given of children intermediate with regard to mode of field approach. Since on the basis of our individual case studies such children did not appear to be different in kind from children at the extremes, and seemed genuinely to belong more or less in the middle of a continuous distribution, this account is very brief.

The material that follows is based on individual case conferences held for most of the 68 10-year boys who served as subjects in the studies already reported. These conferences were particularly intensive for the 30 Group-III boys, who had been studied last. With these boys who, it will be recalled, served as a validation group, the conference took place *after* the special methods for rating the projective test and interview records had already been applied blind. It was in fact the first time that all the material for an individual child was brought together. This material included the original test records for perceptual and intelligence tests, the specially devised learning and problem-solving tests, the three projective tests, the interviews with the child and with his mother, as well as the recorded observations of the child's behavior in the various test situations. The derived scores and ratings for the various tests were available as well. Also available, and representing an intermediate step between the raw data and the final ratings, were impressions from each of the three projective techniques and from the interviews with child and mother, recorded by the staff member responsible for the given technique in the course of arriving at the ratings. These were written prior to knowledge of any other test result for the child. Finally, we had available two blind write-ups for each child, based on his three projective tests. One was prepared by a psychologist who was deliberately kept uninformed about the postulated indicators of differentiation. The other blind write-up was prepared by a psychologist who was asked to center her report around these indicators and was given fairly specific criteria to use with each test.

The method of setting up the two extreme groups and the intermediate group was to divide the distribution of perceptual index scores for the 68 10-year boys into three segments, according to arbitrary cut-off points. In determining these points, natural breaks in the distributions were considered, and an effort was made to have the middle segment extend approximately half a sigma to either side of the mean.

A. CASE STUDIES

1. Highly Differentiated Children

The five cases to be presented include a boy who is active and energetic, though not especially intellectually oriented (Case #1); a gentle child with some feminine characteristics (Case #2); a highly intellectual, emotionally distant and aloof, rather manipulative and competitive child (Case #3); a nonintellectual, socially well-adjusted, unambitious child (Case #4); and finally a severely disturbed child (Case #5).

Keith—Case #1 (Group II). Keith is an example of a highly differentiated child who is active and energetic and not intellectually oriented despite his high intelligence.[1]

[1] His Revised Stanford-Binet, Form L, IQ is 153.

He is the third of five children, with two preschool age brothers, another brother of 11 and a sister of 12. Although the family is financially comfortable (father owns a successful wholesale business and there is ample household help), the mother, a competent, adequate person with an active social and community life of her own, says that she runs her complex household "like an institution," and has early trained all five children to be independent and self-reliant. They have apparently responded to her training, and she is impartially proud of her five competent, "gorgeous-looking," and socially well-behaved children.

Keith has been to camp every summer since age 4. He enjoyed camp activities and there were no complaints of homesickness. For some time now he has gone to the dentist alone, has attended to having his shoes repaired, etc. On two blind write-ups, based on projective tests, he was described as "self-sufficient" and as "highly efficient, self-reliant, resourceful . . . showing remarkable ability to cope actively with his environment, even in adverse circumstances . . . able to assume responsibility . . . showing an over-all high level of differentiation." However, projective tests, particularly the Rorschach, also suggest that his chief problems are in the areas of residual dependency and passivity, and that it is the successful struggle against these that is particularly characteristic of him. As indicated, demands for self-reliance were made on him early; and the mother had regarded as a problem the persistence of what she considered "babyish" traits —e.g., being a poor loser in games and sports and crying when hit by another child. Keith, by age 10, has apparently been able to master these problems at the level of behavior; however, projective tests indicate that the problems have not been fully resolved. (A blind test report refers to "residual dependency needs, and the strong drive to counteract these needs . . . he has developed an attitude of self-sufficiency as a protective device.")

The clarity of Keith's experience of himself and his environment is amply documented. On perceptual tests, he gave the most field-independent performance of the 68 10-year-olds studied.[2]

Keith's mother describes him as having "a crystal clear mind." Because of his tendency to be reserved in the interview with him, the absence of any kind of confusion was more clearly documented than were positive indications of what we called cognitive clarity. Nevertheless, certain things stood out. Against the background of our later knowledge of serious friction between his parents, it seems characteristic of Keith that he was able to "tell

---

[2] His standard scores were −1.02 for the BAT, −1.32 for the RFT, and −1.51 for the EFT; mean, −1.28. He was consistent from test to test and from trial to trial. Thus, on the BAT, in adjusting his body to the vertical, his largest deviation was 8°, with a 35° tilt of the prevailing visual field. On the EFT, thirteen of the twenty-four problems were solved within 5 seconds each. There was one failure within the allotted 5-minute time limit per trial, on the most difficult item in the test. Whatever the nature of the perceptual task, his ability to separate item from context was of a high order.

off" the interviewer politely but firmly when asked about his father. In speaking of vocational plans, although undecided, he clearly distinguished between playing the trumpet, which he regards as a hobby, and serious future plans. His clear perception and awareness of roles within the family circle was illustrated by his comments about his older sister. While expressing some resentment toward her, he commented, "She's the oldest—and she's a girl, but I don't think she should get any special privileges—she wants to change the whole house around, just for her, but I don't agree with that," thus stating both his own position and his perception of the accepted order of things. Equally well defined is Keith's attitude toward his little 4-year-old brother: "He's a regular brat, like the rest of us . . . (When he won't do what I say) . . . I just give him some taps, he's just a baby." He is well informed about his parents' education and earlier work. The clarity of experience is likewise apparent on projective tests. Thus, his TAT characters have quite specific identity and at times very specific relations to each other. On the Rorschach, his perception is exceptionally clear. The human figures he draws are highly sophisticated, with clear assignment of role (see Chapter 7, Figure 7-1).

The impression from all three projective tests is of a well-practiced, highly developed obsessive-compulsive defensive structure. A blind test write-up contained the following comments: "Most striking is his adult capacity to defend himself . . . There are many well-focused mechanisms, including intellectualization, reaction-formation, displacement, and a subtle and complex use of humor . . . Well-developed controls, without too much sacrificing of spontaneity." There is a suggestion, however, both in life and on tests, that aggression has been something of a problem. Thus, his mother describes him as having earlier been destructive and, at the same time, as having until recently been dominated by his older brother. The only present manifestations of earlier impulse problems are reports of his being mischievous and clowning in school. But, over-all, the mother describes him as responsible and trustworthy. Her current concern is that, after having earlier allowed himself to be dominated by the older brother, Keith now tends to dominate and outshine the brother.

An impression of interest in active striving is an unmistakable, salient feature of Keith's projective test productions. Thus, the ambition ascribed to the male he drew was "to conquer the world." On the TAT, the counteraction theme was repeatedly and dramatically emphasized (e.g., on card 5, an invented character, the daughter of the female figure portrayed on the card, had the mumps, with swollen glands as a symptom; when she grew up, she "invents a cure" for swollen glands). Keith is described in one blind write-up as "self-confident . . . but also has confidence in the supportive values and intentions of those around him . . . with evidence of positive identifications . . . he becomes highly involved in tasks, yet is able to maintain critical distance . . . shows a high level of organizational ability."

Keith's social relations outside the home seem limited. His best friend is a boy whom Keith's mother describes as silly and meek, and whom she does not regard as a person of Keith's caliber. Yet she describes Keith as "not a lonely boy." It should be noted, however, that the family itself, with a good deal of companionship among the five children, and an active social life of the whole family group as a unit, provides Keith with social outlets right within the home.

Although he is proud of his high attainment in school, and does not need prodding to get his homework done, his interests, while varied, are not especially intellectual. He reads an occasional book in addition to the conventional comics; he plays the trumpet well enough to participate in school shows; he builds model cars and airplanes; and engages successfully in several sports. The general impression is that whatever Keith does, he does with gusto. The particular content of what he does is somehow of secondary importance to him.

From the mother's account, the impression is that, in addition to encouraging independence and self-reliance, she has respected his development as an individual and, in her rather brusque way, has given warmth and approval. Keith himself gives an over-all impression of adequacy and competence, stressing mastery over the environment rather than need for security or contact as his primary direction.

Chris—Case #2 (Group III). Chris has been chosen to illustrate a high level of differentiation in an emotionally responsive and excitable child, with some feminine characteristics.

He is the middle of three children, with a 12-year-old sister and a 7-year-old brother. The family leads an active social life, including trips, outings, visits to relatives and friends.

Chris was a planned and wanted baby, but the mother, who had derived great satisfaction from her daughter, definitely hoped for a second girl. In describing him, she uses such adjectives as delicious and lovable. On the one hand, she is somewhat troubled about what she calls his effeminacy, and encourages him to develop what she thinks of as boyish activities, such as ball playing and fighting back when necessary. On the other hand, she encourages him in whatever interests he shows spontaneously, even those she considers effeminate for a boy.

In the laboratory Chris was consistently described by all observers as showing excellent task involvement, as being something of a "good boy," but poised and vivacious.

One of the outstanding qualities in Chris is the clarity of his experience of himself and his environment. On cognitive tests, this is shown in his analytical approach in the three perceptual tests [3] and on those parts of the WISC which require analytical competence.[4]

[3] His standard scores were BAT −.79; RFT −.10; EFT −1.60; mean −.83. On the RFT he tended to be variable, occasionally yielding to the influence of

On the basis of the three projective tests, he is described as showing "an unusually high level of awareness . . . his attitude toward the environment appears to be very realistic, with recognition of problems, conflicts . . . (he shows a) high level of discrimination and insight into motives of self and of others." Figure drawings were rated as highly sophisticated, with clear projection of role. However, in view of the mother's comments about his effeminacy, it is of interest that the female drawing shows a higher level of skill than the male drawing (see Chapter 7, Figure 7-2). He identifies the male drawing as a "sailor boy," and adds "I am too old to play sailor," as if dissociating himself from childish things. On the TAT, he created a variety of characters, spelling out the role and identity of each in considerable detail. On the Rorschach, the level of structuring was high, the whole record reflecting richness and variety of experience, without loss of perspective. The clarity of his experience was most directly manifested in the interview with him. His considerable fund of information in many areas of experience was well organized, and was used appropriately and relevantly, reflecting good awareness of relationships, time sequences, etc. He thinks he would like to be a doctor because "doctors help people." He knows that college and "doctors' college" are required, that "you have to get a license, . . . and then you have to get equipment, which is very expensive." In discussing his allowance, he has a clear sense of the relation of amount of allowance to age and grade, accepting the fact that his older sister gets more and his younger brother less than he does. He describes himself, his mother, and his father as persons with identifiable interests and characteristics. For example: "My mother is gentle, she enjoys going out to the theater, and being with her sisters . . . she doesn't actually like to work around the house, but she has to do it, and she likes taking care of my brother and my sister and I, and she likes making us happy . . . she likes shopping, but she doesn't like spending too much money." He describes his family as "a real do-it-yourself family." The over-all impression is of a child with a firm sense of separate identity, a clear grasp of his experience, and a definite orientation in his world.

Chris appears to have internalized the family's values and standards, and to have developed early—perhaps too early—a sense of responsibility. By

the tilted frame, and winding up as an intermediate performer on this test. He was particularly adept at overcoming the embedding context in the EFT, quickly locating the hidden simple figures in all twenty-four complex designs. Where the task was to keep the body separate from the field (BAT), he yielded somewhat to the influence of the visual field on the very first trial, but thereafter he was able to adjust his body to the vertical with a maximum error of only 10°.

[4] Scores on the WISC were generally high, with a full-scale IQ of 138, and IQs of 139 and 131 on the verbal and performance sections, respectively. The intellectual index score, i.e., the sum of weighted scores on Picture Completion, Object Assembly, and Block Design, was 45, high for his group. He did even better on the verbal index, with a summed weighted score of 53 on Vocabulary, Comprehension, and Information.

the time Chris was two-and-a-half years old, he was allowed out alone in the backyard of the apartment house, against the background of the neighbors' disapproval. His mother said she knew that, even at this early age, she could rely on his ability to observe limits, and to understand what he was or was not allowed to do. He has not only been able to take responsibility for bathing for a long time, but recently has voluntarily assumed responsibility for supervising the dressing and bathing of his younger brother.

In a home in which limits are clearly set, though in a general atmosphere of acceptance and approval, it is perhaps not surprising that Chris's controls have developed adequately, though there is evidence both of overcontrol in some respects, and of occasional overexcitability in others. When asked what he does when he is angry Chris told us that he "just gets red in the face and folds his hands," which is consistent with the mother's concern that he is too reticent about expressing anger and resentment. It is of some interest, in the context of other manifestations of developed controls, that in his drawing of a male he included rather primitive and aggressive teeth, suggesting that there is a residual problem in this area. (No parallel intrusion occurs on the other two projective tests.) A blind clinical report, based on all three projective tests, describes him as showing a "highly adaptive use of most of his defenses." The only evidence of difficulty in the control area in his mother's account of Chris is that he "gets so excited" at the thought of special out-of-town trips that "he gets sick." The mother has adopted the tactic of not telling him about a forthcoming trip until just before it takes place, to save him the excitement of anticipation. His teacher is said to describe him as "effervescent . . . he cannot sit still, he has to raise his hand and be active."

Chris's interests are quite diversified. He is not particularly athletic, and is now just learning to play ball. His reading interests include biographies and Westerns, with no special mention of joke books and comics. He likes building model airplanes and reports that his father "stops his work to help me." He spends much of his free time drawing floor plans of houses, much to his father's annoyance; but the mother thinks of this in terms of architecture as a possible occupation and seems satisfied to have his interests develop in any way congenial to him. He collects stamps and matchbook covers. In contrast to the random matchbook cover collections of some of the less differentiated boys, for Chris this activity seems to be a more developed affair. It is one of the activities in the Boys' Club he has joined, where prizes are given for successful collections and albums given for organizing them. Chris enjoys cultural activities such as trips to museums and the theater, to places of historical interest. He has made good progress in playing the piano. The family has apparently provided many cultural opportunities, and has encouraged Chris in his cultural interests. The impression is of a child who gets quite absorbed in his many activities, and who can pursue them both with friends and by himself.

Friendships and getting along socially present no problems. Other boys accept him in spite of his lesser proficiency in athletics, and offer to teach him. He is discriminating in the choice of friends, not depending on boys who happen to live close by, and the friendships tend to be long lasting. There is also no problem in the area of social independence.

His mother describes Chris as gentle, sensitive, affectionate, demonstrative, emotional, and sensible as well. We found in him no special evidence of competitiveness or of ambitious push for achievement, although his standards are high. The emphasis has rather been on the development of resources, interests, and sources of satisfaction. Adaptive, well-functioning controls and internalization of family values and standards to the point where they appear to be truly his own seem especially characteristic of Chris. The tendency to feminine identification has not led to general confusion in role and sense of identity.

Neal—Case #3 (Group I).[5] Neal was chosen to illustrate the emotionally remote, overintellectual children in the highly differentiated group. He shows these qualities to a more extreme degree than any other child we have studied.

Neal is the middle of three children, with a younger and an older sister. The parents are both professionals. The family impressed the interviewer as genuinely enjoying each other's company, with the mother obviously the stronger, and also professionally more successful, of the parents.

This is a cultured though financially modest home, indifferent to money and possessions, highly valuing intellectual achievement. There has been considerable pressure for Neal to attain high scholastic standards; for example, in high school he received a very liberal extra allowance for each grade point attained over 95. Perhaps his repeated reference, in his 10-year-old TAT, to the boy on card 1 being tired and needing a rest, and the rope climber on card 17BM thinking of killing himself—unusual emphases for this group—reflect something of his underlying reactions to the pressures for achievement. In life, however, his reaction to pressures has been to accept the challenge rather than to become discouraged. He works hard, productively as well as originally, in areas of interest to him, but he freely admitted that he did not plug at subjects that failed to stimulate him. "I only like subjects that have a logical system," he told us when he was 14, expressing dislike for subjects in which memorizing was at a premium.

Neal is outstanding in the clarity of his experience. In the perceptual tests he was, on the whole, able to separate an external item from field and overcome the influence of an embedding context at 10, 14, and 17 years.[6]

[5] In the case of Neal and the other boys of Group I, interviews were held with the mothers and the children when the children were 14 and 17, but not when they were 10.

[6] His standard scores for BAT, RFT, and EFT were: at age 10, $-.34$, -1.38, and $-.32$ (mean, $-.68$); at age 14, $-.25$, -1.00, $-.87$ (mean, $-.71$); and at age 17, $+.06$, -1.02, $-.74$ (mean, $-.57$).

However, when the task was to keep the body separate from surrounding field, he acquitted himself less well.[7]

On intelligence tests, Neal turned in a uniformly superior performance, with no significant difference in subtest clusters requiring analytical and verbal abilities.[8]

His intermediate performance on the perceptual test that directly involves the use of the body is consistent with other evidence that the body, with its various implications, is not Neal's favored area. Thus it is no accident that in interview both with him and his mother it is the intellectual side of his development that is most heavily documented.

Both Neal and his mother were most interested in discussing this area. The mother reports that he taught himself to read by the time he went to school, and was reading an encyclopedia when he was 6. During the TAT at age 10, he made reference to the works of Bertrand Russell, and to Huckleberry Finn. At his mother's insistence he took violin lessons between the ages of 8 and 10 and was considered gifted by his teacher. There was apparently an agreement with the parents that he would continue the lessons for two years and then decide on his future course, the parents hoping that by then he would be willing to continue. He stuck it out for two years, practicing without supervision or urging over an hour a day (the more frequent occurrence in our group is a much briefer period of enforced music study, with a constant battle over practicing). At the end of the agreed-upon period he stopped, because he felt it was interfering with his other activities. Only an interest in listening to classical records has remained.

His most developed area of interest has been the field of science, especially on the theoretical side. He has several times been president of mathematics and science clubs; during high school he won several competitive

[7] On the BAT at age 10, for example, his performance was highly variable, with deviations from the true vertical, when he reported himself to be straight, ranging from 2° to 24°. But the variability was systematic rather than random. On the trials in which the body and the room were initially on opposite sides, he was able to utilize the extra clue given by the objective shift in body weight from one side to the other when passing through the true vertical, and, accordingly, showed greater accuracy on these trials in judging his position. On the trials in which body and room were initially to the same side, and in which such extra clues are not available, the pull of the field was much stronger, as judged by his objectively larger errors. The same phenomenon occurred at the two later ages.

[8] At age 14, his Wechsler-Bellevue full-scale IQ was 139, his verbal IQ 147, and his performance IQ 123. His intellectual and verbal index scores were 36 and 42. At age 17, his Wechsler full-scale IQ was 144, and his verbal and performance IQs 144 and 132, respectively; his intellectual and verbal index scores were 42 and 45. The group of which Neal was a member did not have an intelligence test at age 10. His school records show an IQ of 145 on the Pintner-Cunningham at age 6 and an IQ of 150 on the National Intelligence Test at age 9.

national awards in the science and mathematics fields. On the basis of these awards, he was approached by three Ivy League colleges with invitations to apply for admission and has been offered summer jobs in industrial and government research laboratories. At 14, he had initiated and completed an original research project and had returned to our laboratory asking to use statistics books and a calculator so that he could complete data analyses.

By age 17, his vocational choice had crystallized into a preference for theoretical physics; selection of a college was based on its having the best department in pure mathematics. His interests had also broadened, his reading including philosophy of science, as well as biography, history, and economics. He did not read novels, except for selected nineteenth-century classics. Earlier, he had read a good deal of science fiction and was interested in collecting rare issues. For many years he has been interested in chess and has been president of a chess club.

His friendships, which appear to be highly selective and of long duration, are based on mutual interests in chess and science; occasionally he lets friendships drop as interests diverge. By 17, he was dating several girls, again chosen on the basis of mutual interests, managing to find girls with a scientific bent. On a date, he preferred the theater or listening to records to dances or sports events. But, although he can be said to have a normal social life, the impression was that there was not much personal closeness in his friendships.

Neal has not neglected athletic activities. It is characteristic of him and of his determination in pursuing a chosen course that although his motor coordination has never been particularly good, he worked at improving his athletic skills until he could compete with others. In high school he belonged to a social-athletic club.

Although Neal's intellectual interests and pursuits obviously provide inherent satisfaction, they also offer an outlet for his power drive and competitiveness. Thus, when he was 14, he told the interviewer that he disliked a teacher for his modern methods, explaining that the teacher "emphasizes committee work too much . . . marks are given for the group . . . it doesn't give the child a chance to show what he's got." In the same interview, he was most animated when he was discussing his vocational aspirations. Although already considering science at that time, he was apparently considering it primarily as a means to an end. The ultimate end, as he conceived it then, was to be a business executive or the owner of a factory; he considered science, engineering, and law as alternative means of reaching that goal. "A big executive has a lot of people under him. You have authority to carry out what you want. There is a thrill in that." He said he would like to "make a million dollars, get filthy rich . . . If I have money, I can be happy . . . owning a dozen cars, a big house, I can live like a king . . . there is also the prestige." In these interests, he was completely at odds with his family's values and aspirations and admits that they "are a little skeptical, but if I want to try, it's O.K. with them." He thus recognizes himself as different from his family.

Neal's self-concept, and his clarity about it, are not easy to describe. From the purposeful nature of his interests and plans, as given above, the impression is of a person who knows what he wants. But there is also the impression of an obsessivelike split between the intellectual and the emotional-instinctual spheres. It is within the former sphere that he has apparently achieved the greatest clarity, attained self-confidence, and real-istic self-appraisal. This split is documented by two test responses, given at age 14. On card X of the Rorschach, he began with "The blue things on the side look like scorpions with a lot of legs." Then he went on: "Now they look like they are two-headed . . . (each side blue area seen as a two-headed creature). Let's say this one is Jim-John and his two heads are angry at each other." On card 5 of the TAT, he saw a . . . "lady looking into a room . . . she is probably a mother. The part (of the room) you can see is neat and orderly, but the little 5-year-old has been on a rampage in the rest of the room, and it's in a mess." The clinician interpreting the projective test material obtained when Neal was 10 commented: "He will not permit himself to enjoy impulse life . . . has imposed on himself un-bearable restrictions . . . technical relationships are of interest to him, while human beings, and the problem of human relations, are seen as intrusions."

At the end of an extensive interview with Neal at age 14 the inter-viewer recorded his comments concerning Neal's "absence of awareness of deeper needs in himself . . . there is little regard for or interest in the feelings of others . . . overinvestment in his intellectual development oc-curs at the expense of feelings . . . although he is capable of pursuing what he wants with great purposefulness and energy . . . there is too much removal from real feelings, real people, real things." His drawings, at all three ages at which they were obtained (10, 14, 17), are relatively unsophis-ticated, and at 10 both male and female figures lacked facial features, as if deprived of social identity. However, in each case the firm line pressure conveys a certain self-confidence. Awareness, at least at a verbal level, is suggested in his self-description of being somewhat immature, but at least of being able to "recognize my immaturity."

The impression from interviews with both Neal and his mother was that he had experienced enough approval from his family—he is regarded by them as something of a genius—to develop self-respect and a sense of per-sonal worth. Projective tests, however, offer evidence of problems in the area of self-acceptance and identity. For example, in none of the three Rorschachs is he able to see easily the usual people on card III. He ap-proaches the human concept tentatively at age 14, but immediately retreats to "chimps on TV that are dressed up like monkeys." By the age of 17, card IV was "a man walking," but he qualified it as being only "the shape of a man" and, in his characteristically obsessive fashion, criticized the head as "too small" and the feet as "too big."

Controls and defenses are distinctly of the obsessive-compulsive variety. This was commented on independently by two clinicians on the basis of the Rorschach and figure drawings. He told us he seldom got excited over anything, and if he gets angry or annoyed, he just "walks away." He has obviously internalized, in a highly selective manner, many of the family's standards and values, particularly the ability to go his own way and follow his interests, without worrying about what the neighbors will think.

In summary, Neal's investment has been predominantly in achievement and in power, with purposefulness and determination in the pursuit of his goals. The feeling side of life has been correspondingly neglected.

Pete—Case #4 (Group I). Pete has been chosen to illustrate a highly differentiated boy who is nonverbal, nonintellectual, and not especially ambitious or competitive.

When seen in the laboratory at age 17, Pete was almost 6 feet tall, slow-moving, and shy. All examiners commented that he was verbally quite inarticulate. He was self-contained rather than markedly assertive and was consistently described as sober, responsible, and task-oriented even in situations which did not particularly interest him.

Pete is an only child. His father, about whom very little is known to us, died when the boy was 9. Since that time, the mother has supported herself and her son by continuing to run quite successfully their small stationery store. Pete's is a nonintellectual home, without social or intellectual pretensions, oriented to the practical problems of making a living and leading "a decent life." Both physically and psychologically, the home impressed the interviewer as comfortable, with Pete's friends free to drop in. In interviews with her when Pete was 14 and 17, the mother was forthright and brusque, willing to cooperate, but conveying the impression that she felt all this fuss was rather unnecessary. Pete was present during both interviews. For these reasons, the interviews were limited as to both length and coverage. Each time the interviewer described the relation between mother and son as affectionate, good-humored, involving a good deal of casual teasing. The mother handles Pete with a firm hand, on the basis of very clear goals and values of her own. She will stand no nonsense with regard to what she considers to be his responsibilities. However, she is able to leave decisions up to him, for example, concerning the draft and his eventual vocational plans. She can be harsh and directive, but in a context of overall affection and approval. Disagreements are apparently settled without residual resentment.

Considering the apparently close mother-son tie, Pete's sense of separate identity has developed quite satisfactorily. At 17, his goal in life was to marry and to raise and support a family. Neither in interviews with him nor on projective tests was there any evidence of confusion about who he is. Although not spontaneously inclined to talk about himself, in both the 14- and the 17-year interviews he conveyed an impression of a person with a realistic self-appraisal, able to recognize and accept his limitations and the limitations that the home circumstances necessarily impose on him. He showed discriminating appreciation of his mother's problems commenting, for instance, that "she yells at me sometimes, but I realize the circumstances she's in, it is hard for her."

At all three ages (10, 14, 17), his drawings of human figures were clear representations of persons, each with unequivocal identity. The level of sophistication of the drawings at age 10 seemed almost too advanced for a 10-year-old, but at the two later ages it was more appropriate to his chronological age. On the Rorschach, whatever he saw he saw clearly, with a minimum of elaboration and also with a minimum of fussing. On the TAT, characters were for the most part clearly delineated and assigned definite roles.

Articulateness of experience is reflected in Pete's field-independent performance on perceptual tests at all three ages.[9] Consistent with the analytical ability shown on perceptual tests, he is at his best both at 14 and 17 on those subtests of intelligence tests which emphasize analytical ability.[10]

The development of controls and internalization of standards have apparently never been a problem. When asked about his early development, his mother commented repeatedly that he was "never any trouble, always a good boy." He has taken for granted the need to help his mother run the store, and has assumed increasing responsibility for it. In speaking both with him and his mother, we could find little evidence even of adolescent rebellion, although at 17 he did express some resentment about the amount of time the store took and commented that, were it not for being needed at home, he might attend full-time the out-of-town denominational college of his choice, instead of attending at night a municipal college a few blocks from his home.

On blind interpretation of projective tests, Pete was described at age 10 as "cautious," at 17 as showing "a well-developed sense of responsibility," and "strong superego development" . . . with a "marked sense of guilt" at age 14, which had "become less marked by 17." An "obsessive-compulsive type of defensive structure" was suggested. At the same time, in fantasy

[9] His standard scores on BAT, RFT, and EFT were −.96, −.65, and −1.44, with a mean of −1.02, at age 10; −.90, −1.07, −.71, with a mean of −.89, at age 14; and −.31, −1.32, −.68, with a mean of −.56, at age 17. At age 17, he moved somewhat closer to the perceptually intermediate range in over-all score. On the BAT, at that age, his ability to separate his own body from the surrounding field did not improve proportionately to that of the rest of his peer group.

[10] At age 13, as a subject in another study he was given the WISC. His intellectual index score was 42 and his verbal index score was 34. His full-scale IQ at that age was 115, his performance IQ 122, and his verbal IQ 106. At age 17, on the Wechsler-Bellevue, his intellectual index score was 43 and his verbal index score 34. His full-scale IQ was 121 and his performance and verbal IQs 125 and 112, respectively.

(e.g., on the TAT), he allows himself to express far more open aggression and more ambitious striving than he expresses in life situations.

Pete's interests, while fairly well developed, are primarily nonintellectual, and, in adolescence, structured for him by his social group. There is no evidence of initiative or of striking out on his own in the pursuit of interests. Drawing and making things with his hands which, according to his mother, he liked to do at age 10, no longer seemed to interest him at the later ages. Reading was apparently never a favorite occupation. At 17, he read only the Reader's Digest and an occasional book. At 14 and at 17 his interests appeared to center about the activities of the Y and the Young People's group in his church. He has remained a stable member of these groups, and has preferred to stick to these rather than to participate in extracurricular activities in high school and in college. Basketball, social dancing, choral singing have been favorite group activities, with, by age 17, a normal amount of casual dating. He has always been physically strong, energetic, and athletic and, in addition to formal church basketball teams, he has participated in a number of sports. It is perhaps characteristic of Pete that he remained with the Scouts much longer than most other boys whom we have followed into adolescence. His mother describes him as having always been strong, active and energetic, and a regular boy who enjoys everything.

While his best grades in high school were in science courses (performance in other courses having been mediocre in spite of above-average intelligence) his interest in science was not sufficiently developed for him to consider a career in this area. His aim in college is to get "a good education" rather than to pursue any specific course of study. At 17, vocational indecision was a considerable problem to him, but he had actively narrowed down possible choices on the basis of realistic self-appraisal. Thus, he would prefer an occupation that involves contact with people, physical activity, and "seeing the world." He has considered being a telephone lineman, perhaps with work assignments away from home, but with hopes of eventually settling down in Brooklyn.

While his social life centers about group activities, he has individualized and long-lasting friendships as well. He prefers to associate with contemporaries who are "refined" and "well-educated," and has deliberately avoided a rough neighborhood crowd, although some of these youngsters had been his playmates in early childhood.

In several respects projective test material suggests problems which, in life, are perhaps most clearly betrayed in his persistent nailbiting, in intellectual functioning below capacity level, and in a curtailed level of aspirations (e.g., attending college with intention to graduate, but considering becoming a telephone lineman). Thus, tests suggest passivity and a good deal of anxiety in this outwardly active and energetic boy and some doubts about masculine self-assertion. Tests given at the age of 10 suggested a boy who had been pushed into maturity too early. On the TAT, at that age, several stories involved themes filled with adult man-woman (not boy-girl) problems and conflicts, though in other stories he was able to be more appropriately childish. The women drawn at all three ages were "sexy" and seductive-looking, but also looked stronger and more capable than the men he drew. However, the interpreter also commented that, even at the age of 10, Pete was able to manage his "deeper-level" problems, and that by 17 he was pulling through the problems of adolescence "with a very healthy ego." The whole problem of masculine identification with which he has always seemed to struggle—and apparently with a considerable degree of success—is understandable in view of his life situation. Yet the curtailment of goals and the delay in intellectual maturation may perhaps be thought of as part of the price that this battle has cost him.

In summary, in his well-developed control structure, his ability to assume responsibility, his relatively permanent interests which afford him satisfaction, in the clarity of his experience and knowing who he is (in spite of some uncertainty on this score at a deeper level), and in his realistic self-appraisal, Pete, for all his verbal inarticulateness and low drive for achievement, functions in a way that suggests a high level of differentiation.

Nick—Case #5 (Group II). This complex case illustrates a highly differentiated child with serious personality disturbance.

Nick is an only child of divorced parents. The impact of the divorce on him is suggested by a totally unprovoked announcement he made to a staff member he had just met on his first visit to the laboratory: "My father has two wives." The father left home when Nick was 5 and the mother connects a change in his behavior, both temporally and causally, with this event. The mother, with whom he lives, impressed the interviewer as a seriously disturbed person.

Circumstances appear to have made it difficult for Nick to develop a clear sense of separate identity. The conflict concerning his role, which comes through both on projective tests and in interview with him, appears to center about his ambivalent attitude toward his parents. His mother contributes to his uncertainty by treating him in inconsistent ways. She bathes, dresses, and feeds him, but at the same time treats him like a contemporary, commenting that he "likes to be the man of the house," "he won't let me marry—won't let me sing and dance and be gay." His own attitude toward his mother is a mixture of open, clinging attachment and open rebellion. The mother complains that he won't obey. She describes her life with Nick as "a constant battle." Mother and child, according to the interviewer's report, quarrel like a couple of small children. The mother, in her own words, handles his defiance by "beating him until he is red."

In spite of this background, the impression conveyed in direct interview with the boy himself, in projective tests and in perceptual tests, is that at least in some areas he is capable of experiencing in a quite articulated manner.

On all three perceptual tests, he gives a consistently field-independent performance.[11]

On interview he shows considerable clarity of experience. Thus, in speaking of his hobby, playing with clay, he says: "If I want to make anything out of clay, I have to have the radio on, otherwise I am not in the mood to do anything." In describing his social life, he says: "I'll never go out in the street as long as I don't have any friends" and "I don't know how to fight."

He states categorically that a child should "listen to his mother rather than to his father" because "I was born from her." In the test and laboratory situations, he reacted to his surroundings with a super-alertness which amounted to suspiciousness. On projective tests, too, there is conveyed an impression of a much higher sense of awareness and identity than one might expect from his confused home situation. Thus, his two figure drawings are definitely male and female, and each is an identifiable, clearly projected person. On the Rorschach, he shows good ability to define, locate, and elaborate percepts, showing a fairly high level of perceptual clarity. On the TAT, although the characters are frequently referred to as merely "a man" or "a boy," situations are portrayed with fair specificity, though his choice of situations is often quite impersonal. Thus, on 7BM he saw "a counsel and a man . . . (talking) about taxes." A blind test write-up refers to his "good critical ability and a high level of awareness and responsiveness to demands of outer situations . . . but . . . because of his pervasive hostility . . . he is unable to relate to (his environment) in a positive manner." His awareness is perhaps part of his defensive structure, rather than something to be used constructively in the interest of attainment, mastery, or establishing relationships.

The control picture again is mixed. His unmanageable behavior at home, and reports of poor conduct in school, as well as his disturbed and hyperactive behavior in the laboratory, would suggest poor impulse control. However, two different clinicians, in evaluating the control area on the basis of projective tests, saw a more complex constellation. One wrote that "he is remarkably well controlled for his age . . . rigidly defended . . . but anger and rage and destructive impulses, especially concerning his mother . . . might overcome him . . . he uses intellectualization, humor, strives to maintain distance . . . behaviorally, he probably shows spurts of temper . . . (on drawings) the head does not wish to know what the body desires . . ." The other clinician, in discussing his figure drawings, commented on "the controlled angriness of the figures rather than any primitive expression of aggression," thus contrasting Nick with some openly impulse-

[11] Standard scores were -1.06, -1.44, and $-.97$ on BAT, RFT, and EFT, respectively, averaging -1.16. He is easily able to adjust his own body and the rod to the vertical, independently of the position of the surrounding visual field; and he is able quickly to find the "hidden figures" in the EFT against the "pull" of the embedding context. His IQ on Form L of the Revised Stanford-Binet, the test used with Group II, was 120.

ridden children in the poorly differentiated group. On the TAT, he is said to "avoid involvement in what he experiences as major conflict areas." There has apparently been little internalization of standards and little assumption of responsibility for homework and for self-care. This may perhaps be interpreted in the context of both his rebelliousness toward and clinging attachment to his very disturbed mother and her own inability to impose limits and exercise effective firmness in handling Nick.

One gets a fairly characteristic picture of Nick's methods of coping with the environment from his behavior in interview. His behavior can only be described as controlling in a purposeful and manipulative way, so that it was very difficult to conduct the interview as planned. There were many suspicious questions ("What are you writing?" "What are those curtains for?"). He called the interviewer "stupid" and "crazy," told him to "drop dead," and complained that the interviewer talked too much. He insisted that the interviewer accompany him to the bathroom, a request no other child made, and that he be asked questions which he apparently expected. (Incidentally, this behavior is further evidence of his inability to define his role appropriately in the interview situation.) There were angry outbursts about his father ("If I ever see this big butt again, he will get it right in the nose, on the kisser, on the teeth, or in the eyes, or in the ears—boom!"). But when asked about his mother's work, he stated firmly: "She goes to business, and that's all I'm telling you about my family." The projective test write-ups picked up the defensive character of his aggressive behavior. It seems characteristic of Nick that he does not give in to the insecurity which is clearly manifested on projective tests, but energetically uses aggressive-defensive countermeasures which, however, are not socially successful.

Aside from listening to adventure stories on radio and TV, Nick has only one absorbing passion, clay modeling. Judging from the sample figures he showed us, the level of attainment in his one area of meaningful interest is more like the representational play of a very young child, lacking in both skill and realism. (This is in contrast to his human figure drawings, which show both skill and realism in execution.) According to his mother, most of Nick's free time is spent in this kind of solitary play. One can only guess that it represents for him a fantasy life with magical qualities, and affords him an outlet he has not been able to find elsewhere. Although he has an ample supply of other play equipment, he does not use it. There is no interest in reading or sports. He does not play baseball because he "cannot hit a ball." He is afraid to swim and to ride a bicycle.

Nick's social relations appear practically nil. According to his own account, "everybody in my class is my enemy . . . the teacher says they're not my enemies and they admit they're not, but they really are . . . If they're not my enemies, how come they beat me up?" The mother concurs, adding that he comes home crying when boys his age beat him up. (Nick is unusually tall for his age.) She adds that he prefers playing with

2- and 3-year-olds, but their mothers are afraid he will hurt the small children. His mother is his only companion; attending the movies with her is his only recreation outside the home.

In summary, this is a complex boy who illustrates a high level of differentiation in the context of severe personality disturbance. Projective tests highlight more developed resources and greater strength than his overt behavior suggests. Nick apparently seeks to escape from the traumatizing, conflict-provoking situations in which he finds himself by withdrawing into a fantasy world (clay modeling) and by beginning to develop what can only be called paranoid protective mechanisms. (It may be recalled that in our 1954 studies hospitalized paranoid men tended to be perceptually field independent.) However disturbed his overt behavior, there is "fight" in this boy rather than passive abdication to overwhelming odds. It must be added that his mother too, in spite of her severe disturbance, has a similar kind of strength. Although feeling incapable of coping with Nick, she holds a job in which she feels competent. She maintains a home and cares for and supports her son without help from husband or relatives. It is only possible to speculate that, in some way, he reflects his mother's disturbance; and he has some potential, the nature of which is far from clear, that has enabled him to develop and maintain himself as well as he has.

2. Limitedly Differentiated Children

The three cases described below were chosen to illustrate a child primarily characterized by poverty of resources (Case #6); a child with a manifest, pervasive impulse disorder (Case #7); and a child who combines a low level of differentiation with a high level of verbal skill (Case #8).

Phil—Case #6 (Group III). Phil was chosen as the prototype of a limitedly differentiated child, characterized primarily by poverty of resources. Four investigators, each using a different technique of personality study (interview and three projective tests), rated him blind as among the least differentiated children in his group. In spite of average intelligence [12] he is described as doing very poorly in school. Thus, he is functioning below capacity.

He is the younger of two boys, with the mother showing obvious preference for his 13-year-old brother. The father, whose work for an office supply firm involves frequent and sometimes quite long absences from home, does not appear to be an active participant in the rearing of the two boys, but the mother frequently threatens to tell the father when unable to manage the child.

[12] WISC full-scale IQ, 100; verbal IQ, 101, performance IQ, 99; intellectual index score, 27; verbal index score, 29.

The articulateness of Phil's experience is consistently of a low order. This is reflected in his global performance on the perceptual tests.[13]

Blind reports based on projective tests highlight the vagueness of Phil's experience and the lack of developed personality structure. He is described as "amorphous . . . his entire personality is unformed . . . experiencing situations in a vague way . . . he hopes for the best in a confusing, overwhelming world . . . there is little indication of development of self-concept . . . he is confused, but also unaware of his confusion." On the TAT his stories are minimal card descriptions, with the characters given little identity (e.g., "looks like a lady, and she is crying, and I think everything turns out O.K."). On the Rorschach, his perception is vague; he shows little interest in structuring the material. His figure drawings are primitive and poorly organized, the male and female differing only in the presence of a hat on the male and hair on the female. (These drawings are shown in Figure 7-6 of Chapter 7.) The quality of his interview reflects his unfocused view of both himself and of his life. Illustrative is his tangential and confused account of situations in his answer to the question, "Do you have many friends at your summer place?": "The people who live there 'cause our only—we had a hotel—that comes down 'cause the water wasn't pure there, and we had to go up there all the—down the hill—get their friends—'cause it's hard work getting up—and now they have a farm right next door."

Phil's interests appear quite poorly developed. The mother comments that he loses interest quickly in anything he begins. According to his own account, he likes baseball (which he confuses with football), and collects baseball cards, although he says he does not have very many. Reading interests appear restricted to joke books. Asked in interview "what are you

[13] Standard scores for the three tests were BAT, −.03; RFT, +1.10; EFT, +1.73; average, +.93. Although his score on the BAT suggests intermediate ability to keep body separate from field, his performance on separate trials of this test was highly variable. On the most extreme trial, he reported himself as sitting upright when he was actually tilted 22° in the direction of tilt of the room, that is, he tended strongly to accept the axes of the prevailing visual field as a basis for determining body position. In the RFT, he was consistently influenced by the frame to an extreme degree in adjusting the rod; he was unable to separate the rod from its background and to use the position of his own body as a standard of reference. On one trial, he judged the rod to be straight when it was actually tilted by 64° from the true upright. This extreme displacement occurred as a result of a "perceptual shift" in the orientation of the frame; that is, he experienced one of the sides of the frame as topmost and made his judgment of rod position with reference to the shifted axes of the frame, lining up the rod with the frame in its newly perceived orientation. On the EFT, his inability to experience the simple figure as separate from background—i.e., to overcome the influence of the embedding context—was striking. He was unable to find, within the allotted 5-minute time limit, the simple figure within the complex one in seventeen of the twenty-four trials. He commented that the test was hard and boring.

like?" Phil replied: "I like to eat a lot" and "I'm fat." He wants to be a baseball player and offers "owning a candy store" as an alternative. He appears to have a negative attitude toward many things for which he expresses a preference. Thus he refers to the clarinet as "my favorite instrument," but says he gave it up after two months because "I did not like to practice." When asked to tell about "the best teacher he ever had," he named his second grade teacher "because she gave me good marks," but shifted to a much more extended account of another teacher, "the old hag, she stepped on my toes once." When asked about summer vacations he started, promisingly, to refer to "a place all our own," but ended up by telling of being afraid he would "fall off a horse." His frequent references to privileges enjoyed by his older brother which he feels are denied to him add to the impression of a rather unhappy child, who does not really enjoy anything. Projective tests interpretation refers to "limited resources," "emotional and intellectual constriction," and the "dismal" feeling tone of his productions.

Impulse control is poorly developed. His mother refers to him as "independent" but explains that she means that "he wants what he wants when he wants it . . . He cannot be reasoned with . . . they (the two boys) are polite outside, but at home they are just animals . . . I cannot do a thing with him . . . he is too fast for me." In interview with him, there are numerous spontaneous references to fights he has had with other boys. For example, he refers to a boy who "is always picking fights with me—he once lay on my bed—so I knocked him out cold—I wish he's dead, I hate him." He says of another boy "I gave him a sock, I gave him a bloody mouth, a bloody nose." Asked what he does when he is angry, he replied "I yell," and adds that he gets angry often.

The high point of his social independence appears to be his possession of a doorkey. However, the mother reports that he is afraid of being left alone or only with his brother and objects to his mother being out when he is at home. He is not allowed to go about alone, except in the immediate neighborhood, or to take the bus because, according to his mother, "he is too fleety . . . not settled enough." His friendships appear to be based largely on physical proximity, with no indication that they are of long duration or discriminatingly made.

In summary, poorly articulated experience, undeveloped self-concept, limited resources, and poorly developed controls indicate a low over-all level of differentiation.

Arthur—Case #7 (Group I). Arthur is our clearest example of a limitedly differentiated child who is chaotic and whose impulsive, explosive behavior was evident to all observers in the laboratory. Although he is within the average range intellectually, his school work has been for the most part below capacity level. In his first year in a public high school, he failed two subjects in spite of help from a private tutor. At 15, Arthur was sent to an expensive out-of-town boarding school, where his work was reported to have improved. The mother had seriously considered sending him to military school, in the hope that he would "learn discipline."

Arthur's father, a "self-made man," is in a business in which high pressures and daily risks have "taken their toll," according to the mother, and "are making him a nervous wreck." Money and financial standing appear to be important family values. In speaking of her children, the mother stresses the expense and trouble involved, with little expression of affection for them. Arthur is the oldest of four, with one brother who is close to him in age, and two younger sisters. The mother openly prefers the girls, because they are "less trouble." She expresses disappointment with Arthur, especially since, when he was a little boy, she had been told he was "very bright," and made a "good impression" on neighbors and acquaintances.

At age 10, Arthur was described as a small boy who looked like a 6-year-old. By 14, he was 4 feet 10 inches tall, though he told us he was 5 feet 2 inches, and expected to grow to be 6 feet 4 inches tall, because he had been taking "vitamin pills." The mother does not think he is concerned about his height. However, from the laboratory contacts with him it would appear that the problem of height has had deep psychological repercussions of which the mother seems unaware. He himself has made many efforts to improve his physique. He ascribes his poor school work to the fact that he spends so much time in athletics, hoping that body-building will solve the problem of height.

At age 10, Arthur was almost unmanageable in the laboratory because of his restlessness, hyperactivity, and refusal to continue tests unless given a gift. He quickly lost confidence and gave up trying. By the time he was 14, he was superficially more manageable, but problems of control persisted and took new forms. For example, in interview with him, he kept lighting and burning matches, saying that he had had "the habit" for about a year and "couldn't stop." He says he does it when he is mad or bored and adds that he used to set toilet paper on fire in school.

He carried with him, on this occasion, a taped piece of lead, weighing about a pound, explaining, "I have to use it in fights, because I am so short." When a woman staff member came in at this point in the interview, he hit her with it with considerable force, as part of his explanation to her of how it works. He said spontaneously that he has a "terrible temper, the worst in the family . . . When I get mad, you really have trouble . . . I beat up the first person I catch." Hitting seems to be a family custom. Arthur reports, apparently taking it for granted as a normal state of affairs, that his mother hits him with a shoe "once a day." According to his mother, although he has joined several clubs, he just "picks himself up out of them," because he has had a fight. Another manifestation of poor control, as we saw him at 14, was an inability to stay purposefully with a task. There were, during tests, continual intrusions of irrelevant conversation and activity—for example, he started to read a newspaper during the Rorschach; during the interview he abruptly introduced irrelevant topics. In part, this seemed to be a form of leaving the field when the task became difficult or in some way threatening. Projective tests, on the other hand, featured primarily underlying anxiety and inability to disperse and master his fears, "a vague uneasiness, without real awareness, as if trying to pierce through a fog."

The lack of clarity of Arthur's experience of himself and his environment is reflected in perceptual tests. An over-all global mode of perceiving is characteristic of him at age 10, and becomes even more prominent, in comparison with his peers, at ages 14 and 17.[14] He shows relative inferiority on subtests "saturated" with analytical ability on the Wechsler-Bellevue given at age 17, although not on the WISC given at 12.[15]

His poorly developed self-concept and inadequately articulated, confused experience are also reflected in the various techniques of personality study. For example, in blind interpretation of his drawings of human figures, he is described as "archaically attached to his mother in fantasies of violence . . . he cannot bear to tear himself away." He was unable to project graphically a complete human figure, the drawing of the female especially disintegrating below the level of the head into restless scribbling. On the TAT his characters lack identity and are frequently referred to only as "she" or "they"

[14] At age 10, his standard scores for BAT, RFT, and EFT were +.70, +1.00, +.97, respectively, averaging +.89. At age 14, the values for these tests were +1.44, +1.73, −.16, with an average of +1.00. At age 17, the values were +2.12, +2.15, +.14, with an average of +1.47. On the RFT, at age 10, he lined up the rod with the tilted frame on every trial, irrespective of the degree of frame tilt. On the BAT, at the same age, he was quite variable from trial to trial, but even on his most "accurate" trial, he said he was sitting erect when actually tilted by 8°. When this test was repeated at age 17, Arthur, in relation to the 17-year norm, was even more influenced by the tilted room than previously in determining body position. Arthur's EFT performance, at age 10, reflected his inability to overcome the influence of an embedding context in a perceptual task, his control problems, and difficulty in defining his role. This test, especially difficult for Arthur, became a battleground between him and the examiner. Even though three sessions were devoted to the test, it proved impossible to get him to complete it, and his total score on it had to be computed by prorating his score for the twelve completed trials. He insisted on being given a different design from the one presented, clamored for "black-and-white" designs, tore the protective cellophane covers off the design, scratched the walls with the stylus, and jabbed the examiner with it. He was exhilarated when occasionally successful. Under these conditions, it is of course not possible to separate his actual inability to do this task from the influence of his impulsive behavior which made it difficult for him to stay with the task. He did improve markedly at ages 14 and 17 (both in terms of absolute scores and relative to norms for these ages) when his overt behavior had calmed down, turning in an "intermediate" performance on this test.

[15] At age 12, his WISC full-scale IQ was 104, verbal IQ 104, performance IQ 103, intellectual index score 32, and verbal index score 32. At age 17, his Wechsler-Bellevue full-scale IQ was 107, verbal IQ 118, performance IQ 92, intellectual index score 30, and verbal index score 41.

or "might be a girl . . . might be a boy." The Rorschach is totally devoid of human content, with perception conspicuously lacking in clarity. There seems to be little interest in ordering or in structuring his experience. The interviews at ages 14 and 17 bring additional information. Thus, he says that his mother always chooses his books for him to read; without her, he "wouldn't know what to read." His ideal is President Franklin D. Roosevelt, "he had a perfect reason for everything, I never do anything without a reason. He collected stamps, I collect stamps." In his compensatory efforts he gives self-aggrandizing though often confused and contradictory accounts of events and situations, so that it becomes difficult for the observer —if not for Arthur himself—to distinguish fact from fantasy. Thus he tells, at age 14, of his stock market investments. We have made no attempt to check on facts, but he tells of having investments worth $4,000 and, in the next sentence, of owning 15,000 shares of stock worth $5 each. He stated with great conviction in the interview conducted at age 14 that, when tested at 10, he had fallen out of the tilted chair, fractured his ribs, had X-rays taken, "but of course I didn't tell my mother . . . I don't want to start a big thing over nothing . . . I don't want to make enemies." Needless to say, no such mishap had occurred, but inventing the story apparently gave Arthur an opportunity to show his stamina. Poor judgment is implied in the frequent transparent lies which he might know can easily be checked. Another characteristic was the "petering out" phenomenon—i.e., overstating a situation with the overstatement easily collapsing. Thus, he told spontaneously of belonging to a fraternity, but on further question it turned out that he was "only trying to get in." Much of his energy is apparently devoted to an unsuccessful struggle about his status and his identity, but at this stage of his development his efforts take the form of fantasy and talking big, rather than of active dealing with the environment in a directed, purposeful way. Another example of his grandiose though rather vague ambitions is his dream of "making a million dollars and retiring at 30." [16] Asked what he would do after that, he replied, "I don't know, I just want to quit early." Pressed further, he said he wanted to "enjoy himself," but had no idea how.

Arthur's social relations are difficult to evaluate. Both he and his mother frequently refer to fights he had with other boys, but he apparently does have friends who phone him and call for him. The indiscriminate nature of these contacts is suggested in the mother's statement that he has "lots of friends but no buddy." Arthur himself, at 14, when asked if he has a best friend, did not understand what was meant. He finally said: "They are all my friends; they tell me everything and I tell them everything." At the same time, the impression from the two interviews with him and from projective tests is that he does not really feel close to anyone and that capacity for deeper interpersonal contact is limited. Blind interpretation of

[16] Neal, Case #3 above, also wanted to "make millions," but in the meantime was actively pursuing his serious interest in science.

drawings refers to "aggressive, greedy fingers which seem to emphasize the grasping aspects of contact over those of social interaction."

Because of Arthur's tendency to overstatements, which were likely to "peter out" on further probing, the development or substantiality of his interests was difficult to ascertain. With the background of his expressed fear that if he doesn't keep busy he might "get in with a gang" and "get into trouble," the impression was that his interests—ping-pong, outdoor sports, playing cards, collecting stamps—were either transient time fillers or were pursued for ulterior motives. For example, in speaking of stamps and of playing cards, he emphasized almost exclusively the money aspects, while sports and exercise would, he hoped, increase his height.

In summary, Arthur's confused and poorly articulated experience, unclear self-concept, and severe impulse disturbance are indicative of a low overall level of differentiation. He does seem to struggle for some kind of self-definition, but his efforts are unrealistic, unadaptive, and poorly directed.

Ben—Case #8 (Group III). Ben is an example of a child with an extremely uneven development, combining serious limitations in salient aspects of differentiation with a high level of proficiency in some verbal skills.

Ben was born when his sister, an only sibling, was 4. He was a planned baby, although the father had not wanted a second child. The father is apparently a high-strung and demanding person. A combination of his own personal needs and long work hours as a copartner in a retail business results in his having neither the time nor the inclination to participate in the rearing of his children. The mother is necessarily the parent who does the disciplining. ("My husband feels that the children are sort of my department.")

Ben's performance on perceptual tests captures the essence of his inability to get his bearings in his world and to experience it in an articulated manner. He is the most field dependent of the 68 10-year-old boys.[17]

[17] The standard scores for BAT, RFT, and EFT were +1.86, +1.49, and +1.51, respectively, with an average of +1.62. His body is such an uncertain anchorage point for him that, on the BAT, when he was initially tilted 22° to one side and the room tilted 35° to the same side, he requested to be tilted toward the room—i.e., even more than he was already tilted—in order to perceive himself as straight. He did this consistently on all three trials of the series, ending up tilted by 24°, 30°, and 26°. This is the most extreme abdication to the influence of the field that we have yet encountered at age 10. On the RFT, he consistently aligned the rod with the frame, regardless of whether he himself was sitting up straight or tilted. The smallest deviation from the true vertical he achieved in adjusting the rod was 15°. The influence of the frame was so strong for him that he could not escape its influence even on practice trials, with the room fully lit. On the EFT, he failed on fifteen of the twenty-four trials in the 5 minutes allowed, showing how strongly he was influenced by the embedding context. Thus, he was consistently unable to experience either his body or an external object as discrete from the surrounding field.

Consistent with this markedly global perceptual performance is his weakness in handling the WISC subtests which require analytical ability.[18]

Ben's uncertain sense of identity comes through clearly on two of the three projective tests. His drawings of human figures are primitive and unsophisticated, with almost complete absence of detailing and almost no difference between the sexes, suggesting quite literally a poorly differentiated self-concept. Some of his Rorschach contents indicate that the problem of who he is—male or female, person or just the outer appurtenances of a person—is a real problem to him. Moreover, the frequency with which things visualized on the Rorschach are seen as injured and broken (e.g., the figures on Card III are "split up"; on II, "an animal has been badly beaten"; on IV "a telescope is being torn down, it's crumbled") suggests inner fears and undermined self-confidence. However, he gives a different account of himself on the TAT. The characters in his stories have a much better defined identity than one might have expected on the basis of the other two tests. Moreover, some of these characters emerge as victorious rather than defeated at the end of his quite complex and well-organized stories. It seems significant, however, that his stories deal with quite adult worries and concerns, and do not reflect the everyday problems of 10-year-olds that most children in the group go into. The highly verbal nature of the task enables him to capitalize on his verbal capabilities. Asked to "make up a story," he apparently takes full opportunity to escape into the realm of fantasy. By contrast, in the interview, when the focus is directly on him and his experiences, he is less able to make use of his resources. Under these conditions, he is unable to take a stand, express an opinion, tell how he feels. He frequently makes use of the "dependent shift," i.e., quotes another person when asked what he thinks (e.g., "What do you plan to do after high school?" "My mother thinks I'd like to go to an out-of-town college." "What makes a teacher a good teacher?" "Well, my friend has the second-best teacher in Brooklyn." "What do you think about juvenile delinquency?" "My sister wrote a composition about it for school."). Asked in the interview, "What are you like?" he replied: "Well, I never thought about that . . . well . . . I don't know."

The poorly articulated quality of his experience, manifested in perceptual tests, is also expressed on interview in the fuzzy quality of much of his thinking. Although he displays a good deal of knowledge in various areas, his knowledge seems poorly assimilated. He has a marked preference for specific factual things that he can memorize, e.g., populations of states, pictures he has seen on stamps. But his account of events and situations tends to be circumstantial, overconcrete, overspecific. At times he tends to go off on a tangent, as if losing track of what he had been saying. His account of events and situations frequently has an enumerative quality. Thus, asked

[18] His verbal IQ was 140 and his performance IQ 99, with a full-scale IQ of 123; there is a similar discrepancy between his verbal-index score (52) and his intellectual-index score (25).

to "tell a little bit" about his family, Ben gave a conscientious account of place of birth and date of birth, including day of the month and of the week, of all four members of the immediate family. On the other hand, the interview is sprinkled with adultlike comments (e.g., "It's true that if you like something you get a good mark in it," and "I should only watch educational programs on TV") that sound like some of the formulations his mother had used in the interview with her.

In the area of impulse control, the picture is variable. To start with, Ben says of himself, when asked what he does when he gets angry, "I don't show it, I just get angry at myself." In the laboratory, he impressed most observers as subdued, lacking in animation, "like a little old man." His mother describes him as having been "a good, quiet baby," and as currently able to conform to some rather rigid and arbitrary rules (e.g., "my children know better than to sit on beds, they know chairs are for sitting"). The only other approving statement she made in this area was in describing an incident when Ben was five years old. She seemed genuinely moved and appreciative when she spoke of his behavior during his father's serious illness. He was apparently sober, patient, and supportive of her, as if sensing her distress in a very adult way. But dominant in her account were her references to his "terrible temper" and his aggressive outbursts against her. When Ben and his sister fight, which they apparently do frequently, "I get so upset that I just walk away." The over-all impression is of a mother who feels helpless in the face of difficulties and is unable to deal with her child's assertiveness and aggression. In disciplining him, she threatens but does not carry out her threats, alternating between permissive and coercive behavior. With two impulsive parents and inconsistent discipline, Ben's own inconsistencies in managing his temper are perhaps understandable. In areas of socialization other than temper control, the mother describes Ben as dirty and refusing to wash and bathe, but on the other hand as tidy about his room and his possessions. He is not too responsible about his homework, frequently demanding help from his mother and his sister, but at times is perfectly capable of recopying his work several times if he has made even one mistake.

Projective tests also give a variable picture of the control and defense system. Thus, the drawings were described as showing "no manifestations of the more sophisticated controls . . . strong impulses which he cannot master . . . he is a helpless victim of his inner aggressions and fears." Drawings also suggest a child who might lash out blindly out of feelings of weakness and confusion. One clinician, on the basis of projective tests alone, wondered whether Ben is not capable of much better controls and defenses than he is presently using, and whether something had happened in his life situation which had made for regression from a previously higher, perhaps premature, attainment in this area. The previously "good, quiet baby," who, at the age of five, was somehow able to comfort and support his mother in a crisis, may be rebelling now against pressures and expectations which he had accepted too early. From the mother's account, his impulsiveness and aggressiveness seem directed especially at her and his sister.

Ben has some rather sophisticated and well-developed interests. For example, he reads a good deal, and especially enjoys the Landmark Book series; he and a friend are developing their version of the Morse code; he has a stamp collection, which apparently appeals to him as offering a chance to accumulate random information. ("They tell about each stamp, all about Davy Crockett, Daniel Boone, early man, trains, trucks, gliders, airplanes, ships, boats, animals. . . .") He is a good enough athlete so that older boys in the neighborhood ask him to be on their teams; in camp, he has received many athletic awards; on a rainy day, he can amuse himself with games. In contrast, his mother emphasizes that he has no interest at all in making or constructing anything, "not even a jig-saw puzzle," and will not touch tools. She comments that her own competence in many areas—photography, oil painting, handwork, repairing and refinishing furniture—may have discouraged Ben from attempting to meet too high a standard.

On the side of social functioning, the picture is again complex. According to the mother, he "wants to be independent" in some areas. For example, he is one of the very few boys in the group who can take the subway to Manhattan by himself. He has been going to camp since he was 5 years old. During school vacations and weekends, he sometimes spends the whole day outside with friends, only coming in for meals, without reporting to his mother where he is going. She apparently has enough confidence in him to feel that he does not require close supervision. But, on the other hand, his mother still has to bathe him and, on his request, puts on his socks and ties his shoelaces.

His friendships are likely to be of long duration and based on fairly specific mutual interests. ("My friend that I made up the language with . . . my other friend, we like to walk . . . he and I usually talk about sports.")

Unevenness of development is most likely the basis for variability in the major ratings made on the basis of the four techniques for personality evaluation, each rating assigned by a different investigator. These ranged from a high rating for task approach on the TAT to a low rating for cognitive clarity as shown in the interview, with intermediate ratings on figure drawings and the Rorschach. The latter two were explicitly designated by the judges as compromise ratings. Thus, in the drawing of the female, the discrepancy between the high level of sophistication in the drawing of the head and the primitive quality of the rest of the figure is so great that the two parts might have been drawn by two different persons. In the course of assigning a Rorschach rating, the comment was made: "He tries to make up in verbal sophistication what he lacks in genuine perceptual clarity. The final rating probably overrates his level of differentiation." Another clinician, working blind with all three projective tests, summarized her impressions in part as follows: "Mature intellectually, capable of rational planning and good organization . . . but with a serious weakness in self-concept, with confusion and anxiety about role and identity . . . which interfere with otherwise discriminating and assertive dealings with the environment."

In evaluating this complex child with many contradictory trends, the complex and contradictory character of home influences must be considered. Thus there is the psychologically absent father, and a mother who, though competent in many ways, and with well-defined interests and a life of her own, was described on the basis of the interview with her as lacking in security within herself, uncertain about many beliefs and values, helpless in dealing with many aspects of her home and family situation, inconsistent in her rearing practices. This sort of background may have contributed to Ben's uncertainty about his role and his identity. Whether this background has also contributed to Ben's uneven intellectual development as shown, for example, on the WISC, and in his general overinvestment in verbal development, must remain a matter of conjecture. That he has adopted appeasement as one technique for getting along, at least with adults (though probably not with his mother), is suggested both by his projective-test productions and by his behavior with laboratory personnel. Perhaps his developed verbal expressiveness is another such technique. In any event, he can be regarded as a "case illustration" of the finding that highly developed verbal skills may occur in the context of a low level of differentiation.

B. SOME IMPRESSIONS OF THE GROUPS

1. Highly Differentiated Children

We found this group more varied, and therefore more difficult to describe, than the group of limitedly differentiated children. It is likely that the greater individual complexity, implied by more highly developed differentiation, permits more varied forms of integration, thus making for the greater diversity.

The clearer sense of separate identity of these children was commonly manifested in their more definite sense of role in the family. They appeared to recognize and accept their own role as children, and their parents' roles as those of the persons in charge, without either engaging in fruitless attempts to usurp the parental role, or helplessly abdicating to parental authority. In relation to siblings, they appeared to have a clearer sense of themselves as the younger or the older, although friction with siblings was not uncommon. With their roles thus defined, they seemed, nevertheless, to have a realistic expectation that their opinion counts. Some were able to convey this sense of role in the family clearly in verbal communication on interview; others, perhaps less verbally articulate, nevertheless conveyed a sense of being free of serious confusion as to role. As seen later (Chapter 19), the behavior of their parents towards them may have contributed to such role definition.

We often found instances of realistic self-appraisal, modesty, or great dignity among relatively differentiated children. We did not find, as we occasionally did among the less differentiated children, unrealistic bragging about accomplishments and exaggerated self-importance. It is as if their self-appraisal corresponded more nearly to their personal substance.

The picture these children generally presented in the area of friendships is consistent with what we have said of them with regard to their developed sense of separate identity. They are likely to be quite discriminating and selective in their friendships. Friends are likely to be chosen on the basis of congenial qualities, such as common interests or compatible intellectual level. Some of these children showed a quality of self-sufficiency and even aloofness from others, which resulted in a "take-it-or-leave-it" attitude in relation to their friends. The mother of one of these boys commented: "He gets many telephone calls, but he's not dependent on friends. He does not seek them out. He has many interests and is content to be alone." Such a basis for having few friends is quite different from that found among limitedly differentiated children, whose failure to form friendships appeared to be more a matter of inability than of choice.

The relatively high level of cognitive clarity of the more differentiated children, and the articulateness of their awareness of both themselves and of their environment is best illustrated by excerpts from interviews with them.

Thus one child said of his school attainment, "I am one of the good ones," showing his ability to place himself in relation to others. Asked if he is planning to go to college, he replied, "If I have my way, I think so." He expressed his point of view, while at the same time relating it to external realities. His self-awareness was reflected in his self-description: "I work hard, I am quiet when I work."

Another child, when asked about his career plans, said: "I want to be an engineer, like my brother. He says that's why, but I don't think so. I think it's because I like to tinker." This statement reflects an awareness of the motivation for his choice and, again, an ability to distinguish his view from that of another and to hold on to his view despite the difference. It reflects as well a definite orientation toward the future.

A striking capacity for thinking of people's behavior in motivational terms and for maintaining perspective is shown in the comment of one of our differentiated children about his teacher: "She yells a lot, but it isn't her fault. Her father just died." In the same category is the statement of another child: "The best teacher I ever had was strict, but we learned a lot."

The relatively well-developed control structure of the highly differentiated children is illustrated by the following examples.

One child appeared judicious and moderate, almost too much so for a 10-year-old. His mother's main complaint about him was that he was too perfectionistic. A blind interpretation of his Rorschach contained the statement: "He shows good channeling of impulse . . . he is assertive in a contained way." Another description of him, prepared blind on the basis of the three projective tests was: "Intellectualizations are prominent. He effectively uses obsessive defenses. He is overregulated, cautious. He is nevertheless able to acknowledge aggression, at least in fantasy productions, and to express it in modulated form."

Another child was described by his mother as "very disciplined." Comments made in a blind Rorschach interpretation included: "Good ability to rationalize feelings. Remarkable ability to maintain distance from percepts." In his figure-drawing productions, shading was well rationalized and contained, suggesting tight and effective controls. There was an overall impression of marked reliance on intellectualization.

This child also used many sophisticated control measures on the TAT. Some of these served to maintain distance from the themes introduced. They included making the setting unreal (e.g., "it looks like a painting." "This would be like from a motion picture") or making it remote in time and/or space ("This looks like a Roman or Greek . . . picture"). Another kind of control he used on the TAT reflected caution and evasiveness. This involved what we have come to label "interpretative description." Specific features of the card are interpreted in almost Talmudic fashion (e.g., "You can tell it's not a very modern picture since he doesn't have shoes on"). The "story" consists of an elaboration of what is shown on the card itself. Theme development is thereby avoided.[19] This kind of "interpretative description" found among some of the highly differentiated, emotionally distant children is very different from the simple enumeration of details of the card commonly observed in the TAT records of the less differentiated children.

Still another child gave the impression, on the basis of all available data, of being socially overadjusted, with a strong orientation toward social conformity. There was evidence to suggest, however, that the family standards and values he follows have become his own. This evidence came from the

[19] Holt (1951) describes a similar phenomenon in adults. He writes: "Paranoid cautiousness . . . may make itself known through an inferential, descriptive approach that *derives,* often by explicit steps, everything in the story from the details of the picture itself" (p. 211).

interview with the mother as well as from the projective test data for the child. A blind write-up, based on these tests, contained the comment: "He has had to sacrifice much to live up to his parents' standards, which have now definitely become his own." His mother commented that even as a very small child he never broke anything. His figure drawings contained much careful, obsessive detailing, and suggested controls which are effective, though tight and effortful, rather than natural and flexible. His TAT productions again showed much obsessive detailing, with avoidance of commitment by means of the liberal use of alternatives. On this test, however, he at times used a "pollyanna type" of denial, together with breakthrough of aggressive fantasy when the stimulus became too strong for denial to be effective.

Individual case studies led to two further impressions. First, when an occasional breakthrough of impulse occurred in everyday life or in projective test material among these children, it was in a setting of generally highly developed controls. Second, as a manifestation of their relatively well-developed control structure, many of these children showed a clear sense of responsibility, and appeared to have a formulated set of standards. Though these standards were sometimes conventional, they were internalized and had become the children's own. There is the impression that when conventionality does occur among highly differentiated children, it has a very different basis than it does among the less differentiated children. Thus, among children at least, conventionality or conformity as such is not incompatible with developed differentiation. In fact, conventionality was encountered more often among such children than we might have anticipated.

In general, the children in this group, particularly in contrast to the limitedly differentiated children, showed relatively well-developed interests, which appeared to be meaningful to them and were actively pursued. Such a development of interests may require initiative and ability to pursue remote goals and carry on on one's own, without the need for constant stimulation from the outside.

The interests of the highly differentiated children were quite sophisticated—for example, chess as contrasted to collecting pictures of baseball players, a favorite occupation among the less differentiated children. When a more conventional interest was pursued, it was likely to be only one of a number of interests. While variety of interests seemed characteristic of some children in the group, at least as impressive was the fact that they appeared to derive genuine satisfaction out of their activities.

One child's interests included science, chess, and going to museums. On TV, he watched, by preference, some quite adult programs along with the more childish ones. His parents stressed culture and education and encouraged him in his interests. At the same time, the motive force for his interests seemed to stem from within himself.

The range of interests of another boy included fish, flowers, reading, playing ball. His mother described him as "good at constructing things," "appreciative of artistic things," and "always able to amuse himself."

A difference among children in the highly differentiated group that emerged in the course of the case studies concerned an aspect of emotional make-up. Some children were emotionally quite passive, compliant, conforming, even placating, compassionate, emotionally accessible, and not afraid of emotional involvements. We have designated such children as "emotionally soft." They contrasted with other children in the group who are best described as "emotionally hard." The latter children tended to be distant and aloof, showing a quality of emotional remoteness. They were mainly interested in their own value system, and mastery over and manipulation of the environment appeared to be salient goals. Some of these characteristics are similar to those found by Crutchfield and Starkweather (1953) among their extremely field-independent Air Force captains, for example "cold and distant in relationships with others," "unaware of his stimulus value," "manipulates people as a means of achieving personal ends."

The "hard" quality, when it occurs, is most likely to be found among the more highly differentiated children. We have never encountered it among limitedly differentiated children.

While the "emotionally hard" children manifested a quality of directedness in their activity in quite apparent form, the "emotionally soft" children were as capable of giving direction to their lives, though perhaps in less obvious ways. The sense of directedness of the latter children was shown, for example, in their long-range pursuit of meaningful interests and friendships and in their ability to persist in the face of difficulties, to set and maintain their own high standards of achievement, and to take on and carry through responsibilities appropriate to their age.

The highly differentiated children had their share of problems. These included special fears of the dark, of swimming and going into the water, of dirt and germs, and even of lighting matches. These fears appeared to be specific and localized, and did not lead to a generalized hampering fearfulness, as was the case with some of the less differentiated youngsters. We are, of course, inclined to regard the special fears as problems any child might have, rather than as a distinguishing characteristic of the highly differentiated group. We would be inclined to assign a similar status to occasional reports that a child was sensitive and easily hurt. On the other hand, the tendency to be too perfectionistic, overcontrolled, or emotionally distant is consistent with the obsessive-compulsive structure which is often found in children of this group.

2. Limitedly Differentiated Children

While these children also showed variety along with essential similarities, they were a good deal easier to characterize as a group than the highly differentiated children, perhaps because limitedly developed individual complexity permits less varied forms of integration.

Their poorly developed sense of separate identity manifested itself in a variety of ways. For example, in interviews with them, their lack of developed views of their own, and their consequent reliance on others for a definition of their attitudes and sentiments expressed itself in a phenomenon we have come to call the "dependent shift." When asked for their opinion on a given issue, they were likely to cite the judgment of a source which to them is authoritative. One child, asked "What are you like?" answered: "I don't know, my friends do." Another, asked how he likes his teacher, answered: "Everybody says she's nice."

Suggestive of the same phenomenon was the repeated use by one of these children of the collective "we" where "I" would have been more appropriate. This behavior seemed to reflect an inability to separate himself from others in his environment.

In the blind case write-ups of children in this group comments concerning "poorly developed self-concept" and "confusion about role" were recurrent. One child was described as showing a "hazy and dissolving sense of personal identity," another as "confused, often losing his bearings, unable to find a nucleus of values around which to develop an orientation toward both himself and the outside world."

The peer-relationships of these children tended to show some of the qualities which might be anticipated on the basis of their relatively undeveloped sense of identity. Lasting friendships, selectively and discriminatively formed, were rare. Friendships tended to be casual and transient in nature, with the choice of friends dictated by circumstances. Some of these youngsters show an undiscriminative gregariousness, and tend to go with the crowd, but have no individualized friendships. For example, the mother of one boy (Case #7) described him as having "a lot of friends but no buddy." Even with the limited friendships, there was often friction and difficulty in getting along, although some of the more gregarious and more compliant boys in the group did present a picture of good social adjustment in the sense of getting on well with other children.

The poorly articulated experience of these children was particularly evident in the interviews with them. Often their responses had only a tangential relation to the questions asked, or showed irrelevant over-inclusiveness, combined with inability to generalize. For example, one child, asked whether he had any cousins of his own age, gave a long list of his many cousins, specifying the age and school grade of each. What we have come to call "overspecificity in a sea of vagueness" was illustrated by one child who, in response to a question about juvenile delinquency, answered: "That's when a big boy breaks a store window like on the corner." Another common phenomenon in describing an event or activity was that of "petering out." An impressive account of a particular activity in which a child was presumably involved was given, but on further questioning it developed that the child had just started on the activity, or was only thinking of engaging in it. The low level of awareness of themselves and of others was evident in their descriptions of people. One child, for instance, described his father, mother, sister, and teacher indiscriminately as "nice," with no indication that they were experienced as persons with individualized characteristics. Another aspect of the same phenomenon was the tendency to describe persons in terms of "external constructs"—for example, "my father has a big moustache on him" and "my mother likes to go to second-alarm fires."

The poorly developed controls often found in this group of children were manifested both directly (on projective tests, in their mothers' accounts of "constant fighting," in the reports of the children themselves—e.g., "when I get mad, I scream"), and indirectly (in the relative absence of internalized standards). A lack of developed standards was shown in two main ways: acceptance of very infantile, externally imposed standards, and inability to assume responsibility. The lack of responsibility was particularly evident in the complaints made by mothers of such children that the child lacks interest in school work, and "cannot be trusted" to go about by himself, be left on his own, or do assigned tasks at home without constant reminders and supervision.

The records of these children provide impressive illustrations of their poorly developed controls and lack of internalized standards.

The blind write-up of one child described him as "a helpless prey to any strong impulse from within or any stimulus from without." Another was described as "easily distracted, especially by his own thoughts and im-

pulses, against which he has been too weak to build up effective defenses
. . . His thought processes are characterized by chaotic rambling." In
the various test and laboratory situations, this child was hyperactive, constantly asking irrelevant questions. His figure drawings were chaotic, again
suggesting serious problems with impulse control.

Another child in this group was described in the blind write-up as follows: "Defenses are easily penetrable . . . shows little complexity either in
the development of active conflicts, or of defenses against them . . . assumes little responsibility for handling his feelings." His mother complained
that he was lazy, needed constant reminders, "doesn't care about his homework."

In contrast to the highly differentiated children, the youngsters
in this group showed, in a variety of ways, failure to function as "going concerns." Some manifested it primarily in a low level of energy
and resources, others in limited meaningful involvement with the environment, still others in a lack of responsibility, limited ability for
self-care, and general social dependency, and some in babyish or demanding behavior at home.

Thus, one child, at age 10, was still dressed by his mother; his mother
drove him to music lessons in the neighborhood, although he was perfectly
capable of taking the bus by himself; he told us he "missed his mummy"
when away at camp for 3 weeks. Another child never buys anything out
of his allowance without asking his mother. Several staff members commented that while being tested he tended to give up quickly when he encountered any difficulty. His energy seemed invested more in impulsive
behavior than in constructive pursuits. In a blind write-up it was said of
him that there is "very little display of energy or of motivating purposefulness in any of his test productions . . . he seems passive and immobilized
. . . experiences a constant fear of failure."

Evidence of lack of developed interests was striking in this group.
The over-all impression was that interests were casually pursued, and
with the exception of single passions—baseball in one case, fishing in
another—they seemed to be time fillers rather than genuine sources of
satisfaction. The mother of one boy complained that he "has no interests . . . if he can't finish something right away, he doesn't have
the patience to finish."

Several mothers of children in the group complained that they have
to entertain their child, a complaint not made about any child in the
highly differentiated group. The most dramatic illustration of lack
of direction, purpose, and meaningful involvement was supplied by a
child who told us in interview that he spends most of his time in empty
lots, "just jumping around."

The difficulties of children in this group seemed to stem largely from impulse control problems, lack of resources, and poorly developed sense of responsibility.

As in the case of the more highly differentiated children, several subgroups emerged on intensive individual case study of the limitedly differentiated children.

The largest subgroup presented a picture of a strikingly low level of differentiation in over-all development. They showed poverty of resources, lack of enterprise and initiative, poorly developed interests, lack of well-structured controls and defenses, and marked dependence on external sources of support and guidance. Problems of impulse control did occur in this subgroup, but not as a primary feature. In the behavior observations these youngsters were often characterized as fearful, apprehensive, ill at ease, uninterested, but not as primarily impulsive. Children showing this constellation are perhaps the prototype of poorly differentiated youngsters. Case #6 is illustrative of this subgroup.

A smaller group of children, although also showing the poverty of resources found in the first group, was characterized primarily by severe problems of impulse control. As we saw them in the laboratory, these children appeared overactive, unmanageable, difficult to handle. Their projective test productions usually gave a strong impression of poor channeling of aggression, poor controls, chaotic personality organization. Children in the first subgroup, who secondarily presented an impulse control problem, were at least able to mobilize their controls sufficiently so that they were not unmanageable in their laboratory contact with strange adults. Case #7 illustrates the impulse-driven subgroup.

Still another kind of limitedly differentiated child, represented by only 2 boys in our sample, is distinctive enough to be placed in a separate subgroup. (Ben, Case #8, is one of these.) An outstanding characteristic of the 2 boys, evident in our contacts with them, as well as in their test productions, was a high level of verbal skills. In fact two different staff members, working blind with the TAT and the Rorschach, respectively, commented that, because of the verbal sophistication of these two children, they might be overrating them. A comment made on the basis of the Rorschachs of both these boys, prior to knowledge of their performance on any other tests, referred to "oversophistication in the absence of a sufficiently developed inner structure." In both cases, a discrepancy of over 40 points between the verbal and performance sections of the WISC, in favor of the former, supported the impression of extremely uneven development in the direction of overinvestment in verbal skills. A discrepancy of such magnitude between verbal and analytical development has thus far not been encountered even once in a highly differentiated or intermediate youngster. We learned from these cases that a high level of verbal skills is not an adequate basis for predicting a high level of differentiation when this verbal achievement is unsupported by a sufficiently developed underlying structure.

Despite the high level of verbal skills of these 2 boys, in their interviews they gave an unmistakable impression of a low level of cognitive clarity. Both had a wide fund of information on many subjects, but the information was poorly assimilated. They gave the impression of trying hard to impress adults and, as far as the personnel of the laboratory was concerned, they succeeded in this attempt.

We do not regard these 2 boys as exceptions to the essential picture presented by limitedly differentiated children. The existence of such cases serves as a reminder that children who are limitedly differentiated cannot be thought of as showing a similar degree of development in all areas.

One final observation must be made about the emotional quality of children in the limitedly differentiated group.

In considering certain descriptive terms used to characterize some of the highly differentiated children, e.g., overcontrolled, emotionally aloof, interested in mastering and manipulating the environment, one is perhaps likely to anticipate that the limitedly differentiated children, free of such emotionally hampering qualities, would show the opposite characteristics; that the freedom from the rigidities and emotional distance would lead to such social qualities as capacity for empathy and greater freedom in interpersonal contact. At least in our limited sample of 68 children, only 10 years old and drawn from a socially and culturally homogeneous population, this expectation was not borne out. Sensitivity to the moods, needs, and characteristics of others, which genuine empathy implies, and interest in interpersonal relations, as well as freedom to engage in them, characteristically were found not among the limitedly differentiated children, but among those in the highly differentiated group whom we have called "emotionally soft." Certainly empathy involves more than, for example, the greater alertness to facial expression found among the less differentiated children (see Chapter 8), an alertness which reflects need for acceptance and approval, rather than a genuine response to and regard for another person.

3. Intermediate Children [20]

The most important fact about the children in this group is that on intensive study they showed themselves not to be unique in kind, as compared to children in the two extreme groups. They could be described with reference to the dimensions which distinguished the groups at the extremes from each other.

Using these dimensions the intermediates may be characterized as follows: In articulateness of experience, including sense of separate identity and body concept, they seemed genuinely intermediate with very few showing the high level of articulation found in the more differentiated group, but none showing the marked confusion and lack of clarity found in the limitedly differentiated group. In the area of controls, the picture was more variable. They seemed closer to the highly differentiated group, though the quality of overcontrol and overintellectualization that was seen among children in the latter group did not occur among the intermediates. In the development of interests, the intermediates were on the whole "in-between," showing quite a range, from obvious paucity of resources in one case and "not knowing what to do with his free time" in another, to several whose interests appeared to have depth and had meaning for them. Finally, in quality of social relations, only two of the intermediates showed the self-sufficiency and aloofness that were seen among the "hard," highly differentiated children.

[20] Each child in this group had a perceptual index score (the mean of the standard scores for BAT, RFT, and EFT) which fell in the middle range of the distribution of these scores for the entire group of 10-year-olds. These intermediate index scores may be composed of individual test scores which are consistently intermediate or which vary widely. Our previous work (1954) suggested that when a person shows marked variability in individual test scores, the variations may be related to differences in the structure of the task presented by the individual tests—particularly, the degree to which task structure facilitates or hinders the separation of item from field. We considered the possibility that the individual's ability to capitalize upon the assistance which the structure of the task offers him may provide an important clue to his general functioning. Accordingly, we gave attention to the patterning of the scores for the individual perceptual tests which made up the composite perceptual index score of each child in the intermediate group. In our intensive study of individual children, however, we were unable to discern any distinct relation between perceptual patterning and psychological functioning in general. Accordingly, the intermediate children are considered together as a group.

C. SUMMARY

Following the analyses of specific characteristics of children, described in the preceding chapters, case conferences were held on individual children in the groups on which these analyses were based. All the test material available for the child, as well as scores and ratings derived from this material, were considered at the conferences, along with the records and ratings of the interviews with the mothers.

One outcome of these case studies was the clear impression that the pictures of more differentiated and less differentiated children, suggested by the previously established patterns of significantly interrelated characteristics, are not "abstractions." They seemed generally consistent with the pictures of children that emerged from our intensive study of them as individuals.

The case studies also provided an opportunity to identify other differences between more differentiated and less differentiated children than those previously considered. These differences, which at present represent observations yet to be checked systematically, included capacity for self-care, ability to assume responsibility, nature and bases of friendships, and kinds and depth of interests. In addition, the case conferences provided an opportunity to document with material closer to life some of the relations identified in our earlier statistical analyses.

The case studies further highlighted the impression, already evident from our earlier studies, that children who are similar with respect to the development of differentiation may still in many ways be different. Our particular concern with the diversity in the course of the case conferences led to the identification of several subgroups among children brought together as being more differentiated or less differentiated. Among the relatively differentiated children, there was one subgroup designated "emotionally soft" because they showed such qualities as emotional accessibility, compassion, and apparent absence of fear of emotional involvement. A contrasting subgroup was designated "emotionally hard." Children in this group tended to be distant and aloof, and particularly interested in their own value system and in mastery over and manipulation of the environment. Among the limitedly differentiated children, we found one subgroup, the largest, characterized by poverty of resources, lack of enterprise and initiative, undeveloped interests, lack of well-structured controls and defenses, and marked dependence on others. Children showing this constellation are perhaps the prototype of limitedly differentiated youngsters. A second subgroup showed as an outstanding characteristic severe problems of impulse control, though also giving evidence of marked poverty of resources. Finally, the third and smallest subgroup consisted of children whose outstanding characteristic was a high level of verbal skills in the absence of developed underlying structure. They thus presented a picture of uneven development.

Finally, the case studies suggested that children who are intermediate in mode of field approach, considered a major indicator of extent of differentiation, are not different in kind, but can be described along the same dimensions which distinguished the extreme groups from each other.

16

THE PROBLEM OF
ORIGINS OF DIFFERENCES
IN LEVEL OF
DIFFERENTIATION

The problem of how differences in level of differentiation arise leads to such questions as these: In what ways may early characteristics of children, possibly constitutional in character, contribute to the differences? In what ways may the differences be determined by life experiences, both in the family and in society?

To obtain effective answers to these questions, an extensive program of research is obviously required. We have made a start on such a program. In one line of research we have sought to explore the relation between early observable characteristics of children and their functioning at later ages in the psychological areas with which we have been particularly concerned. This study has been completed, but its results are not yet analyzed. The approach used is described in Chapter 23, along with studies of stability of functioning during later periods of development. The second, and at this time main approach to the problem of "origins" has been through studies of children's interactions with their families—particularly their mothers—in the course of growing up. These studies are described in Chapters 17 through 22.

The studies we have done on the possible role of constitutional and experiential factors in the development of differentiation were guided by an interaction approach. Thinking in the field of child development has long departed from the view, on the one hand, that the child is a piece of passive clay in the hands of the mother, who makes of him whatever her own needs and wishes dictate and, on the other hand, that the child's growth is simply an unfolding along the predestined course laid down in his genetic make-up. An interaction approach is also consistent with current views of the nature of gene action (see, for example, Sinnott, Dunn, and Dobzhansky, 1958). Genes do not enforce a given inevitable expression "from within themselves"; genic expression depends, in varying degree, on the environmental conditions that obtain during development.

The appropriateness of an interaction approach to the particular issues with which we are concerned is suggested by the results of a study by Vandenberg.[1] As part of a general investigation of hereditary factors in psychological traits, Vandenberg administered the RFT to groups of fraternal and identical twins. Identical twins were found to be significantly more similar in RFT performance than fraternal twins.[2] As in any study of identical twins reared together, this finding can be explained on two alternative bases. Identical twins have the same genetic make-up, and so the greater similarity in RFT performance may reflect the influence of genetic factors. On the other hand, it may be reasoned that identical twins have more similar "stimulus value" to their parents (and others) than do fraternal twins. They therefore elicit similar reactions with the result that the forces acting on them during development tend to be more similar than for fraternal twins. Only a study of identical twins reared apart would permit a choice between these alternatives.

The results of the Vandenberg study seem, however, to rule out the possibility that the nature of the child's perceptual functioning—and the psychological constellation of which it is a part—can be explained on the basis of a purely "environmental" hypothesis. Although we have no evidence from the studies reported below or from other sources that would contradict a pure genetic explanation, we are not inclined to accept it on the grounds set forth above.[3] This leaves the interaction hypothesis as the most tenable one.

[1] Personal communication from Steven G. Vandenberg.

[2] Identical female twins were significantly more similar than identical male twins.

[3] In the course of our studies of children we have had the opportunity to study two pairs of 10-year-old identical twins. One of these pairs had similar perceptual test results, the other pair had quite different results. In a study of two pairs of identical adult twins, we again found that one pair had very similar perceptual results and the other rather different results. The existence of differences in even a single pair of identical twins would argue against a strict genetic interpretation of perceptual performance.

The concept of interaction, considered thus far in relation to the roles of constitutional and experiential factors, is specifically applicable when viewing the child's experiences in the family. The mother's influence on the growing child must be viewed in terms of a mother-child relation, involving a complex, continuous interaction between characteristics of each. As a hypothetical example, a given mother's pattern of behavior may be different with an active than with a lethargic child. In turn, the effect of a coercive mother may be quite different on a child who initially is highly active than on one who is extremely lethargic. In such an interaction view, it does not seem meaningful to ask whether the child's initial make-up or the mother's behavior is generally more important for the child's development.

An interaction view of the kind we have sketched suggests that the ideal study for answering the questions we posed is a longitudinal one, starting with observations of the family even prior to the birth of the child. Because of its demands in personnel, facilities, and time, we were unable to undertake studies based on this method. As an alternative, we have carried out cross-sectional studies of mother-child relationships and, as mentioned, have begun longitudinal studies in the period from infancy to the 6–9 year age range. Despite the limitations of this approach, we felt the information and insights gained about the relation between the child's level of differentiation and the nature of his experiences in the family would be useful in planning the comprehensive longitudinal studies which alone can provide full answers to the questions we have posed.

In approaching the problem of the influence of life experiences on a child's progress toward greater differentiation we recognized that it is necessary to consider the wide range of relations children have with their environment. We chose to start with the child's relation to his family and particularly to his mother. The mother is generally the more important parent in relation to rearing. This is true in general for our culture. That it is true as well for the children we studied is suggested by the finding that in the majority of these children's TAT parent-child stories the parental figure was the mother. Our decision to focus on the mother was determined also by the practical consideration of choosing the parent who had both the time and interest to take part in a rather extended interview. In taking the child's relation to his mother as the starting point of our studies, we realize that the role of the father, siblings, and other important persons in the child's environment will also need to be investigated.

We used two approaches to obtain evidence about the relations between mothers and children. Our main approach was through the mother. A secondary approach was through the child. Each provided a partial view of the interaction process.

An impression of a mother's relation to her child from the mother's view was obtained through an interview with her. In this she gave an account of her feelings, attitudes, and behavior toward her child and her child's responses to these. Although the categories used in evaluating mother-child relations on the basis of interviews with the mother are all necessarily oriented toward the mother's views and behavior, they must be considered as aspects of mother-child interactions.

In a second approach to the study of mother-child relations we sought evidence from the child himself. One source of information was the child's account of parental role as projected in the TAT. Another source was an interview conducted with the child. Since in these interviews we deliberately refrained from probing too deeply into the child's relations to and feelings about his family this source was of limited usefulness.

The studies with both approaches were guided by the broad hypothesis that children whose differentiation is limited have had relations with their mothers of such a nature as to interfere with the opportunities for psychological differentiation; and that highly differentiated children have had relations with their mothers of a nature that permitted or even fostered progress toward differentiation.

In Chapters 17, 18, and 19 we describe our studies of mother-child relations based on interviews with the mother. In Chapter 20 we describe an investigation carried out to test the hypothesis, suggested by these studies, that mothers who are themselves more differentiated tend to have more differentiated children. Studies of mother-child interaction conducted from the standpoint of the child are described in Chapter 21. Finally, in Chapter 22 we bring together the results of our studies of mother-child relations and discuss some processes of interaction which may lead to the development of greater or less differentiation in children.

17

INTERVIEWS WITH
MOTHERS: PROCEDURE
AND MAIN RESULTS

This chapter describes the general procedure followed in obtaining information about mother-child interactions through interviews with mothers, and the methods used in analyzing the interview data. The main quantitative results of the study are presented, particularly evidence on the relation between ratings of mother-child interactions, based on these interviews, and measures reflecting children's mode of field approach. The two chapters that follow give a more extensive account of the impressions and "clues" within the data on which the ratings were based.

A. PROCEDURE

Home interviews with mothers were conducted by a staff member who is a social worker by training. At the time of the interview, and during the period when she analyzed and judged the interview records, she had no knowledge of the children's performances in any of the tests conducted in the laboratory. The interview was held with the child's knowledge and agreement after the study of the child had been completed. The purpose of the interview, as told to both mother and child, was to obtain information about certain aspects of early development.

Mothers were seen by appointment. With a few exceptions they seemed well motivated to participate in the interview which lasted approximately 2 hours. They were a more or less self-selected group since they had given permission for their children to come to the laboratory and had collaborated with the staff in working out arrangements for the completion of tests. Most mothers were more than willing to talk about their children either because of pride in them, a desire to complain about them, or the wish to obtain advice or assistance with problems.

In accordance with the mothers' as well as the interviewer's preference the interviews were generally held on school days during the morning or early afternoon. The children usually were not present. However, some children were briefly seen when the interview began or terminated. In five instances, a child was present during the entire interview.[1] In four instances the father was present during the interview.

Within the general framework of a focused interview, flexibility and adaptation of technique to particular circumstances took precedence over standardization of questioning, sequence of topics, or even completeness of topic coverage. In the interest of rapport the interviewer refrained from taking notes. With the Group-I and Group-II mothers, notes were made of the interview in as full detail as possible immediately following the home visit. Interviews with Group-III mothers were tape recorded.[2] For all groups observations of the interrelationship between mother and interviewer and behavior of other family members, if present, were fully noted afterwards.

Interviews with Group-II mothers were conducted first. For cross-validation purposes, the study was repeated with the Group-I and Group-III mothers. In the case of Group I, the interviews were not held until the children who had first been tested at age 10 were restudied at age 14.[3] In the other two groups, interviews with the mothers were held when the children were 10. In Group II, one "mother" proved to be a recently acquired stepmother. One Group-I mother could not be interviewed because of protracted illness, another because she refused cooperation. In Group III, one mother had died and another had deserted; in both instances the father was interviewed instead. Of the five cases in which mothers were not seen four were not considered in the analyses carried out. The mother who had deserted was judged on the basis of the fact that she had deserted. Further, the records of six of the interviews held were too

[1] Relationships considered in the analyses presented were not affected when results for children seen by the interviewer were excluded.

[2] Only one mother, though otherwise collaborating fully, refused to permit use of the recorder. Another mother asked that the recording be delayed until she had expressed certain criticism of the laboratory. One father initially did not wish to have the interview recorded but agreed to it after he had finished talking about his wife's desertion.

[3] Home interviews were not introduced until 1953. This group was first studied in 1949, when the boys were 10.

sparse to permit evaluation. In all, then, the analyses reported are based on fifty-eight cases.

B. CONTENT OF THE INTERVIEW

Six general areas, listed below, were covered. Within the flexible structure of the interview, the attempt was made to gather information within these areas, even if such information was not spontaneously given. In each of the areas, both the mother's and the child's attitudes were sought, as well as the mother's modes of handling specific situations. Such questions as "What could you do?" or "How would you handle that?" seemed quite rewarding in providing insight into practices about which a mother might have been expected to be relatively reticent. Furthermore, within each area inquiry was also made concerning earlier attitudes and behavior in order to obtain a retrospective account and not merely a cross-sectional view of mother-child interaction. It will be noted that the content of these areas concerns the child and the mother-child relation. Information about the mother as a person was usually elicited as well, directly or indirectly. It is obvious that whatever they talked about, mothers did provide information about themselves. The six areas and topics covered within each area, as well as questions uniformly phrased, were:

1. Physical care
   Prior experiences with and preparations for child care.
   Resources utilized for advice or help, including physicians, nurse, relatives, books, etc.
   Experiences of pregnancy.
   Account of early development.
   Mother's behavior and feeling regarding feeding, toilet training, dressing, duration of such care, and child's and mother's attitudes toward continuing or discontinuing.
   Account of illness. Child's and mother's responses.
   Questions:
   Which do you prefer, demand or scheduled care in feeding, toilet training? How has _____'s father participated in the caring for _____? How do you feel about this?
2. Child's past and current adaptation to school
   Facts about accomplishments and behavior in school.
   Recall about mother's and child's behavior in first school experience.
   Handling of difficulties.
   Questions:
   How do you feel about _____'s school progress, compared with his abilities and your hopes and expectations?

How do you feel about teachers _____ has had?

What makes a good teacher or a bad teacher?

What have you done about _____'s doing his homework?

How do you feel about parents helping their children with school work?

3. Child's social relationships and activities

Account of child's relationships with friends.

Changes in relationships mother would consider desirable.

Special friends mother approves or disapproves of and steps she has taken to encourage or discourage such friends.

Handling of fighting or quarreling with friends or siblings.

Mother's participation in child's hobbies or special interests.

Questions:

How have you handled _____'s fighting?

What activities have you restricted or encouraged?

Why did you restrict these activities?

How did _____ feel about these restrictions?

Do you let _____ travel alone, stay in the house alone?

When did you first let _____ play alone outside?

4. Discipline (specific inquiry was made unless this area was covered under other topics)

Mother's usual mood in punishing.

Methods used in particular situations.

Father's and mother's role in disciplining.

Child's reaction to discipline.

5. Mother's attitudes toward child

Goals for child, including career preferred by parents and child.

Abilities or talents which might point to a particular career.

Questions:

What are you most proud of in _____?

What do you enjoy most about _____?

What annoys you most about _____?

At what age have you enjoyed _____ most?

At what age have you found _____ most difficult?

How would you feel about _____'s having a job like his father's?

6. Family members

Recreation and chores shared, vacations, weekends, holidays.

Father (information generally obtained under other topics, as discipline, activities, physical care). Father's job.

Mother (information about job and social activities usually obtained under other topics).

Siblings. Relationships among siblings.

Data about siblings in areas 1 to 5 were often elicited to encourage mother's recall about child studied or to define mother's practices in particular areas.

C. METHOD OF ANALYSIS OF DATA

The analysis of the interview records was guided by the hypothesis that one source of difference in extent of differentiation among children would be the kinds of relations they had had with their mothers. Specifically we expected that characteristics of mother as a person and the nature of a mother's interaction with her child would be related to the child's level of differentiation. Thus in analyzing the records we aimed, by evaluating data concerning both mother as a person and her relationship with her child, to judge whether the impact of the mother's interaction with her child tended mainly to foster or to interfere with the development of differentiation in the child. Although a variety of mother-child interactions was the most reasonable expectation, a twofold classification of mothers seemed most feasible at this early stage of our work. Our general aim, then, was to arrive at a global judgment for each mother as to whether her interaction with her child tended to foster or inhibit differentiation.

It should be stressed that the judgment concerned only the mother's role in the development of differentiation and did not refer to her contribution to her child's adjustment. Although in many instances a given quality of interaction seemed associated with the development of both differentiation and adjustment in the child, there were also instances, as we shall see in the two chapters that follow, where a relationship that seemed to foster differentiation contributed, at the same time, to serious problems in adjustment.

In making judgments we were mainly concerned with whether a mother, considering her characteristics as a person and the nature of her interaction with her child, had permitted her child to separate from her and to have an identity of his own; whether she herself had developed personal values and standards so that she could help her child achieve an articulated sense of himself and the world; and, finally, whether she had related to him in a way which would help him develop control over his impulses.

Studies of parent-child relationships reported by others provided a background for exploration of these issues. To the extent that many of these studies have been concerned with general "adjustment" of the child they were not relevant to the issues with which we were concerned. Studies, however, which considered dependency and behavior expressing presence or absence of impulse control, either as the antecedent or consequent variable, seemed more relevant to our study. For example, associations between dependent behavior in the child and the following parental attitudes have been reported: maternal overprotection of a dominant nature (Levy, 1943); parental overattentiveness (Hattwick and Stowell, 1936); severity of punishment for aggression toward parents and use of withdrawal of love as a disciplinary technique (Sears, Maccoby, and Levin, 1957); lack of assurance and poise in the mother (MacFarlane, Allen, and Honzik, 1954). Associations have been found between behavior suggestive of lack of impulse control in the child and lack of assurance and poise in the mother (MacFarlane, Allen, and Honzik, 1954); parental "rejection" (Symonds, 1939; Newell, 1934, 1936); lack of early family relationships (Goldfarb, 1955); maternal overprotection with indulgence (Levy, 1943); autocratic home atmosphere (Radke, 1946); "actively-rejectant" homes (Baldwin, Kalhorn, and Breese, 1945).

These studies suggested some parental attitudes and behavior which might influence the development of differentiation. Thus, for instance, it seemed reasonable to expect that overprotective, overattentive maternal behavior would handicap the development of a sense of separate identity; lack of assurance in the mother would interfere with the development of articulated experiences for the child; and indulgent submissive behavior on the part of the mother would not give a child adequate support for controlling his impulses.

Such considerations as well as an intensive study of interview records of Group-II mothers (the first group interviewed), both during the process of evaluating these mothers and after the classification of these mothers had been completed, led to the formulation of a series of indicators, referring both to mother as a person and to her behavior with her child. These indicators were used as guideposts for judging mothers as fostering or interfering with the development of differentiation. When indicators described behavior in quite general terms it seemed necessary to spell out more clearly what was to be assessed. The indicators and specific behavior thus formulated, with one exception, were used in the validation studies carried out with mothers of Group-I and Group-III children.

We did not conduct a study designed to check on the communicability of the rating method. However, an independent validation study by Seder (1957), reported in detail in Chapter 22, has confirmed many of our findings.

We present below, under the headings "mother as a person" and "interaction with the child," the indicators which guided the over-all classification of mothers, as mainly differentiation fostering or inhibiting. The more specific kinds of behavior which, in turn, were used in forming impressions about a given indicator are also presented. These are cast in terms of maternal characteristics and behavior considered to be inhibiting of differentiation in the children.

Characteristics of mother as a person

(Indicators in this area focused on the extent of the mother's assurance or trust in herself and the degree of her sense of self-realization.)

Indicator 1: Mother in rearing child does not have assurance in herself.
Specific behavior:
Mother tends to blame herself for mistakes in rearing.
Mother attempts to rely on authorities rather than her own judgment or "intuition."

Indicator 2: Mother does not have feeling of self-realization in her own life.
Specific behavior:
Complaints predominate in mother's account of her relationship with her husband both as marital partner and as parent.
Complaints about child predominate.
Lacks sense of achievement in homemaker role.
Complains of nervousness, fatigue, being worn out.
Lacks satisfaction in general social relationships.

Indicator 3: Impact of mother on interviewer.
Specific behavior:
This indicator was not formulated until after evaluations of Groups I and II had been completed.
Interviewer felt pity, solicitude, nurturance, constraint (expected of mothers whose relations to children inhibited differentiation) vs. interviewer felt stimulated, refreshed (even if annoyed) and put on her toes, so to speak (expected of mothers whose relations to children contributed to differentiation).
Interviewer felt like a professional therapist and counselor (expected of mothers whose relations inhibited differentiation) vs. felt as in a woman-to-woman role (expected of mothers whose relationships contributed to differentiation).

Interaction with child

A. Mother's attitude toward child

Indicator 2: (Parts of indicator "mother does not have feeling of self-realization in her own life" as this feeling relates specifically to her role as a mother of this particular child.)

Indicator 4: Regards child as delicate, in need of special attention or protection, or as irresponsible.

Indicator 5: Does not accept masculine role for child.

B. Rearing procedures

(Indicators focused on training for independence, training for control of aggressive behavior, and rearing relating more specifically to intellectual development.)

Indicator 6: Through fears and anxieties for or ties to child mother markedly limits child's activities and his going out into community.

Indicator 7: Physical care of child seems inappropriate to age.

Indicator 8: Maternal control is not in the direction of child's achieving mature goals or becoming responsible or is consistently directed against child's asserting himself.

Specific behavior:

Mother's attitude in punishing is emotional, irrational; discipline is severe.

Indicator 9: Limits curiosity, stresses conformity.

A more detailed account of these indicators and specific kinds of behavior is given in the two chapters that follow, together with illustrative material selected from the interview records.

The way in which these indicators, formulated in terms of relations considered as inhibiting differentiation in the child, were used in the final dichotomous classification of mothers was as follows:

As a first step in the analysis of an interview record, all evidence of behavior relevant to each indicator was summarized. On the basis of this evidence a rating of "+" was assigned to a mother for this indicator if she showed the characteristics in the above listing (stated in terms of inhibition of differentiation) or a rating of "−" if she did not show these characteristics. Since the behavior evaluated for a given mother often showed conflicting trends, the rating assigned necessarily represented a judgment of the over-all impact of the evidence. This was the case, for instance, when major changes in attitudes were reported by a mother over the period covered in the interview.

The separate indicator ratings were then used as a basis for a final global judgment of a mother—as fostering or inhibiting differentiation. In making this final judgment it was again necessary to take account both of conflicting trends between ratings of mothers according to individual indicators and conflicting trends in the original evidence which had been resolved earlier when the indicator ratings were made. There were few "pure" cases where the evidence considered in the final judgment of a record was entirely consistent or unambiguous.

In view of the retrospective nature of the mother's account of early events, the way in which information about early training was treated deserves special attention. In evaluating these accounts, the mother's attitude was considered, rather than the facts she gave—for example, whether toilet training seemed to have proceeded with an attitude of coerciveness or permissiveness, rather than the age at which toilet training began. Such evaluations depended less on the reliability of the mother's memory than would evaluations of factual data.

For Group-III mothers, used as a validation group, the ratings of separate indicators, except indicator 6 (limits child's activities), were highly and significantly related to the final over-all judgment and to each other. It seems likely that these high intercorrelations are a function of overlap in the information used for the various indicators and/or the influence of a "halo" effect in the ratings. We shall accordingly present statistical results for the over-all ratings only, and not for the separate indicators.

In making a final over-all rating, a summary was prepared of each record, giving a general impression of the mother and her relation to her child. These summaries were prepared prior to knowledge of the child's test results. Following are two illustrative summary accounts of mothers who, in their relations with their children, present markedly contrasting pictures.

Example of a mother whose interaction with her child was judged as inhibiting differentiation [4]

Especially characteristic of this mother is her lack of approval of her child. Complaints about him predominate. She did not want him when he was a baby; he was sick, troublesome, and has persisted in making her "nervous." She has a marked and undisguised preference for her older son. Feeling unable to cope with her younger son, she is at times pressuring and coercive, "yells" about his school work, threatens to use his father as a "big stick," slaps him in anger. At other times, she indulges him, is unable to refuse sweets, although he is overweight and supposed to be on a diet. She is afraid he will be angry if she does not have his meals ready on time. She has not particularly restricted his activities. Though she does not let him travel alone because she regards him as irresponsible, she gives him a house key and allows him to stay at home alone. However, he recently went through a period of being afraid to stay alone even in the daytime, and she was forced to curtail her own social activities in order to stay with him. She places great emphasis on conformity, aspects of dress, appearance, and manners. She impresses me as a superficial, shallow, pleasure-loving person, who resents responsibility and the trouble her son has given her. In addition to failing to provide the secure kind of rearing in which he could develop control, she provides for him a pattern of an angry, impulsive, immature person. In the interview, mother constantly asked for advice or approval.

[4] The child is Phil, Case #6, in Chapter 15.

Example of a mother whose interaction with her child was judged as fostering differentiation [5]

Mother is essentially a high spirited, active, vital woman. She believes in having fun and a "life of her own." She describes herself as a "natural mother" who "instinctively" knows how to bring up children and who relies on her own judgment rather than on authorities. She states that she has a definite "philosophy" of child rearing and acts on it without much conflict, though she is aware that she is criticized by some people in the community. The essence of her philosophy is to make her children independent, not to supervise them too closely, and to let them "grow from within." Although she says she runs the home "like an institution," and can do little more than attend to physical needs of her 5 children for shelter, food, and clothing, she tries to give special attention to the special needs of each child. She is definitely approving of all her children whom she regards as lusty and intelligent. All the children, including the son we studied, have been early "shoved out into the world" (camp at 4 years, Sunday School, etc.), to get them "out of the house." Punishment, according to mother, has generally been meted out by plan and firmly administered. In spite of bickering and fighting between parents, mother seems to be a confident woman who enjoys life. She deals with situations directly, actively "managing" her husband but at the same time deferring to him. In the interview she was direct, forthright, and stimulating to the interviewer.

Thus, guided by the various indicators cited, each mother was placed in one of two groups. In one group were placed mothers whose interaction with the particular child we had studied (as evaluated through the personal characteristics of the mother, her attitudes toward her child, and her rearing procedures) seemed predominantly to foster the development of differentiation in the child. Such mothers, for convenience of designation, are referred to as "IFD" mothers (interaction fostering differentiation). In the second group were placed mothers who, judged on a similar basis, interacted with their children in a way that seemed predominantly to inhibit the children's differentiation. Such mothers have accordingly been designated "IID" mothers (interaction inhibiting differentiation). It must be stressed again that this twofold classification of mothers was made independently of whether the mother's relation with her child had been "optimal," in terms of contributing to the child's "good adjustment" and "mental health."

[5] The child is Keith, Case #1, in Chapter 15.

D. MAIN RESULTS

As noted, interviews were first conducted with the mothers of Group-II boys; and it was in the course of analysis of the interview records of this group that the method of rating the interview data was evolved. The final ratings of mothers of this group as IID or IFD were compared to the perceptual index scores of their children. The resulting point biserial r of .85 ($P < .01$, $N = 21$) [6] confirms our expectations.

For validation purposes, the home interview study was repeated with Groups I and III.

For Group I, the point biserial r between the ratings of the mothers and perceptual index scores of the children at 14 was .82 ($P < .01$, $N = 10$), in the expected direction.

For Group III the correlation between ratings of mothers and children's perceptual index scores was .65 ($P < .01$, $N = 27$). The correlations of mothers' ratings with children's intellectual index and cognitive index scores were .41 ($P < .05$) and .57 ($P < .01$), respectively. All values are in the expected direction. [7]

Our starting hypothesis is substantially confirmed. As expected, the mothers of children with a more global field approach have had the kinds of relations with their children which tended to inhibit the children's progress toward differentiation; mothers of children with a more analytical field approach have interacted with their children in a way which tended to foster the development of differentiation in their children. [8]

Going beyond these quantitative results we give, in the next two chapters, more extended descriptions of maternal characteristics, attitudes, and behavior which entered into our judgments of mothers. In Chapter 18 we discuss characteristics of mother as a person and in

[6] The number of mothers rated in the three groups is less than the total number of children studied. For reasons previously stated, some mothers had not been interviewed and, in six cases, the interview record was too sparse to permit a rating. For 10 of the 68 boys in the three groups ratings of their mothers could not be made.

[7] The correlation between mothers' ratings and verbal index scores of the children is .15 (not significant). This finding suggests that the evaluation made of the mothers did not encompass every aspect of their possible influence upon their children. The fact that the ratings of the mothers did not relate to the degree of verbal skill of their children is of particular interest in view of the discussion in Chapter 11 concerning the relationship between verbal skills and differentiation.

[8] Relations between ratings of mothers and other measures for the children are reported in Chapter 22.

Chapter 19 attitudes toward her child and rearing procedures which were evaluated. Though, for convenience of description, we have chosen to consider these aspects separately, they are obviously dynamically interrelated and closely interwoven. Thus, the attitude a mother has toward a child and her rearing practices with him are very much related to the nature of her own personality. Again, various aspects of a mother's personality work together in complexly interrelated ways to influence the quality of help she gives or fails to give her child. In view of such considerations we give attention, wherever possible, to the interrelatedness of the areas discussed.

E. SUMMARY

In this chapter we described the procedures and main results of our studies of mother-child interaction based on interviews with mothers. The areas covered in the interview and the method of analysis of interview data were described. In this analysis an evaluation was made of whether a mother in interaction with her child tended mainly to foster or interfere with the development of differentiation in the child. Indicators used to guide these judgments were listed, leaving for the two subsequent chapters a more detailed description of maternal characteristics and behavior which entered into our evaluations. Mothers of children in Groups I, II, and III were classified as IID (interaction inhibiting differentiation) and IFD (interaction fostering differentiation). The classification was independent of whether a mother's relationship with her child had been optimal in terms of her contribution to a child's "good adjustment" and "mental health." Significant relations were found between judgments of mothers and perceptual index scores of their children for Groups I, II, and III. For Group III significant relations were also found between judgments of mothers and children's intellectual index and cognitive index scores. Our starting hypothesis is thus confirmed.

18

CHARACTERISTICS OF
MOTHER AS A PERSON

We discuss in this chapter the personal characteristics of mothers which contributed to their classification into IFD and IID groups. Some impressions obtained from a review of the interview records after this classification had been made also are considered.

The personal characteristics of mothers considered in judging them as IID and IFD were self-assurance and self-realization. In the process of making judgments of Group-II mothers, these characteristics were selected as important aspects of the mother's contribution to the development of differentiation in her child. It was our expectation that a mother who has herself achieved a sense of self-realization would be better able to permit her child to separate from her and to develop as an individual than a mother who lacks it. We also expected that mothers who are self-assured would have less hesitation about setting and maintaining limits for their children, and so help them develop impulse control. Mothers who lack self-assurance might be inconsistent and wavering and thus fail to give support to a child's development of controls.[1]

In selecting self-assurance and self-realization we were, then, focusing on characteristics we thought important for the development of differentiation in the child. We were not necessarily selecting characteristics most important for the development of good adjustment. For example a mother who was judged as having a sense of self-realization might not show warmth toward her child which would help him develop trusting attitudes toward other people. A mother judged as self-assured might be overly meticulous and compulsive and in this way set standards which are unrealistic and difficult for the child to meet.

[1] These issues are discussed in Chapter 22.

Moreover in choosing to focus on self-assurance and a sense of self-realization we excluded a number of aspects of the mother's personal functioning which had at first seemed important with respect to the development of differentiation in the child. In the course of the analysis of Group-II records these aspects did not seem directly relevant to judgments of mothers as IID and IFD. For instance the interviewer's impression that a mother was psychologically disturbed did not necessarily contribute to judging her as either IID or IFD. Nor did marital status, as divorce or separation, employment status (whether a mother was a homemaker or had gainful employment outside the home), or the status of the family with respect to domestic help (whether a mother was the mistress of a large home with domestic assistance or the chief cook and bottle washer) in themselves contribute to a judgment of IID and IFD.

Evidence which contributed to evaluating a mother in terms of her self-assurance and sense of self-realization is discussed in the context of her relations within the family and her general social relations.

A. MOTHER'S SENSE OF SELF-REALIZATION AND SELF-ASSURANCE IN THE FAMILY

1. Evidence Suggesting Lack of Self-Assurance and Self-Realization

Complaints of being tired, worn out, tense and nervous, and feeling unable to cope with family situations or problems in everyday living entered into judging a mother as IID. An example of a statement contributing to such a judgment is the following:

M: I know my husband was very interested in having a third child, but I really wouldn't care to. You give too much of yourself to each child. Maybe if you have an awful lot to give—I don't feel—it's just my nerves you know. I can't absorb it. It's too much of a strain on me . . . It's just that my husband is a demanding person. He always wanted things just so, whether I had help or I didn't have help. And as a result, the burden of the two children and my husband and the house and the quarters were all crowded . . . Everything all rolled into one. I just couldn't take it . . . I was sick for a long while . . . just a bad state of nerves.

Predominantly complaining attitudes about their children were considered evidence of a lack of self-realization in motherhood. In the following chapter such complaints are discussed in the context of mothers' attitudes toward the specific children studied. Complaints of both material and emotional deprivation and neglect by husbands provided further evidence of a lack of self-realization, although it was not known whether such complaints were based on fact. The mother's experience was considered without taking into account whether or not her complaints had a realistic basis.

Some complaints which contributed to a judgment of IID concerned the vocational failure of their husbands. In making such complaints mothers often expressed lack of esteem and regard for their husbands. One mother stated: "He never found himself; I don't want (our son) to be a work horse like his father (a factory worker). I want him to have a white collar job." Others who felt deprived and complained of inadequate incomes and crowded apartments still showed understanding of the reasons for their husbands' failures.

Lack of satisfactory companionship with their husbands was another complaint which suggested lack of self-realization in marriage. For instance some mothers stated that frustration and fatigue at work meant that their husbands just "ate and slept at home." One mother said her husband got tired at work and "let loose and screamed" as soon as he got home. Still another, whose husband was highly successful in his job, felt that his vocational achievements had "taken a toll" and left him irritable, with little energy to give to family life. Complaints concerning personal characteristics of their husbands such as immature or childish behavior were also considered as evidence of a lack of self-realization. Mothers who made such complaints might describe their husbands as making unreasonable demands, which they felt unable to meet. For instance, they told of their husbands' insistence on perfectly kept, orderly homes even when the children were young, on special foods to suit their idiosyncratic tastes, or the preparation of food at all hours of the day without regard to other household tasks.

Complaints that father and son were aligned against the mother were also considered indicative of a lack of self-realization. Some mothers reported that the close relation between father and son had left them out and made them feel "unloved."

Lack of self-realization was also indicated when a mother stated that absence of practical assistance or emotional support from her husband in bringing up the children had created burdens she did not feel adequate to assume.

M: I did it all myself. He never got up with any of my children . . . at night he would never get up for them . . . Their cries never disturbed him.

I: How do you feel about sharing it (getting up at night)?

M: Well, I used to hear stories, "My husband gets up during the night." I used to feel so envious that mine never did. I didn't resent it, but of course I would wish each night that I could get really a night's sleep.

Indulgence of a son by his father might also be sensed by a mother as depriving her of proper support. This was expressed by one mother as follows:

I: What did your husband do about bringing him up when he was little?
M: He gave him everything his heart desired. Anything—it would get me. Like, he'd give him a dishpan full of water and put in soap powder. Learn to make bubbles . . . anything to make him quiet, he would give him. The mess was there for *me* to clean up but he would give him anything just to amuse him.

The manner in which a mother resolved conflicts with her husband about child care provided evidence for judging both her sense of self-realization and self-assurance. When, in the face of such conflicts, a mother abandoned her own goals, or ways of implementing these goals, and felt dissatisfied in doing so, a rating of IID was indicated. One mother, for instance, felt that her husband's insistence that a mother's place was in the home had deprived her of outlets which might have made her a better mother, yet she "submitted" to his demands. She gave the following response to the question, "Have you ever worked?"

M: Well, I'd love to work. But I don't have anyone, and my husband doesn't trust the children alone in the house. So I can't go . . . And to me it's the best thing for a mother to get away from the children and go to work.
I: What's your husband's feeling about it?
M: He doesn't think the mother should go to work and leave the children on their own . . . He says anything can happen, you know, when no one's around and then it's on your conscience. . . . My husband says, "That's all you have to do is watch them. That's your job, watching" (laughs). So I guess I got into the habit of it.
Another mother who could not assert herself complained that her husband left the discipline to her and indulged their son by taking him to shows and keeping him up late. As a consequence she stated that her son regards her as a nagger—but his father is the person who gives him good times.

We considered it particularly suggestive of a lack of self-assurance in child rearing if a mother searched for and sought to elicit rules for child care from "the books," physicians, or theories in vogue among neighbors or friends, and yet derived little comfort or security from the advice she obtained.

A mother who failed to find comfort and support might, for instance, continue to blame herself for mistakes in child rearing or she might continue to search for the "right formula," even with regard to how much love to give a child. One mother stated that it is difficult to know how to bring up a child. She added that she really didn't know what to do since if you do too much for your children they think you don't give them enough freedom but if you don't do enough, they think you don't love them.

2. Evidence Suggesting Self-Assurance and Self-Realization

Among manifestations of self-assurance and self-realization used in making judgments were mothers' direct reports that they felt vigorous and energetic. Another manifestation, more often inferred from a mother's statements, was of efforts to master their tasks at home even in the face of experiencing serious realistic difficulties. For instance, a mother of four children, who had been confronted with problems of low income, small quarters, lack of help from her husband, who had been seriously ill and was often away in the evening attending school, stated that she had been quite able to manage the care of the children herself. A "no surrender" attitude seemed to characterize her approach to life.

Evidence of self-realization was often obtained from descriptions of husband-wife relations and activities. Expressions of satisfaction in shared interests with their husbands and joint social activities, regard and esteem for their husbands as people, contributed to ratings of IFD. For example one mother stated, "We like to dance together. We are both pretty expert." And then the mother commented that although her husband does not spend much time with their sons, in a few minutes he gives them as much help with sports as many fathers would give in a day. Still another mother stated that her husband, like her son, has a "crystal-clear mind."

Further evidence of self-realization in marriage was obtained from mothers' views of their husbands' roles in child rearing. For example, a mother might express approval of father-son "men only" activities, such as hunting, fishing, or going to ball games. Compatibility and agreement with her husband, suggesting self-realization in marriage, might be indicated in the use of "we" by a mother in speaking of parental attitudes toward the child. For example, "Both of us hate to spank him." "We agreed we wanted him to go to Hebrew School, not for religious education but to learn something about Jewish culture." "We both feel we don't care to have him cop all the honors."

In cases of disagreement with their husbands about child rearing, mothers who appeared able to present their own viewpoints in discussing differences of opinion with their husbands were considered to display self-assurance and self-realization. One mother made the following statements which suggested that she could maintain her convictions about bringing up her child:

M: Sometimes he (my son) rubs my husband the wrong way, and he does things my husband thinks a boy shouldn't do. Like (my son) likes to sit and draw floor plans for homes . . . my husband gets annoyed . . . it isn't masculine enough for him. And I tell my husband, "Leave him alone. Architects are born from children like that. We never know. Don't curb him. It interests him."

I: He leaves him alone?

M: Yes. My husband listens to me. We get along well that way.

When husbands did not participate in child rearing, mothers were considered IFD if they were concerned with the effect of a father's nonparticipation on the child rather than complaining of their own increased burdens. The following example is illustrative:

M: When I came home from the hospital, I took charge of the children . . . I seemed to be well enough and strong enough to be able to handle my own chores.

I: How about your husband's helping you with the youngsters?

M: No—I wouldn't say that—but of course, I never encouraged it, you see . . . today I'm a little bit sorry that I didn't give him that opportunity, because I think that a father ah—understands a child a little better and gets better acquainted . . . but they really should start as an infant.

Statements such as the following which suggest a mother's ability to cope with situations when their husbands did not help them also contributed to IFD ratings. One mother stated that since her husband does not perform his duty as a Jewish father by taking the boys to High Holy Day services, she takes responsibility for seeing that the boys go. Another mother described her husband as "never able to take action" when the children were sick but stated quite factually that she can manage such situations alone.

Self-assurance and self-realization were indicated when a mother expressed confidence in or satisfaction with her own handling of the rearing situation. A review of the interview records suggested that these attitudes might be found in mothers who varied in methods of child care. Such confidence and satisfaction might or might not be associated with help and assistance from husbands. For instance, there were mothers who stated that their husbands' approval and/or active participation in child rearing had contributed to their own self-realization and self-assurance. One mother, who described her husband as an active copartner in child rearing, stated, "I think basically we are a healthy family, but it is just normal . . . I mean you just get upset and worry about little things . . . My husband, fortunately, is a much calmer person than I am. So, if anything goes wrong, I always have him to sort of balance me." Another mother stated that, although she enjoyed bringing up her children and felt quite secure about it, her husband's approval of her role and the status he gave her as a mother added to her pleasure in and assurance about being a mother. On the other hand, mothers might be judged self-assured and to have a sense of self-realization in their motherhood, despite disagreements with their husbands and despite the lack of the husband's participation or even interest in the rearing of the children.

Some mothers showed self-assurance by commenting that they knew their own children better than did other people such as physicians or teachers. Other mothers who tended to look to outside authorities nevertheless indicated self-assurance by stating that they used their own common sense in applying what they read or had been told. This might involve, for example, selective use of a physician's recommendations to fit their own particular child, the needs of the whole family, or the mother's special needs.

The ability to define for themselves their roles as mothers was considered as evidence of self-assurance. Such role definition was manifested, for example, when mothers continued to do what was "natural" for them, even if criticized by neighbors or friends, or if their methods of child care were not consistent with current theories of child rearing. This was implied in the phrase "natural mother" used by some women in describing themselves. Though their interpretation of the maternal role might vary and their performances as well (for instance, a mother might stay home to care for her children or she might be gainfully employed), mothers indicated self-assurance if they felt whatever role they assumed had not been thrust upon them from the outside by their husbands or other people or circumstances. For example, one mother said that while at times she had felt "confined" when her children were little, she now feels this was a worthwhile choice since her children now have the interests and values she had tried to inculcate in them.

A mother might be evaluated as self-assured even if she identified various areas in which she had made or was still making "mistakes." Mothers were considered as self-assured when they approached such mistakes in a factual and forthright manner, in a spirit of "everyone makes mistakes."

B. MOTHER'S SENSE OF SELF-REALIZATION AND SELF-ASSURANCE IN GENERAL SOCIAL RELATIONS

1. Lack of Self-Assurance and Self-Realization

Expression of feelings of deprivation or neglect by others contributed to a judgment of IID. For instance one mother said she longed for neighbors with whom she could live as "one happy family" and that she felt unwanted and isolated when no one "knocked at the door" of her apartment. She had felt "like a person" only when she had worked in a factory during the war, and had thus associated with other people. Similarly, a mother commenting on her eagerness for gainful employment stated: "That way you meet people and have an environment." In expressing a sense of deprivation some mothers stated that household chores and child care had limited their social relations. Others mentioned as handicaps their own personal characteristics, as being shy, reserved, lacking in self-confidence, or feeling physically unattractive (being "too tall" or not having a "pretty face"). An inability to measure up to expected standards of behavior was also mentioned, as in the following excerpt:

M: I'm not one of these card sharks. And I never took an interest in rummy or bridge or poker. You know I play—but I'm a poor loser, and I never wanted to get interested in bridge and things because I know I wouldn't be good—I would be too bad a loser.

I: What would you do if you lost?

M: I'd get mad (laughs) so I feel that rather than play and be a poor loser I won't play. I'd rather say I don't know how to play and that's all. They don't have to know I'm a sore loser.

Restriction of relations outside the home accompanied by feelings of deprivation provided the main evidence of a lack of self-realization in social relations. However, on later review of interview records we found that a few mothers judged IID were not restricted in social relations but rather had achieved satisfaction and status in social life in a variety of community activities. However, strict conformity to values and manners of the social group with which they sought to identify was characteristic of IID mothers who achieved satisfaction in social life.

2. Evidence Suggesting Self-Assurance and Self-Realization

Varied interests outside the home were considered evidence of self-realization. Activities reflecting such interests might include participation in community organizations, such as Cub Scouts and PTA groups, social life with their husbands or other women, or sponsorship or leadership in women's religious or charitable organizations. As just noted, however, a review of the interview records suggested that participation in varied activities might be consistent with an IID rating, especially if the mother stressed conformity to outside standards and values.

A sense of self-realization might be conveyed when strong ties with friends and relatives were described as the following example suggests:

I: What do you do on Sundays?
M: Sundays we're doing things. We're going. We're coming. We're busy. I mean we have family to see, we have friends to see. So far this summer the children have been away (at camp) but Sunday we'll visit my brother . . . my mother-in-law . . .   Our friends, barbeques, picnics. We're hardly ever home.

Even when ties were restricted to the immediate family, so that its members seemed to be living on a little island, mothers might be judged as having a sense of self-realization if, despite this isolation, they seemed secure in their own superior status.   The following excerpt from a summary of an interview record suggests such attitudes:

Mother stated that their family is very similar to one portrayed in a story of a current woman's magazine.   She described the family as highly individualistic, absent minded, unable to accumulate material goods, oblivious to community standards, but very much enjoying themselves and their free way of life.

C. IMPACT OF MOTHER ON INTERVIEWER

Another source of evidence for judging the mother as a person was her behavior during the interview itself, considered as a sample of the mother's behavior in a social situation.   The interviewer, as already indicated, did not attempt to structure the interview uniformly, but rather adapted herself to the particular mother or situation in the home as she found it.   Mothers behaved quite individualistically in their use of the interview and their reactions to the interviewer.

For example, a mother might attempt to use the interview to solve her problems, to obtain guidance from test results, or to elicit the interviewer's impression of the child we had studied.   She might give information in an objective, straightforward, and pertinent way.   She might treat the interviewer as an authority or she might herself assume an authoritative manner.   She might be easy and informal or she might be stiff, reserved, or inept in receiving the interviewer as her "guest."   If she served refreshments, she might eat with the interviewer in the kitchen or serve her more formally, join the interviewer in eating, or wait on her.   With regard to the child's participation in the research program, she might be appreciative of the research aims, grateful that the child had had a "good time," or she might be critical of special laboratory procedures.   In her communication she might be restrained, give "yes" or "no" answers, hesitantly wait for the interviewer to question her; she might begin with a flow and continue with a flood of conversation, terminated only by the interviewer's departure; or she might give appropriate, well-organized responses.

In the course of interviewing and evaluating the mothers of Groups I and II the interviewer, as noted in Chapter 17, recognized that mothers judged as IFD had quite a different impact on her than did those judged IID. Analysis of the interview records for Groups I and II showed that the role the interviewer assumed and the quality of her feelings in response to a mother were characteristically different for mothers judged IID than for mothers judged IFD. An indicator was formulated on the basis of these differences. This indicator was subsequently used in judging Group-III mothers. Reactions of pity, solicitude, nurturance, the assumption of the role of professional therapist or counselor, and feelings of constraint contributed to judgments of IID. In contrast when the interviewer felt stimulated, refreshed, even if annoyed, and "put on her toes," and when she felt as in a "woman-to-woman role," implying a sense of talking with an equal, an IFD rating was suggested.

Responses evoked in the interviewer which contributed to ratings of IID and IFD will perhaps clarify the above descriptions of the indicator. Each of the following paragraphs is taken from a different interview record.

1. Interviewer's Responses Contributing to an IID Rating

I had to be watchful to preserve a proper tenor and tempo in the interview (an interview during which a rather formal and elegant luncheon was served by a maid). I felt cautious and brought out an overlay of manners, the just-so wiping of the mouth, the waiting for the correct moment to have cigarettes passed, initiating conversation so my hostess could eat. Care, constriction, proper social behavior was my keynote. Everything should be reasonable, not exceeding correct manners. (General effect judged as constraining on interviewer.)

I felt like a professional social worker or marriage counselor who must give mother acceptance and support and was continually conscious of the need to remain nonjudgmental. I was active in encouraging mother to define problems about which she initially said, "I hate to have to let you know these things about our home." (Interviewer felt like a professional social worker.)

2. Interviewer's Responses Contributing to an IFD Rating

After the first few minutes, I did not have to encourage her to talk, felt she understood what the interview was about, and that her interest in the laboratory extended beyond her interest in her own child. I felt spontaneous, lively, had pleasure and enjoyment in talking with mother. I did not need to give her a boost, but felt that she could stand on her own feet. I was interested in information she gave on handling various parent-child situations and felt admiration for her handling of her daughter's problem of deafness. (General effect on interviewer judged as stimulating.)

I felt that mother was easy to talk with and friendly. I felt comfortable and could drink coffee and enjoy it, and enjoyed looking about the apartment as mother invited me to in order to see various arrangements she had made in dividing and decorating the rooms. Mother seemed to like and enjoy me also. There was no tension as I talked with her. I felt some admiration for her making a comfortable, homey, attractive place with their limited income. (Interviewer felt as in a "woman-to-woman" relationship.)

D. SUMMARY

The personal characteristics of mothers considered particularly important to the development of differentiation in their children, and used in judging them as IID or IFD, are self-assurance and self-realization. These characteristics were evaluated in the context of the family and social situations outside the family.

Predominance of complaints about their husbands and children suggested a lack of self-realization. Inability to cope with problems of everyday living and failure to define their roles as mothers suggested a lack of self-assurance and self-realization. Mothers who felt deprived and neglected in social relations were judged to show a lack of self-realization. However, a review of the interview records after the child's mode of perception was known suggested that some mothers judged as IID obtained status and satisfaction from outside relations.

The predominance of approving attitudes toward their children, relations with husbands which were not regarded as depriving, a capacity to define their own roles as mothers, and the absence of exaggerated self-blame when mistakes were made, contributed to judgments of mothers as self-assured and as having a sense of self-realization. Self-realization in social relationships outside the home which contributed to an evaluation of mothers as IFD included a variety of social interactions.

Characteristics of mothers were also evaluated by using the interview as a social situation in which a mother's impact on the interviewer was considered. Interviewer reactions of pity, solicitude, constraint toward the mother, and the assumption of a role of "professional therapist" or counselor contributed to judgments of IID. In contrast, reactions of being stimulated or refreshed or the assumption of a "woman-to-woman role" contributed to judgments of IFD.

19

MOTHERS' INTERACTIONS
WITH CHILDREN

Having considered personal characteristics of mothers which contributed to their classification as IID or IFD, we turn to their attitudes toward and rearing procedures with the specific children studied in the laboratory.

A. MATERNAL ATTITUDES TOWARD CHILDREN

Three indicators used in judging mothers as IID or IFD served as focal points: "Mother does not have feeling of self-realization in her own life (as mother of this specific child)"; "regards child as delicate, in need of special attention and protection or as irresponsible"; and "does not accept masculine role for child."

Evaluation of maternal attitudes was based on explicit statements made by the mother concerning her feelings about her child, and on inferences from the quality of her interaction with him.

1. Explicit Statements of Approval and Disapproval

The complaints verbalized by a mother as well as the characteristics she approved of in her child provided one basis for judging the mother's attitudes toward her child. Such expressions of complaints and approval provided information concerning the quality and content of her feelings and her sense of self-realization or lack of self-realization in him. A mother's attitudes were expressed either spontaneously or in answer to specific questions, as "What are you most proud of in _____?"; "What annoys you most about _____?"

a. Characteristics contributing to judgments of mothers as IID.

When the over-all tenor of the mother's statements about her children was one of complaints, with expressions of approval minimal and hard to come by even on specific questioning, an IID rating was suggested. In some instances mothers expressed negative feelings with self-reproach or at least doubt as to whether they should feel as they did. In other cases, even when approval was expressed, it was conditional, i.e., dependent on the child's living up to the mother's demands and expectations.

Such complaints often concerned the child's failure to satisfy the mother's standards of achievement (most frequently in the intellectual area); his failure to conform to standards of social behavior and appearance, which would enhance her status in the public eye; his being too great a care and responsibility, or too demanding of her energy; his aggressive and assertive behavior with her. The following excerpts from summaries of individual interview records illustrate complaints in these areas.

Intellectual achievement:
Mother is disappointed in his intellectual development because of her earlier impression that he was a very bright child. He had been "sociable," and had talked early. He is a behavior problem in school, inattentive, does not bother to complete his work; homework is sloppy and he makes no effort. Mother wonders whether he is "dumb." (At age 10 his WISC IQ was 106.)

Social behavior and physical appearance:
He pays little attention to good grooming, is careless about personal appearance, is overweight. This has handicapped his social relationships. Mother thinks people judge one on how one looks.

Demands made by child:
Earlier when he had no friends, he "drove her crazy" wanting her to play games with him or to "take him places." He wants attention, can't be trusted to be left alone, and he is always "on top of" mother. Depends on mother to do things for him—make his bed, tie his shoes, put his things away.

Aggression and assertion:
Difficult to manage, fights mother about clothes and meals, picks fights, "screams and hollers" at her. "Disturbs the peace" at home.

Conditional approval was often based on the child being good, obedient, not troublesome or demanding of care, not rebellious or aggressive; and being affectionate, easy to care for, socially acceptable, respectful with neighbors, well mannered and polite in public.

b. Characteristics contributing to judgments of mothers as IFD. When the over-all tenor of the mother's statements was one of approval, even in the face of the child's behaving in ways not consistent with her ideals or standards, a rating of IFD was suggested. Characteristics of which they approved included school achievement, creativity, independence, responsibility, sensitivity to other people's feelings, affection toward parents or siblings. Emphasis on how her son's behavior might affect him rather than on the annoyance or inconvenience it might create for the mother also contributed to an IFD rating. Behavior which mothers thought might handicap a child often included passive, insufficiently assertive tendencies. The following examples are illustrative of concerns expressed:

His modesty and fear of the dark or of being alone are of concern to mother.

Somewhat babyish, wants to lie down with mother. She thinks taking a doll to bed with him is babyish.

He is shy about making contacts, going alone to a new organization; mother wishes he were more forward and aggressive, as one needs to be in the "jungle of New York."

Mother somewhat concerned that he has "effeminate tendencies." He has a good sense of rhythm, might be a good dancer, but she would hesitate to have him specialize in dancing.

2. Attitudes Suggested by Mothers' Descriptions of Their Interaction with Their Children

In their descriptions of their rearing procedures, mothers gave further information bearing on their attitudes toward their children. The excerpts below illustrate attitudes contributing to classification as IID or IFD. They are taken from summaries made to aid the classification of mothers.

a. Attitudes contributing to judgments of IID.

(1) Possessive attitude toward child (mother is intensely involved with child in terms of regarding him as her possession)

This is a mother who clearly lacks the ability to differentiate her child from herself or permit him to be separated from her. She would "die without him." She makes him feel guilty if he is separated from her. "Like I said, in due time if he felt that he didn't want to be with me, I'd allow him to do what he wants to. He's perfectly free. I wouldn't care how he'd break my heart . . . But all I say is I just don't want to be forgotten, that's all. I put his happiness before anything."

(2) Anxious, solicitous attitude

This mother tries to protect her child from harm by preventing him from overexercising, and by seeing that he eats on time, eats the right food, etc.

She states that she has babied him, telling him what to do, making decisions, and has been "watchful."

(3) Cold, unsympathetic, hostile attitude

This mother has apparently rejected her son from the beginning, and even in pregnancy had a sense of being injured by him. Subsequently she felt that he "took a toll" of her by crying, being difficult to feed, by his constant need to be taken to clinics for physical care. She now refers to him as a "leech," "sucking her life blood" in his constant demands for attention and affection.

(4) Amused, indulgent attitudes alternating with hostile attitudes (mother does not indicate deep feeling or concern about her child)

Mother states that she does not spend much time with her son. When he was a baby, she regarded him as a toy to be exhibited. She found him attractive and later enjoyed his good manners. She has, however, found him difficult to cope with because of his excessive temper. Though she is amused by him, wheedles and indulges him, she also beats him. Her concern about his behavior seems to be geared to her own comfort, rather than to her son's development.

b. Attitudes contributing to judgments of IFD.

(1) Warm affectionate feelings, high involvement with child

Mother thoroughly enjoys being with her son, appreciates his humor, his curiosity, his assertiveness which she has encouraged. Though her children seem to be the focus of her interest and activity, she has also been sensitive to her son's needs for independence.

(2) Warm accepting attitude, not highly involved

Mother expressed warmth toward her son and approval of him. She is neither babying nor overprotective. Her permissiveness, her noninterference seem at times carried to extremes—e.g., when her two sons fight, and the older boy is rough and abusive toward the younger one, she does not "step in." She states that she knows very little about her son's activities with friends and comments that we would have to ask him about these.

(3) Accepting attitude, not warm

Mother is proud of her son's self-sufficiency. She describes herself as "not warm as some mothers are."

It should be noted that such characteristics as warmth toward or involvement with the child did not, by themselves, contribute toward one or the other kind of judgment of a mother; the apparent reasons for such attitudes, however, were considered. Thus, a mother highly involved with her child might be extremely possessive and protective and discourage separation and independence of the child, whereas another highly involved mother might still encourage his development as a separate individual. The former constellation would contribute to a judgment of IID and the latter to a judgment of IFD, although a high degree of involvement characterized both mothers.

B. REARING PROCEDURES

Rearing must be regarded as a continuous, reciprocal process in which the parent influences the child, whose reactions, in turn, influence the parent. To get an impression of the impact of given rearing procedures upon the growing child, it is necessary to consider the nature of these procedures over the child's entire life span. With this in view we evaluated rearing procedures in historical perspective. This process is illustrated in the selected episodes cited in this chapter. These episodes refer to various periods in the child's life—infancy, a mid-period beginning when the child started school or when a sibling was born, and the current period when the mother was being interviewed.

While we regard rearing as a reciprocal process, in this chapter we view this process from the perspective of the mother's behavior as she recounted it. In Chapter 21 we describe the maternal role from the standpoint of the child, and in Chapter 22 we consider the total process of mother-child interaction.

Mothers' rearing procedures were evaluated mainly with regard to the extent to which these procedures had encouraged or discouraged separation from her and her part in helping her child develop impulse control. Particular aspects of the separation and controls issues were emphasized in specific indicators as follows: tying the child to her, keeping him more or less infantile through giving physical care inappropriate for his age; constricting development through prohibiting or not tolerating assertiveness; limiting the child's going out into the community; limiting curiosity, stressing conformity. Two summary evaluations are given below to illustrate contrasting kinds of rearing which contributed to our judgments of mothers.

Example of rearing contributing to an IID rating
Mother has had a great deal of anxiety about her son's health and her concern over preventing illness has circumscribed the family life, limiting excursions and vacations. She has gone to extreme lengths to prevent her son from being harmed by dirt or from being exposed to crowds.

Though the boy's illnesses have been only minor, she regards him as "sickness prone." She has frequently given him enemas as disease-preventing and purging. She imbued him with a sense of shame in relation to urinating on the floor when he was very young. She still bathes her 10-year-old son and lays out clean clothes for him. She comments on "a mother's tendency to do the thing yourself if a child doesn't do it when you want it done." Her son is apparently never free from her care and supervision.

Example of rearing contributing to an IFD rating

Mother has given her son [1] a sense of pride in being Jewish, though she is not conforming or orthodox in religious ideas. She was not impressed with the values of the more fashionable temple many of the neighborhood children attended and selected a Hebrew school they could afford. She has expressed to the children her appreciation of the warmth and beauty of all religions. She is aware of the children's individual needs and their needs at different periods of development, though preserving a common core of values and standards on which she insists.

She states that it is better to "talk out your feelings" than to suppress anger as her son sometimes does. She adds that she can now accept, without retaliation, the children's saying that they hate her and each other, but that earlier she used to react with anger when she was upset by the children's behavior. She makes many references to her son's making his own decisions. She does not worry about what other mothers believe is the correct time for a child to walk, talk, or go out in the street alone, but is generally guided by her own knowledge and awareness of a child's readiness.

Each of these two mothers presents a quite consistent picture in terms of the indicators related to rearing procedures. Other mothers gave evidence of what appeared as contradictory trends or atypical manifestations. For instance one mother had sent her child to camp at age 5, prided herself on not keeping him tied to her apron strings, and was nonchalant about giving physical care. However, she was intolerant of his being "fresh" with her, punished severely for misbehavior, insisted on perfect dress and manners. Another mother stated that she had been quite anxious and protective and "too cautious" and restrictive about letting her son play in the road or schoolyard. However, she appeared as outstanding in stimulating curiosity by answering questions, finding resources for encouraging her son's interests in gardening and history.

We turn now to a more detailed account of rearing procedures which contributed to ratings of mothers as IID or IFD. Rearing procedures are considered under two headings: training for independence (evaluated under indicators "through fears and anxieties for, or ties to child, markedly limits child's activities and his going out into community," "physical care of child seems inappropriate to age," "limits curiosity, stresses conformity," "maternal control is not in the direction of a child's achieving mature goals or becoming responsible or is con-

[1] The son is Chris, Case #2, in Chapter 15.

sistently directed against child's asserting himself"); and training for control of aggressive, assertive behavior (evaluated under the "maternal control" indicator just mentioned). Of necessity procedures considered under each heading have important implications for procedures under the other headings.

1. Training for Independence

a. Mother-child interactions contributing to rating as IID. There are many ways in which a mother may prevent a child from separating from her. The most obvious one is to baby her child and protect him excessively. In such cases, both physical and psychological separation from the mother is made difficult for the child.

The indicator "physical care of child seems inappropriate to age" referred to a rather specific type of infantilizing at the level of body care, such as dressing, feeding, helping with toilet functions long past the usual time reported by other mothers. The limitation of the assumption of other types of responsibilities was evaluated in the indicator "control is not in the direction of the child's achieving mature goals, or becoming responsible, or is consistently directed against the child's asserting himself." This included prohibition of such activities as lighting the stove, remaining alone at home, even for short periods of time during the day, or choosing what clothes to wear. Some mothers, for example, constantly sat with their children to make sure homework was done. Others frequently used the phrase "too young," suggesting that they considered the child incapable of doing anything on his own.

The limitation of the assumption of responsibilities by the child was also represented in the indicator "through fears and anxieties for, or ties to child, mother markedly limits the child's activities and his going out into community."

Restriction of activities might include using public transportation, as bus or subway, walking to school alone, going away to camp, playing in areas outside the immediate neighborhood, or, at younger ages, playing outside the home or apartment without the mother's presence. Only when there was evidence of marked and comprehensive restriction and the mother's fears and anxiety were given as motivation for restriction were mothers judged as inhibiting with reference to this indicator. Restrictions which appeared realistically based (e.g., in response to a child's physical handicap) were excluded by this definition.

In applying the indicator, rearing which did not markedly restrict the child's activities in the manner indicated suggested an IFD judgment. A review of the interview data after mothers had been classified suggested that even when mothers gave their children considerable freedom to go out into the community, and did not restrict their activities, they might still fail to permit their children to develop as separate individuals. For example, some mothers who sent their children to camp at a very early age or allowed bicycle riding "anywhere" permitted such activities in the spirit of getting rid of their children rather than in the interest of individual development. It now appears that a more discriminating application of this indicator, taking into consideration the motives of mothers who allow their children opportunities for physical separation from them, would contribute substantially to the usefulness of this indicator in judging mothers. In fact as reported in Chapter 17 this was the only indicator that failed to relate significantly to our over-all judgments of mothers.

Training which on the surface appeared to be the very opposite of babying a child was also considered as handicapping separation from a mother. This training referred to pressing for early development in the area of social skills. Such behavior was reported by mothers who were evaluated on the indicator "limits curiosity, stresses conformity" as interfering with the development of differentiation. These mothers had very early expected their children to live up to adult standards of social conformity such as neatness, cleanliness, tidiness and had attempted to make "little gentlemen" of them. One mother, for example, stated that she had expected her son at age 2 to eat in a restaurant without spilling food. Other mothers had pressed their children to walk, talk, feed, or care for themselves at an early age. In some instances this was associated with a desire to "keep up with the Jones'," or to achieve some prescribed norm suggested by "authorities." In other instances, efforts to make a child "grow up too soon" were based on the mother's desire to be relieved of some of the burden of child care by shedding parental responsibilities, as the following example suggests.

I: Could you say at what age you enjoyed him most?
M: Well, I'm sorry to say I didn't appreciate him when he was a baby, because of the closeness of the two children. We considered him an old man when he was really a baby. It was always when he was small, "Watch out for the baby!" whereas he was a baby himself. He's only a year-and-a-half older . . . And I was rushing them, I rushed their lives away. I was always forcing them to do things.

One might speculate that both trying to make a child behave like a grownup and infantilizing him, though involving very different rearing procedures, have the common property of permitting the mother to avoid coping with the changes of growth in the child. One might further suggest that both infantilizing a child and making an adult of him prematurely may be manifestations of lack of awareness of the child as a separate individual. To maintain the child as a baby is, in extreme form, to keep him as one with the mother, perpetuating the pattern that existed at the beginning. To expect "adult conformity" is another manifestation of fusion of the child and herself, this time at an adult level.

b. Mother-child interaction contributing to judgments of IFD. The indicator "physical care of child seems inappropriate to age" provided a guide for judging mothers as IID or IFD. Where no evidence of inappropriate physical care was present in a record, this was considered as consistent with judgment of mother as IFD.

A second indicator bearing upon a mother's encouragement of separation was "through fears and anxieties for or ties to child, mother markedly limits child's activities and his going out into community," discussed above with reference to mothers judged as IID. Evidence suggesting that a mother permitted and even encouraged her child to separate from her was considered as consistent with an IFD rating.

One mother, for example, stated that both she and her husband had decided at whatever cost to themselves they would let their son be independent as soon as he was able. When he entered first grade she let him start out alone but "tailed" him until she had assured herself that he knew how to watch the lights and cross the street. She said, as did some other IFD mothers, that her "heart was in her mouth" when she let him ride his bicycle, but felt that she must not let her fears stand in the way of his achieving the independence he wanted and was ready to assume.

A third indicator considered was "maternal control is not in the direction of a child's achieving mature goals, or becoming responsible, or is consistently directed against child's asserting himself."

Mothers who permitted or encouraged a child to assume various kinds of responsibilities, as carrying through with household chores, staying alone in the house, caring for pets, keeping appointments, were viewed as interacting with their children in a manner which encouraged the development of differentiation. Such women often displayed trust and confidence in their children's ability to be discriminating and selective in choosing friends and were not afraid of "bad companions," or of the contagion of delinquent activities (reported by mothers who were judged as handicapping the development of responsibility).

Evidence in this area was also obtained from mothers' descriptions and views of their children's schoolwork. Where a mother considered such schoolwork the child's own, though she might help or encourage him, this was seen as consistent with an IFD rating. For example, one mother said:

I: What's your feeling about helping him with homework?
M: Well, as I say, he doesn't ask for too much help and I don't believe in pushing him, standing next to a child watching him do his homework . . . it's *his* homework. If he makes mistakes, that's the only way of doing it to find out what's wrong . . . If he asks, like he often asks for help with sentence structure, I mean we do that, but that's about all.

Encouragement of the development of curiosity was also considered as evidence of permitting a child to separate from a mother. This was evaluated in the indicator "limits curiosity, stresses conformity." Evidence of this came from the mothers' attitudes toward their children's interests and attempts to explore and find things out on their own. Mothers who encouraged questioning, who offered their children an opportunity to understand "how things are," who, in disciplining their children, explained "why," gave evidence of encouraging curiosity. One mother instead of punishing her small son when he spilled cereal on the floor explained "how things fall to the ground." Such mothers took it for granted that their children would be interested in the adult world, for example, what the mother did on her job.

Further analysis of the interview records after the child's mode of perception was known suggested that, in general, mothers who had permitted or encouraged separation from them took into account their children's readiness for such separation.

In such mothers recognition of readiness implied that a mother had understanding of and was sensitive to what her child was capable of doing. The following example suggests such an attitude.

M: I let my children go down (alone) very early. At 2½ they went into the back yard (of the apartment house) by themselves. And many times I had mothers tell me they would report me. They thought he was too young. But I knew my child. I knew that if I told them to stay in the back yard, and I gave them the wagon, and whatever they needed, they would stay in the back yard. And that if they needed me, they'd call me.

Sensitivity to the child's needs might also include a sense of discrimination of a given child's needs as different from those of his siblings, or as different at various stages of his own development. Some examples may clarify this kind of "awareness."

With a family of five, mother always gives special attention to whichever child appeared to her to be the "underdog" at the time.

Mother recognized child's need to have special status of older brother when sibling was born. Father gave him a watch at this time.

Mother understood that her son was disturbed by the divorced father's absence and that this was having an adverse effect on his schoolwork. Therefore she let father visit frequently.

However, opportunity for separation from a mother did not always involve a recognition of the child's readiness for such separation. Some mothers even pushed their children to assume responsibilities, to take care of themselves, to go out into the community, or to strive for intellectual achievement, disregarding their children's own pace and readiness for such activities. However, such "overacceleration," though not a manifestation of regard for the particular individual needs of their children, sometimes seemed motivated by a desire to make their children self-regulating, self-sufficient, and in effect separate individuals. Such mothers differed from other mothers who accelerated their children by letting them go out into the community, or by attempting to make adults of their children at an early age through emphasizing social conformity. Such maternal attitudes which were usually specific to certain areas of training did not seem to be motivated by a desire to make their children independent in any general sense. In fact we have suggested that acceleration which involves demands of adult conformity may indeed be a manifestation of failure to encourage "real" separation from a mother.

2. Training for Control of Aggressive, Assertive Behavior

a. Mother-child interaction contributing to ratings of IID. As stated earlier, mothers' complaints of aggressive behavior in their children, especially directed toward themselves, contributed to a rating of IID. Such specific behavior as being impulsive, stubborn, disobedient, headstrong, fresh, demanding might be included in what they disapproved of or disliked in their children, whereas being quiet, mannerly, compliant might be approved.

The specific kinds of efforts made by the mothers studied to control their children and, in particular, to deal with aggressive and assertive behavior varied, but could be grouped as follows: (1) indulgent, submissive reaction; (2) coercive training, severe punishment; (3) combination of indulgence and severe discipline; (4) control by irrational threats.

(1) SUBMISSIVE, INDULGENT REACTION ON MOTHER'S PART

Such behavior was reported particularly by mothers who felt overwhelmed by the demands of motherhood. They often were unsure of themselves, dependent on others for guidance, and seemed incapable of either defining standards of behavior for their children or of adhering to whatever standards or limits they had set. Such mothers frequently expressed a feeling of desperation or helplessness in coping with their children. They often seemed actually to be afraid of them and their indulgence seemed to serve as a device to prevent attack, argument, or criticism from the child. In such homes one often wondered who was in command, the mother or child. In the face of opposition, these mothers characteristically wilted, dissolved, or abdicated after an initial unsuccessful attempt to dominate or to insist on a given type of behavior from the child. They sometimes attempted to turn over discipline to the father, or utilized him as a "big stick." Their threats, however, were characteristically not carried out.

The following excerpt from an interview illustrates indulgent maternal behavior:

I: What do you do now if he doesn't eat (something you serve)?
M: Well, like my husband says, a restaurant—you have to make what they want. (My child) loves pot roast. If you don't make him pot roast he gets mad. "What's the matter, you don't have enough time to make it?"

Sometimes indulgence—as failure to insist on a child keeping to a prescribed diet, waiting on him or servicing him—was seen by a mother as a manifestation of her love for him, or was justified in order to preserve a child's love.

One mother's failure to insist that her child diet, though he was very much overweight, unhappy about his obesity, and handicapped in many activities and social relationships with other boys, was reported as follows:

I: Has he had to diet in the meantime?
M: Yes, he's dieted ever since he was 6 years old. He's been off and on a diet. It's really nerve-racking . . . he resented the fact that his brother was allowed to eat so much and that I had to limit the amount of sweets and starches he could take . . . so I just couldn't deprive him.

(2) COERCIVE TRAINING, SEVERE PUNISHMENT

A rigorous, exacting, pressuring kind of control contributed to an IID rating. Mothers displaying such attitudes toward their children were generally curbing, insistent on unquestioning, immediate obedience. They allowed no decision making on the child's part.

Some mothers were particularly coercive in the area of school performance. When the child had done poorly in school they pressured, nagged, or punished him. This often was accompanied by a lack of awareness of why the child was not doing well, or why the steps they had taken had not promoted achievement. This was indicated by such statements as: "I don't understand why he isn't doing well." "He's just lazy and lacks ambition." "He has no inclination to learn." A driving, pushing determination to make the child successful was sometimes portrayed, even in the face of the teacher's opinion or their own suspicion that the child did not have the capacity to live up to the mother's very high expectations. This was particularly likely when the child had early given promise of being bright by talking early, or being socially very responsive.

Mothers seen as coercive often spontaneously reported episodes involving punishment of their children. Discipline tended to be severe, harsh, or inappropriate relative to the offense. It was also often arbitrary with no understandable reason given the child as to why he was being punished. Such mothers tended to show bias when they dealt with social situations involving their children. Within the family they often spared a preferred child and discriminated against the nonpreferred. Moreover, these mothers tended to punish impulsively and reported feelings of hostility while punishing the child. The types of punishment most frequently reported by such mothers were beating, hitting, or nagging.

The following examples are illustrative:

I: What did you do when they found him lighting matches at school?
M: I took him home, and I told him, "You want to feel the heat of them? All right, you can stick your finger in them." He started to cry, and I hit him. I gave him a beating, a real hard beating, and I had him in the house for a week, he couldn't go out. And ah—ever since then, he doesn't touch it . . .

I: Can you tell me something about it (training for bowel control)?
M: He just never wanted to sit on his potty. And I'd sit there and read him stories. I never left him alone. But he just didn't want to sit on his chair . . .
I: Sure. And what could you do?
M: I used to hit him.

(3) COMBINATION OF INDULGENCE AND SEVERE DISCIPLINE
A wavering between indulgence and severe discipline was another pattern for dealing with aggressive behavior which contributed to an IID rating. Mothers showing this pattern were apt to be impulsive

and irrational in disciplining their children. Episodes depicting inter-action between them and their children sometimes sounded like re-ports of fights between equals. Indeed, "fighting" was a term often used by such mothers when they described interaction with the child.

I: What annoys you the most about him?

M: I think what unnerves me the most . . . is his temper and the fact that he doesn't wash . . . I'll tell (my son), "Go up and take a bath." See, he can't take a bath himself because he comes out dirtier than when he went in . . . I said, "Come up and you'll take a shower." So . . . he doesn't want to. I said, "Yes you will," and I literally dragged him up . . . put him in the shower. So he just stood there. And I can't go in with him, I'll get my hair wet. So I said to him, "Have you washed?" "No," or "I won't tell you," or whatever it was. His legs and ankles, the dirt was so embedded it looked like it had to soak for a year to get it off. What hap-pened was in rage I finally shut the shower off. So he said he'd get out. I said, "You won't get out. I'll let water in the tub." "Don't put water in the tub." He started screaming—started in with cursing. The end of it was I let some water into the tub and I had to climb into the tub and wrestle with him. Have you tried wrestling with a wet soapy kid? Well, he fell down about seven times . . . splashed me from head to foot. And if I grabbed a foot, I had to scrub it real fast 'cause he'd pull it away. We were up there for about an hour fighting like that . . . And he won't give in. Called me every name under the sun.

(4) CONTROL BY IRRATIONAL THREATS

Some mothers attempted to control aggressive behavior toward themselves or toward other children by using irrational threats. These mothers tended to be especially disturbed by expressions of aggres-sion toward themselves. The following example is illustrative.

M: He has a terrible temper. He told me to "drop dead" any number of times—"you shut up, you bastard"—things like that.

I: What do you do about it then?

M: Well, once I explained to him that you don't talk that way. "For one reason, suppose you tell me to drop dead, and suppose by some freak acci-dent I happened to drop dead. You would feel that you caused me to die, which isn't so, you don't really mean it." Then after, he'll tell you he's sorry, he lost his temper. So I said to him, "That's how murders are committed. People lose . . . control of themselves. They don't know what they're do-ing. I said, "You can't allow yourself to lose complete control of yourself." . . . And yet it happens, you know, again and again.

b. Mother-child interaction contributing to ratings of IFD. When mothers tended to be definite about standards of behavior expected of their children, made such standards meaningful and clear to them, and were, on the whole, consistent about enforcing the limits which they had imposed, an IFD rating was suggested.

The setting of excessively high standards did not preclude a judgment of IFD. For instance, one mother emphasized neatness and orderliness. Her child, however, seemed to have been able thoroughly to adopt such standards as his own, even to the point where his mother complained of his "perfectionism."

Control measures evaluated as consistent with IFD judgments included the use of reasoning and explanation as the preferred method of discipline. One mother made the following comments about her discipline:

> I'm not strict . . . I think basically they're both very good children. I think children need guidance. We do a lot of talking to them and we do a lot of explaining. I feel maybe that will be just as well as punishing them. Don't misunderstand me, I don't say that I never raise my voice. I can't say that and be honest with you.

The use of reasoning and explanation requires a greater tolerance of the child's assertiveness since explanation allows for the possibility of a child questioning, answering, or arguing with the mother. Such techniques also give the child some understanding of what he has done and provides a guide for future behavior. The use of reasoning and explanation was one indication of the mother's own self-control and her less emotional manner in disciplining. Whereas expressions of generalized anger and hostility toward children contributed to an IID rating, attempts to weigh situations and to apportion punishment equitably according to misdemeanor suggested IFD rating. However, occasionally mothers presenting a picture consistent with IFD classification reported the use of physical punishment, at times when specific situations got "beyond" them and they got "red hot mad." Such episodes of anger seemed sporadic in otherwise well-controlled mothers and specific to the occasion rather than expressions of generalized frustration by the child.

In general, as suggested by the indicator "control is not in the direction of the child's achieving mature goals or becoming responsible, or is consistently directed against the child's asserting himself," control by mothers which involved either coercion or, at the other extreme, indulgence contributed to IID rating. In contrast, a nonindulging but nevertheless directing attitude, free of coercion, contributed to an IFD rating. An example of a mother's comments reflecting noncoercive attitudes is the following:

I: At what age have you enjoyed him the most?

M: Well—he's always been a source of pleasure. I'm enjoying him now. He's really coming out . . . I don't believe in saying to a child jump and they jump, and if you say hop, they hop. What a child does on his or her own, or their own ingenuity, to me I enjoy that . . . it's like you teach a dog to sit, and you say "sit" and the dog sits. I can't see my child doing that. I can't say "sit" and then they sit.

C. SUMMARY

We have discussed attitudes toward the child studied and rearing procedures which contributed to classification of mothers as IID or IFD. Evaluation of maternal attitudes was based on explicit statements made by the mother and inferences from her interaction with her child.

The predominance of complaints about a child contributed to an evaluation of a mother as lacking a sense of self-realization. These complaints were expressed by mothers in terms of personal grievances. They included the child's failure to live up to maternal expectations, particularly in the intellectual area, lack of conformity to mother's standards of physical appearance or social behavior, aggressive, assertive behavior especially when directed against the mother. When mothers resented demands for special care or attention they were considered as lacking self-realization. Approval which was contingent on the child's being good, compliant, not troublesome, not demanding of care was considered evidence of lack of self-realization in regard to this particular child.

On the other hand, the predominance of expressions of approval for their children was evidence of self-realization in mothering. Such approval focused on school achievement, creativity, the assumption of responsibilities by a child. Maternal attitudes which indicated that a mother was more concerned with the effect of problem behavior on the child than on her suggested a judgment of IFD. Characteristics such as warmth toward or involvement with a child did not by themselves contribute to one or the other kind of judgment of a mother. Rather the apparent reason for and purpose of such attitudes was considered.

Rearing procedures which contributed to judgments of IID or IFD were described: rearing which interfered with separation from the mother included giving physical care inappropriate to age, preventing the assumption of responsibility, markedly limiting a child's activities because of fears or anxieties, stressing conformity, especially pressing for adult behavior when children were very young. Submissive, indulgent maternal behavior, severe punishment, training which combined indulgence and severe discipline, and attempts to control by irrational threats were taken as evidence for judging mothers as handicapping the development of impulse control.

An IFD rating was suggested when mothers adapted their physical care for the child to his age, encouraged him to assume age-adequate responsibilities and activities, and stimulated his curiosity and interests.

A review of interview records after the child's mode of field approach was known suggested that separation from a mother was most frequently encouraged by mothers who were sensitive to their children's readiness for such separation. However, overacceleration which was a manifestation of a mother's desire to make a child self-sufficient and self-regulating and, in effect, a separate individual may be consistent with "real" separation from a mother. Acceleration which stressed social conformity or was primarily motivated by the mother's desire to get rid of her child or reflected primarily the needs of the mother rather than of the child may not contribute to the development of a sense of separate identity in the child.

Setting of definite standards of behavior which were made meaningful and clear to a child and were consistently enforced were used to judge mothers as contributing to the development of impulse controls. However, the setting of excessively high standards did not preclude an evaluation of fostering impulse control.

In general, maternal control which involved either coercion or at the other extreme indulgence contributed to an IID rating. A nonindulging, noncoercive but directing attitude contributed to an IFD rating.

20

FURTHER STUDIES OF THE "MOTHER AS A PERSON"

Classification of mothers as IID or IFD was based on global impressions from the interview records as a whole. Though these classifications were oriented to specific issues and grounded in particular indicators, no effort was made to weigh systematically the contribution of individual indicators to the final classification. It is clear that the classifications are based on a large complex of factors which require more specific identification. In the present chapter we describe a study which represents an initial step in this direction.

The particular component of the complex of factors with which we chose to begin is in the area of "characteristics of mother as a person." As we examined our characterizations of the mothers with regard to both their attributes as persons and their interaction with their children, it became apparent that included were many attributes which, in the children, we had regarded as indicators of extent of differentiation. Thus, IID mothers were described as having failed to develop a stable sense of self, reflected, for example, in a lack of definition of their roles as wives and mothers. In rearing their children they lacked clarity as to how to implement their goals and lacked realization of their children's needs as individuals. IFD mothers, on the other hand, had more clearly defined their roles. They had developed more sense of direction and inner values in their own lives. They had more clearly defined ways of implementing goals and standards for their children. They were less impulsive and more rational in interaction with their children and they seemed more aware of their children as separate persons. In classifying mothers as IFD and IID we were, in effect, including some evaluation of the mother's own level of development with respect to sense of separate identity, impulse control, and capacity for articulated experience, which we have considered indicators of differentiation.

These considerations suggested two hypotheses which we have tested: 1. The degree of differentiation of the mother herself was part of the basis on which the over-all global ratings of IID and IFD rested. 2. The more undifferentiated children are likely to have more undifferentiated mothers. The latter hypothesis seems tenable if we consider the ways in which mothers who lack the qualities we have taken as indicators of differentiation might handicap their children's progress toward differentiation. For instance, a mother who has not developed a sense of her own identity, as a person separate from others, would be less likely to permit her child to separate from her or to develop as an individual. If a mother's own experience is not articulated she cannot help her child achieve articulation. Her own failure to develop internalized frames of reference would not permit her to communicate to the child a clear, consistent, and meaningful view of himself and others. Both by her own example and by inconsistencies in experiences offered to her child she would handicap his development of impulse control. Thus it seemed reasonable to hypothesize that mothers who are themselves limitedly differentiated would tend to have relatively undifferentiated children and that mothers who are more differentiated would tend to have relatively differentiated children.

A. METHOD OF STUDY

As a first step in the testing of the two hypotheses, we made a partial evaluation of extent of differentiation of mothers previously interviewed. Two of the techniques used to assess differentiation in the children were used, the EFT and figure-drawing test.

This study has several features which deserve comment. First, it provides an opportunity to assess the mother as a person directly, apart from her role as mother. Further, compared to the complex clinical judgments involved in ratings of interviews, the measures derived from the EFT and figure drawings are based on more limited and therefore more easily identifiable information. Finally, from our earlier work we had well-established, reliable methods for evaluating EFT performance and figure-drawing productions.

1. Procedure. Twenty-six [1] of the 28 Group-III mothers previously interviewed were revisited by the same staff member, 2 to 3 years after the inter-

---

[1] Two mothers in the original group had moved outside the state; because of traveling distance involved they were not accessible for testing.

view.[2]   At the time of testing the mothers ranged in age from 35 to 47 years, with a mean of 41.3 years.   Mothers were, in general, cooperative about the revisit.   The reason given for the visit was to study the congruence of perceptual functioning in mothers and sons, and to maintain contact with the family.

The visit began with a brief inquiry concerning major changes in the family and the child studied.   The EFT and figure-drawing test were then administered, in that order.

2. Tests.   Because it was felt that many of these busy mothers might refuse to come to the laboratory for extended testing, and might have only limited time to give us, the choice of tests was restricted to those which could be administered at home, and which would require a minimum of time.   These considerations led us to use the EFT, in a shortened form (first six figures) and the figure-drawing test.   We decided on testing in the home even though we expected and actually did encounter in the home situation interruptions and distractions, such as the presence of other family members, including young children who required attention, repeated phone calls, or frequent ringing of door bells.

Though its choice was dictated by practical requirements, the EFT was perhaps the least desirable of the tests of perceptual field dependence to use for this particular group of women.   Unlike the BAT and RFT, the EFT has a correct response on each trial and the subject knows when he is not doing well or has failed.   This may have made the test less suitable for women far removed from their school days.   Moreover, as will be recalled from Chapter 5, performance in the EFT probably involves an attention-concentration factor.   Among women approaching the period of menopause with its associated anxieties there might be some for whom the maintenance of focused attention would be a problem.   In such cases, a high EFT time score might reflect an attention difficulty rather than the preferred mode of field approach.   Interruptions inevitable in home testing might also affect the time score.

Administration of the figure-drawing test in the home, we recognized, might also present disadvantages, but these did not appear as great as in the case of the EFT.   Interruptions and distractions while figures are being drawn are of course undesirable; since performance is not timed, however, they are not likely to have the marked adverse effect possible with the EFT.   Moreover, the feeling of failure which the EFT permits is not to the same degree possible with the figure-drawing test.

3. Method of rating figure drawings.   The sophistication-of-body-concept scale, described in Chapter 7, was first developed for rating the drawings of 10-year-old boys and subsequently modified for application to a college group.   It was felt that further modification might be necessary in order to apply the scale to a group of women in their late 30's and 40's.   The

---

[2] This interval was consumed in evaluating the initial interviews.   On the basis of the results obtained the decision was made to test the mothers.

drawings were therefore given to the psychologist who had developed these scales with instructions to apply the "adult" version of the scale, if it seemed appropriate, or to modify it, if necessary, to cover the range of performances of this particular age-sex group.

The adult version of the sophistication-of-body-concept scale proved applicable, with one modification, to this group of drawings. Because of special problems in rating the drawings of 5 women, a sixth category was added to the five which make up the adult version of the scale. Drawings in this sixth or "special-group" category were described by the rater as follows: "(They) differ from the drawings in category 1, the most primitive group, in that they do not look like the simple, completely immature, and undifferentiated drawings placed in that category. Nor do they resemble the productions of a slightly higher developmental level found in category 2. They are essentially regressive and inconsistent, rather than undeveloped (and) primitive. Thus they cannot be placed unequivocally in any of the five categories." Certainly, it is not surprising that regressive trends would be found among some women who were of an age when problems of menopause would be common. Nor is it surprising that the figure drawings obtained from the younger age groups with which we have worked, and for which the sophistication scale was developed, did not include any showing as markedly regressive features as those encountered in the drawings of the mothers.

Since the "special-group" drawings were thus not considered ratable on the same dimension as the other drawings, they were excluded in advance from the quantitative analyses to be described.

B. RESULTS

1. General Impressions of Mothers on Revisit

The investigator's focus in this home visit was on giving tests rather than on evaluating mothers through a new interview. However, in this second meeting some impressions were inevitably formed concerning change or lack of change in these mothers. The interviewer found that, on the basis of her previous interview and subsequent intensive study of the interview records, she had retained vivid memories of these mothers. These were compared to impressions formed on revisit.

Many mothers gave the interviewer essentially the same impression they did previously. For example, the interviewer recorded the following comments about one mother after the revisit: "No doubt about this mother. She is the 'no-surrender' person of the first interview." Of another mother she noted: "Her complaints are similar to and often identical with those of the first interview. 'He opens his big mouth and screams' sounds familiar, as does 'He's not the kind of child you can love.'"

In other mothers changes were apparent, mostly in the direction of reduced self-confidence. The comment made about one mother was, "Her anxiety about bringing up her son is more apparent in this interview"; of another, "Mother seems more excitable and unsure of herself than in the previous interview."

Five mothers, however, appeared to have changed so markedly that the interviewer experienced what can only be described as immediate "shock" at the apparent change in them. Changes noted were mainly in the direction of appearing markedly more anxious, more depressed, more dependent, less energetic. These impressions were more or less cursory and cannot be thought of as representing any systematic evaluation of change. They suggest, however, that the test performance of these mothers might have been different at the time the initial home interviews were held. Since in some of our analyses we compare scores for the EFT and figure drawings obtained at this time, and interview ratings of the mother and various scores for the children obtained 2 to 3 years earlier, the occurrence of such changes may have affected the relationships obtained.

It is noteworthy that the drawings of 3 of the 5 mothers independently identified by the interviewer as giving evidence of marked change were placed, because of regressive qualities, in the unratable "special group."

2. Main Findings

In our studies of children we considered that EFT performance provides a measure of articulateness of experience and that sophistication-scale scores provide measures of development of body concept. Both these characteristics, we have postulated, reflect extent of development of differentiation. The correlation of .65 ($P < .01$, $N = 21$) between EFT and sophistication-scale scores in Group-III mothers shows a high relation between the two aspects of differentiation. The relation between perceptual performance and sophistication-scale scores established with 10-year-olds and young adult men (Chapter 7) is now confirmed for a group of women in the middle years of life.

To test the hypothesis that ratings made on the basis of interviews with mothers were in part based upon impressions of extent of mothers' differentiation, the original interview ratings of mothers were compared to their sophistication-of-body-concept scores, with a resulting correlation of .53 ($P < .05$), in the expected direction. As anticipated, mothers judged IFD drew figures reflecting a more sophisticated body concept than mothers judged IID. The correlation of .20 between EFT scores and judgments of mothers as IID or IFD is in the expected direction, but not significant.

Taken together the results suggest that the global evaluations of mothers as IID or IFD in part reflected their level of differentiation. However, from the size of the correlations between the measures of differentiation used and judgments of IID and IFD, it is evident that other factors entered into the final, over-all interview judgments, and that level of differentiation was only part of what was being assessed.

To test the hypothesis that relatively differentiated children are likely to have mothers who are themselves more differentiated, the sophistication-scale and EFT scores of mothers were compared to their children's cognitive performances. Mothers' figure-drawing scores correlated .48 ($P < .05$) with their children's perceptual index scores, .41 (not significant) with children's intellectual index scores, and .49 ($P < .05$) with children's cognitive index scores, all in the expected direction. Mothers' EFT scores correlated .37 (not significant) [3] with their children's perceptual index scores, .15 (not significant) with intellectual index scores, and .29 (not significant) with cognitive index scores. Though all the correlations with mothers' EFT scores are in the expected direction, none is significant by our standards.

Thus, the relation between extent of differentiation of mother and child tends to be significant, as expected, when the mothers' figure-drawing scores are used to reflect differentiation, but are not significant, though in the expected direction, when the mothers' EFT scores are used to reflect differentiation.[4]

We do not have sufficient data to account for the lack of a significant relation between mothers' EFT scores and measures of differentiation for their children. One possible basis, unreliability of the shortened EFT, seems unlikely in view of an internal consistency reliability coefficient of .78 obtained for this group of mothers with the six figures used. The special difficulties in test administration already mentioned may have contributed to the lack of relationship by bringing the attention-concentration component of performance on the EFT (see Chapter 5) to the fore. The problem requires further study.

[3] By a one-tail test, used by many investigators in circumstances where a definite outcome has been predicted, this correlation is significant ($P < .05$).

[4] In Chapter 22 we compare the measures derived from studies of the mother (interview ratings, sophistication-of-body-concept-scale scores, and EFT scores) to various other measures of differentiation of their children. As we shall see, except for EFT scores the picture is one of generally significant relationships.

Our starting hypotheses that the degree of differentiation of the mother herself was part of the basis on which the over-all global ratings of IID and IFD rested, and that less differentiated children are likely to have less differentiated mothers, have received partial support from the evidence. The findings raise several issues that require further consideration.

We are, of course, not implying that the mother is the only person who contributes to the development of differentiation in a child nor that parental characteristics are static or operate in a void without regard to the child's contribution. Within the interaction point of view, we have suggested merely that differentiation of the mother contributes to a large complex of parent-child interactions relevant to the child's development of differentiation. There is the question, however, of whether a mother who is highly differentiated may lack qualities, not necessarily related to her own level of differentiation, of importance for the development of differentiation in her child. Thus, a mother who is highly differentiated may not accept a particular child and her lack of acceptance may handicap his development toward differentiation. On the other hand, it is difficult to imagine how a mother who is herself limitedly differentiated could by her upbringing help her child become highly differentiated. Mothers whose drawings were rated at the "primitive" end (categories 1 and 2) of the sophistication-of-body-concept scale had, with one exception, children who were relatively undifferentiated, according to their perceptual performance and various other measures of differentiation (see Chapter 22). In this exceptional case, impressions of the mother obtained by both the interviewer and the psychologist who, as we describe later in this chapter, used the figure drawings to make a clinical evaluation of the mothers, are of interest. Both described this mother as giving an impression that she had earlier achieved better integration and better defenses than she was presently utilizing. Thus, in spite of the fact that her drawings had not been rated in the "special group" (regressive trends) we may perhaps speculate that earlier she was better equipped to furnish opportunities for the development of differentiation in her child.

3. Clinical Evaluation of Figure Drawings of IID and IFD Mothers

Evaluations of mothers by a second psychologist, Meta Steiner, using the same sets of drawings gave further support to the hypothesis that in judging mothers as IID or IFD we were in part assessing level of differentiation. The psychologist was asked to evaluate the drawings of 26 mothers of Group-III boys particularly with reference to areas previously considered by the interviewer in making judgments of mothers as IID or IFD. She was asked to comment on each mother's self-realization, coping mechanisms, and social relationships, to the extent that the drawings permitted such judgments. Specific definition of these areas was left entirely to her. After her preliminary individual evaluations were completed, the mothers were identified for her as belonging to the IID or IFD groups. She was then asked to generalize about possible common characteristics of mothers within each group and about characteristics which seemed to distinguish the two groups from each other. Her method of evaluations of figure drawings differed from that already described inasmuch as she did not "rate" the drawings but used the raw data for clinical evaluation of particular aspects of personality.

We give below descriptions of IFD and IID mothers based on clinical evaluations of drawings of both male and female figures.

IID Mothers

The most outstanding common trend of the group of IID mothers was their relative lack of developed controls. Control features, such as the zoning of specific body portions, were strikingly lacking. Shading tended to spill over the boundaries. Often some body parts were missing, such as arms, legs, nose, or more characteristically hipline or waistline, so that the body appeared as a sack or a nonselective container. Circles, ovals, or squares represented the trunks in some of these drawings; the top of the figure was not clearly demarcated from the rest of the body, as if the functioning of the body occurred in the form of one over-all undifferentiated reaction.

Such underplaying of the body and by implication of its functions may be taken as a graphic representation of the rejection of the body aspects of the self, including the sexual aspects. Self-rejection in the area of sex-role identification was suggested by the fact that 7 of the IID mothers drew the male figure first. This occurred only once in the IFD group. One of the IID mothers commented about her first drawing: "It is either a man or a woman, you would have to ask for a label," thus verbalizing her difficulty in role-delineation. She projected this difficulty graphically in a shapeless figure with minimal indications of sex identity. Along with a rejection of the feminine role, or at least with a lack of special pride in or enjoyment of the role, there was often a suggestion in the drawings of IID mothers of an underaccentuation of the maternal role. Thus the breast area might be neglected or minimized rather than stressed.

In social adjustment, these mothers seemed anxious, and fearful of rejection. Fear of a critical and rejecting world was portrayed, for example, in facial features suggestive of suspiciousness. Some of these mothers also seemed passive and dependent in social relationships. Features suggestive of dependency—such as passive, helplessly extended arms, often short and faintly drawn—were common. Executive organs were characteristically underplayed (e.g., hands were often missing, or barely indicated). Though interaction with the environment as portrayed was predominantly passive, there were occasional indications of a potential for sporadic impulsive outbursts (e.g., heavy slashed lines for the mouth, suggestive of bursts of verbal aggression). The drawings, even when large, had little vigor in line treatment, reflected no pleasure in performance, and indicated little effort in the execution of the task. There were indications of fantasies of success, social status, or prestige in many of the drawings but few indications of active striving. The contrast between lack of "personal substance" and fantasied aspirations is illustrated in one drawing, for example, in which a tall hat was put on a rather primitive drawing of a man with no other indication of clothing and little body detailing.

As might be anticipated, some mothers in the group showed these characteristics more clearly than others. Nine of the 13 IID mothers produced drawings in which the characteristics described above occurred with frequency and intensity, while the drawings of 3 mothers had some admixture of features more frequently seen in the drawings of the IFD group, described below. Finally, one IID mother projected in her drawings a personality as well developed and organized as most of the IFD mothers. It is of interest that the interviewer, in independently evaluating this mother 3 years earlier, though rating her IID, had judged her as being like the IFD mothers on the indicator "mother in rearing child does not have assurance in herself."

IFD Mothers

The drawings of IFD mothers gave an impression of richer personalities with better developed abilities for coping with life situations in more varied and subtle ways. Representations of human figures were more adequate, the drawings better organized, individual features delineated and separated from each other.

While IFD mothers showed acute distress as often as IID mothers (e.g., various graphic indications of conflict: disproportions, multiple lines, erasures, and reinforcements), they also gave evidence of capacity to handle and absorb their anxieties, aggressions, and depressions. They strove to intellectualize, to erect boundaries, to segregate conflict. For example, shading tended to be rationalized; compulsive controls were likely to be indicated in an emphasis on symmetry and careful attention to details and boundaries; erasures were followed by attempts at more acceptable solutions. One would infer that the better integration of the self, as projected in the drawings, enabled these mothers to develop a stronger sense of identity.

Greater acceptance of their role was, for the group, indicated in two ways. First, 12 of 13 IFD mothers (compared to 6 of the 13 IID mothers) drew the female figure first. Second, pleasurable acceptance of femininity, sometimes to the point of narcissistic concentration on body functioning and glamour, was suggested in the elaboration of feminine accoutrements such as necklaces, earrings, ruffles, ornaments on a purse, and, in one case, an evening gown. While such "seductive" features were emphasized in some cases maternal aspects of the figure were stressed in other cases (e.g., emphasis on large and heavy breasts, wide hips, a pregnant look). The males drawn by these women were clearly identifiable as males in terms both of clothing and of features traditionally assigned to the male, such as broad shoulders, wide stance, "solid-looking" feet. Differentiation between male and female drawings was far clearer than in drawings of IID mothers. The "weak" males, more characteristically drawn by IID mothers, were conspicuously absent among the IFD mothers.

As a group, these women showed an interest in striving for executive functioning and activity. Thus, a high energy level was suggested in vigorous line treatment. More active contact with the environment was suggested by clearer articulation of hands than was the case with IID mothers. In general, contact features—e.g., hands, arms, feet—were not underemphasized in comparison with the amount of attention given to faces, as was the case with IID mothers. Arms tended to be of adequate length, hands and fingers were sometimes portrayed in action. Sensitive and better modulated lines were further indications of a greater variety and subtlety in social contacts.

Women in the IFD group were by no means free of problems and conflicts in the area of social interaction. But their manner of handling these conflicts appeared to be more sophisticated and purposeful. Thus, instead of omitting or barely indicating hands, as did IID mothers, the IFD mothers might hold their arms and hands close to the body or draw them hidden behind the back. Whatever problems these women might have in the areas of social contact and activity, the discrepancy noted in IID mothers between "personal substance" and fantasied level of aspiration was not characteristic of this group.

Three sets of drawings did not conform to these group trends. In each of the three, there was an overlay of pathology, along with residual indications of previously better developed defenses and resources. The degree to which the defenses had been developed was difficult to assess because of the dominance of current pathology.

These clinical evaluations of mothers' figure drawings add to the impression that extent of differentiation is relevant to classifying mothers as IID and IFD. As seen through the medium of this projective test core groups of IID and IFD mothers differ markedly in the complexity of their controls and in their definition of their social relationships and their role as women.

C. SUMMARY

On the basis of impressions of personal characteristics of mothers formed through interviews with them, two hypotheses were formulated. The first stated that mothers judged as IID on the basis of interviews were less differentiated than mothers judged as IFD. The second proposed that more differentiated children would tend to have more differentiated mothers. To test these hypotheses, mothers who had previously been interviewed, and whose children had been studied in the laboratory, were revisited at home and given a shortened version of the EFT and the figure-drawing test. We considered, on the basis of our studies with children reported in Chapters 4 through 15, that EFT performance and ratings of sophistication of body concept may be taken as measures of extent of differentiation.

The two measures of extent of differentiation proved to be highly and significantly related.

To test the first hypothesis, mothers' interview ratings were compared to their EFT and figure-drawing sophistication-scale scores. To test the second hypothesis, mothers' EFT and sophistication-scale scores were compared to their children's scores on tests of mode of field approach. Figure-drawing sophistication-scale ratings of mothers related significantly to interview judgments of mothers as IID or IFD. As expected, IFD mothers drew figures which suggested a more developed conception of the body. Sophistication-scale ratings of mothers also tended to correlate significantly with measures of mode of field approach of their children, reflecting extent of differentiation. Mothers whose figure drawings showed a sophisticated conception of the body tended to have children with an analytical field approach. Mothers' EFT scores did not relate significantly to judgments of mothers as IID or IFD, or to measures of mode of field approach of their children, although all relations were in the expected direction. The basis of this outcome is not clear and requires further study.

Both starting hypotheses receive partial support from these results. Mothers who had been judged as IID tend to be less differentiated, according to the measures used, than IFD mothers, and to have children whose cognitive scores reflect less differentiation.

Finally, impressions formed from a clinical evaluation of figure drawings of IID and IFD mothers added to the impression that level of differentiation was relevant to classifying mothers as IID and IFD.

21

CHILDREN'S VIEWS
OF PARENTS

Our investigations of parent-child relations among children differing in extent of differentiation followed two lines. In the first approach, already described, we studied mothers in terms of both their personal characteristics and interactions with their children. In a complementary approach we sought evidence from the children themselves. To this end we investigated children's views of parents expressed in TAT stories and interviews. These studies are described in the present chapter.

Studies of the child's viewpoint reflected in TAT stories and in interviews were conducted by different staff members, and were carried out independently of the studies made of mothers. Whereas the studies in the three preceding chapters and the study based on the children's interviews were limited to mothers' relations with their children, the TAT study considered the role of fathers as well.

The same general hypothesis which guided the studies of mothers was also the basis of the TAT and interview studies of children. It led us to expect differences between relatively more differentiated and relatively less differentiated children in the views they hold of parental role and parental attitudes. Particularly, it seemed likely that parents showing the kinds of characteristics observed among mothers judged, on the interview, as IFD (Chapters 19 and 20) would tend to be experienced by their children as essentially supportive; on the other hand, parents with characteristics common to mothers judged, on the interview, as IID would more likely be experienced as non-supportive. Parental support might be expressed in the TAT stories in a variety of ways, for example, in giving guidance and help and imparting standards for growth; in showing positive attitudes and acceptance; in acting in a reasonable way, and for the child's own good. Lack of support might also be shown in varied forms, as for example, in inability or unwillingness to give guidance, help and standards for growth; in attitudes of complaints and nonacceptance; in the exercise of authority in an arbitrary and severe fashion, and with little regard for the child's good.

A supportive parental role does not necessarily imply a smooth, conflict-free, happy relation between parent and child. Such a role may be found in a context of conflict, and resentful feeling and resistant action on the child's part. In the same way, a nonsupportive parental role need not mean conflict and hostility. A parent may be unable to give the child the guidance the child feels he needs, but this lack may or may not be accompanied by warm feelings toward the child.

We recognize that what a child says about parents in the TAT or on interview need not always express the real views and sentiments he holds. His account may at times represent wish fulfillment rather than things as they are; or, particularly in the interview, it may at times be colored by attempts to present as benign a picture as possible. We have chosen in these first studies to base our analyses directly on the content of the account given by the child, with the expectation that the flavor of the child's view of parental role and attitudes, which we were seeking to identify, would generally be captured in such analyses.

A. STUDY OF TAT STORIES

1. Group-I and -II Boys

a. Stories available. Since parent-child themes were rather frequent in the TAT productions of our children, ample material was available for this analysis. Of the total of 435 stories obtained from the 38 children in Groups I and II, 135 or 31% included parental figures, with the frequency about the same for children with a relatively analytical or relatively global field approach. In 21% of the total stories the role of the parent in relation to the child was sufficiently spelled out to permit an evaluation of parental role.

The greater involvement of these 10-year-old boys with their mothers is suggested by the fact that in 50% of all stories involving parents the parent was a mother alone, and in 21% the mother was referred to along with the father. This outcome is not easily attributable to the pictures themselves, for in the series used, figures who looked like mothers were no more frequent than figures who looked like fathers.[1]

It is also noteworthy that in 79% of all parent-child stories the child was specifically designated as a "boy." This suggests a high degree of opportunity for identification with characters in the stories. Actually, the cards used (see Chapter 3) were selected to include several showing a boy in order to permit an opportunity for self-identification.

b. Method of rating stories. The nature of the parental role projected was evaluated in the following manner. Each story involving a parent was first separated from the child's TAT record by a staff member who took no further part in the study. The stories thus remained unidentified as to "author." The parent-child stories obtained from all the children for each specific card were then evaluated. The set of stories for one card was rated before the set for the next card was considered. This procedure retained the anonymity of the child who produced the story and reduced any halo effect that might come from reading through all of a given child's productions.

Among stories with a parent-child theme, there were some in which the relation between parent and child was not sufficiently spelled out to permit evaluation. Such stories were regarded as unratable. The remaining stories were classified according to the eight categories described below.[2] In the first four of these, with an "N" designation, the parent was portrayed as being, in one way or another, nonsupportive toward the child; in the last four, with an "S" designation, the parent was portrayed as being supportive toward the child. This classification was applied to stories involving only mothers, stories involving only fathers, and stories involving both parents considered as a unit.

The eight categories used in the classification of stories, with sample stories for each category, follow:

1. Parent nonsupportive

N-1: The parent is coercive toward the child—as, for example, the child is prevented from doing something he wants to do or is forced to do something he does not want to do. In stories in this category, the child is expected to conform with an arbitrary wish or demand of

[1] The card which elicited the largest number of stories in which a mother appeared was card 1, which portrays a boy alone with a violin.

[2] In instances where the parent was portrayed in more than one role, the story received a multiple rating—that is, it was placed in more than one category. Also, when a story made reference to both a mother and a father, and the role of each was specified, a separate rating was made of each parental figure.

the parent. Stories were not placed in this category when the parent forces the child to practice, do homework, etc., in the spirit of wanting the child to learn or improve.

Example. Card 5. This looks like a boy's room and the mother came to say good night to the boy and the boy isn't in the bed. The boy ran away because he didn't like his mother—she looks like she has a mean face in the picture. (Why doesn't he like her?) She was mean to him. She won't let him play. She don't let him do what the boys do . . . play ball, bicycle. Won't let him go into the gutter and play.

N-2: The parent has a negative feeling toward the child, as for example, the parent is described as angry with the child, dislikes the child, disapproves of the child or of his actions or feelings, treats the child badly, is not helpful to the child.

Example. Card 14. The boy had an argument with his father and he feels pretty badly about it and is going to jump out the window and I think he's going to end up in the hospital (pause) or in the cemetery. (Which do you think it might be?) What? (Hospital or cemetery?) Cemetery—if it's on the sixth floor. (You say they had an argument?) Yes. (What might the argument have been about?)—About school marks. Like my father will be with me tonight, he's going to kill me . . . I got 64 in spelling.

N-3: The parent punishes the child but the punishment is not of a physical nature.

Example. Card 3BM. Looks like a boy and he's laying against his couch and crying because he did something bad—his mother or father took something he liked away from him. (What did he do bad?) Let's see—he hurt his brother—a little brother about one year old maybe.

N-4: The parent administers physical punishment or injures or kills the child.

Example. Card 18GF. Uuh, this is a killing one. Alrightee. Well—this, this lady—got—um—was a very nervous lady and her son came home and—came behind her and scared her and she got up and she went to kill him, choke 'im and she must have killed him—I guess—unless he's superman. That's all. (And then what might have happened?) Get caught by the cops.

2. Parent supportive

S-1: The parent gives guidance or direction to the child. For example, the parent arranges for the child to study, teaches him a skill or principle, gives him a standard for behavior by means of which he can improve himself, wants him to learn or improve himself. In stories placed in this category, the parent may be acting against the child's immediate wishes, provided that this is done in the spirit of being interested in having the child learn or involves moderate urging to learn.

Example. *Card 7BM.* Once there was this man who thought that he was the wisest man in the world. But he went out once to a foreign land. He tried to speak their language, but could not—but still he thought he was the wisest man in the world. He went to another country, and tried to speak their language—but could not. Still he thought he was the wisest man in the world. Finally, after going to about a dozen—a dozen countries and not being able to speak their language, he gave up. His father came over to 'm and told him that no one could be the wisest—no one could know every language—or everything in the world, no one can be that smart, and then the man realized that—it's best that he should work hard at knowing his own language, than knowing the whole world's language.

S-2: The parents' attitudes and behavior toward the child are helpful. For example, the parent takes care of the child when the child is ill or in difficulty, helps him overcome some difficulty, gives him a gift, replaces something he lost or broke, rewards the child for something he did.

Example. *Card 5.* Well, a girl is sick and—and she has the mumps and she's calling on—uh—her mother to come in because she—uh—uh—her glands are starting to hurt (uh huh) and then a—at the end she—uh—gets well again (uh huh). And—uh—and she becomes a nurse only for swollen glands, and she invents—for—uh—mumps—and she invents a cure for it.

S-3: The parent loves or likes the child, approves of the child, is proud of him, is concerned for him, has warm feelings toward him. Included here were stories in which the parent is worried or crying because the child is ill or injured or dead.

Example. *Card 7BM.* Well it's about this—uh—two—these two—well uh, there's this lawyer, this, the—the young one, this young man over here is a lawyer about 35 years old, and the, and the—and this—his father is next to him who is about 60 years old (uh huh) and uh, and this man, the lawyer, defend—uh—what happened is, the lawyer defended another man who—who was not guilty and everybody thought he was guilty and he—and he proved it, that he wasn't guilty and his father is smiling down on him because he thinks that his son is very smart.

S-4: The parent may in part be characterized in any of the ways described in N-1 through N-4 above, but the child is specifically described as being improved thereby. For example, the child learns a lesson or draws a moral from the experience, he becomes more skilled or his performance improves. Stories were not included in this category if the child simply succumbs, as by saying he is sorry.

Example. *Card 1.* Uh, should I tell what the picture is about first? (Yes . . . as I told you . . . interrupts examiner) OK. Well, this boy was studying his homework and he didn't like to study homework (uh huh) and he didn't like to do homework, so he, so he—sneaked down—so he sneaked up to his room and he started playing with his electric train (uh huh) and he feels very happy—that he doesn't have to do his homework and he's watching the train go along . . . and all of a sudden his mother comes (laughs) (uh huh) and she grabs him out of the room and she makes him do his homework (uh huh) and she has—and he has to do more homework than he did before because he was bad (uh huh) and he has to go to bed early, (uh huh) and that—and the moral of the story is you should always do your homework.

Each story with a rating of N-1 through N-4 was assigned a score of "+1" and each story with a rating of S-1 through S-4 a score of "−1." Stories in which a parental figure was cast in more than one role, and so received a multiple rating, were scored "+1" if N ratings for that story predominated over S ratings, "−1" if the S ratings predominated, and "0" if there was an equal number of N and S ratings. By computing the sum of the scores for individual stories total scores were obtained for each child for his "mother" stories and his "father" stories separately. Finally, a "combined score" was determined; in computing this score, the ratings for all of the child's "mother" stories and "father" stories were considered along with stories in which parents had been treated as a unit. Thus, each child received three scores. In each instance, the higher the score in a "plus" direction, the greater the preponderance of stories in which the parent was portrayed as nonsupporting toward the child.

To test the reliability of the ratings, the TAT stories were categorized by a second judge using the above system of classification. The correlation between total scores ("mother" and "father" stories combined) achieved by each child, according to the ratings made by the two judges, was .94 ($P < .01$), suggesting good interjudge agreement.

Scores were obtained for 32 children for mother stories, for 28 children for father stories, and for 34 children for stories referring to both parents combined.[3] For the last mentioned measure, for example, the range of scores was from +3 to −4.

[3] Some of the 38 children produced no stories at all or no rateable stories about mothers and/or fathers.

c. Results. We expected, on the basis of our starting hypothesis, that the less differentiated children would tend to have relatively many parent-child stories in which the parent was portrayed as nonsupportive toward the child, in the specific manner defined. The results are consistent with this expectation. The correlation of perceptual index scores with TAT measures of maternal role was .64 ($P < .01$), with measures of paternal role .35 (not significant), and with combined measures .63 ($P < .01$). Although the relation with ratings of "father" stories tends to be lower than the relation with ratings of "mother" stories, there is the suggestion that in these fantasy productions children with a more global field approach portray both parents in a relatively nonsupporting relation toward themselves and children with a more analytical approach in a relatively supportive relation.

A qualitative study of the specific themes of the TAT parent-child stories contributes further to the impression of marked differences in views about the relations of parents to their children between more differentiated and less differentiated children. Dividing the 38 Group-I and -II boys, according to perceptual performance, into analytical, intermediate, and global subgroups, we find that children in the global group often portray parents as physically aggressive, brutalizing, and overpowering toward their children. Not only do parents in the stories hit their children, but they even kill them. Thus, of the 9 boys in the global group 4 had a story in which a mother kills her child for disobeying her or for upsetting her, or because she dislikes the child. In contrast, there was not a single instance of a mother killing a child in the stories of the analytical group. Moreover, in response to card 14, 4 of the 5 boys with a global approach to whom the card was given created stories in which a child commits suicide or runs away from home for such reasons as being hit too many times, or being unloved. In contrast, not one of the 7 children with an analytical approach to whom card 14 was given produced stories in which parents are cast in such extremely terrorizing and unloving roles.

Children in the global and analytical groups also differ in the views they project regarding the manner in which parental authority is exercised. Thus, in the stories of boys with a global approach parents tend characteristically to be arbitrary, tyrannical, and inflexible. The child is often simply required to comply with the parents' wishes, with no reason given or implied. By contrast, in the stories of children with an analytical approach, parents tend more commonly to be seen as reasonable, flexible, and mild in the pressures they apply. Standards which such fantasied parents introduce for their children's behavior are likely to be based on moral principles. Compliance with these standards usually pays off for the child in that, through identifying with the parent, he can achieve a directive useful later in life. Even though such a parent may be acting against the child's immediate wishes, his actions are likely to have positive consequences for the child's later life, and hence, in the long run, "for the child's good." The exercise of parental authority is thus seen as one aspect of parents' interest in loving the child. Other manifestations of parental support in the stories of children with an analytical approach are the help and comfort given the child in adversity, actions taken to make the child happy, expressions of concern and feeling for the child. These parents are often able to offer informed guidance to the child or to seek the guidance of experts. They understand and foster the child's need for proficiency and achievement and they offer help toward these goals.

2. Validation Studies

For validation purposes, the study was repeated with the 30 10-year-old boys of Group III and 13 14-year-old boys taking part in one of our longitudinal studies.

a. Group-III boys. Correlations of perceptual index scores were significant with ratings of father stories ($r = .41$, $P < .05$) but not with ratings of mother stories ($r = .01$) or with combined ratings ($r = .29$). With intellectual and cognitive index scores, the ratings of father stories correlated .24 and .35, the ratings of mother stories −.10 and +.05, and the combined ratings .09 and .21. None of these values is significant. Only for the ratings of father stories is there a trend apparent.

The low, nonsignificant correlations with ratings of mother stories for the Group-III boys may be due in part to the generally more "benign" view of mothers projected in the TAT stories of this group as a whole, compared to the stories of Group-I and -II boys. Whereas 14 of the 38 Group-I and -II children received "+" total scores for ratings of mother stories (reflecting a tendency for mothers to be cast in nonsupportive roles), only 4 of 30 of the Group-III boys received "+" scores. It is possible that this shift, whatever its source, made the rating scale developed for the original 10-year group less applicable to them.

b. Fourteen-year boys. The second validation group consisted of 13 of the 27 14-year boys who had taken part in the longitudinal study.[4] For this group the correlations of perceptual index scores with ratings of mother stories, father stories, and combined ratings are .69 ($P < .01$),

---

[4] Fourteen of the 27 14-year boys had received the TAT at age 10 as Group-I boys. Since their TAT records were thus among the 38 records of Group-I and -II boys used in developing the TAT parent-child rating scale they were not included in this validation study.

.31 (not significant) and .71 ($P < .01$), respectively. All three values are in the expected direction and two are significant.

The results for the three groups of boys studied (the 10-year boys of Groups I and II, the 10-year boys of Group III, and the 14-year boys) suggests a tendency for children with a global field approach to cast parents in a relatively nonsupportive role in their TAT stories and for children with an analytical approach to cast them in a more supportive role. This tendency is consistent with our starting hypothesis.

3. Role of Fathers as Portrayed in TAT Stories

The TAT analysis of parental role suggests that there are differences in how children with different modes of field approach experience their fathers, as well as their mothers. The evidence indicates that children with a global approach tend to see fathers also as nonsupportive toward their children, in contrast to children with a more analytical approach, who see fathers as relatively supportive. This finding concerning fathers of course requires further investigation.

In interpreting the results for fathers, and mothers as well, it must be considered that in the TAT, feelings toward one parent may be displaced onto the other parental figure, or that one parental figure may be used as a vehicle for expressing a fusion of the child's feelings toward both parents. These possibilities suggest that the score for mother and father stories combined perhaps reflects the child's impression of the role of parents, experienced as an "atmosphere effect," even if this impression has been created mainly through the quality of feelings and actions of one parent.

4. Relation between Children's Views of Parents in TAT Stories and Views of Parents Based on Interviews with Mothers

The analyses of parent-child relations based on children's TAT parent-child stories and the study based on interviews with mothers were used as complementary research approaches to the study of the relations children with different modes of field approach may have had with their parents. If the two approaches were in fact concerned with the same aspects of parent-child relations, we would expect the separate ratings to be related. This is actually the outcome. Correlating the children's TAT combined ratings (taken as the best measure of children's views of parental role) with ratings of their mothers as IID or IFD, we find for the boys of Group II a point-biserial r of .75 ($P < .01$) and for the boys of Group III, used as our validation group, a point-biserial r of .48 ($P < .01$).[5] The finding, that impressions formed from children's TATs of their views of parents are in fact confirmed when these parents are studied directly, is also noteworthy from the standpoint of TAT methodology.

Allowing for differences in specific content, determined by differences in test medium used, the results of the analyses of the children's TAT stories and of the interviews with the mothers seem consistent. The characteristics assigned to mothers by children in their TATs, though often taking the exaggerated and caricatured form which the permissive fantasy setting of the TAT makes possible, are congruent with the impressions derived from interviews with their mothers. Thus, mother-child interactions, described by children with a relatively global field approach in their TAT stories, often portray mothers as unloving, punitive, unable to give help and guidance, exercising parental authority in arbitrary fashion. Corresponding to these characterizations of mother-child interactions given by the children themselves, the mothers of these children, on interview, often gave the impression of inability to guide their children toward assumption of responsibility and self-assertion, of disciplining severely and in an irrational mood, of limiting their children's activities because of their own fears and anxieties. A consistent picture is also found for the children with a relatively analytical approach when their views of mothers, expressed in the TAT, are compared to the impressions given by the mothers on interview.

B. CHILDREN'S VIEWS OF MOTHERS AS REFLECTED IN INTERVIEWS WITH CHILDREN

Another source of information about mother-child relations, as seen from the standpoint of the child, was the interviews conducted with the 24 boys of Group II. As described in Chapter 11, the interviews with this group sought mainly to survey the child's present and earlier life situation. Although an attempt was made to obtain some general information about the child's relation to and feelings about his parents, we deliberately refrained from too probing an exploration of this area, keeping the interview at a fairly factual level. Moreover, at the time the interview was conducted it was not anticipated that it would be used for systematic study of parent-child relations. Thus, the data available in many records for evaluating the child's relations

---

[5] For 7 of the Group-I boys, we had both mothers' interview ratings and children's TAT ratings when the boys were retested at age 14. These measures also correlated significantly ($r = .82$, $P < .05$).

to his parents and his feelings toward them are sparse. The study reported must therefore be considered a preliminary one.

1. Method

In order to minimize the possible "halo effect" upon judgments that might come from reading the entire interview record, the following procedure was adopted: Two staff members not otherwise involved in this part of the study went through the interview records, selecting excerpts to be judged.

In this selection process, all sections of the interview in which the child's account did not include references to the mother were eliminated first. Ordinarily, for example, the child's account of his school activities, sports, clubs, etc., did not involve mention of the mother. Any interchange between child and interviewer was included if the mother was mentioned specifically or by implication, unless the mention of the mother was purely incidental (e.g., where the child referred to a playmate as "my mother's friend's little girl"). Purely factual interchanges—e.g., concerning the mother's age or work—were included. The areas which most frequently afforded some view of the mother were physical care, punishment, family rules and procedures, recreation, household responsibilities. Excerpts dealing with other family members were excluded, unless the child involved the mother in such an account. The child's description of the immediate family constellation and of the physical setting of the home was included, in order to give the judge minimal background information.

By this method a selected set of excerpts from the interview record was prepared for each of 22 of the 24 children in Group II. The excerpts were arranged in the same sequence as they occurred in the interview. These excerpts varied in number per record from four to fifteen, and in length from one to fifteen lines; and they were uneven with regard to pertinent information. Direct and verbalized appraisal of mothers was relatively infrequent and the child's attitude toward her had to be inferred from whatever material he gave.

The following directions were presented the rater, Meta Steiner, as a guide to making judgments:
a. "Dimension" to be rated: Child's view of mother, as it is expressed in, or inferred from, the interview with him.
b. The "dimension" to be rated is further defined in terms of the extremes of a continuum.[6]

[6] It can be seen that, adapted to the medium of interview material, this classification in many ways parallels the classification used in rating TAT stories.

(1) "Positive" pole. Child's view of the mother is entirely or predominantly positive. By "positive" is meant that the mother is *experienced by him* as giving, supporting, comforting, reliable, to be trusted; child does not feel discriminated against, e.g., in favor of a sibling; child feels that punishment, even if severe, is "for his own good."

(2) "Negative" pole. Child's view of the mother is entirely or predominantly negative. By "negative" is meant that the mother is experienced by him as depriving, nonsupportive, not comforting, not reliable, not trustworthy; child feels discriminated against, e.g., in favor of a sibling; child feels that punishment is undeserved, and not "for his own good."

Manner of rating:

a. The "poles" described represent extremes. The criteria are suggestive rather than exhaustive. A child's view of the mother which is rated as "positive" need not include all of the specific positive feelings mentioned. It is, for example, possible that the child's view of the mother is rated as positive even though his feelings about her do not fit exactly any of the specifics given above. Similar considerations apply to ratings of the child's view of his mother as negative.

b. It is anticipated that most children will not experience their mothers in entirely positive or entirely negative terms, and that there will be shades and gradations of attitude. The question of "weighting" the "positive" and the "negative" in evaluating a given child's experience is left to the rater. The rater is free to formulate, or not formulate, more specific steps or categories in rating the experience of children who do not fall at one or the other extreme of the total "experience continuum."

c. A rating is to be assigned to each child, except where the rater feels that the material is too sparse to make a rating possible.

d. For each child, the basis for judgment should be written out.

As a first step in making a final judgment for a given child the rater examined each excerpt separately and judged it as "noncontributory," or as reflecting "positive," "negative," or "neutral" views of the mother. The second step was an integration of the evaluations of the excerpts into a final total judgment. This judgment was based on a clinical weighing of the composite impressions rather than on a counting or summation of judgments of separate excerpts. In this way trends which had not been clear as long as the excerpts had been treated as discrete units entered into and helped to modify the final judgment, if they appeared to have gained importance by frequency or psychological congruence.

The following are examples of excerpts considered as not contributing to an evaluation of the child's view of his mother and excerpts reflecting either neutral, positive, or negative views according to the definitions given.

Statement evaluated as *noncontributory:*

Everybody in the family has their own room, except my father and mother sleep in the same room.

Statement evaluated as *neutral:*

Once in a while my mother is strict, and once in a while she isn't.

Statements evaluated as *positive,* reflecting the boy's view that the mother is comforting, approving, trustworthy, fair, and not discriminating against him:

(What happens when you scream in your sleep?) My mother comes in and she quiets me down. (Mother seen as a comforter.)

That's one thing my mother and father brag about (refers to no longer needing a baby sitter) . . . they are proud of me. (Mother seen as approving.)

(Does your mother ever work?) No, she threatens, but she never does it. (What does she threaten to do if she works?) . . . if we're bad she threatens, she threatens us, "I'm going to go to work, and you're going to have to take care of yourself at all times" (laughs). She never does it though, I trust her. (Mother seen as trustworthy.)

Well . . . I, they don't whip me or anything for instance if I do something wrong which . . . well I hardly remember . . . I hardly get really punished. If I have only a little punishment, I don't get candy or I don't get this or something or I'll get a certain card taken away from me, that you're saving up for or something like that. (What's the last time you remember?) Last time I remember I was punished, oh for refusing to eat a carrot. (And so what happened?) Oh I got a card taken away from me until I finally ate it and I (laughs) got my card given back again. (Mother seen as fair in punishing.)

Statements evaluated as *negative,* reflecting the view that the mother is depriving, not approving, not trustworthy, or as discriminating against him in punishment:

(Other) kids were allowed to climb, and I wasn't allowed to do that. They could do everything my mother did not like (me to do) because she said I can kill myself doing that. (Mother seen as depriving, obstructing his development.)

(Well what I mean is if you did something and your mother didn't like what you did.) Sometimes, she'd hit me. Sometimes she would . . . I don't know, she'd turn me out. (Mother seen as hostile, not approving.)

My mother told my father about it (reporting misbehavior toward sister). (Mother seen as not trustworthy.)

(What do your mother and father say when you have a fight with your sister?) Her . . . she always gets the best part. (You feel your sister does? What'd they say to you?) You shouldn't . . . I always get hit and hit, and she never gets hit. (Mother seen as unfair in punishment.)

It was possible to assign a final rating of "positive" or "negative" view of the mother to 14 of the 22 children. In the case of the remaining 8 children, the excerpts did not provide enough unambiguous material to justify a rating.

To determine the relation of these ratings to mode of field approach, the perceptual index scores of children rated as having a "positive" or "negative" view of the mother were compared. A point biserial r of .52 was obtained, in the expected direction but not significant. The tendency was for children with a more analytical field approach to experience their mothers as supporting, giving, comforting, reliable, approving of them, and fair in punishment, and for children with a global approach to view their mothers as depriving, not trustworthy, hostile and not approving, and unfair or discriminating against them in punishment.

Views of the mother suggested in this preliminary study of interviews with children are consistent in direction with the views indicated in children's portrayals of mothers in TAT stories.

C. OTHER STUDIES

The results of two recent studies are consistent with our findings.

Bieri (1960), as one part of a larger study, investigated the parental identifications of groups of college men and women whose mode of field approach had been evaluated on the basis of EFT performance. The aspect of identification considered in this study was the extent to which the subject perceived himself as similar to either parent. The semantic differential was used as the measuring instrument. The subject rated himself, his mother, and his father according to a 7-point scale, on each of 12 bipolar adjectives. The disparity between the subject's self-ratings and his ratings of each parent was taken as an index of his parental identification.[7] He was considered to identify more strongly with that parent in relation to whom the disparity in ratings was smaller. On the assumption that persons of either sex who identify with their fathers are apt to show greater independence, assertive and active coping behavior, Bieri hypothesized that subjects who were relatively field independent on the EFT would be more apt to be "father identifiers." As predicted, women who identified with fathers were found to have significantly lower EFT scores than those who identified with mothers. For men and for both sexes combined the difference was in the expected direction, but not significant.

Bieri's study of parental identification touches upon an aspect of parent-child relations on which we did not obtain direct information

[7] It is perhaps possible that such scores may reflect masculine-feminine identification as well as parental identification.

in our own study. His findings are, however, consistent with ours in suggesting that a person's mode of field approach is related to the kind of experience he has had in his family.

Mussen and Kagan (1958) compared differences in views of parents to differences in behavior related to mode of field approach. On the basis of performance in an Asch-type group pressure situation, a group of "conforming" and a group of "independent" college men were set up. (It will be recalled from Chapter 8 that in situations of this kind persons with a global field approach tend to be more conforming than persons with an analytical approach.) Each story in the TAT records of these subjects was rated "blind" for presence or absence of parental punishment themes. Such a theme was considered present if parents —individually or together—deprived, rejected, and/or physically or verbally punished their child. This method of evaluating parent-child TAT stories is in many ways similar to ours. A "parental-punishment" score was computed for each subject, representing the number of punishment themes in his stories. The distribution was dichotomized into negative (no parental punishment themes) and positive (one or more parental punishment themes) groups. As hypothesized, a significant tendency was found for conformers to fall in the positive group and independents in the negative group. Thus, employing an aspect of behavior similar in some ways to that we have studied, but using an older age group and a somewhat different method of TAT evaluation, this study yielded results that are in essential agreement with our own.

D. SUMMARY

Complementing the studies reported in preceding chapters of mother-child relations viewed from the standpoint of the mother, we undertook studies of interaction between parent and child, as portrayed by the child himself.

The child's view of parental role was investigated, first, through an analysis of the way in which children portrayed parents—fathers as well as mothers—in their TAT stories. The scale developed for rating stories consisted of categories in which the parent was portrayed as supportive toward a child and others in which the parent was portrayed as nonsupportive. As anticipated, in these fantasy productions boys with a relatively global field approach tended to create parental figures who, in their feelings and actions toward their children, were essentially nonsupportive. In contrast, boys with a more analytical field approach tended to create parental figures who, in a variety of ways, were supportive toward their children. This difference was found for father figures as well as mother figures. The evaluations of mother-child relations based on interviews with mothers and evaluations made on the basis of the TAT stories of their children were, by and large, in significant agreement.

As a second and more preliminary approach to the child's view of maternal role an analysis was made of excerpts from interviews with children in which reference to the mother was made. The set of excerpts for each child was rated as to whether the child seemed to experience his mother primarily as giving, supporting, comforting, reliable, trustworthy or primarily as depriving, nonsupportive, not comforting, not reliable, not trustworthy in her feelings and actions toward him. The relation between these ratings and children's perceptual index scores was in the expected direction, although it did not reach significance.

The findings are generally consistent with results on mother-child relationships based on interviews with mothers. This congruence justifies greater confidence in the results of these independent studies.

22

PARENT-CHILD
RELATIONSHIPS:
AN OVERVIEW

In the preceding chapters (17–21), we described our first attempts to explore sources of differences in differentiation among children. In this chapter the main results of the studies are briefly reviewed and some additional evidence presented. We also consider certain issues of parental influence which require clarification and present the results of a study confirming our hypothesis about the relation between mother-child interactions and the development of differentiation in the child. Finally, processes of mother-child interaction which may contribute to or hinder a child's progress toward differentiation are discussed.

A. EXTENT OF DIFFERENTIATION OF CHILDREN AS RELATED TO CHARACTERISTICS OF MOTHERS AND MOTHER-CHILD INTERACTIONS

In the analyses presented in the preceding chapters, the three measures obtained from studies of mothers—ratings as IFD or IID, based on interviews; sophistication-of-body-concept scale scores derived from figure drawings; and EFT scores—have been compared to only two of the measures of differentiation for children—perceptual index and intellectual index scores. We extend our comparison of mothers and children by considering several additional measures available for the children: Rorschach ratings, cognitive clarity ratings, and scores reflecting sophistication-of-body concept, sense of separate identity, and nature of defenses and controls.

341

Table 22-1 presents the correlations between the three measures available for the mothers and nine measures reflecting extent of differentiation for the children.[1]

Examination of Table 22-1 shows that interview ratings and sophistication-of-body-concept measures of mothers tend to relate significantly to the various measures of differentiation for the children. Of fifteen correlations between mothers' interview ratings and children's measures, eleven are significant. Significant relationships are found both for Group II, on which the procedure for rating mothers' interviews was first developed and applied, and for Group III, the validation group.

Mothers' sophistication-of-body-concept scores tend to relate to measures of extent of differentiation of the children. Seven correlations are in the expected direction and five are significant.[2] EFT scores of mothers, however, do not relate significantly to any of the children's measures. As suggested in Chapter 20 the basis of this lack of significant relation requires further study.

Thus, children whose mothers were judged from interviews to have contributed to the development of differentiation in their children and children whose mothers were relatively differentiated (according to sophistication-of-body-concept measures but not according to EFT scores) gave evidence of developed differentiation in various areas of functioning. The specific measures available for the children suggest that they tend to experience in articulated fashion, to have a developed concept of their bodies, a sense of separate identity, and structured defenses and controls. In contrast, children whose mothers were judged to have inhibited the development of differentiation in their children and who showed a poorly developed body concept presented a picture of limited differentiation according to various indicators.

Stating these relations in terms of the specific behavioral manifestations used to infer extent of differentiation in children, we see how extensive are the characteristics of children associated with the aspects of mother-child interaction considered. Thus, children of mothers

[1] Sophistication-of-body-concept and EFT measures were available for Group-III mothers only.

Also, the mothers of Group-I boys were not interviewed until their children were 14. The children's personality test productions at this age have not yet been analyzed. As noted in Chapter 17, however, the perceptual index scores for the boys at age 14 did relate significantly to ratings of mothers as IID or IFD.

[2] The denial-scale scores from the TAT, which related to none of the measures for mothers in Group III, did not relate to the perceptual index scores of the children of that group. It is the only measure for children in the table of which this was true.

Table 22-1. Relations between measures for mothers and children

Indicator	Children Area	Scale and Tests	IFD-IID Ratings (home interview)		Mothers Soph. body concept [a] (figure drawing)	EFT [a]
			Group II N = 21	Group III N = 27	Group III N = 21	Group III N = 26
Articulateness of experience	Mode of field approach	Perceptual index (BAT, RFT, EFT)	.85 **	.65 **b	.48 *	.37
		Intellectual index (WISC)	—c	.41 *	.41	.15
	Structuring	Rorschach percepts	.54 *	.35 *b	.54 *	.34
	Articulateness in "real life"	Cognitive clarity	—	.65 **	.43 *	.16
	Nature of body concept	Sophistication-of-body concept (figure drawing)	.40 d	.35 *b	.63 **	.29
	Sense of separate identity	Approach to task (TAT)	.60 **d	.47 **b	.46 *	.00
Defenses and controls		Structure of defenses (TAT, Rorschach, drawings)	.42	—	—	—
		Handling of aggression (TAT)	.48 *	.25 *b	-.04	-.10
		Denial (TAT)	.40	.03 b	.15	.11

* Significant at .05 level. ** Significant at .01 level.
a Group-II mothers were not given the figure-drawing test and EFT.
b One-tail test of significance was used for these correlations.
c A "—" indicates that the particular analysis was not performed for this group.
d N = 20.

judged IFD and having a sophisticated body concept tend to show analytical ability in their performance in both perceptual and intellectual situations; a high degree of cognitive clarity in interviews; ability to structure the ambiguous stimuli presented by Rorschach ink-blots; a well-articulated concept of their bodies; ability to perform a task without reliance on the examiner for definition and guidance; and ability to handle aggressive impulses.

B. SOME FURTHER ISSUES IN THE STUDY OF PARENT-CHILD RELATIONS

Several problems bearing on the results of our studies need to be discussed. First, we consider aspects of children's development which do not appear related to characteristics of the mother-child interactions studied. Second, we consider issues that require further investigation.

1. Characteristics of Children Unrelated to Features of Mother-Child Interactions Studied

a. Verbal skills. As suggested in Chapter 11 the development of some verbal skills may follow a different pathway than the development of differentiation. The evidence we now have indicates that proficiency in some kinds of verbal skills is unrelated to extent of differentiation. We might expect, therefore, that the evaluations made of mothers and of mother-child interactions, oriented toward the development of differentiation in children, would be unrelated to the children's development of at least some verbal skills.

Our evidence on this point is very limited, but the results now on hand are consistent with this expectation. For Group-III children [3] verbal index scores, based on scaled scores from three WISC subtests (Vocabulary, Comprehension, and Information), show low, nonsignificant correlations with interview ratings of mothers as IID or IFD, with mothers' sophistication-of-body-concept scores, and with mothers' EFT scores (.15, .23, and .06, respectively). Thus, development of verbal comprehension appears unrelated to the particular characteristics of mothers and mother-child interactions evaluated.

On the basis of the negligible correlations just cited it is possible that in some cases at least mothers who, in interaction with their children, handicap the growth of differentiation, may yet contribute to the development of some verbal skills. We have in fact encountered

[3] Since the WISC was not given to children in Groups I and II, verbal index scores could not be computed for them.

such instances in our individual case studies. In considering how this may come about, we can only offer some speculations, since at the time the mothers were interviewed we were not specifically concerned with this issue, and did not seek evidence about it. The suggestions offered below are all in line with the hypothesis that aspects of mother-child interaction which serve to inhibit the development of differentiation in children may help foster some verbal skills.

One factor to consider is that in the cultural subgroup from which most of our children were drawn intellectual achievement is highly valued. Verbal facility as an early expression of "brightness" was particularly emphasized by mothers of some poorly differentiated children. Such mothers also tended to be much concerned with conformity to cultural standards, and with the opinions of neighbors and friends. As part of their emphasis on conforming behavior, they seemed to encourage verbal development in their children, considering it socially pleasing. Though emphasis on conformity seemed to interfere with the development of differentiation, it might have contributed to the development of some verbal skills.

Haggard (1957), in the study considered in Chapter 11, suggests a way in which certain conforming attitudes may contribute to the development of particular verbal skills. In describing children who were high achievers in spelling and language, he reports that the intellectual passivity and obedient carrying out of rules, required for success in these areas, are found in children who, feeling rejected, attempt to gain parental acceptance by strict adherence to parental regulations. High achievers in spelling and language, who seemed strikingly similar to some of our limitedly differentiated boys, showed just such a pattern. According to Haggard, these children viewed parental figures as omnipotent, rejecting, generally punitive, and nonsupportive. Such attitudes toward parents seem similar to those portrayed by some of our less differentiated children in their TAT stories and were consistent with our characterization of some IID mothers. We observed also that mothers of some less differentiated children engendered in their children the attitudes of intellectual passivity and rule-following that Haggard found in children who were high achievers in spelling and language; and that the children themselves strove to gain acceptance by conforming to parental standards and expectations. Thus, some of our less differentiated children might have invested in verbal skills for the reasons suggested by Haggard.

Levy (1943), whose overprotective mothers seem similar to some of our IID mothers in their attempts to maintain prolonged and intense contact with their children, advances other possible reasons for the development of language skills in the children of such mothers. He found that children of overprotective mothers tended to excel in subjects requiring language skills, in comparison to their lesser attainment in arithmetic and natural science. As reasons for the special development of language skills, he considered the close association with the mother and identification with her; and the absence of contacts with peers which might prevent the use of adult language. He explained the relatively low grades in arithmetic and natural sciences on the basis of lack of involvement of verbal skills in these disciplines. Levy also emphasized the inability of these mothers to coach their children in arithmetic; the lack of experience of overprotected children with number concepts acquired through doing errands; and the greater "self-discipline" which arithmetic requires.

For some of our less differentiated children the quality of contact with adults which may have been important in the special development of language skills seemed to limit the development of differentiation. It is of interest that the mother of one of the relatively undifferentiated boys whose verbal expressiveness was particularly developed was the prototype of a possessive mother.

The factors considered thus far may contribute to development of some verbal skills among less differentiated children. Particular kinds of mother-child relations which seem to limit differentiation may, however, also adversely affect the development of some verbal skills. For example, a mother's nonaccepting attitude may lead her child to hostile rebellion and refusal to strive for achievement in areas she stresses. The development of verbal skills may suffer if it is one of these areas. Maternal attitudes of nonacceptance may push a child into social withdrawal, a condition in which the development of verbal communication will be hampered.

Further studies are needed to follow up the suggestions that have been given concerning the role of mother-child interactions in the development of differentiation and verbal skills.

b. Effectiveness of adjustment. The question of whether mothers who interact with their children in such a way as to foster differentiation are "better mothers" than those who interfere with this development was raised in Chapter 18. From the standpoint of what mothers are able to offer to the development of their children, it is clear that IFD mothers, who themselves showed relatively structured controls and defenses and a developed sense of separate identity, were better equipped to help their children develop control over impulses and a sense of their own identity. On the other hand, some of the very characteristics which enabled these mothers to contribute to the development of differentiation in their children tended, in some cases, to interfere with the help they could give them in working out an effective adjustment.

Some IFD mothers seemed to have contributed to their children's emotional aloofness, resistance to emotional involvement, and tendencies to be overintellectual, overcontrolled, and perfectionistic. Among these were mothers who were proud of their children, yet not warm and giving in their relations with them. For instance, a mother who was an athlete and a business woman very early trained her child to care for himself, was seldom at home when he came from school, and took great pride in her child's ability to look after himself. She stated that she was "not warm as many mothers are." Though the training in self-reliance she gave seemed to contribute to her son's becoming differentiated, it apparently did not provide an experience of warm, interpersonal relationships for him. Rather it seemed to accentuate his isolation, his inability to relate to others, and may have undermined his trust in others.

The tight family units found in families of some highly differentiated children isolated them from others. Though such families seemed secure in their own feelings of superiority, thus providing security and a sense of strength in the child, their failure to assimilate themselves into the neighborhood and community tended to perpetuate a sense of aloofness in their children.

Other patterns of highly individualized values may also have contributed to development of differentiation but not adjustment in a child. For instance, in the home of Neal, an overintellectual and remote child (Case #3, Chapter 15), we found high value placed on intellectual achievement, with emphasis on the development of the intellectual side at the expense of the emotional and social aspects of living. He had obviously internalized the family standards and values, including the ability to go his own way and follow intellectual and theoretical interests. At the same time, we had an impression of a split between the intellectual and emotional-instinctual sphere and of achievement of clarity and realistic self-appraisal mainly in the intellectual sphere.

Other IFD mothers seemed overexacting in the standards they imposed on their children since they themselves were rigid and overcontrolled. They emphasized values such as neatness, orderliness, perfectionism. One IFD mother reported that her child was unable to submit any papers to his teacher which did not meet his (the child's) criteria of excellence. She added that he seemed to lack creativity and imagination, was obsessively clean and neat, and had many fears of contamination by dirt and bugs. She commented that the father also was so neat that "you'd never know there was a man in the house." The child had apparently internalized the standards which were emphasized so clearly in the home, and his behavior reflected the "family pattern." The highly controlled family atmosphere seemed to contribute to the child's differentiation but his adaptation was one of exaggerated "perfectionism."

On the other hand, some IID mothers, who did not provide experiences which would help their children develop differentiation, nevertheless, by emphasizing conformity and good manners, seemed to contribute to "social adjustment" of a specific kind. For instance, one IID mother pointed to the fact that her child was well liked by other children because he was agreeable and noncompetitive. Still another stated that her son was much admired in the neighborhood for his "respectful ways" with older people. Their children's conformity in school situations was considered a virtue by these mothers. However, though such behavior may have been helpful to immediate cultural adaptation, the cost to the children's development as individuals may have been excessive.

Thus, though IFD mothers, relative to IID mothers, seemed to have more to contribute to the development of differentiation in their children, each group may aid or hamper their children's adjustment. The nature of the help or hindrance to adjustment seems, however, to have been different for the two kinds of mothers.

2. Further Areas of Parent-Child Relations Which Need Investigation

It is apparent that many aspects of children's experiences in the family, in addition to those considered, may enter into the development of differentiation.

First, the father's contribution to the child's development needs to be considered. The TAT analysis of parental roles (Chapter 21) suggests that there are differences in how children with different modes of field approach experience their fathers as well as their mothers. The evidence indicates that children whose global field approach reflected limited differentiation tend to see fathers as nonsupportive, in contrast to more analytical children who see fathers as relatively helpful.

In home interviews mothers described father-child relations in ways consistent with views the children themselves expressed about their fathers. IID mothers frequently referred to what we called the "psychologically absentee" father and IFD mothers to the presence of a more supportive "man of the house." Of course, one could not be sure whether a mother's description of the father-son relation concurred with reality or reflected her own attitudes toward both father and son. In a few instances a mother's description of the paternal role was quite different from that given by the child on interview. These mothers tended to depreciate the father-son relation while the children conveyed an impression of strong positive attitude toward their fathers. Seder (1957), in a study considered in the next section, found that fathers of children with a global field approach played a relatively passive role in some aspects of child rearing. However, her evaluations of fathers were also based on evidence from interviews with mothers.

The father's influence on a boy's progress toward differentiation is, of course, important in its own right, especially since we are concerned with the boy's concept of himself. But the father's role in the family may also influence the mother's attitudes and behavior with her child. For instance, whether a father gives his wife a feeling of prestige and of status within the family, or sees her function as that of "watchdog" and regards the child as the rightful master in the mother-child relation, is important for the mother's self-concept and thus indirectly affects her maternal role.

Future studies also need to consider "family patterns." It may be, for example, that when we observed in a mother such characteristics as exaggerated cleanliness and neatness, or deeper expressions of an obsessional picture, we were in fact dealing with a dimension of the total family matrix. It also seems important to consider the distribution of authority in the family as a whole as well as points of stress and potential for disorganization in the family structure.

Further studies are also needed of parent-child interaction from the standpoint of the child's contribution to the development of patterns of interaction. The variety of ways in which children may reenforce or elicit particular kinds of behavior and attitudes from a mother were spontaneously mentioned in the course of the home interviews. Some mothers stated, implicitly or explicitly, "he is the kind of child who," and described the way in which the particular characteristics of a child had influenced their rearing and attitudes toward this child: for instance, "He is the kind of child who is by nature slow and easy going so that there has never been a particular need for me to discipline him"; "He's never been able to stick to things so I've had to watch that a lot, especially his homework"; "He's always been a lazy child so I've had to push him"; "He's always been a delicate child so I've had to be careful about letting him overexert"; "One reason I've always disliked him was his being in perpetual motion from the day he was born and causing me a lot of trouble." These excerpts refer to concepts a mother has about her child, and do not tell us about either the mother's part or the child's part in the formation of the concepts. Possible effects of the child's early characteristics on the development of the mother's behavior toward him are suggested, however.

The possible role of the child in shaping the mother's behavior was also apparent in the responses of mothers to children of different sex. For instance, school achievement seemed to be stressed more with sons than daughters, "since he's the one who's got to earn a living." For this reason, some mothers reported selecting boys as the ones who should have "educational advantages" if schooling could not be financed for all children.   Among IFD mothers there seemed to be greater acceptance and encouragement of assertiveness for their sons, but greater emphasis on social training for their daughters.   An unusually dramatic contrast between her feeling for her son and her daughter was described by one mother who was extremely insecure in her role as a woman.   She reported a "nervous breakdown" with severe depression when she gave birth to a daughter.   She stated that giving birth to a daughter symbolized her inadequacy as a woman.   Having a son, on the other hand, had been a continuing source of pride and pleasure to her.   It seems quite possible that the differences in attitudes toward the rearing of sons and of daughters in the cultural group from which our subjects have come may have contributed to differences found in the development of males and females with respect to some aspects of differentiation (Chapter 13).[4]

The importance of studying not only characteristics of the mother, but also the child's impact on her and the interaction between mother and child, has been pointed out in many studies.   Fries (1944, 1953) has described the effect upon maternal attitudes of the sex, activity, and normality of infants, and the ways in which such attitudes are conveyed to the children.   Coleman, Kris, and Provence (1953), using illustrations from four cases included in longitudinal studies, emphasize—perhaps overstress—the influence of the child's development on the mother in modifying her attitudes and behavior toward him.

---

[4] We have on hand data for a group of girls similar to those presented in this book for boys. Included are records of various tests given to the children and interviews conducted with their mothers. When these data are analyzed, there will be a particularly good opportunity to compare mothers' rearing practices with boys and girls, and to explore the effect of differences in practices on the development of differentiation in the two sexes.

C. INDEPENDENT VALIDATION STUDY

Supplementing the validation studies we have ourselves carried out is an independent study by Seder (1957). Our impressions of differences in the rearing procedures and attitudes of mothers of relatively field-dependent or field-independent boys find support in the Seder study. This study had its origins in our general hypothesis and early findings concerning the relation between children's mode of field approach and the nature of parent-child relationships. Seder formulated a number of specific hypotheses which she tested through an exploration of the family influences to which children differing in extent of field dependence had been subjected.

Seder's results are in general consistent with ours. Such confirmation is of particular value since both her population and her methods were different from our own. While in our study a clinical interview was used to obtain information about parent-child relationships, with evaluations taking the form of global ratings, Seder used a questionnaire and rated separately a large number of fairly specific rearing procedures. The influence of mothers as well as fathers and "parents" was considered though only mothers were interviewed. Both boys and girls were included in the study.

Groups of 60 boys and 60 girls approximately 10 years old, who had been given the EFT and WISC, were drawn from a group of 225 children in the Newton (Massachusetts) Reading Project. The mothers had been visited at home by an interviewer other than Seder. Through a detailed questionnaire information was obtained about various areas of child rearing and family relations.

On the basis of their EFT results, children of each sex were divided into three groups of 20 each. For each sex, the highest scoring 20 constituted the field-dependent group, the lowest scoring 20 the field-independent group. In a second analysis, with groups of 20 field-dependent and 20 field-independent children matched for IQ, Seder obtained results generally confirmatory of the findings of the main study which is reported.

Each of Seder's hypotheses is presented below with a listing under each of the characteristics which significantly distinguished parents of field-dependent and field-independent boys and girls. The relation of Seder's findings to the indicators which guided our over-all ratings of mothers as IID and IFD is also noted.

Hypothesis 1: "Field-dependent subjects have been subjected to 'coercive' or 'infantilizing' child-rearing procedures, with great stress upon conformity and authority."

Mothers of field-dependent boys and girls were significantly more severe in their toilet training procedures than mothers of field-independent children.

The age at which bladder training or weaning from the bottle was completed did not significantly distinguish field-dependent and field-independent children. With respect to weaning from breast or bottle, mothers of field-dependent children tended to have been either infantilizing or coercive. Mothers of field-independent children tended to take a more moderate course; this finding was significant for boys only. The age at which bowel training was completed was significantly related to field approach for girls only.

Field-dependent boys were, as infants, kept physically closer to their parents during the night and shared their parents' room or even their parents' bed. This result was not significant for girls with respect to sharing room with parents.[5]

These findings partially confirm Hypothesis 1. They also tend to be consistent with two indicators of IID ratings, "control is not in the direction of a child's achieving mature goals or becoming responsible, or is consistently directed against child's asserting himself" and "physical care of child seems inappropriate for his age."

Hypothesis 2: "Field-dependent subjects have been submitted to harsh training for aggressive control."

Parents of field-dependent boys and girls significantly more often punished them for aggressive or assertive behavior than did parents of field-independent children who, in turn, more often punished their children for passive and immature behavior.

These results tend to support Hypothesis 2 and are consistent with our own indicator, "control is not in the direction of a child's achieving mature goals or becoming responsible, or is consistently directed against child's asserting himself."

Hypothesis 3: "Parents of field-dependent children will have prevented the growth of independent, assertive mastery of the environment and the assumption of an adult role."

Mothers of field-dependent boys and girls tended to "jump in" to settle disputes and protect their children from attack by others, whereas mothers of field-independent children significantly more often let them settle disputes themselves.

[5] The information used by Seder in the analyses carried out to test Hypothesis 1 depended on the mother's recall of early events. Such memories may not always be accurate. It will be recalled (Chapter 17) that because of this we based our judgments of mothers as IID or IFD on attitudes expressed rather than facts reported.

Father-son activities were significantly more "active" (involving sports, excursions, travel, etc.) when sons were field independent than when they were field dependent. This result was not significant for girls.

Parents of field-dependent boys and girls consistently pushed their children toward goals and standards which the parents had set, whereas parents of field-independent children tended to allow their children to set their own standards and to meet them on their own terms. The results were significant for both boys and girls.

Discipline of parents of field-dependent boys was "authoritarian," including physical and verbal aggression, ridicule, shame, threats of withdrawal of love; discipline of parents of field-independent boys was significantly more often "democratic," including denial of privileges, isolation, reasoning. This result was not significant for girls.

In addition to these analyses, Seder also considered under this hypothesis the analysis used under Hypothesis 2.

These results tend to confirm Hypothesis 3. They are consistent with two of the indicators of IID ratings, "through fears and anxieties for, or ties to the child, markedly limits child's activities and his going out into community" and "control is not in the direction of a child's achieving mature goals, or becoming responsible, or is consistently directed against child's asserting himself."

Hypothesis 4: "Field-dependent children have been reared in generally less accepting, warm, and permissive homes than the field-independent subjects."

The principal analysis relevant to this hypothesis was based upon a "warmth-evaluation score" derived from general interview impressions, as well as some specific questions. The homes of field-dependent girls were characterized by less warmth and greater hostility. The results were significant for girls but not for boys.

None of our indicators evaluated "warmth." In fact, some of the mothers of the relatively differentiated boys seemed to lack warmth though approving of their children. Seder's variable included both warmth and acceptance, but it is not clear how these were weighted. Thus, we cannot judge whether her evidence is consistent with any of our indicators.

Hypothesis 5: "Field-dependent subjects, in general, have been reared by less consistent methods than field-independent subjects."

Mothers of field-dependent girls often tend to make threats which are not followed through, whereas parents of field-independent girls make fewer threats which are usually carried through. This result was significant for girls but not for boys.

Punishment by mothers of field-dependent boys tends to be dictated by personal moods and whims of parents. Punishment by parents of field-independent boys is the result of objective standards of behavior mutually agreed upon by parents and children. Although significant for boys the result did not hold up for girls.

Another measure considered by Seder to reflect consistency in rearing concerned parental agreement in matters of discipline. This measure did not distinguish parents of field-dependent and field-independent boys or girls.

Hypothesis 5 is only partially supported by the evidence. The result for boys concerning moods, whims vs. standards mutually agreed on, seems consistent with the indicator "control is not in the direction of a child's achieving mature goals, or becoming responsible or is consistently directed against child's asserting himself."

Hypothesis 6: "Mothers of field-dependent children are anxious and emotional in dealing with their children, and insecure in their own judgments about child rearing."

One analysis used to test this hypothesis evaluated the degree to which a mother relied on her doctor (rather than herself) for the decision as to whether or not to breast feed her child. Mothers of field-independent girls significantly more often relied on themselves in making this decision than did mothers of field-dependent girls. This finding was not significant for boys.

In addition to this analysis, Seder also considered as relevant to this hypothesis two of the analyses described under Hypothesis 5.

Seder's results only partially support her hypothesis. Her evaluation of maternal reliance on a doctor again brings in the problem of the accuracy of the mother's recall of the infancy period.

Hypothesis 7: "Field-dependent subjects come from maternally dominated homes, with a passive father providing an inadequate role model for assertive, aggressive behavior."

The principal evidence bearing upon this hypothesis came from an analysis of which parent was the agent of punishment. Field-independent boys were significantly more often punished by their fathers. This result was not significant for girls.

We did not consider the agent of punishment separately in judging mothers.

In general, Seder's findings seem consistent with our own, though obtained by quite different methods. They suggest too that, when taken by themselves, some of the indicators we considered in making global ratings of mothers as IID or IFD discriminate between the two groups of mothers.[6]

D. SOME SPECULATIONS ABOUT PROCESSES OF MOTHER-CHILD INTERACTION AND THE DEVELOPMENT OF DIFFERENTIATION

Our studies have made it possible to describe general patterns of mother-child relations associated with greater or limited differentiation of children. We should like now to consider, in a speculative way, the processes by which mothers' interactions with their children may contribute to or interfere with the development of differentiation. Since the routes by which a child may become differentiated are multiple and complex, this account can hardly do more than suggest some directions for further research. It must also be recognized that we cannot consider with any degree of uniformity the different levels at which interactions between mother and child take place. In the discussion that follows we give attention to the development of articulateness of experience and impulse control. Some possible characteristic patterns of mother-child interactions associated with such development are suggested.

1. Articulateness of Experience

We suggested in Chapter 2 that the separation of the "me" from the "not me," or the process of segregation of the self, is an early stage in the development of articulation of experience. Taking into consideration reactions of both mother and child, we may speculate about some of the routes by which a mother may actively contribute to, permit, or handicap such a separation.

In the initial stages of her relation to a new baby a mother may literally maintain contact with her child beyond a hypothetical optimum, and thus reflect an attitude which may hinder separation. A mother's motivation for maintaining contact with her child is complex and var-

---

[6] Ribback (1957), in a study of a group of progressive-school children and their mothers, found an absence of consistently significant correlations between maternal attitudes to child rearing and the perceptual-analytic ability of their children. The Picture and Patch test she used, despite its apparent similarity to the EFT, may not involve overcoming an embedding context. Moreover, the definition of maternal behavior factors derived from the PARI scale which Ribback used suggests that the maternal attitudes she considered may have been quite different from the ones on which our judgments of mothers were based.

ied. For example, the maintenance of contact might continue the kind of satisfaction she had felt during pregnancy, especially if possessiveness and a desire for union with her baby played a prominent role in the pregnancy experience. The mother's own failure to achieve a sense of separate identity may prevent her from separating from her child. Lack of personal and sexual fulfillment with her husband may lead her to attempt to substitute the son's responses for her husband's. Again, for some mothers physical contact appears to be the preferred way to help and comfort the child. Some mothers feel that they alone can comfort their children. For instance, one IID mother, when she was ill, would not entrust her baby to her husband or her nurse, and refused hospital care lest her child should "die" without her.

A mother may force her physical presence on the child indiscriminately, regardless of his needs, age, and developmental stage. She may handle him, stroke him, pick him up, hold him, walk about with him, whether he is asleep or awake. Our emphasis here is on handling which primarily arises from the mother's own needs, although she may rationalize her behavior as being in the service of the baby. Persistence of such possessiveness was seen, for instance, in a mother who still referred to her 10-year-old son as "my baby."

Such mothers may be contrasted with those who, while feeling strong ties to the children and gaining satisfaction from physical contact with them, are early able to recognize their children as individuals, both physically and psychologically. For these mothers the amount of physical contact is determined by the baby's own needs for comfort and support as well as by the mother's pleasure in contact with him. They do not, out of their own need, perpetuate a pattern of mother-child symbiosis.

Physical contacts, exaggerated both in intensity and duration, may have a variety of outcomes. These depend on variations in the strength of the baby's need for physical contact, as well as on the mother's attitudes toward such contacts. If a mother's own need for contact is strong and her particular baby, for physical or psychological reasons, is especially in need of such contact, physical unity with her baby will be prolonged and eventual separation delayed, handicapping the development of self-differentiation. On the other hand, a more active, robust child may early rebel against his mother's excessive physical closeness to him. He may kick her, squirm, or simply fail to nestle in her arms. Such resistive behavior on the baby's part may be quite traumatizing to a mother who especially needs to evoke a positive response from her child. She may react to his resistance by clinging to him even more strongly. If the child counters with further resistance, she may feel rejected by and resentful toward him. Since the clinging mother is likely to be an anxious mother, her feeling of being rejected by the child may further exaggerate her anxiety. If, in her resentment, she gives up and ceases to caress and fondle her child, the effect on him may be just as handicapping to the development of separation as the effect of too close a union. In either case, a mother will not contribute to the interaction necessary for the child's progress toward separation from her as a step toward differentiation of the self.

We must consider the effect on the child's self-differentiation of a mother who is initially too distant. The mother's distance from her child may express itself in letting the child repeatedly "cry it out," keeping him in bed or in his playpen most of his waking time, offering no closeness or physical contact during feeding, and in general reducing physical contact to a minimum. Some of our mothers rationalized their reduced physical contact with the child as being "for his own good," showing him that his "whims" have no effect on his environment. The consequences of such behavior will depend in part on the constellation of feelings and attitudes which brought it about. But whatever the constellation, being "left alone" in this way reduces access to objects around the child, deprives him of the chance to explore his world and thus limits, in these important initial stages, his first steps toward articulation of his experience of himself and the world. One might anticipate that if a mother thus fails to offer stimulation a more passive child of low energy level might reach out less to his environment than a child with greater energy. Variations in the quality of early physical contacts between mother and child have only been touched upon here. Research is needed into the ways in which early bodily contacts contribute to the development of articulation of experience.

The development of a child's concept of his body is basic for the formation of his self-concept. A mother's negative attitude toward the body and its functioning may curtail important primary sources of information and satisfaction which a child may derive from his own body. In particular a mother who feels threatened when a child handles and touches his sex organs may convey her fears to her child at a very early age. Such mothers may interfere with the child's investigation of his body, either by imposing physical restraints or later by punishment if the child handles his sex organs. An early sense that his own body is "dangerous" may discourage body exploration so that his body image tends to remain undifferentiated. Such attitudes may limit the development of curiosity in a more general sense. Thus negative attitudes toward the body may interfere with early progress toward articulation of experience of the self and the world.

Yet there are children who in spite of maternal protection and shielding manage to develop some sense of separate identity. We recall for instance a mother of a quite differentiated child who stated, "He simply wouldn't let me baby him." Another mother who had kept her child in close contact with her, for instance walking him to school daily until age 8 and pulling him away from children who to her looked dangerous or aggressive, stated: "He just would not let me take care of him any longer." In the absence of knowledge of earliest mother-child relations we cannot tell what enabled these boys to resist their mothers so effectively. A child's experiences of protection and shielding are fundamentally different in different mother-child relations. For example, a mother's anxiety, even if diffuse, may be expected to have a very different effect when accompanied by warm sympathetic feeling than when accompanied by feelings of noninvolvement or rejection. Also, other relations than those between mother and child are important in the child's development of a differentiated self. For example, we have not considered the role of the father. He may, in a variety of ways, modify the mother's attitudes and he will certainly modify the impact of such attitudes on the child. Siblings and other relatives, in their prolonged contacts with the child, are also very important. Finally, little is known about the role of constitutional factors in the development of articulateness of experiences. Further research is needed in all these areas.

Apparently similar maternal patterns are never exactly the same and cannot be expected to have consistently similar results. Not only the mother's attitudes, but her underlying motivation, her warmth, her temperament and its compatibility with the temperament of a specific child, are part of a field to which the child has originally contributed his own endowment. In this interaction, in which neither mother nor child remains static, all processes become reciprocal.

Development of an articulated way of experiencing is furthered by exploration of the outside environment beyond the mother-child field. Such exploration permits comparison and contrasting of the self with others and thus provides opportunities for constantly growing awareness of the self.

Conceiving of the mother as an interpreter of the world, let us first consider mothers who see the world as dangerous and threatening, and therefore cannot help but communicate such an image to their children. Dangers are experienced by such mothers as general and vague and, if expressed to the child, are likely to be cast in nonspecific terms. Long before they are verbalized, and simultaneously with verbalized expressions, fears are transmitted from mother to child by actions, by avoidance, by gestures of disgust and shame, often as an ever-present accompaniment to any number of maternal activities. When expressed to the child, the fears are formulated in broad and general terms such as "don't climb," "don't talk to people," "don't ever fight," "you should always do as mother tells you." For mothers who sense dangers as global in content, the means of meeting the dangers may consist of general proscriptions to avoid everything. Since general dangers can be met only by general measures, withdrawal or denial might be the child's preferred choice. Following the spirit of such exhortations, children would limit their activities and the scope of many interests which contribute to articulation of experience. For example, some mothers of limitedly differentiated children reported that their children's anxieties and fears were so encompassing that the children were depressed and unhappy and their activities constricted. One mother described her son as a "sad sack" who did nothing but "mope on the lounge." Still other children, feeling that they live in a dangerous world, may become submissive in order to get the reassurance and protection of others. If a mother is anxious about a hostile world she may welcome submission to and dependence on her as a tribute of love, reenforcing the cycle of excessive dependence and hindering self-differentiation of a growing child.

In marked contrast with the more general definition of dangers and means of coping with them are more specific and delimited prohibitions to be met by specific action: "This tree does not have limbs strong enough to hold you"; "if someone hits you fight back with your mean left, daddy will show you how." When the difficulties and problems of life are thus formulated to the child they appear better defined and may therefore be countered by specific measures. Mastering these difficulties may even have a certain appeal to the child, and be accepted by him as a challenge. Such an interaction may contribute to the emergence of a clear awareness of self, of a field around the self, and of potential interaction between them.

The process of structuring of experience begins very early in infancy. A mother may handle a baby with sensitivity to his needs and to the occasion, rather than indiscriminately perceiving every situation as an emergency. There are mothers who know when to cuddle a baby, when to feed him, when to leave him alone, mothers who are able to identify particular cries of their babies which they meet with particular responses. As a consequence, the child himself is in a better position to become more specifically aware of his different needs.

Such awareness would seem to be a necessary condition for forming a concept of his body, which in turn is central for the articulation of experience of the self.

In contrast there are mothers who have only global perception and global methods; some pick a child up, some feed him, push a pacifier into his mouth, or let him cry it out indiscriminately because of dimly felt notions that the child is always hungry, or always in need of attention. Specifically, there are mothers who regularly respond with floods of stimuli, rattles, and noisemakers, in order to drown the child's discontent, which they may interpret for their own reasons as the child's lack of outside excitation. Such indiscriminate responses of a mother handicap a child's development of awareness of his own specific needs. Lack of maternal sensitivity in giving care, moreover, handicaps a child's learning the shadings and specific meanings of objects in his environment, and thus helps to perpetuate a more global way of experiencing. The ways in which a mother contributes to an articulated mode of experiencing through her perceptiveness and sensitivity in handling a child merits further study.

Later in childhood mothers continue in varying degree to define the world for their children, depending largely on the ways in which they themselves experience the world. If a mother selects and times certain experiences for which she feels a child is ready, she can help him avoid confusion as he becomes gradually aware of an ever increasingly complex world. We were impressed by the ways in which some of our IFD mothers tended to take account of the children's readiness, as they set goals for their achievements. They spoke of "knowing my child," of the child having "his own pace." Selective presentation of experience is in marked contrast to an oversupply of experience, an indiscriminate showering of the child with love, toys, or food by mothers who are quite blind to the various needs of their children at different stages of development.

Again, depending on the child, such an oversupply of experiences may have various results. When a mother does not provide the necessary screening of the environment we would postulate that a child of strong intense needs whose stimulus threshold is low would easily become confused and overwhelmed. He would then have difficulty in experiencing the world in an articulated way.

The definite and strong preferences which some children seem to develop early in life may help to insulate them against the effect of an oversupply of experiences. We would expect that such children would not be as easily overwhelmed by a "flooding" mother as would children who do not have such discriminating preferences. A "capacity to focus" which may appear very early in childhood sets natural limits to the effects of overstimulation by a mother. As an example, the effect of being presented with an array of toys is different for a child who has a capacity to focus on one of them, to establish a preference quickly, than for a child who is helpless when exposed to choices he cannot make. An irritable child, when overstimulated in this manner, may react with confusion and outright panic, since without having structure within himself he cannot structure an external situation. On the other hand, a capacity to focus and choose may enable a child himself to delimit the field to some extent; at the same time, excessive delimitation of the field may lead to constriction of experience.

In order to help a child develop articulateness of experience, a mother, as we have suggested, must not only give him an opportunity to separate from her, to make choices, but she must also actively help him structure those experiences. The development of values and standards is a most important part of the process.

It seems necessary for the absorption and integration of values that the child be able to understand the broader meaning underlying specific regulations. The mother of Chris (a highly differentiated child, Case #2 in Chapter 15) offered him a set of values selected from her religious background which seemed to have meaning to herself. The values she offered were thus made personally meaningful and could be applied by him with discrimination to specific situations. Such values may be contrasted with values which are stereotyped and take a generalized form as "I want you to be good," or "you should make yourself liked by other people" which can be applied only mechanically.

The mother's own development of a cohesive set of values is important if she is to offer her child the inherent meanings of regulations. We have already mentioned the mother of a less differentiated child who, fearful of being identified as a member of a minority group in the neighborhood, insisted on her child's conforming to the standards of the prevailing culture which differed from her own. Thus she confused his sense of values, passing on to him outside regulations which he could not link to his own traditions but could only apply by rote.

We should mention here other situations which interfere with the child's internalization of values. A child may be quite clear about his roles at home, his position in the family, the restrictions to which he must comply, behavior that will be punished or rewarded, the sequence and order of daily life in the household. However, clarity and consistency do not seem to be enough to provide a well-operating value system for internalization. The psychologist who analyzed an interview with a relatively undifferentiated child described him as follows:

"He is a little boy, hemmed in by careful restrictions, who does what he is told. He seems clear within a narrow range set by adults, a range from which he does not wander. However, if he leaves his framework, imposed and managed by adults, he becomes vague and uncertain." This illustrates a case where not only individual rules, but whole sets of consistent rules were transmitted by the mother, yet in such a way as to make internalization by the child difficult. As long as the child remained with his mother and under her supervision, the outer frames of reference he was following were adequate for him. However, one could foresee that without such outside props the orientation of the child might collapse.

A mother may also deprive a child of an opportunity to digest or absorb values by pushing him prematurely into adult forms of behavior. Such pushing is characteristic of mothers who attempt to force their children into a pattern of conformity to outside standards rather than of mothers whose acceleration of their children's development stresses responsibility and independence. Premature pushing often takes the form of a demand that the child be "a little gentleman" at an early age. Pressed too early into adult patterns, a child can accept this role only by adhering to stereotypes which are indiscriminately parroted.

Thus, not only the properties of value systems and the readiness of the specific child for assimilating regulations, but also the specific manner in which the mother transmits these values, affect the internalization of standards by a child.

The complex process of internalization of values has been only touched upon in this discussion. The dynamics of the mother-child interaction in this process would certainly deserve much deeper exploration. It is clear that a mother finds satisfaction in her child's developing values and standards which are meaningful to him in his culture. However, it is also clear that every step that brings her child nearer to this goal brings her important task to a close. Therefore she has some, often unconscious, interest in delaying the process. This means that the transmission of values may often be accompanied by conflict in a mother. It seems important to follow up the dynamics of this conflict in further research.

2. Development of Controls

The development of articulateness of experience of the self and of the outside world and the development of a system of impulse control are reciprocal processes. In the beginning a mother plays a most important role in the child's control of impulses. Gradually the child must be able to take over and develop his own system of controls. A mother may help or interfere with the establishment of controls in various ways. Which she does will depend in part on her own control structure, and in part on characteristics of the child. Children seem to differ with regard to the strength and urgency of their needs and also in their threshold for stimulation. A child who lacks the ability to postpone gratification—and this would seem to be observable very early—would be more prone to be overwhelmed by stimulation from his mother, or at least to react with greater intensity to such stimulation. A child's physiological equipment—for instance, skin sensitivity —would seem to be important for his response to stimulation.

If we look at the development of impulse control of a child as a common task for mother and child, we might expect that a moderate amount of energy combined with a capacity for smooth discharge would provide for both partners in this task the easiest condition for channelization of impulses. The problem of channelization would perhaps be most difficult in a child with a high level of energy combined with jerky modes of release sometimes seen in brain-damaged cases. Whether a child's pattern of release of energy and amount of energy is acceptable to a mother's temperament, temper, and aspirations may also be a factor in her contribution to the child's development of impulse control. She may, for instance, neglect or overstimulate her child if his low level of energy is not congenial to her. On the other hand, she might fail to provide the necessary control if her child's uncontrolled high energy level gratifies her own needs. In such instances adequate channelization of the child's energies might become difficult.

The type and effectiveness of a mother's own control system is important in the common endeavor of mother and child to establish a structured system of controls and defenses in a child.

A mother who can tolerate her own impulses and yet has well-structured controls and defenses would seem most likely to help her child develop his own system of controls. At any stage of development a child needs a mother's tolerance in order to allow himself the freedom to gratify his impulses. He needs his mother's controls as an aid to withhold the expression of his impulses until he himself can master or manage them. By necessity a mother must use at least some restrictive measures. But these measures may be applied by mothers in such ways that they are sensed by a child as guidance and orientation and thus contribute to optimal success in channelization.

A fair degree of consistency in a mother's response would seem necessary for the formation of an internalized system of controls by a child. The child of a predictable mother knows what is expected of him, what will pass as acceptable and how much aggression, for instance, he can safely express and in what fashion. If a mother herself is able to control her impulses she is better able to provide such an experience for a child. A mother of this kind contrasts with a mother whose own controls are undeveloped and who may, for instance, react at one time by meeting aggression with aggression and at another time by passively succumbing to the child's aggression, depending on her mood and circumstances of the moment. Thus a child does not have a basis for forming standards. Such ambivalence in a mother deprives her child of guide lines for controlling his impulses.

Direct imitation of a mother by a child may play but a relatively unimportant role in this process of the development of controls. If a mother is secure in her own controls she may not insist that the child adopt her specific control measures. For instance, the mother of a quite well-differentiated, well-controlled child who described herself as a pacifist stated about her son's fighting, in response to aggressive attacks by other children, "His way is not my way but it is right for him."

But even a mother who has developed a system of impulse controls does not necessarily foster the development of impulse control in her child. For instance, if a mother's defenses are rigid her conviction about order and regularity will most likely express itself early in the child's life in strict regulations such as scheduling of feeding and toilet training. If her scheduling, even strict scheduling, is compatible with basic patterns of energy and its discharge in the child, and if, at the same time, a mother is warm and accepting of her child, we might expect that channelization of impulses might be fostered and the child himself might gradually develop his own system of controls. However, if a mother is not only rigid but also a stern disciplinarian, whatever controls her child might try to develop on his own may soon be supplanted by the mother's more powerful regulations. In a passive and unassertive child severe punishment may seriously undermine his ability to express aggression directly. Such a child might resort to repression and denial of his needs, and be unlikely to develop a variety and complexity of controls. We recall, for instance, a mother who stated that her child had lacked "energy, drive, ambition," from the time he was born, was "too easily influenced" when she imposed her will on him, and was constricted in his interests and activities. In this case the psychologically absentee father offered the child no escape from the dominant, controlling mother. In other cases, however, a child might be partially immunized against a mother's rigid restrictions by a father's stimulation and warmth. A more energetic child whose mother is a rigid disciplinarian may react with outbursts of aggression, making controls still more difficult to achieve, and create a cycle of hostility difficult to break down.

Turning to mothers who themselves have not developed ways of coping with their impulses we may mention some mother-child interactions which may interfere with or at least may not be helpful to the development of controls in a child. If such a mother has an overly demanding child she may submit and abdicate to him. Her surrender may pervade the whole pattern of her interaction with her child and prevent him from developing the amount of inhibition necessary for control of his impulses. Later on, mothers who are indulgent, who give in to their children's needs at whatever cost to themselves or others, deprive their children of opportunities to bring into play those controls which a child might establish on his own. Thus a child does not learn how to weigh conflicting needs or to permit values and reasoning to enter into his reactions, which are essential for the development of controls. Such maternal overindulgence not only fails to offer support to a child in controlling his impulses but may even increase their intensity. For instance, a mother previously referred to could not bear to deprive her child of sweets, though he was overweight and was under doctors' orders to diet. This seemed partly based on her own problems about food, and particularly on her fear that any restrictions on her part would be interpreted by her child as deprivation and would lead to loss of his affection for her. Another mother who vaguely recognized her own temper tantrums as a problem found temper in her son when he was a baby "cute" and "amusing" but also annoying. She considered her son a "toy" and showed him off to her friends, in order to exhibit his "masculinity." At times she alternated between giving in to his tantrums and beating him, and feeling "helpless" in dealing with him. Approval and surrender to these tantrums and her inconsistency in dealing with them seemed to contribute to the perpetuation of his "primitive" patterns of attempting to master his environment.

Again a mother, perhaps fearful of aggression because she cannot tolerate her own aggressions, may protect her child from conflicts with other children. Thus one of our mothers consistently pulled her child out of fights. In this way she restricted his opportunities to assess his own strength and thus learn how to express and to limit his aggression in accordance with realistic factors.

Difficulties in establishing control may also arise from increased tension in the child through excessive stimulation. For example, an IID mother who considered her child as particularly brilliant and socially responsible reported that she had constantly showed off her infant to relatives. She commented that it was small wonder he had turned out (at age 14) to be an excitable, poorly controlled boy. In such instances we would wish to know more about the child's potentials for defending himself against excessive stimulation from his mother. If his threshold for stimulation had been higher he might have been less disturbed at an early age.

As life situations grow more varied, controls have to become correspondingly more structured. If a mother, in her own development, has arrived at a stage which allows her to wait and to exercise her own regulative ability in a way compatible with the specific child at a specific stage, the child can gradually try out new types of control and adapt them to changing situations.

The ways in which mothers with different types of controls and defenses affect the development of controls and defenses in their children merits further study.

In the above discussion of the development of controls and articulateness of experience the variety of possible parent-child interactions has barely been touched upon. We have suggested only a few of the routes by which a child may become more differentiated and have been able to point to only a limited number of directions for further research.

E. SUMMARY

The main results of our studies of mother-child relations as a source of differences in extent of differentiation among children were briefly reviewed. A more extended comparison of characteristics of children with evaluations made of their mothers gave substantial support to the picture of relations reported in preceding chapters. In this comparison we used for the children a variety of measures devised to reflect extent of differentiation in various areas of functioning. For the mothers we used the ratings made of them as IID or IFD on the basis of interviews as well as sophistication-of-body-concept and EFT scores. As in our studies of the children, we considered the latter two measures to reflect extent of mothers' differentiation. The interview ratings and sophistication-of-body-concept scores of mothers, although not their EFT scores, showed generally high and significant correlations with the various measures of differentiation for their children. Mothers judged on the basis of the interview to have fostered the development of differentiation in their children and mothers giving evidence of a developed body concept tended to have children who showed articulateness of experience of the field, a developed body concept, a sense of separate identity, and structured defenses and controls. Mothers judged as having inhibited their children's progress toward differentiation and mothers with a poorly developed body concept were apt to have children who gave evidence of limited differentiation in these various areas.

We saw earlier that in children level of some verbal skills and effectiveness of adjustment do not relate to extent of differentiation. As might have been expected, we have now found that interview ratings and sophistication-of-body-concept scores of mothers do not relate to measures of verbal comprehension for their children. Some suggestions were offered as to how aspects of mother-child interactions which inhibit the development of differentiation in children may actually contribute to the development of some verbal skills. Regarding effectiveness of children's adjustments, we have suggested that though IFD mothers have more to contribute than IID mothers to the development of differentiation in their children, each kind of mother may aid or hamper the development of effective adjustment, though in different ways.

We have identified some of the areas of parent-child relations which require further investigation from the standpoint of their effect on the development of differentiation of children. One is father-child relations. The variety of ways in which children may reenforce or elicit particular behavior and attitudes from their mothers points to the importance of further studies of mother-child interactions considered from the standpoint of the child. A study of differences in the reactions that boys and girls may elicit from the same mothers would be of particular interest in view of the possibility raised in Chapter 13 of sex differences in extent of differentiation.

Results of a study by Seder (1957), in which mothers' responses to a questionnaire filled out in a home interview were used to evaluate a large number of fairly specific rearing procedures, generally confirmed our own findings. This confirmation is of particular interest in view of the difference in methodology between Seder's study and our own.

Some speculations were offered concerning processes of mother-child interaction which may contribute to or hinder the development of differentiation of children. These were presented in order to suggest directions of research which might be pursued in giving greater specificity to the general patterns of mother-child relationships identified to this point.

23

STABILITY OF
PSYCHOLOGICAL PATTERNS
DURING GROWTH
AND IN ADULTHOOD

Our concern in this chapter is with the stability of the psychological patterns that have been described. The issue is whether a child who, compared to other children of his age, shows greater differentiation in many areas of functioning at one stage of growth is likely to hold a similar position at later stages as well. The same question may be raised about stability in adulthood.

It was suggested in Chapter 2 that "formal" features of an individual's psychological make-up, of the kind represented by differentiation, are likely to show considerable stability, as compared to "content" features. Consistent with this view, we find Escalona and Heider (1959) concluding from their recent study of continuity in early development that "our best predictive successes have occurred in regard to the formal aspects of behavior. With few exceptions we have been better able to forecast *how* a child goes about moving, thinking, speaking, playing, than *what* he is likely to do, think, say, or play" (p. 73). Stability is likely to be found during the growth years though not to so great an extent as in adulthood, making for continuity in individual psychological patterns from one stage of development to another. The particular ways in which the indicators of differentiation investigated may show themselves are of course likely to vary at different stages of growth. Thus, a developed sense of separate identity takes quite different forms when the child is 8 than when he is 18, even though at both ages he may be considered to have a relatively poorly developed or well-developed sense of separate identity. Particularly in children, stability must be considered in a setting of ever ongoing change.

We have done considerable work on the problem of stability in the form of longitudinal studies of children and adults. The data-gathering phase of most of these studies has been completed. Relatively little has been done, however, on the analysis of these data. We describe below the studies done and the results now on hand. For convenience the studies are presented according to the ages of the subjects used: one group of studies is concerned with stability during childhood and adolescence, a second group with stability during adulthood.

In addition to the longitudinal studies, investigations of another kind bearing on the stability problem are described. These investigations, carried out for the most part in other laboratories, attempted to change the person's mode of field approach by direct experimental means.

A. STUDIES OF STABILITY DURING ADULTHOOD

1. Longitudinal Studies

Two groups of young adults have been studied longitudinally. One group of 103 college students received at first, as described in detail in our 1954 report, our battery of tests of perceptual field dependence and a series of personality tests. One year later they were recalled for retesting with the perceptual battery, and 3 years later they were recalled (by Bauman, 1951) for perceptual and personality retesting.

Subjects of the second group were first seen at 17 years of age, when they were seniors in high school, receiving a battery of perceptual and personality tests. They were restudied 3 years later (by Fliegel, 1955) with the perceptual battery, the figure-drawing test, the Rorschach, and an interview.

Test-retest correlations for perceptual measures (Table 23-1) are extremely high, suggesting striking stability in mode of field approach over periods ranging from 1 to 3 years. In fact, many of the stability coefficients in Table 23-1 compare favorably with the split-half reliability coefficients for these same tests, reported in Chapter 4.

An evaluation of the figure drawings of the men in our original college group indicates striking stability in extent of articulation of body concept. The figure drawings, obtained by us at the time of initial testing and again by Bauman at the time of retesting 3 years later, were rated according to the sophistication-of-body-concept scale

Table 23-1. Coefficients of stability for perceptual test scores: adults

Investigator Subjects [a] Retest Interval		Witkin, et al. College stud. 1 year	Bauman College stud. 3 years	Fliegel 17-year-olds 3 years
BAT	Men	.82 (32) [b, c]	.77 (32) [d]	— [e]
	Women	.73 (30)	.74 (30) [d]	—
RFT	Men	.88 (32)	.84 (32)	— [e]
	Women	.75 (30)	.66 (30)	—
EFT	Men	— [f]	.89 (32)	.97 (13)
	Women	—	.89 (30)	.68 (14)
Index	Men	— [f]	.91 (32) [d]	.85 (13)
	Women	—	.74 (30) [d]	.80 (14)

[a] Refers to age or status of subjects at time of original testing.

[b] Number in parentheses refers to number of cases.

[c] In computing these correlations only the cases employed by Bauman, selected from our larger group, were used in order to make the studies for the 1- and 3-year intervals comparable. The 1-year interval correlations for the entire sample are roughly equivalent to those reported here and may be found in our 1954 report.

[d] Recomputed from Bauman's original data.

[e] For these tests, test-retest correlations are reported by Fliegel for separate series only, rather than for each test as a whole.

[f] The EFT was not given to these subjects. In the absence of EFT scores, total index scores could not be computed.

(Chapter 7). The test-retest correlation of these ratings was .86 ($P < .01$, $N = 24$).

Another kind of evidence of continuity in functioning emerged from the Bauman study when certain life experiences of subjects were considered. In addition to giving them the tests cited, Bauman interviewed his subjects with the aim of obtaining evidence of important changes in life circumstances during the 3-year period since initial testing (as marriage); opportunities for personality change (through psychotherapy); and occurrence of psychological trauma (as divorce). No significant difference was found in extent of change of perceptual performance from test to retest between a group of subjects who had had major changes in these areas and a group who did not.

2. Experimental Attempts to Alter Mode of Field Approach

Another approach to the problem of stability in adulthood is found in the many studies which attempted to bring about a change in people's mode of field approach through the use of various direct experimental means. The techniques used consisted of drugs, convulsive seizures, stress, or special training.

Franks (1956) found no significant differences in RFT performance among groups of subjects given sodium amytal (a barbiturate), dexedrine (an amphetamine), a placebo, or nothing. A person's preferred mode of field approach thus seems to "survive" the transient changes in psychological state induced by drugs. To this extent mode of field approach must be considered a stable characteristic.

As part of a study mentioned briefly in Chapter 12, we found that alcoholics showed no significant change in RFT or BAT performance with alcoholization. A significant change was found, however, in EFT performance, ingestion of alcohol leading to higher time scores. Of the three perceptual measures only the EFT involves speed of performance, and it may be that difficulty in maintaining attention, produced by drinking, may have a marked effect upon speed of EFT performance without a corresponding change in mode of perception itself.

A third study, by Pollack, Kahn, Karp, and Fink (1960), examined the effects of a course of tranquilizer therapy (chlorpromazine or promazine), anti-depressant (imipremine), or convulsive therapy (electric or inhalant) upon RFT performance of patients in a voluntary psychiatric hospital. The RFT was administered prior to, during the fourth week of, and following treatment. Neither the drug nor convulsive-therapy groups showed any significant change in mean RFT scores during treatment. Moreover, test-retest correlations were very high for both groups, .86 and .88 ($P < .01$ in each instance), respectively. It is interesting that the convulsive-therapy subjects suffered retrograde amnesia for the first test, experiencing retesting as an entirely new situation. The drug-therapy group showed no significant change in extent of field dependence following cessation of treatment although, for reasons that are not clear, the convulsive-therapy group showed a reduction. Again, the convulsive-therapy subjects suffered retrograde amnesia for the previous test.

In general, the results of these three studies are consistent in suggesting that mode of field approach tends to remain stable with changes in psychological state induced by various kinds of drugs although apparently not by convulsive seizures.

Findings of studies designed to assess the effects of stress upon performance in tests of mode of field approach are generally consistent with the results of the drug studies.

Kraidman (1959) tested a group of patients on the EFT, immediately prior to heart surgery and 5 to 6 weeks later, during convalescence. The presurgery situation was considered a "natural" source of stress. No significant change in EFT performance was found from test to retest.

Prolonged confinement in a sensory-isolation situation, which for many people is highly stressful, failed to have a significant effect on EFT performance in one study (Davis, McCourt, and Solomon, 1958). In another study (Scott, Bexton, Heron, and Doane, 1959), no change was found in performance on the Thurstone Gottschaldt taken before and after a period of isolation; however, a control group showed improvement when retested after the same interval of time without exposure to isolation.

Other studies suggest that special training may affect performance in our perceptual tests, but apparently perception itself is not altered and there is little transfer of training between tests. In one of our earlier studies (Witkin, 1948) we attempted to bring about a change in perception by means of special training procedures, which included discussions of problems of orientation and practical demonstrations in which the subject participated. These training methods improved scores in the test in which the training was given (TRTC) and in a highly similar test (rotating-room test),[1] but not in a different kind of test (RFT). These results suggest that no fundamental change in mode of field approach, in the sense of alteration of the subject's characteristic way of perceiving, occurred in consequence of training. Our observations of subjects during training tended to confirm this impression. We noted that subjects who improved their scores in the test on which they received training accomplished this apparently by the acquisition of special techniques or "tricks" useful in correcting the immediate impression of the location of the upright.

A preliminary study by Schneck and Wexler [2] is of particular interest, with regard to the effect of training, because of the method employed. Using only four subjects, they found that suggestions made under hypnosis to "rely less on the visual field" in the TRTC did not change performance during the posthypnotic period. In contrast,

---

[1] Weiner (1955) also found that training affected performance in a situation involving perception of the upright (a luminous cube test); and the training was transferred to a similar situation (a rod-and-cube test).

[2] Personal communication from Rochelle M. Wexler.

suggestions made with regard to Rorschach responses were effective in producing change.

In another study, Gruen (1955) investigated the perceptual performances of a group of professional dancers. The dancers, particularly trained to utilize body cues, did significantly better than control subjects on the BAT,[3] but no difference was found in performance on the RFT and EFT. It is possible that the finding for the BAT is an artifact attributable to the particular control group used. Gruen's control subjects were the college men of our 1954 study. Recently, we studied a less selected group of subjects than the college students, comparable in age to Gruen's dancers. Using these subjects as a control group we found, in analyses we have done, no significant difference in the BAT between them and the dancers.

The studies of the effect of drugs, stress, and training suggest that mode of field approach is, on the whole, resistant to change by experimental means, and thus appears to be a stable characteristic of a person. Where change was noted, it seemed to involve the subject's *performance*, leading to a change in his score, but not in his actual mode of field approach. Convulsive shock therapy apparently did affect field approach.

The results of the longitudinal investigations described at the beginning of this section, together with the findings of the experimental studies just considered, suggest that, in adulthood, measures reflecting the particular aspects of differentiation considered tend to remain stable. They tend to be stable over a period of years, even when important life experiences intervene, and in the face of deliberate attempts to bring about a change.

B. STUDIES OF STABILITY DURING GROWTH

These studies also employed the longitudinal method, and made use of several groups of children. The data obtained have been only partially analyzed and, for one group, no analyses have yet been performed.

1. Studies of Children in the 8–13- and 10–17-Year Period

These groups of children were recruited from a public school in the neighborhood of our laboratory.

The 10–17-year group consisted of 30 boys and 30 girls. When first

---

[3] For this analysis, total BAT scores were computed from the scores for separate series reported by Gruen.

studied at age 10, all of them received the RFT, BAT, RAT, and EFT; and half received, in addition, a Rorschach, TAT, figure-drawing test, and miniature-toys-play test. The entire group was studied again at 14 and 17, when they received the entire battery of perceptual, and a series of personality tests; and at 17 they were given the Wechsler-Bellevue. At both 14 and 17 they were also interviewed and an interview was conducted with their mothers as well. We expect to recall this group for further study in the near future, when they will be 24 years old.

The second group of children followed longitudinally, consisting of 26 boys and 27 girls, was first studied at age 8 and recalled for further study at age 13. The testing procedures at age 8 were the same as those followed at age 10 for the 10–17 group, except that the EFT was omitted as too difficult; again, the testing procedures at 13 were the same as those at age 14 for the latter group, with the omission of home interviews.

To this point we have analyzed stability only with regard to mode of field approach (for both groups) and sophistication of body concept (for the 10–17-year group).

a. Stability of mode of field approach. Our 1954 report described cross-sectional studies of perceptual development, concerned with changes in extent of field dependence as measured by our battery of perceptual tests. Since then, we have extended these cross-sectional studies to include additional age groups, and we have conducted longitudinal studies as well (Witkin, Goodenough, and Karp, 1961).

The same developmental trend is revealed by the results of both the cross-sectional and longitudinal studies: children tend to be relatively field dependent early in their perceptual development and to become more field independent as they grow older. The ability to determine the position of the body apart from the tilted room, to perceive the position of a rod independently of the tilted frame, to pick out a simple figure obscured by a complex design, tends to improve, on the whole, until about the age of 17. Thereafter, there is a tendency towards increased field dependence, particularly in the case of women, although the increase is relatively slight compared to the earlier decline.

Stability coefficients for the three perceptual tests and the perceptual index, for the 8–13- and 10–17-year groups in our longitudinal studies, are presented in Table 23-2. In general, the coefficients of stability for the RFT and EFT are high, particularly in view of the length

Table 23-2. Coefficients of stability for perceptual test scores: children

Age of subjects	Retest interval	N M	N F	BAT M	BAT F	RFT M	RFT F	EFT M	EFT F	Index M	Index F
10–14	4 years	27	24	.58	.66	.56	.57	.51	.69	.64	.88
14–17	3 years	27	24	.68	.88	.82	.75	.95	.95	.87	.94
10–17	7 years	27	24	.31	.63	.49	.53	.48	.68	.50	.79
8–13	5 years	26	22	.14	.36	.71	.61	—ᵃ —		—ᵃ —	

ᵃ The EFT was not given to this group at 8. In the absence of EFT scores, total index scores could not be computed.

of the test-retest intervals. Performance in the BAT reaches a fairly high order of stability in the 10–17-year period.

If we evaluate perceptual stability on the most comprehensive basis available—that is, with scores for the three perceptual tests combined—the results are indeed striking with reference to the 10–17 group. As shown in Table 23-2, we find coefficients of stability for boys of .64 for the 10–14 period, .87 for the 14–17 period, and .50 for the 10–17 period. The corresponding values for girls are .88, .94, and .79.[4]

The evidence of stability provided by these results is particularly impressive since it covers a period when the child is entering many new areas of life, when important new needs within himself are emerging, and when ways of coping with these new life circumstances and needs are being developed. Of course, in terms of group means, there is a marked trend toward reduction in extent of field dependence, so that these general changes are in fact associated with changes in perception. What is of interest, however, is that under the impact of new demands and new opportunities in living, individual children do not change their relative positions in the group during this period more than is implied by the magnitude of the correlations obtained. These results suggest that basic characteristics of the individual reflected in

[4] The very high coefficients of stability, together with the systematic changes in group means, suggest little likelihood of "reversals" during development in the sense of change, counter to the group trend, from a more field-independent to a more field-dependent way of perceiving. This is supported by examination of individual cases in our longitudinally studied group. Almost all children showed continuous movement toward a more analytical field approach throughout the age range studied. It is thus indicated that among children differences in mode of field approach are most often a consequence of differences in pace of development or perhaps in starting point.

his mode of field approach are established relatively early in life and tend to persist through the changes that accompany development and altered relations with the environment.

b. Stability of sophistication of body concept. The results of a study of the body concept of children in the 10–17 group provide further evidence of stability.

Figure drawings were obtained from 14 of the boys in this group at age 10 and again at age 17. The drawings at 10 were rated according to the children's version of the sophistication-of-body-concept scale, and the drawings at 17 according to the slightly different "adult" version (Chapter 7). The ratings were made by the same judge at different times and without knowledge that the drawings came from the same subjects.[5] The correlation between ratings of the 10-year and 17-year drawings was .73 ($P < .01$). Children who showed a relatively articulated body concept at 10 showed it 7 years later as well, even though the drawings at the two ages gave evidence of a general change toward more sophisticated representation of the human body.

The extent of the change that did occur is shown by the results of a subsidiary analysis. After her ratings had been completed, the judge was told that the drawings had been made by the same boys and asked to match them. She was successful with only four of the fourteen sets of drawings.

A post hoc study by the rater of the ten sets of drawings which had not been correctly matched led to the impression that, in addition to marked changes in characteristics reflecting greater differentiation, the following changes in the drawings of individual subjects contributed to difficulty in matching: 1. Vast changes in kinds of interests (as suggested, for example, by roles portrayed) which resulted in marked differences in content of drawings by the same child. 2. Marked decrease in drawing features suggestive of disturbance or pathology. 3. Changes in main conflict areas. Thus, the large and varied changes that occur in this period of life are reflected in the drawings; some of the changes are in content aspects of personality, others refer to nature of integration, still others to extent of differentiation. Yet, in the context of such large change, and over so long a period of time, we find marked stability in relative extent of sophistication-of-body concept.

We shall have an opportunity to check these findings through anal-

[5] To eliminate number of drawings as a clue, an extra set was added to the 17-year drawings.

ysis of the figure drawings we have for girls in the 10–17-year group and for boys and girls in the 8–13-year group.

c. *Stability of measures reflecting extent of differentiation in other areas.* Although they are yet to be analyzed, we have on hand a large body of data which will permit us to evaluate stability in other aspects of functioning from the standpoint of differentiation. As noted, children in both the 8–13 and 10–17 groups received the battery of perceptual tests on each test occasion, and most of these times they also received the Rorschach, TAT, miniature-toys-play test, and intelligence test; and they were interviewed. This material will be analyzed further with regard to articulateness of experience and sophistication-of-body concept; and we shall also explore the areas of sense of separate identity, and nature of controls and defenses.

Obviously, stability must be considered in relation to nature of life circumstances obtaining in the period during which stability is being evaluated. Certain kinds of unstable life situations, or important changes in life circumstances, may reduce continuity in form of functioning from one stage of growth to another. On the other hand, stable life conditions, for example, in the area of the child's relation to his mother, are apt to make for greater continuity. The interviews with the mothers, conducted at different points in the children's lives, should provide information on life circumstances particularly useful for understanding extent of stability or change in individual cases. In this regard, children who show very marked changes during growth, in the areas we are studying, will be of special interest.

2. Studies in the Period from Infancy to 9 Years

It is reasonable to consider that evidence of development of differentiation, in however primitive a form, is to be found fairly early in infancy. In the preceding chapter, we commented on some characteristics that emerge in the first months of life, which may suggest progress toward differentiation. There is also the impression from a number of studies that infants are different from each other in ways suggestive of differences in extent of differentiation. To the extent that this is so, it should be possible to investigate stability from infancy to later childhood. In this period particularly we may expect that evidence of continuity from one stage to another needs to be sought in kinds of behavior which may in many ways appear different. And here again, the study of stability requires knowledge, during the period considered, of characteristics of the child and of his life situation (particularly his family setting), viewed in their interaction.

It seems particularly important to push the study of stability to the infancy period. The evidence presented earlier suggests that greater or more limited differentiation is a stable characteristic of a person in adulthood and it may even be so as early as age 8 or 10. The factors contributing to individual differences in pace of development of differentiation must therefore be operative, to an important degree, at very early ages. Studies starting in infancy are apt to be especially useful in shedding light on the nature of these factors and their mode of operation.

Closely related to the problem of stability is the problem of "precursors," i.e., characteristics which contribute to the development of differentiation, though they do not themselves reflect developed differentiation. As an example, a readily available fund of energy, though not in itself a feature of differentiation, may be found to aid in a variety of ways in the development of differentiation. Identification of such precursors may help provide another route through which continuity between early and later functioning may be studied. Here again, extent of continuity may be expected to depend upon conditions prevailing during development.

Problems of stability in pace of development of differentiation and of precursors of differentiation need to be studied in relation to each other. The ideal setting for their investigation is a longitudinal study, beginning with intensive evaluation of the parents of the child before the child is born, and of the child himself at the time of birth. The child's development would then need to be followed in relation to his interactions with his family and with his environment at large. The longitudinal study we have undertaken, starting in infancy, falls far short of this ideal, but it represents a useful step in that direction, and offers promise of contributing to a further understanding of the origins of individual differences in development of differentiation.

The study of children from infancy to the 6- to 9-year period was made possible through the generous cooperation of Dr. Sibylle Escalona and Dr. Lois Murphy. Although the data-collection phase of the study has been completed, analysis of the data has not yet begun, so that only the plan of the study can be described at this time.

The children for the study were drawn from a larger sample originally studied by Escalona and her coworkers when the children were between 4- and 32-weeks old. The procedures used in studying the infants have been described in detail by Escalona, Leitch, et al. (1952). They included extensive observations of behavior in a variety of situations, including standard and specially devised infant tests. Most of the observations were made with the mother present, and interviews conducted with the mother were focused on the child. The records available for each infant are extraordinarily rich in detail and in depth.

With the help of L. Murphy and the staff of the "Coping Project" of the Menninger Foundation, it was possible to locate and restudy, in Topeka, Kansas, 72 of the original 128 cases seen by Escalona. They were then 6–9 years old and included 27 of the 30 cases followed by L. Murphy for the coping project.[6] In the restudy by us, all the children received the Rorschach, TAT, and the figure-drawing test, and an interview was carried out with their mothers along the lines of the interviews described in Chapters 17–19. The children were also given a battery of perceptual tests, specially developed for use with children in the 6- to 9-year age range. These tests were modified versions of the BAT, RFT, and EFT. In general, the modifications were designed to make the tests easier, more concrete, and of greater interest to children.

Thus we have on hand extensive data for each of 72 children both when they were infants and when they were 6–9 years old. Information is also available for the mothers, from the standpoint of their relationships to their children, for both these periods. The material will be evaluated in relation to the problems of relative stability in pace of development of differentiation and precursors of differentiation. An added value of this study is the opportunity it provides to investigate mother-child relationships much earlier in the child's life than was possible in the studies we have conducted thus far.

C. SUMMARY

The first steps in investigating stability in aspects of individual functioning reflecting more developed or less developed differentiation were described. The studies were undertaken with the expectation that there would be stability in adulthood and, to a lesser degree, during periods of growth as well.

Long-range studies of adults, some extending over a period of more than 3 years, showed a pattern of generally high and significant test-retest correlations for measures reflecting extent of development of differentiation in the areas of functioning considered. Stability in other areas remains to be determined. In a series of studies with adults, done mainly by others, it has been found that drugs, stress,

[6] Some of these children have also been used in other investigations, as the study of maternal behavior of Brody (1956) and the prediction study of Escalona and Heider (1959).

and training had little or no effect on mode of field approach, pointing in another way to the stability of this aspect of differentiation.

To investigate stability during the growth years, longitudinal studies were carried out with three groups of children; one group was studied in the period from infancy to 9 years; another in the period from 8–13 years; and a third in the period from 10–17 years. Though all these studies have been carried through the data-gathering stage, no analyses have yet been performed on the data for the first group, and only a partial analysis has been made of the data for the second and third groups. The analyses already done show striking stability over a period of 7 years in the two areas considered, mode of field approach and extent of articulation of body concept. There was a change in the group as a whole toward more analytical perception, suggestive of a relatively articulated way of experiencing, and the drawings of these children reflected a generally more sophisticated body concept. Moreover, there was evidence of changes in the group in content aspects of personality and in pathology. Yet, in the context of vast psychological change, children who at age 10, relative to their group, gave evidence of more developed differentiation in the areas considered, tended to have the same relative standing in the group at age 17. These findings suggest that relatively more developed or less developed differentiation in many areas of functioning may be a stable characteristic of the growing child, even though the manner in which differentiation expresses itself varies from one age to another.

The data on hand will permit us to check these findings with additional groups, and to extend our investigation of stability to other areas of functioning. The material for the children studied in infancy and again in the 6- to 9-year period will make it possible to carry the study of stability down to a very early age. The infancy records will also be explored from the standpoint of early "precursors" of differentiation. At issue in the study of stability and of "precursors" is the problem of continuity in individual psychological patterns over time.

24

PSYCHOLOGICAL INDIVIDUALITY

Many themes were woven into the research account that has been given. An outstanding theme, sketched in the first chapter and continuously amplified, as evidence accumulated, has been that of psychological individuality. An interest in individuality implies concern both with patterns of characteristics within persons and with variations in patterning among persons, i.e., diversity. We have pursued this interest mainly through studies of development of children.

Werner (1957) recently commented on the need for greater attention, both in research and theory, to the problem of individuality in development:

The original aim of developmental theory, directed toward the study of universal genetic changes, is still one of its main concerns; but side by side with this concern, the conviction has been growing in recent years that developmental conceptualization, in order to reaffirm its truly organismic character, has to expand its orbit of interest to include as a central problem the study of individuality (p. 146).

In the area of development, the study of individuality concerns itself with several issues, each of which we have to some degree investigated. One is individual variations in pace and direction of development. Bearing on this problem are our studies of differences among children in extent of differentiation. Another issue is self-consistency, or how "things hang together" in an individual child at any stage of development. We approached this problem by viewing children's performances across a series of situations, reflecting various areas of functioning. A related issue concerns stability of patterns of individual functioning from one stage of development to another. Our longitudinal studies attempted to deal with this problem. Finally, there is the issue of sources of individual differences in psychological growth patterns. Related to this problem are our studies of mother-child interactions, and of the relation between characteristics present in infancy and patterns found in later development.

The necessity of considering individuals in their unique make-up when investigating problems of psychological functioning and development has been repeatedly demonstrated in our work.

It was perhaps most dramatically illustrated in the early observation that marked differences among people are to be found even in the "cold," narrow laboratory situations used in our studies of space orientation, where stimulus conditions were carefully kept uniform. This finding quickly led us to realize that in its neglect of individual determinants of perception the problem we undertook to solve was inadequately conceived. We had set out to discover which of the two standards used in perception of the upright—the "visual" or "postural" —is more important under various conditions and we found that our question was unanswerable. It was not possible to respond in the form of a simple generalization; the question needed to be rephrased to ask as well "more important for whom?"

The value of knowing about variations in people's performances is not simply to extend the existing catalogue of individual differences, which is already very long. By establishing the way in which individual differences may affect a given function it is possible to obtain a fuller understanding of the nature of that function. The effect of factors within the person must be considered along with the effect of situational determinants, as we have consistently attempted to do in our studies.

Another illustration of the importance of considering individuals in their uniqueness comes from the repeated observation that though to characterize a person as more differentiated or less differentiated is to say a great deal about him, it is far from a sufficient account. In considering indicators of developed differentiation we found that they occurred in very varied individual psychological settings. To make a person "come to life," in the sense of obtaining a feeling of what he is like dynamically and in action, it is necessary to add a whole series of uniquely individual qualifications to the statement that he shows a particular characteristic or set of characteristics of a high level of differentiation. To recall, we found a developed sense of separate identity in emotionally cold, isolated, overintellectual children as well as in emotionally warm children, capable of great empathy and deep, meaningful involvements with others. Again, an articulated way of experiencing was encountered in children with developed or limited verbal skills. Even more striking, persons showing many characteristics of developed differentiation could be functioning effectively or be so disturbed as to require institutional care.

The studies we performed out of an interest in issues of individuality have shown that people may be characterized in ways that cut across traditional categories of perceiving, intelligence, and personality. This finding highlights the difficulty in attempting to consider these categories in isolation from each other. Are we describing a person's perception when we say of him that he spontaneously experiences his body as an entity apart from the surroundings, that he has an immediate impression of himself as a person separate from others? Or are we describing his personality? The identification of individual ways of functioning, expressed in diverse areas of psychological activity, causes us more and more to look across the traditional categories into which man's psychological life has often been divided.

To stress the importance of considering the unique constellation of characteristics each individual presents may seem almost trite. However obvious, such an emphasis is particularly necessary in research, where the need to establish generalizations may lead to disregard of individuality, and in the field of development, where concern with the normative requires balance by attention to individuals.

The pursuit of issues of individuality required the development of methods appropriate to their study. Several features of the methodology that emerged are worth noting.

First, techniques have been made available for a more experimental approach to the study of personal functioning. Of the cluster of characteristics found to be interrelated and interpreted as manifestations of more developed or less developed differentiation, some are particularly amenable to study by experimental means. This is particularly true of the characteristics of cognitive functioning represented in the cluster. To the extent that a child's mode of field approach "stands for" the larger cluster and can be evaluated in an objective way, it serves as a "tracer element" which pegs the child's developmental status with regard to level of differentiation. The aim of studying personal functioning by techniques which permit manipulation and control of conditions is thereby aided. It is in part for this reason that the study of cognitive functions has come to serve increasingly in recent years as a route to the understanding of psychological organization and functioning.

A second methodological outcome of the pursuit of problems of individuality has been to bring our studies somewhat closer to life. Our interest in self-consistency led us to explore various aspects of children's behavior under a variety of conditions. In one phase of this effort the child's dealings with the examiner were used to evaluate his characteristic way of relating to adults in a real encounter. In another phase we made a first attempt to explore articulateness of experience under everyday circumstances. Our interest in how children come to be different from each other, in the ways observed, led us to examine their experiences in the family. This effort, most of all, engaged us in studies outside the laboratory. The complementary use of information from the laboratory and from life itself became an increasingly salient feature of methodology as our research progressed.

Just as the pursuit of problems of individuality demanded a suitable research methodology, so did it require an appropriate conceptual framework. This need became particularly pressing with the accumulation of results from studies of self-consistency, the issue of individuality in which our greatest research effort has been invested. The concept of differentiation, which has had long usage in psychology, seemed to offer the best basis for tying together the many diverse segments of behavior we had found to be associated.

The idea that even quite different kinds of behavior may have a common core is hardly a new one; it finds support in evidence from systematic studies and in everyday experience alike. A familiar example may be cited.

A recent popular magazine survey of the segregation problem in the South contained an interview with a prosegregationist. In the course of the interview he expressed his views on a number of issues: he strongly opposed foreign aid, favored restricting the power of the Supreme Court, supported the House Un-American Activities Committee, and was against federal aid to education. As he himself put it, the segregation fight is "only one part of a larger battle." These apparently disparate sentiments may be tied together by conceiving of them as parts of a conservative attitudinal system, in the same way that the differentiation concept has been used to relate a number of segments of behavior. Other parallels may be drawn to sharpen the sense of our use of the concept of differentiation. Like the differentiation concept, the concept of "conservative" serves the very useful function of providing a basis for predicting a person's behavior from one situation to another. Again, paralleling a limitation of the role served by the differentiation concept, to characterize someone as conservative in his attitudes is not to explain how the particular attitudinal system arose or how its parts came to be linked during development. As still another similarity, the components of such an attitudinal system may be discrepant or "unevenly developed"; for example, particular life experiences may make for an out-of-character positive view toward foreign aid.

The theoretical framework we have been using, based on the differentiation concept, is patently in the midstream of its development. Just as it underwent continuous change as our work progressed—a fact amply demonstrated in this book—so will future work inevitably result in considerable further change. With regard both to conceptual clarity and supporting evidence the theoretical framework is at this moment more developed in some of its areas than in others. Much additional work is needed, aimed at the reciprocal goals of further development of theory and application of theory to particular problems.

Some potentially useful directions for further work may be cited as illustrative.

One is concerned with the problem of continuity or stability in psychological functioning during development. The search for continuity in the context of the ever ongoing change which development brings about has two requirements. First, particular aspects of functioning that are apt to remain relatively stable during growth need to be identified. Second, the modes of expression of a particular kind of functioning at different stages of development, which though different in content are equivalent with regard to formal characteristics, need to be established. The differentiation concept appears useful in meeting both requirements. Differentiation refers to structural aspects of psychological make-up, which, as compared to content aspects, may be expected to remain relatively stable during development. Moreover, the differentiation concept offers a basis for identifying segments of behavior at different age levels as equivalent. That the differentiation concept does in fact offer a useful guide to the study of stability during development is suggested by the first results of the longitudinal studies reported in the preceding chapter.

The studies already done suggest that the differentiation concept provides a useful focus in the study of parent-child relations. It served to direct attention to particular facets of behavior of mother and child and of the interaction between them. To have such a focus is especially useful in the study of the large, complex area of parent-child relations.

The existence of a connection between extent of children's differentiation and their experiences in the family, as well as the nature of the associations observed, suggest that learning is important in the development of differentiation. The learning that takes place in the course of growing up, which has greater or more limited differentiation as its end-product, needs to be identified. Studies of the learning involved in particular phases of mother-child relations, along lines suggested in Chapter 22, should be useful for this purpose.

The main evidence bearing on our theoretical framework has come from studies with children. There is every reason to believe that this framework is generally applicable to the psychological functioning of adults as well. It is also to be anticipated, however, that differences between adults and children may make for differences in the intrapsychic relations with which we have been dealing. One difference between adults and children may be particularly important. In children, our findings suggest, limited differentiation is most often, although not always, the result of some kind of developmental "arrest." Among adults, it may also be a consequence of regression, coming after earlier achievement of a more differentiated level of functioning.

Limited differentiation may present a different picture when it is the result of regression than when it is due to developmental arrest. For example, regression may be markedly unequal in different areas of functioning. To the extent that limited differentiation on a regressive basis is more common in adults, "unevenness" from area to area with regard to extent of differentiation may be greater than in children. Regression is a pathological development; it may provide an overlay that makes identification of the relations we have observed difficult, or even alters the relations in some ways. Possibilities such as these need to be explored.

Another issue of interest is how the various manifestations of developed differentiation come to be "linked" in the manner observed. At various points we have speculated about the ways in which the achievement of articulated experience of the world, for example, may help the development of a sense of separate identity, or the development of structured defenses and controls may contribute to articulation of experience, etc. Research directed at illuminating the "pathways" of interrelations is needed. It is noteworthy that the differentiation concept provokes inquiry into the relations among disparate areas of functioning and provides a useful approach to the study of these relations.

Problems of psychopathology may also be fruitfully approached from the standpoint of the differentiation concept. Studies already performed suggest that impairment of integration, and hence pathology, is likely to take different forms in more differentiated and less differentiated people when they become psychologically ill. The concept of level of differentiation seems to provide a partial basis for interpreting differences among people in direction of pathological development and in choice of symptoms. It also seems to offer a useful approach to the study of particular pathological entities.

Mode of field approach, used as an indicator of extent of differentiation, has been found to cut across some of the conventional nosological categories. As one example, patients bearing a hospital diagnosis of schizophrenia gave perceptual performances ranging along the whole field-dependence-independence continuum. On the other hand, when these same patients were considered from the standpoint of such characteristics as extent of self-differentiation, meaningful relations were apparent between the kind of pathology they showed and their mode of field approach. There is the possibility that mode of field approach, and hence extent of differentiation, may provide a useful basis for sharpening some of our diagnostic classifications.

Sex differences have been a constant feature of the results of our studies of perceptual and intellectual functioning, in both adults and children. Though the differences have been small, compared to variations within each sex, they have been stable and persistent. The studies we performed were not designed to yield information about other differences between the sexes which might shed light on the differences observed in mode of field approach. The differentiation concept may provide a useful approach in the research now needed, which has the sex differences problem as its focus. We saw in Chapter 13 that this concept seemed useful in bringing together a variety of evidence on sex differences from investigations of perceptual and intellectual functioning and from studies of social relationships.

The particular sex differences with which we have been concerned seem to bear on differences between men and women in biological and cultural roles. These sex differences may therefore provide a useful medium in which to study the important problem of sex roles. The availability of effective techniques for evaluating these sex differences should be a particular asset in such studies.

Another important direction for further conceptual development and research is the relation between the findings and concepts that have been presented and some of the concepts of ego psychology. In common usage "ego" refers to the psychological "apparatus" which mediates functions such as perceiving, learning, thinking, motility, and which is the "seat" of the defenses. It is the ego which would in this usage be the agency responsible for such achievements as articulation of experience, and the kinds of defensive operations characteristic of people who tend to experience in articulated fashion. The qualities of experience and characteristics of defenses we have been investigating could thus be considered expressions of ego functioning, and the contrasting constellations studied conceived as products of different kinds of egos, specifically of a more differentiated or less differentiated ego. Another point of contact between what we have been considering and ego psychology lies in the nature of the relation between ego and self. The experience of one's own activities which registers in the self includes at least some of the ego's activities. In studying the self, as we have attempted to do, there is inevitably an opportunity to obtain information about the ego as well. Although we have based our theorizing on the phenomena immediately at issue in the studies performed, extensions both in conceptualization and research to current thinking in ego psychology seem readily possible.

A final suggestion for research represents a marked departure from the work done thus far. It concerns the mediating neurophysiological mechanisms involved in experiencing in a relatively global or articulated fashion. What, for example, is the underlying "machinery" which causes a previously seen simple figure to "pop out" of the background for one person and remain submerged for another? Recent advances in neurophysiology may provide an approach to research on questions such as this.

Central to individual differences in performance in our perceptual tests is the extent to which the person is able to keep an item apart from a context. It is possible to translate such effects into the operation of neural traces. Taking the embedded-figures test as illustrative, we may presume that the simple design creates a trace which remains after the design is removed. Upon this memory trace is superimposed the trace of the complex design which contains the simple figure. We may speculate that the memory trace of the simple figure has a different fate, in the presence of the new trace, for the person who easily finds the simple figure than for the person who has great difficulty. In the first instance, it may be considered, the boundaries of the memory trace remain firm; in the second they do not, with the result that the trace readily fuses with the new trace or is in other ways affected by it. The techniques devised by Köhler and Wallach (1944) for their studies of figural aftereffects may provide one means of testing the hypothesis that traces have firmer boundaries, and so remain discrete, in persons whose experience is relatively articulated. It seems possible by these techniques to control the nature and locus of registration of traces and to study their fate in interaction with other traces registered either simultaneously or subsequently.

Implicit in this approach is the idea that differences in extent of articulation of experience may be related to identifiable differences in neural functioning. The studies suggested provide an opportunity to use perceiving as a route to better understanding of neural mechanisms. The stability of the particular mode of perceiving involved, and its pervasiveness in individual functioning, make it a particularly useful one for the kind of study proposed.

We have no doubt that as the conceptual framework that has been presented is tested in further research it will undergo considerable correction and acquire greater specificity. The usefulness of the framework, even in its present form, is reflected in the scope of the areas already investigated and amenable to investigation under its guidance, and the variety of evidence it has helped to interpret and integrate.

REFERENCES

Adamson, R. E. and Taylor, D. W., 1954. Functional fixedness as related to elapsed time and set. *J. exp. Psychol.*, 47, 122–126.

Alexander, F., 1950. *Psychosomatic medicine.* New York: Norton.

Allport, G. W., 1960. The open system in personality theory. *J. abnorm. soc. Psychol.*, 61, 301–310.

Anastasi, Anne, 1958. *Differential psychology: individual and group differences in behavior.* (3rd Ed.) New York: Macmillan.

Andrieux, C., 1955. Contribution a l'etude des differences entre hommes et femmes dans la perception spatiale. *L'annee Psychologique*, 55, 41–60.

Aronson, Harriet J., 1957. The influence of training and field dependency on the modification of misperception. Unpublished doctor's dissertation, Purdue University.

Asch, S. E., 1952. *Social psychology.* New York: Prenctice-Hall.

Asch, S. E., 1956. Studies of independence and conformity (Part 1), a minority of one against a unanimous majority. *Psychol. Monogr.*, 70 (Whole No. 416).

Asch, S. E. and Witkin, H. A., 1948a. Studies in space orientation: 1. Perception of the upright with displaced visual fields. *J. exp. Psychol.*, 38, 325–337.

Asch, S. E. and Witkin, H. A., 1948b. Studies in space orientation: 2. Perception of the upright with displaced visual fields and with body tilted. *J. exp. Psychol.*, 38, 455–477.

Bailey, W., Hustmyer, F., and Kristofferson, A., 1961. Alcoholism, brain damage and perceptual dependence. *Quart. J. stud. Alc.*, 22, 387–393.

Baldwin, A. L., Kalhorn, Joan, and Breese, Fay H., 1945. Patterns of parent behavior. *Psychol. Monogr.*, 58 (Whole No. 268).

Bales, R. F. and Couch, A., 1956. A factor analysis of values. Unpublished study, Lab. Soc. Relat., Harvard University.

Baroff, G. S., 1959. WISC patterning in endogenous mental deficiency. *Amer. J. ment. Defic.*, 64, 482–485.

Barry, H., Bacon, Margaret K., and Child, I. L., 1957. A cross-cultural survey of some sex differences in socialization. *J. abnorm. soc. Psychol.*, 55, 327–332.

Bauman, G., 1951. The stability of the individual's mode of perception, and of perception-personality relationships. Unpublished doctor's dissertation, New York University.

Bechtoldt, H. P., 1947. Factorial study of perceptual speed. Unpublished doctor's dissertation, University of Chicago.

Bell, Elaine G., 1955. Inner-directed and other-directed attitudes. Unpublished doctor's dissertation, Yale University.

Beller, E., 1958. A study of dependency and perceptual orientation. Paper read at Amer. Psychol. Assn., Washington.

Bennett, D. H., 1956. Perception of the upright in relation to body image. *J. ment. Sci.*, 102, 487–506.

Bertini, M., 1960. Traits somatiques aptitudes perceptives et traits superieurs de personalité. Paper read at Inter. Congr. Psychol., Bonn, Germany.

Bieri, J., 1960. Parental identification, acceptance of authority and within-sex differences in cognitive behavior. *J. abnorm. soc. Psychol.*, 60, 76–79.

Bieri, J., Bradburn, Wendy M., and Galinsky, M. D., 1958. Sex differences in perceptual behavior. *J. Pers.*, 26, 1–12.

Bieri, J. and Lobeck, Robin, 1959. Acceptance of authority and parental identification. *J. Pers.*, 27, 74–86.

Block, J., 1957. A study of affective responsiveness in a lie-detector situation. *J. abnorm. soc. Psychol.*, 55, 11–15.

Botzum, W. A., 1951. A factorial study of the reasoning and closure factors. *Psychometrika*, 16, 361–386.

Bound, Mae M., 1957. A study of the relationship between Witkin's indices of field dependency and Eysenck's indices of neuroticism. Unpublished doctor's dissertation, Purdue University.

Brody, Sylvia, 1956. *Patterns of mothering.* New York: International Universities Press.

Bruell, J. H. and Peszczynski, M. D., 1958. Perception of verticality in hemiplegic patients in relation to rehabilitation. *Clin. Orthopaedics*, No. 12, 124–130.

Bruell, J. H., Peszczynski, M., and Albee, G. W., 1956. Disturbance of perception of verticality in patients with hemiplegia: a preliminary report. *Arch. phys. Med.*, 37, 677.

Bruell, J. H., Peszczynski, M., and Volk, D., 1957. Disturbance of perception of verticality in patients with hemiplegia: second report. *Arch. phys. Med.*, 38, 677.

Brunswik, E., 1933. Untersuchungen über Wahrnehmungsgegenstände, I. Die Zugänglichkeit von Gegenstanden fur die Wahrnehmung und deren quantitative Bestimmung. *Arch. ges. Psychol.*, 88, 377–418.

Brunswik, E., 1944. Distal focusing of perception: size-constancy in a representative sample of situations. *Psychol. Monogr.*, 56 (Whole No. 254).

Carden, Joyce A., 1958. Field dependence, anxiety, and sociometric status in children. Unpublished master's thesis, University of Texas.

Cattell, R. B., 1952. *Factor analysis.* New York: Harper.

Chateau, J., 1959. Le test de structuration spatiale TIB.I.S. *Le travail humain*, 22, 281–297.

Chein, I., 1944. The awareness of self and the structure of the ego. *Psychol. Rev.*, 51, 304–314.

Cohen, J., 1957. The factorial structure of the WAIS between early adulthood and old age. *J. consult. Psychol.*, 21, 283–290.

Cohen, J., 1959. The factorial structure of the WISC at ages 7–6, 10–6, and 13–6. *J. consult. Psychol.*, 23, 285–299.

Cohen, S. I. and Silverman, A. J., 1961. Psychophysiological mechanisms of stress responsivity. Annual Rep., Div. Psychophysiol. Res., Dept. Psychiatry, Duke University Medical Center.

Cohen, S. I., Silverman, A. J., and Shmavonian, B. M., 1959. Psychophysiological mechanisms of stress responsivity. Semi-annual Rep., Div. Psychophysiol. Res., Dept. Psychiatry, Duke University Medical Center.

Cohen, S. I., Silverman, A. J., and Shmavonian, B. M., 1961. The body field dimension in perceptual isolation studies. Paper read at World Congr. Psychiatry, Montreal.

Coleman, Rose W., Kris, E., and Provence, Sally, 1953. The study of variations of early parental attitudes. Psychoanal. Stud. Child, 8, 20–47.

Crudden, C. H., 1941. Form abstraction by children. J. genet. Psychol., 58, 113–129.

Crutchfield, R. S., 1955. Conformity and character. Amer. Psychologist, 10, 191–198.

Crutchfield, R. S., 1957. Personal and situational factors in conformity to group pressure. Paper read at 15th Int. Congr. Psychol., Brussels.

Crutchfield, R. S. and Starkweather, J. A., 1953. Differences among officer personnel in perception of the vertical under distorting influence of a tilted frame. Res. Memorandum, IPAR, University of California.

Crutchfield, R. S., Woodworth, D. G., and Albrecht, Ruth E., 1958. Perceptual performance and the effective person. Lackland AFB, Texas, Personnel Lab. Rep. WADC-TN-58-60. ASTIA Doc. No. AD 151 039.

Dana, R. H. and Goocher, B., 1959. Embedded-figures and personality. Percept. Mot. Skills, 9, 99–102.

Davis, J. M., McCourt, W. F., and Solomon, P., 1958. Sensory deprivation: (1) effects of social contact, (2) effects of random visual stimulation. Paper read at Amer. Psychiat. Assn. meeting, Philadelphia.

Davis, P. C., 1956. A factor-analysis of the Wechsler-Bellevue Scale. Educ. psychol. Measmt., 16, 127–146.

Dement, W. and Kleitman, N., 1957. The relation of eye movements during sleep to dream activity: an objective method for the study of dreaming. J. exp. Psychol., 53, 339–346.

De Varis, D., 1955. Field dependence and self-recognition. Unpublished study.

Doob, L. W., 1958. Behavior and grammatical style. J. abnorm. soc. Psychol., 56, 398–400.

Dubno, P., 1954. An introductory study of the relationship of some personality characteristics to patterns of intelligence test performance. Unpublished master's thesis, Brooklyn College.

Duncker, K., 1945. On problem-solving. Psychol. Monogr., 58 (Whole No. 270).

Eagle, Carol Johnson, 1959. An exploratory study of the relationships between cognitive and perceptual styles and drives and defenses in differing states of awareness. Unpublished study.

Eagle, Carol Johnson. Personal communication.

Edwards, A. L., 1954. Manual for Edwards Personal Preference Schedule. New York: Psychological Corp.

Epstein, L., 1957. The relationship of certain aspects of the body image to the perception of the upright. Unpublished doctor's dissertation, New York University.

Erikson, E. H., 1959. Identity and the life cycle: selected papers. *Psychol. Issues*, 1 (Whole No. 1).

Escalona, Sibylle and Heider, Grace M., 1959. *Prediction and outcome*. New York: Basic Books.

Escalona, Sibylle, Leitch, Mary, and others, 1952. Early phases of personality development: a non-normative study of infant behavior. *Monogr. Soc. Res. Child Develpm.*, 17, No. 1.

Eskin, L. D., 1960. A study of some possible connections between criminal behavior and perceptual behavior. Unpublished doctor's dissertation, New York University.

Eysenck, H. J. and Furneaux, W. D., 1945. Primary and secondary suggestibility: an experimental and statistical study. *J. exp. Psychol.*, 35, 485–503.

Feinberg, I. R., 1951. Sex differences in resistance to group pressure. Unpublished master's thesis, Swarthmore College.

Fenchel, G. H., 1958. Cognitive rigidity as a behavioral variable manifested in intellectual and perceptual tasks by an outpatient population. Unpublished doctor's dissertation, New York University.

Fenichel, O., 1945. *The psychoanalytic theory of neurosis*. New York: Norton.

Fink, D. M., 1959. Sex differences in perceptual tasks in relation to selected personality variables. Unpublished doctor's dissertation, Rutgers University.

Fishbein, G. M., 1958. The relationship between modes of perception and asthmatic symptomatology. Unpublished doctor's dissertation, University of Denver.

Fisher, S. Personal communication.

Fisher, S. and Cleveland, S. E., 1958. *Body image and personality*. Princeton: Van Nostrand.

Fliegel, Zenia O., 1955. Stability and change in perceptual performance of a late adolescent group in relation to personality variables. Unpublished doctor's dissertation, New School for Social Research.

Forehand, G. A., 1958. Cognitive correlates of response style. Unpublished doctor's dissertation, University of Illinois.

Franks, C. M., 1956. Differences déterminées par le personalité dans la perception visuelle de la verticalité. *Revue de psychol. Appliquée*, 6, 235–246.

French, J. W. (Ed.), 1954. *Manual for kit of selected tests for reference aptitude and achievement factors*. Princeton: Educational Testing Service.

Frenkel-Brunswik, Else, 1949. Intolerance of ambiguity as an emotional and perceptual personality variable. *J. Pers.*, 18, 108–143.

Freud, Anna, 1946. *The ego and the mechanisms of defense*. New York: International Universities Press.

Friedman, E., 1960. The effects of unilateral auditory stimulation on the perception of the visual upright in muscular dystrophy. Unpublished doctor's dissertation, Yeshiva University.

Fries, Margaret E., 1944. Psychosomatic relationships between mother and infant. *Psychosom. Med.*, 6, 159–162.

Fries, Margaret E. and Woolf, P. J., 1953. Some hypotheses on the role of the congenital activity type in personality development. *Psychoanal. Stud. Child*, 8, 48–62.

Gardner, R. W., 1957. Field-dependence as a determinant of susceptibility to certain illusions. *Amer. Psychologist*, 12, 397. (Abstract)

Gardner, R. W., Holzman, P. S., Klein, G. S., Linton, Harriet B., and Spence, D. P., 1959. Cognitive control, a study of individual consistencies in cognitive behavior. *Psychol. Issues,* 1 (Whole No. 4).

Gardner, R. W., Jackson, D. N., and Messick, S. J., 1960. Personality organization in cognitive controls and intellectual abilities. *Psychol. Issues,* 2 (Whole No. 8).

Gardner, R. W. and Long, R. I., 1961. Field-articulation in recall. *Psychol. Rec.,* 11, 305–310.

Goldfarb, W., 1955. Emotional and intellectual consequences of psychologic deprivation in infancy: a reevaluation. In Hoch, P. H. and Zubin, J. (Eds.), *Psychopathology of childhood.* New York: Grune & Stratton.

Gollin, E. and Baron, A., 1954. Response consistency in perception and retention. *J. exp. Psychol.,* 47, 259–262.

Goodenough, D. R. and Eagle, Carol J., in press. A modification of the embedded-figures test for use with young children. *J. genet. Psychol.*

Goodenough, D. R. and Karp, S. A., 1961. Field dependence and intellectual functioning. *J. abnorm. soc. Psychol.,* 63, in press.

Goodenough, D. R., Shapiro, A., Holden, M., and Steinschriber, L., 1959. A comparison of "dreamers" and "non-dreamers": eye movements, electroencephalograms, and the recall of dreams. *J. abnorm. soc. Psychol.,* 59, 295–302.

Goodenough, Florence L., 1926. *Measurement of intelligence by drawings.* Yonkers-on-Hudson, New York: World Book.

Goodman, Beverly, 1955. A study of the consistency of performance in perception and concept formation. Unpublished master's thesis, Brooklyn College.

Goodman, Beverly, 1960. Field dependence and the closure factors. Unpublished study.

Goodnow, R. Personal communication.

Gordon, B., 1953. An experimental study of dependence-independence in a social and laboratory setting. Unpublished doctor's dissertation, University of Southern California.

Gottschaldt, K., 1926. Über den Einfluss der Erfahrung auf die Wahrnehmung von Figuren, I; Über den Einfluss gehäufter Einprägung von Figuren auf ihre Sichtbarkeit in umfassenden Konfigurationen. *Psychol. Forsch.,* 8, 261–317.

Greenberg, G., 1960. Visual induction of eye torsion, as measured with an after-image technique, in relation to visual perception of the vertical. Unpublished doctor's dissertation, Duke University.

Gross, Frances, 1959. The role of set in perception of the upright. *J. Pers.,* 27, 95–103.

Gruen, A., 1951. Visual and postural determinants of perceptual organization in subjects having special postural training. Unpublished doctor's dissertation, New York University.

Gruen, A., 1955. The relation of dancing experience and personality to perception. *Psychol. Monogr.,* 69 (Whole No. 399).

Guetzkow, H., 1947. An analysis of the operation of set in problem-solving behavior. Unpublished doctor's dissertation, University of Michigan.

Guetzkow, H., 1951. An analysis of the operation of set in problem-solving behavior. *J. gen. Psychol.,* 45, 219–244.

Guilford, J. P., 1957. A revised structure of intellect. *Rep. psychol. Lab.,* No. 19, Los Angeles, University of Southern California.

Guilford, J. P., Berger, R. M., and Christensen, P. R., 1955a. A factor-analytic study of planning, II. Administration of tests and analysis of results. *Rep. psychol. Lab.*, No. 12, Los Angeles, University of Southern California.

Guilford, J. P., Frick, J. W., Christensen, P. R., and Merrifield, P. R., 1957. A factor-analytic study of flexibility in thinking. *Rep. psychol. Lab.*, No. 18, Los Angeles, University of Southern California.

Guilford, J. P., Kettner, N. W., and Christensen, P. R., 1955b. The relation of certain thinking factors to training criteria in the U. S. Coast Guard Academy. *Rep. psychol. Lab.*, No. 13, Los Angeles, University of Southern California.

Guilford, J. P., Wilson, R. C., and Christensen, P. R., 1952. A factor-analytic study of creative thinking, II. Administration of tests and analysis of results. *Rep. psychol. Lab.*, No. 8, Los Angeles, University of Southern California.

Gump, P. V., 1955. Relation of efficiency of recognition to personality variables. Unpublished doctor's dissertation, University of Colorado.

Guskin, S. L., 1955. Individual differences in dependence on visual or kinesthetic cues. Unpublished master's thesis, University of North Carolina.

Haggard, E. A., 1957. Socialization, personality and academic achievement in gifted children. *Sch. Rev.*, Winter issue.

Harris, Frances. Personal communication.

Harris, I. D., 1948. Observations concerning typical anxiety dreams. *Psychiatry*, 11, 301–309.

Harris, I. D., 1951. Characterological significance of the typical anxiety dreams. *Psychiatry*, 14, 279–294.

Harris, R. A., 1950. The effects of stress on rigidity of mental set in problem solution. Unpublished doctor's dissertation, Harvard University.

Hattwick, Berta W. and Stowell, Margaret, 1936. The relationship of parental over-attentiveness to children's work habits and social adjustment in kindergarten and the first six grades of school. *J. educ. Res.*, 30, 169–176.

Hemmendinger, L., 1953. Perceptual organization and development as reflected in the structure of Rorschach test responses. *J. proj. Tech.*, 17, 162–170.

Henneman, R. H., 1935. A photometric study of the perception of object-color. *Arch. Psychol.*, 27, 1–88.

Holt, R. R., 1951. The Thematic Apperception Test. In Anderson, H. H. and Anderson, Gladys L. (Eds.). *An introduction to projective techniques.* Englewood Cliffs, N. J.: Prentice-Hall.

Holt, R. R. and Goldberger, L., 1959. Personological correlates of reactions to perceptual isolation. *WADC Tech. Rep.* 59–735, Wright-Patterson AFB, Ohio.

Holtzman, W. H., 1955. *Tentative manual, the Holtzman Form-Recognition Test.* Austin: University of Texas (Mimeo).

Holtzman, W. H., 1956. Progress report of research on the development of a new inkblot test. Austin: University of Texas (Mimeo).

Holtzman, W. H. and Bitterman, M. E., 1956. A factorial study of adjustment to stress. *J. abnorm. soc. Psychol.*, 52, 179–185.

Honigfeld, G. and Spigel, I. M., 1960. Achievement motivation and field independence. *J. consult. Psychol.*, 24, 550–551.

Iscoe, I. and Carden, Joyce A., 1961. Field dependence, manifest anxiety, and sociometric status in children. *J. consult. Psychol.*, 25, 184.

Jackson, D. N., 1955. Stability in resistance to field forces. Unpublished doctor's dissertation, Purdue University.

Jackson, D. N., 1956. A short form of Witkin's Embedded-Figures Test. *J. abnorm. soc. Psychol.*, 53, 254–255.

Jackson, D. N., 1957. Intellectual ability and mode of perception. *J. consult. Psychol.*, 21, 458.

Jackson, D. N., 1958. Independence and resistance to perceptual field forces. *J. abnorm. soc. Psychol.*, 56, 279–281.

Jahoda, Marie, 1959. Conformity and independence: a psychological analysis. *Human Relations*, 12, 99–120.

James, W., 1908. *The principles of psychology.* Vol. I. New York: Holt.

Janis, I. L., et al., 1959. *Personality and persuasibility.* New Haven: Yale University Press.

Jeffreys, A. W., Jr., 1953. An exploratory study of perceptual attitudes. Unpublished doctor's dissertation, University of Houston.

Jones, L. V. and Fiske, D. W., 1953. Models for testing the significance of combined results. *Psychol. Bull.*, 50, 375–382.

Kalis, Betty L., 1957. Some relationships between size perception and ego adequacy. *J. Pers.*, 25, 439–450.

Karp, S. A., 1957. Field dependence and occupational preference. Unpublished study.

Karp, S. A., 1962. Overcoming embeddedness in perceptual and intellectual functioning. Unpublished study.

Karp, S. A. and Marlens, Hanna, 1958. Field dependence in relation to miniature-toys play. Unpublished study.

Karp, S. A., Poster, Dorothy, and Goodman, A., 1960. Differentiation in alcoholic women. Unpublished study.

Katona, G., 1940. *Organizing and memorizing.* New York: Columbia University Press.

Kelly, G. A., 1955. *The psychology of personal constructs.* New York: Norton.

Klopfer, B., Ainsworth, Mary D., Klopfer, W. G., and Holt, R. R., 1954. *Developments in the Rorschach technique.* Vol. 1, Technique and theory. Yonkers-on-Hudson, New York: World Book.

Köhler, W. and Wallach, H., 1944. Figural after-effects: an investigation of visual processes. *Proc. Amer. phil. Soc.*, 88, 269–357.

Kolb, L. C., 1959. Disturbances of the body-image. In Arieti, S. *American handbook of psychiatry*, Vol. I. New York: Basic Books.

Konstadt, Norma, 1961. Factors in mirror tracing. Unpublished honors thesis, City College of N. Y.

Korchin, S. Personal communication.

Kraidman, Emma, 1959. Developmental analysis of conceptual and perceptual functioning under stress and non-stress conditions. Unpublished doctor's dissertation, Clark University.

Kruse, H. D. (Ed.), 1957. *Integrating the approaches to mental disease.* New York: Harper.

League, Betty J. and Jackson, D. N., 1961. Activity and passivity as correlates of field-independence. *Percept. Mot. Skills*, 12, 291–298.

Levine, H. L., 1957. The role of the E-effect on perceptual shifts in the rod-and-frame test with body tilted to left and right. Unpublished study.

Levitt, E. E., 1956. The water-jar Einstellung test as a measure of rigidity. *Psychol. Bull.*, 53, 347–370.

Levitt, E. E. and Zelen, S. L., 1953. The validity of the Einstellung test as a measure of rigidity. *J. abnorm. soc. Psychol.*, 48, 573–580.

Levitt, E. E. and Zuckerman, M., 1959. The water-jar test revisited: the replication of a review. *Psychol. Rep.*, **5**, 365–380.

Levy, D. M., 1943. *Maternal overprotection.* New York: Columbia University Press.

Lewin, K., 1935. *A dynamic theory of personality.* New York: McGraw-Hill.

Lewis, Helen B., 1958. Over-differentiation and under-individuation of the self. *Psychoanalysis psychoanal. Rev.*, **45**, 3–24.

Linton, Harriet B., 1952. Relations between mode of perception and tendency to conform. Unpublished doctor's dissertation, Yale University.

Linton, Harriet B., 1955. Dependence on external influence: correlates in perception, attitudes, and judgment. *J. abnorm. soc. Psychol.*, **51**, 502–507.

Linton, Harriet B. Personal communication.

Linton, Harriet and Graham, Elaine, 1959. Personality correlates of persuasibility. In Janis, I. L., et al. *Personality and persuasibility.* New Haven: Yale University Press.

Loeff, R. G., 1961. Embedding and distracting field contexts as related to the field dependence dimension. Unpublished master's thesis, Brooklyn College.

Longenecker, E. D., 1956. Form perception as a function of anxiety, motivation, and the testing situation. Unpublished doctor's dissertation, University of Texas.

Lorr, M., 1953. Multidimensional scale for rating psychiatric patients. Hospital Form. *VA Tech. Bull.*, TB 10-507. Washington, D. C.

Luchins, A. S., 1951. On recent usage of the Einstellung effect as a test of rigidity. *J. consult. Psychol.*, **15**, 89-94.

Macfarlane, Jean W., Allen, Lucille, and Honzik, Marjorie P., 1954. *A developmental study of the behavior problems of normal children between twenty-one months and fourteen years.* Berkeley and Los Angeles: University of California Press.

Maier, N. R. F., 1933. An aspect of human reasoning. *Brit. J. Psychol.*, **24**, 144–155.

Maier, N. R. F., 1940. The behavior mechanisms concerned with problem solving. *Psychol. Rev.*, **47**, 43–58.

Marlowe, D., 1958. Some psychological correlates of field independence. *J. consult. Psychol.*, **22**, 334.

McClelland, D., Atkinson, J. W., Clark, R. A., and Lowell, E. L., 1953. *The achievement motive.* New York: Appleton-Century-Crofts.

McFarland, R. A. and Channell, R. C., 1944. A revised two-hand coordination test. *Rep. No. 36*, Airman Develpm. Div., CAA, Washington, D. C.

Mednick, S. A. Personal communication.

Meresko, R., Mandel, R., Shoutz, F. C., and Morrow, W. R., 1954. Rigidity of attitudes regarding personal habits and its ideological correlates. *J. abnorm. soc. Psychol.*, **49**, 89–93.

Miller, Ann S., 1953. An investigation of some hypothetical relationships of rigidity and strength and speed of perceptual closure. Unpublished doctor's dissertation, University of California.

Milton, G. A., 1957. The effects of sex-role identification upon problem solving skill. *J. abnorm. soc. Psychol.*, **55**, 208–212.

Mooney, C. M., 1954. A factorial study of closure. *Canad. J. Psychol.*, **8**, 51–60.

Mooney, C. M. and Ferguson, G. A., 1951. A new closure test. *Canad. J. Psychol.*, **5**, 129–133.

Murphy, Lois B., 1960a. The child's way of coping: a longitudinal study of normal children. Bull. Menninger Clinic, 24, 97–103.

Murphy, Lois B., 1960b. Coping devices and defense mechanisms in relation to autonomous ego function. Bull. Menninger Clinic, 24, 144–153.

Murray, H. A., et al., 1943. Thematic Apperception Test manual. Cambridge: Harvard University Press.

Mussen, P. H. and Kagan, J., 1958. Group conformity and perceptions of parents. Child Develpm., 29, 57–60.

Nakamura, C. Y., 1955. The relation between conformity and problem solving. Tech. Rep. No. 11, Dept. Psychol., Stanford University.

Nakamura, C. Y., 1958. Conformity and problem solving. J. abnorm. soc. Psychol., 56, 315–320.

Newbigging, P. L., 1952. Individual differences in the effects of subjective and objective organising factors on perception. Unpublished doctor's dissertation, University Coll., University of London.

Newbigging, P. L., 1954. The relationship between reversible perspective and embedded figures. Canad. J. Psychol., 8, 204–208.

Newell, H. W., 1934. The psychodynamics of maternal rejection. Amer. J. Orthopsychiat., 4, 387–401.

Newell, H. W., 1936. A further study of maternal rejection. Amer. J. Orthopsychiat., 6, 576–589.

Newman, E. B., 1939. Forgetting of meaningful material during sleep and waking. Amer. J. Psychol., 52, 65–71.

Osgood, C. E., 1952. The nature and measurement of meaning. Psychol. Bull., 49, 197–237.

Overlade, D. C., 1954. Humor perception as abstraction ability. Unpublished doctor's dissertation, Purdue University.

Overlade, D. C., 1955. Humor: its relation to abstraction. Paper read at Midwest. Psychol. Assn., Chicago.

Pardes, H. and Karp, S. A., 1958. Field dependence in obese women. Unpublished study.

Patel, A. S. and Gordon, J. E., 1961. Some personal and situational determinants of yielding to influence. J. abnorm. soc. Psychol., 61, 411–418.

Pemberton, Carol L., 1952a. The closure factors related to other cognitive processes. Psychometrika, 17, 267–288.

Pemberton, Carol L., 1952b. The closure factors related to temperament. J. Pers., 21, 159–175.

Perez, P., 1955. Experimental instructions and stimulus content as variables in the size constancy perception of schizophrenics and normals. Unpublished doctor's dissertation, New York University.

Phillips, L., et al., 1957. The application of developmental theory to problems of social adaptation. Prog. Rep. No. 2 to USPHS, Worcester State Hospital, Massachusetts.

Piaget, J., 1952. The origins of intelligence in children. New York: International Universities Press.

Podell, J. E., 1957. Personality and stimulus factors in adult cognition: a developmental analysis of decontextualization. Unpublished doctor's dissertation, Clark University.

Podell, J. E. and Phillips, L., 1959. A developmental analysis of cognition as observed in dimensions of Rorschach and objective test performance. J. Pers., 27, 439–463.

Pollack, M., 1955. Effect of brain tumor on perception of hidden figures, sorting behavior and problem solving performance. Unpublished doctor's dissertation, New York University.

Pollack, M. Personal communication.

Pollack, M., Kahn, R. L., Karp, E., and Fink, M., 1960. Individual differences in the perception of the upright in hospitalized psychiatric patients. Paper read at East. Psychol. Assn., New York.

Radke, Marian J., 1946. The relation of parental authority to children's behavior and attitudes. *University of Minn. Instit. Child Welf. Monogr.*, No. 22.

Rechtschaffen, A. and Mednick, S. A., 1955. The autokinetic word technique. *J. abnorm. soc. Psychol.*, 51, 346.

Ribback, Beatrice H., 1957. Factors related to the perceptual-analytic ability of children. Unpublished doctor's dissertation, Purdue University.

Rieff, R. and Scheerer, M., 1959. Memory and hypnotic regression. New York: International Universities Press.

Riesman, D., 1950. *The lonely crowd.* New Haven: Yale University Press.

Rodgin, D. W., 1955. A factor analytic study of fallacies in logical thinking. Unpublished doctor's dissertation, Purdue University.

Rokeach, M., 1960. *The open and closed mind.* New York: Basic Books.

Rosenfeld, I. J., 1958. Mathematical ability as a function of perceptual field-dependency and certain personality variables. Unpublished doctor's dissertation, University of Oklahoma.

Rosner, S., 1956. Studies of group pressure. Unpublished doctor's dissertation, New School for Social Research.

Rosner, S., 1957. Consistency in response to group pressure. *J. abnorm. soc. Psychol.*, 55, 145–146.

Rudin, S. A. and Stagner, R., 1958. Figure-ground phenomena in the perception of physical and social stimuli. *J. Psychol.*, 45, 213–225.

Sangiuliano, Iris A., 1951. An investigation of the relationship between the perception of the upright in space and several factors in personality organization. Unpublished doctor's dissertation, Fordham University.

Saugstad, P., 1951. Incidental memory and problem solving. *Psychometric Lab. Rep.* No. 66, University of Chicago.

Schafer, R., 1954. *Psychoanalytic interpretation in Rorschach testing.* New York: Grune & Stratton.

Schilder, P., 1935. *The image and appearance of the human body.* London: Kegan Paul.

Schwartz, D. and Karp, S. A., 1960. Field dependence in a geriatric population. Paper read at October meeting of Brooklyn Psychiatric Society.

Scott, T. H., Bexton, W. H., Heron, W., and Doane, B. K., 1959. Cognitive effects of perceptual isolation. *Canad. J. Psychol.*, 13, 200–209.

Sears, R. R., Maccoby, Eleanor E., and Levin, H., 1957. *Patterns of child rearing.* Evanston, Ill.: Row, Peterson.

Seder, Judith A., 1957. The origin of differences in extent of independence in children: developmental factors in perceptual field dependence. Unpublished bachelor's thesis, Radcliffe College.

Silberman, L., 1961. Verbal and perceptual abilities in middle- and lower-class 12-year-old boys. Unpublished study.

Silverman, A. J., Cohen, S. I., and Shmavonian, B. M., 1961. The body field dimension in perceptual isolation situations. Paper read at World Congr. Psychiatry, Montreal.

Silverman, A. J., Cohen, S. I., Shmavonian, B. M., and Greenberg, G., 1961. Psychophysical investigations in sensory deprivation: the body-field dimension. *Psychosom. Med.*, 23, 48–61.

Sinclair, Edith J., 1956. The relationship of color- and form-dominance to perception. Unpublished doctor's dissertation, University of Chicago.

Sinnott, E. W., Dunn, L. C., and Dobzhansky, T., 1958. *Principles of genetics.* (5th ed.) New York: McGraw-Hill.

Stark, Ruth, Parker, Ann, and Iverson, M., 1959. Field dependency and response to ego orientation. Paper read at Eastern Psychol. Assn., Atlantic City.

Street, R. F., 1931. *A gestalt completion test.* New York: Teachers Coll., Columbia University.

Strong, E. K., 1943. *Vocational interests of men and women.* Stanford, California: Stanford University Press.

Stroop, J. R., 1935. Studies of interference in serial verbal reactions. *J. exp. Psychol.*, 18, 643–662.

Sullivan, H. S., 1947. *Conceptions of modern psychiatry.* New York: Norton.

Sweeney, E. J., 1953. Sex differences in problem solving. *Tech. Rep.* No. 1, Dept. Psychol., Stanford University.

Symonds, P. M., 1939. *The psychology of parent-child relationships.* New York: Appleton-Century-Crofts.

Taft, R., 1956. Some characteristics of good judges of others. *Brit. J. Psychol.*, 47, 19–29.

Taft, R. and Coventry, J., 1958. Neuroticism, extraversion, and the perception of the vertical. *J. abnorm. soc. Psychol.*, 56, 139–140.

Taylor, J. M., 1956. A comparison of delusional and hallucinatory individuals using field dependency as a measure. Unpublished doctor's dissertation, Purdue University.

Thetford, W. N., Molish, H. B., and Beck, S. J., 1951. Developmental aspects of personality structure in normal children. *J. proj. Tech.*, 15, 58–78.

Thurstone, L. L., 1944. *A factorial study of perception.* Chicago: University of Chicago Press.

Thurstone, L. L., 1949. Mechanical aptitude III: analysis of group tests. *Psychometric Lab. Rep.* No. 55, University of Chicago.

Titus, H. E. and Hollander, E. P., 1957. The California F Scale in psychological research: 1950–1955. *Psychol. Bull.*, 54, 47–64.

Tuddenham, R. D., 1951. Studies in reputation: III. Correlates of popularity among elementary school children. *J. educ. Psychol.*, 42, 257–276.

Tuddenham, R. D., 1952. Studies in reputation: I. Sex and grade differences in school children's evaluations of their peers. *Psychol. Monogr.*, 66 (Whole No. 333).

Tyler, Leona E., 1956. *The psychology of human differences.* (2nd ed.) New York: Appleton-Century-Crofts.

Vandenberg, S. Personal communication.

von Bertalanffy, L., 1950. The theory of open systems in Physics and Biology. *Science*, 111, 23.

Wapner, S. Personal communication.

Wapner, S. and Witkin, H. A., 1950. The role of visual factors in the maintenance of body-balance. *Amer. J. Psychol.*, 63, 385–408.

Weiner, M., 1955. Effects of training in space orientation on perception of the upright. *J. exp. Psychol.*, 49, 367–373.

Werner, H., 1948. *Comparative psychology of mental development* (Rev. ed.). Chicago: Follett.

Werner, H., 1957. The concept of development from a comparative and organismic point of view. In Harris, D. B. (Ed.). *The concept of development: an issue in the study of human behavior.* Minneapolis: University of Minnesota Press.

Werner, H. and Wapner, S., 1952. Experiments on sensory-tonic field theory of perception: IV. Effect of initial position of a rod on apparent verticality. *J. exp. Psychol.*, 43, 68–74.

Wertheim, J. and Mednick, S. A., 1958. The achievement motive and field independence. *J. consult. Psychol.*, 22, 38.

Wertheimer, M., 1945. *Productive thinking.* New York: Harper.

Wexler, Rochelle M. Personal communication.

Wit, O. C., 1955. Sex differences in perception. Unpublished master's thesis, University of Utrecht.

Witkin, H. A., 1948. The effect of training and of structural aids on performance in three tests of space orientation. *Rep. No. 80,* Div. Res., CAA, Washington, D. C.

Witkin, H. A., 1949a. Perception of body position and of the position of the visual field. *Psychol. Monogr.*, 63 (Whole No. 302).

Witkin, H. A., 1949b. Sex differences in perception. *Trans. N. Y. Acad. Sci.*, 12, 22–26.

Witkin, H. A., 1949c. The nature and importance of individual differences in perception. *J. Pers.*, 18, 145–170.

Witkin, H. A., 1950a. Perception of the upright when the direction of force acting on the body is changed. *J. exp. Psychol.*, 40, 93–106.

Witkin, H. A., 1950b. Individual differences in ease of perception of embedded figures. *J. Pers.*, 19, 1–15.

Witkin, H. A., 1952. Further studies of perception of the upright when the direction of the force acting on the body is changed. *J. exp. Psychol.*, 43, 9–20.

Witkin, H. A. and Asch, S. E., 1948a. Studies in space orientation: III. Perception of the upright in the absence of a visual field. *J. exp. Psychol.*, 38, 603–614.

Witkin, H. A. and Asch, S. E., 1948b. Studies in space orientation: IV. Further experiments on perception of the upright with displaced visual fields. *J. exp. Psychol.*, 38, 762–782.

Witkin, H. A., Goodenough, D. R., and Karp, S. A., 1959. Developmental changes in perception. Unpublished study.

Witkin, H. A., Karp, S. A., and Goodenough, D. R., 1959. Dependence in alcoholics. *Quart. J. stud. Alc.*, 20, 493–504.

Witkin, H. A., Lewis, Helen B., Hertzman, M., Machover, Karen, Meissner, Pearl B., and Wapner, S., 1954. *Personality through perception.* New York: Harper.

Witkin, H. A. and Wapner, S., 1950. Visual factors in the maintenance of upright posture. *Amer. J. Psychol.*, 63, 31–50.

Witkin, H. A., Wapner, S., and Leventhal, T., 1952. Sound localization with conflicting visual and auditory cues. *J. exp. Psychol.*, 43, 58–67.

Witryol, S. L. and Kaess, W. A., 1957. Sex differences in social memory tasks. *J. abnorm. soc. Psychol.*, 54, 343–346.

Woerner, Margaret and Levine, T., 1950. A preliminary study of the relation between perception and thinking in children. Unpublished study.

Young, H. H., Jr., 1957. Personality test correlates of orientation to the vertical: a test of Witkin's field-dependency hypothesis. Unpublished doctor's dissertation, University of Texas.

Young, H. H., Jr., 1959. A test of Witkin's field-dependence hypothesis. *J. abnorm. soc. Psychol.*, **59**, 188–192.

Zaks, M. S., 1954. Perseveration of set, a determinant in problem-solving rigidity. Unpublished master's thesis, Roosevelt College of Chicago.

Zukmann, L., 1957. Hysteric compulsive factors in perceptual organization. Unpublished doctor's dissertation, New School for Social Research.

NAME INDEX*

Adamson, R. E., 76, 77, **391**
Ainsworth, Mary D., **397**
Albee, G. W., 132, **392**
Albrecht, Ruth E., **393**
Alexander, F., 207, **391**
Allen, Lucille, 279, **398**
Allport, G. W., 10, **391**
Anastasi, Anne, 218, **391**
Andrieux, C., 214, 215, **391**
Aronson, Harriet J., 57, **391**
Asch, S. E., 36, 41, 151, 153, **391, 402**
Atkinson, J. W., **398**

Bacon, Margaret K., 220, **391**
Bailey, W., 205, 206, **391**
Baldwin, A. L., 279, **391**
Bales, R. F., 146, **391**
Baroff, G. S., 195, **391**
Baron, A., 100, 101, **395**
Barry, H., 220, **391**
Bauman, G., 40, 369, 370, **391**
Bechtoldt, H. P., 50, **392**
Beck, S. J., 96, **401**
Bell, Elaine G., 60, 145, **392**
Beller, E., 147, **392**
Bennett, D. H., 132, 205, 214, 215, **392**

Berger, R. M., **396**
Bertini, M.,·174, 175, **392**
Bexton, W. H., 372, **400**
Bieri, J., 67, 73, 112, 146, 214, 338, **392**
Bitterman, M. E., 53, 216, **396**
Block, J., 167, **392**
Botzum, W. A., 49, 50, 56, **392**
Bound, Mae M., 43, 60, 205, **392**
Bradburn, Wendy M., 112, 214, **392**
Breese, Fay H., 279, **391**
Brody, Sylvia, 379, **392**
Bruell, J. H., 132, **392**
Brunswik, E., 52, **392**

Carden, Joyce A., 60, 200, 214, 221, **392, 396**
Cattell, R. B., 64, **392**
Channell, R. C., 50, **398**
Chateau, J., 214, 215, **392**
Chein, I., 12, **392**
Child, I. L., 220, **391**
Christensen, P. R., **396**
Clark, R. A., **398**
Cleveland, S. E., 131, 132, **394**
Cohen, J., 61, 64, 66, 208, **392**

* Numbers in **boldface** refer to entries in the bibliography.

405

SUBJECT INDEX

416

PMA Space and Reasoning subtests, 51
Problem-solving ability, 59
  and conformity, 152
  and field dependence, 71–75, 79n
  sex differences, 217
Projection, 211
Projective tests, *see* Personality-assessment techniques
Psychiatric patients, 9, 44, 126, *see also* Pathology

Reading ability, 200
Recognition-efficiency test, 62, 93–95
Reconciliation-of-opposites test, 63, 196–197
Regression, 317, 386
Repression, 157, 169, 172–173, 179
Retroactive inhibition, 100
Reversible figures, 54–55
RAPH scale, 146
- Rod-and-frame test (RFT) described, 36–37
Room-adjustment test (RAT) described, 39
Rorschach test, measures, related to, differentiation, 193
  field approach, 93, 163, 183–184, 225
  ratings of mothers, 343
  verbal skills, 193
Rorschach test, studies, active attitude, 183–184
  body-concept articulation, 131–132
  case studies, 229 et seq.
  defensive structure, 160–164
  impulse control, 166
  isolation, 174–175
  secondary suggestibility, 152–153
  self-consistency, 26, 28–30
  stability under hypnosis, 372–373
  structuring of experience, 81–93
Rotating-room test described, 42

Schizophrenia, 205, 208n
Self-awareness, 171–172
Self-concept, *see* Body-concept articulation, Sense of separate identity
Self-confidence, 168
Self-consistency, 25–30, 222–228

Self Contextual Influence Test, 154
Self-view, 154–155
Semantic differential, 154
Sense of separate identity, 134–156
  and adjustment, 20
  and mother-child interaction, 355–358
  as differentiation indicator, 12–13
  in psychiatric patients, 209
  manifestations of, 134–135
  sex differences, 218–219
  see also, Body-concept articulation
Sense of separate identity, studies of, 136–155
  attentiveness to others, 147–149
  attitude formation, 149–154
  conformity, 140–141, 149–152
  dependent attitudes, 142–146
  incidental learning, 141–142
  "real-life" situations, 147
  reliance on self vs. others, 135–149
  routinized-task performance, 140–141
  stability of self view, 154–155
  suggestibility, 152–154
  task attitude in TAT, 136–140
    criteria for rating, 136–139
    relation to field approach, 140, 225
    relation to maternal characteristics, 343
    relation to other indicators of differentiation, 193
    relation to verbal skills, 193
    reliability of ratings, 140
    scaling procedure, 139
Sensory isolation, 168, 208n, 372
Set, breaking, 76–79, 146
  susceptivity to, 77–78
Sex differences, 214–221
  and age, 215
  in articulation of experience, 216
  in differentiation, origins of, 220–221
  in intellectual functioning, 216–218
  in memory, 103, 216
  in mother-child interaction, 350
  in perception, 214–216
  in sense of separate identity, 218–219
  in verbal skills, 219–220
Social perception, 112–113, 147–149, 266